PROFESSIONAL STUDIES IN PRIMARY EDUCATION

Praise for the second edition

'This is a really excellent book that is packed with information. Each chapter provides a rigorous overview of theoretical perspectives combined with a clear examination of Teaching Standards and sound professional advice. I would recommend this text to anyone interested in teaching and especially to those who aspire to the profession.'

Mark Brundrett, Liverpool John Moores University

'A wonderful resource! As a lecturer, the chapters supported teaching and learning for the Professional Studies module. The text gave necessary insight to trainee teachers in understanding their roles and responsibilities while reflecting on their impact on teaching and learning. The History of Education and Learning Teaching in School encouraged useful debate and dialogue and an awareness of the importance of ongoing professional development.'

Janet Douglas Gardner, London Metropolitan University

'A substantial, practical and valuable read for any trainee teacher. Each chapter carefully focuses on a key aspect of Primary Education, unpicking and exploring issues and offering several points for reflection.'

Sarah Wright, Edge Hill University

'This is a text that supplements early years focused texts. It helps look at the wider school and covers important aspects of the role, reflexivity, inclusion, safeguarding. Really clearly laid out and student friendly!'

Catherine Farnon, Highlands College

'This is an essential read for teacher training students. It is easy to read and well signposted.'

Sarah Martin-Denham, Sunderland University

3RD EDITION

PROFESSIONAL STUDIES IN PRIMARY EDUCATION

EDITED BY
HILARY COOPER
SALLY ELTON-CHALCRAFT

Los Angeles | London | New Delhi
Singapore | Washington DC | Melbourne

Los Angeles | London | New Delhi
Singapore | Washington DC | Melbourne

SAGE Publications Ltd
1 Oliver's Yard
55 City Road
London EC1Y 1SP

SAGE Publications Inc.
2455 Teller Road
Thousand Oaks, California 91320

SAGE Publications India Pvt Ltd
B 1/I 1 Mohan Cooperative Industrial Area
Mathura Road
New Delhi 110 044

SAGE Publications Asia-Pacific Pte Ltd
3 Church Street
#10-04 Samsung Hub
Singapore 049483

Editor: James Clark
Assistant editor: Rob Patterson
Production editor: Tom Bedford
Marketing manager: Lorna Patkai
Cover design: Sheila Tong
Typeset by: C&M Digitals (P) Ltd, Chennai, India
Printed in the UK

Library of Congress Control Number: 2017946070

British Library Cataloguing in Publication data

A catalogue record for this book is available from the British Library

ISBN 978-1-5264-0967-6
ISBN 978-1-5264-0968-3 (pbk)

At SAGE we take sustainability seriously. Most of our products are printed in the UK using FSC papers and boards. When we print overseas we ensure sustainable papers are used as measured by the PREPS grading system. We undertake an annual audit to monitor our sustainability.

Contents

About the Editors

Hilary Cooper is Professor Emeritus of History and Pedagogy at the University of Cumbria. After many years teaching in London primary schools and undertaking her doctoral research on child development using data collected as a class teacher, she lectured in education at Goldsmiths' College, London University. In 1993 she became Director of Professional Studies in the Department of Education at Lancaster University, then Reader, and later Professor of Education at St Martin's College, now the University of Cumbria. She has published widely and has an international reputation.

Sally Elton-Chalcraft is Reader (Associate Professor) in Education, University of Cumbria, where she works with learners on UG, PG, MA and PhD programmes. Her most recent research projects, which inform her teaching, include collaborative work investigating the imposition of fundamental British values into teacher education and school settings, teaching and learning creatively particularly religious education in the primary phase, an evaluation of senior leadership courses with an emphasis on black and minority ethnic (BME) and women aspirant leaders, and a collaborative research project with other Cathedrals Group universities and partnership schools resulting in some fit-for-purpose guidelines for ethical research in school settings. She has been lead investigator collecting data over two summers in six Indian states investigating the impact of Christian faith in schools and also attitudes towards special educational needs (SEN).

About the Contributors

Jan Ashbridge is Principal Lecturer in the Institute of Education at the University of Cumbria. She spent her time in school enjoying the company of the children in early years and Key Stage 1 classrooms in Burnley and in the South of Cumbria. She left to become a Senior Advisory Teacher for Cumbria Local Education Authority. Jan has been planning a range of continuing professional development (CPD) programmes and training in early years provision and in phonics for students and teachers across the north-west of England, and has published a number of chapters in books.

Nicky Batty is a Senior Lecturer and Principal Safeguarding Officer for the Institute of Education at the University of Cumbria. Her professional areas of interest and study are safeguarding and primary English education. She graduated from Charlotte Mason College and has always upheld the philosophy: 'for the children's sake'. She taught for 12 years in several schools in Cumbria and Stockport. Her Master's research had a focus on applied linguistics, which has continued to inform her teaching and learning in curriculum and specialist English modules.

Pete Boyd is Professor of Professional Learning at the University of Cumbria in England. He has a research capacity-building role within the Institute of Education and teaches undergraduate education studies, as well as contributing to initial teacher education programmes. He supervises educational research by teachers and lecturers completing Master's and Doctoral level studies. Pete's most recent research includes collaborating with teacher researchers in investigations into classroom practice focusing on dialogue, mastery approaches, developing learner dispositions and learner response technology. Pete also has research interests in higher education, including assessment for learning, the pedagogy of professional education, and the work and identity of professional educators. His co-authored books include *Developing Effective Assessment in Higher Education: A Practical Guide* (Open University Press, 2007) and *Learning Teaching: Becoming an Inspirational Teacher* (Northwich Critical Publishing, 2015).

Jean Conteh has worked in multilingual contexts for her whole career, first as a primary teacher and teacher educator in different countries, and then as an academic at the University of York from 2003, and Leeds University, where she took up a senior lectureship and was in charge of Postgraduate Certificate in Education (PGCE) Primary English from 2007. She has a particular interest in the roles of language and culture in the processes of learning, and has published many books, chapters and articles about these issues, including *The Multilingual Turn in Languages Education* (Multilingual Matters, 2014). Jean has been involved in many projects relating to researching English as an additional language (EAL) in teacher education and development.

Carol Darbyshire taught in primary schools before moving to higher education. She is Subject Leader in Primary Computing initial teacher education (ITE) and Senior Lecturer within the Department of Children, Education and Communities at Edge Hill University. Carol has been involved in numerous fund-related technology projects, including the development of Control Technology in Primary Schools, a Curriculum Review of information and communication technology (ICT), and Supporting Schools in Implementing the New Computing Curriculum. She co-authored *Understanding and Teaching the New ICT Curriculum* (David Fulton, 2005). Her research interests include the role of technology in education and the emerging pedagogies associated with computer science in primary classrooms. Carol's doctoral study examined the social shaping of technology and how the theme of power and control relates to the alienation of those who feel disconnected from an increasingly technology-dominated society. Her current research focus is on technology and community education.

Nerina Díaz has had extensive experience in education. She has taught all age ranges, from 2–72, in a variety of formal and informal contexts. She has taught in primary, tertiary and higher education in the UK, New Zealand and the Middle East, and has always been interested in how examining comparative systems can or can not provide suggestions or models for improvement. Now retired from the University of Cumbria, she nevertheless continues to engage with learners through coaching activities and consultancy contracts.

Vicky Duckworth is a Reader in Education at Edge Hill University. Vicky has developed considerable expertise as an educationalist and researcher in the field of adult literacy and education. She is deeply committed to challenging inequality and emancipatory approaches to education, widening participation and inclusion, community action and engaging in research with a strong social justice agenda. Presently she is leading a University and College Union (UCU) funded research project, with Dr Rob Smith, which aims to understand and provide evidence of how the further education sector is vital in transforming lives and communities in twenty-first-century Britain.

Simon Ellis is a Senior Lecturer in the Faculty of Education at Canterbury Christ Church University. He currently teaches on the Master's in Education programme and the National Award for SEN Coordination course. He also contributes regularly to a range of the university's initial teacher education programmes. His areas of interest are pupil behaviour and the education of pupils identified with social, emotional and behavioural difficulties. He has co-authored two books on *Behaviour for Learning* (Ellis and Tod, Routledge, 2009, 2015). Prior to joining the university, Simon worked as a Key Stage 3 National Strategy Behaviour and Attendance Consultant and a Local Authority Behaviour Support Service specialist teacher and manager. He originally trained and taught as a primary teacher and also has experience of working as an SEN coordinator. Simon's doctoral thesis focused on the development of beginning teachers' thinking and practice in relation to pupil behaviour.

Kim Harris is a Senior Lecturer at the University of Worcester. Her background is in primary teaching and she has taught children aged 5–11 at schools in Berkshire and Cumbria as a class teacher and as a maths, history and music subject coordinator. Prior to moving to Worcester, she worked as a Senior Lecturer at the University of Cumbria for 8 years leading the 3-year BA with qualified teacher status (QTS) music specialism, teaching professional studies and as Year 3 Cohort Leader. Her current responsibilities include leadership of an undergraduate research methods module and a postgraduate subject specialism research module, as well as teaching music and professional studies. In addition, she supports trainee teachers as a personal academic tutor, as a Partnership Tutor and as a member of the newly qualified teacher/recently qualified teacher (NQT/RQT) committee. Her research interests focus on teacher development in primary music education, and the induction and professional development of academic staff in teacher education.

Sue Harrop is a Senior Lecturer and Year 2 Undergraduate Leader working in the Faculty of Education at Edge Hill University. She taught for 16 years, and supported school improvement through the role of an Advanced Skilled Teacher. During this time she supported trainee teachers on the graduate teaching programme. She has been involved in teacher education working with universities in the north-west, and coordinated a project in schools where Master's students could gain experience of researching. She has published an article that highlights the needs of NQTs. Her doctoral research is focused on CPD opportunities within working communities.

Donna Hurford works as an Educational Consultant at the University of Southern Denmark, where she focuses on internationalising the curriculum and students as learners. Having taught primary classes in Lancashire schools, Donna worked as a Senior Lecturer and latterly a Programme Leader in the Faculty of Education, University of Cumbria, where she specialised in education studies and global citizenship. Donna contributed a chapter on teaching pupils global citizenship through P4C to Rowley and Cooper (*Cross-Curricular Approaches to Teaching and Learning*, Sage, 2009). Donna's research collaboration with Andrew Read led to presentations and articles on students' approaches to assessment for learning (AfL) and independent learning. Inspired by student teachers and AfL Donna recently completed her PhD on student teachers' perceptions of their development as AfL practitioners.

Jo Josephidou was a primary school teacher, specialising in early years before joining the University of Cumbria in 2009. Here she was Programme Leader for the BA Hons in early years education (with QTS), teaching predominantly early years pedagogy, inclusion and early literacy. She joined the Early Childhood Studies team at Canterbury Christ Church University in 2014, and teaches on a variety of modules in this programme. Jo is presently compiling her doctoral research, which focuses on practitioner gender and the pedagogy of play.

Vini Lander is Professor of Race and Teacher Education in the School of Education at the University of Roehampton, UK. Her passion for teaching about race equality arose from her childhood experiences as an immigrant to Britain. As a teacher and teacher educator Vini has been committed to improving professional understanding of race and racism in education. The persistence of race inequality has been Vini's driving force to educate teachers to think beyond the status quo that may perpetuate these inequalities. Her dedication to promoting race equality and her long-held belief that teachers can make a difference underpins her teaching, publications and research.

Suzanne Lowe is currently employed as Lead External Examiner for the BA primary programme at Kingston University. She worked for 10 years as a Senior Lecturer, teaching educational studies, inclusion and science modules to ITE students at the University of Cumbria. She was a leading teacher of mathematics in Cumbria Local Educational Authority (LEA) for 4 years. Suzanne has also been involved in education in local museums. Her particular areas of interest lie in inclusion and in science education. Suzanne's MA in education examined aspects of educational leadership, curriculum development and children's cognitive processes.

Jayne Metcalfe taught in primary schools in Cheshire and Cumbria before becoming a Senior Lecturer in Computing in the Institute of Education at the University of Cumbria, where she is also one of the safeguarding leads. Her professional areas of interest include the role of technology in enhancing teaching and learning and safeguarding, in particular online safety. She is passionate about raising trainee teachers` awareness of risks online and how they can protect themselves, as well as the children in their care. Her Master's research focused on this area and has helped inform practice in the institution, she has also previously published chapters on keeping safe online.

Richard Palmer is an education consultant for personal social and health education (PSHE) and for religious education (RE). Richard worked as a specialist Local Authority adviser for PSHE in the south-west, and was also seconded as a regional subject adviser for London between 2008 and 2010. He has taught across Key Stages in a number of schools and developed PSHE-related projects within early years settings. Whilst teaching education studies as a Senior Lecturer at the University of Cumbria, he completed his MA focusing on homophobic bullying in primary school. Wider interests include developing teaching materials and programmes to support PSHE in family settings.

Andrew Read is Head of Undergraduate Education programmes at London South Bank University. He read music at Oxford then returned to London and completed a Primary PGCE at the Institute of Education. He worked in primary schools in Tower Hamlets for some 14 years, teaching pupils from the early years to Year 6, and coordinating music and English. From 2010 to 2016 he was Head of Primary Initial Teacher Education at the University of East London. In 2004, he completed an MA in feature film screenwriting at Royal Holloway College, University of London. Andrew is particularly interested in independent learning, and exploring ways in which learners in schools and universities can take greater ownership of assessment. He has also researched into student teachers' thinking about 'good practice' for pupils with English as an additional language. In 2017 at the sixth Annual PedRIO Conference he presented work on co-constructing assessment criteria with undergraduates.

Anne Renwick was a Senior Lecturer at the University of Cumbria, teaching across the full range of early years programmes until her recent retirement. She has worked in a number of primary schools in Cumbria and the north-east of England, teaching Nursery, Reception and Key Stage 1 children. Before joining Cumbria University, Anne was employed as a Senior Early Years Advisory Teacher for Cumbria Children's Services, supporting practitioners in a range of early years schools and settings. Anne has developed her own research on the subject of professional development for the children's workforce and her Master's dissertation focused on support for teachers working in children's centres. Recent research centres on transition into higher education and the development of teacher identity in undergraduate QTS students.

Lynne Revell is a Reader of Religion and Education at Canterbury Christ Church University. She is Programme Director for the doctorate in education and previously worked with specialists in RE and citizenship in teacher education. Her areas of research include Islam and education, extremism and teacher professionalism. She is currently co-convener of the British Educational Research Association Special Interest Group on religious and moral education and co-convenor of a World Education Research Association research network on extremism and education.

Lin Savage was a Principal Lecturer at the University of Cumbria until her recent retirement. She had responsibility for early years programmes between 2009 and 2013. Previously Lin had over 25 years of experience teaching early years and primary children in Cumbria and London. She was an Advanced Skills teacher and worked as an early years advisory teacher and area special educational needs coordinator (SENCO) for Cumbria LEA, supporting practitioners and delivering professional training for leaders and practitioners. Lin is interested in all aspects of early years education. Her Master's research focused on early years students' experience of joining the workforce. Recent research has included a consideration of the professional status of early years educators and analysis of practitioner's conversations with young children. Lin retired from the University of Cumbria in April 2013.

Susan Shaw is Primary PGCE Programmes Leader, including the Schools Direct programme at Edge Hill University. Previously she was Principal Lecturer in the Faculty of Education at the University of Cumbria. She spent 20 years in primary schools, with positions ranging from class teacher to head teacher before becoming a lecturer. She has a National Professional Qualification for Headship (NPQH) and is a Fellow of the Higher Education Academy. She is passionate about preparing ITE students to understand the holistic development of the child as well as curriculum development, and is shaping her ITE programme around this.

Ian Shirley is Senior Lecturer in Primary Music Education and Subject Leader for Primary Foundation Subjects at Edge Hill University. He is a Board Member of the UK Orff (music education) Society and he sits on the Editorial Board of the *British Journal of Music Education*. Ian's current research interests concern critical policy sociology. Ian's doctoral research focused on the constitution of music education policy and in how policy indicates the kinds of identities and practices that are validated within the ever-changing policy context. Ian conducts the Edge Hill Community choir and has worked as both musical director and accompanist on a number of amateur music theatre productions.

Sue Soan is a Senior Lecturer at Canterbury Christ Church University (CCCU). She works with Master's level and doctoral students on all subject areas relating to additional needs. She also undertakes supervision sessions, supports local schools and is a Governor for a CCCU-sponsored academy. Sue has also worked on a number of national and international projects, and has published regularly since 2003 on many aspects of additional educational needs and joint professional working. Sue's doctoral thesis (2013) is entitled 'An exploration through a small number of case studies of the education provision for Looked after Children who have experienced early life abuse or neglect'. She is an external examiner and adviser for universities and undertakes consultancy and supervision work as well as having been the Editor for a specialist academic journal until January 2017. Sue is also an Education Panel Member for a couple of fostering agencies. In her spare time Sue is a Trustee of the national charity for SEN professionals, 'nasen'. Prior to joining the university in 2003 Sue taught in nursery settings, primary and secondary mainstream and special schools for over 25 years, working as a classroom teacher, a subject coordinator (mathematics) and for over a decade as a Senior Leader, including Head of Secondary and SENCO. Her areas of expertise and research interest are Looked After Children, autism, SENCO, motor and coordination development, multi-professional working, supervision and Video Interaction Guidance (VIG).

Janet Tod is Emeritus Professor of Education at Canterbury Christ Church University. She is a qualified speech therapist and British Psychological Society (BPS) Chartered

Educational and Clinical Psychologist. She led the 2004 TTA funded Evidence for Policy and Practice Information (EPPI) review (Powell and Tod, 'A systematic review of how theories explain learning behaviour in school contexts', 2004) that produced the Behaviour for Learning conceptual framework. She has subsequently worked with Dr Simon Ellis to develop the Behaviour for Learning approach based on this framework that is now widely used on a range of teacher education programmes. Their work has been further disseminated through two books, *Behaviour for Learning: Proactive Approaches to Behaviour Management* (Ellis and Tod, Routledge, 2009) and *Promoting Behaviour for Learning in the Classroom: Effective Strategies, Personal Style and Professionalism* (Ellis and Tod, Routledge, 2015).

Diane Warner is a Senior Lecturer at the University of Cumbria, where she teaches both undergraduate and Master's level students, in primary education. Her area of special interest is race, culture and ethnicity issues in higher education. Her research for her Master's degree investigated how white student teachers viewed using multicultural books, while her current PhD studies focus on the journey of black and minority ethnic student teachers in initial teacher training. She is the joint coordinator of English in Education for all teaching students at the university, ranging from London to the north-west campuses. She is also interested in, and has led modules on pupils learning English as an additional language. She sits on a number of university committees.

Foreword: Why Do You Need This Book?

Hilary Cooper and Sally Elton-Chalcraft

Many of us wanted to be teachers in order to be different from some of the teachers we had known, and to be inspiring, as some of our teachers were. At a time of continuously changing expectations and prescriptions, often politically driven, how free are we to do this? The answer is, remarkably free, if we have a confident and secure understanding of the professional choices we are able to make.

Making professional choices

It sometimes seems that, because everyone has been to school, they all feel entitled to a valid opinion about how children should be taught. This can be very frustrating! Learning how to be a primary school teacher – deciding how and what to teach, discerning high-quality research with political awareness and criticality – is like learning how to play three-dimensional chess, challenging in its complexity but not impossible. The ability to make informed professional choices is what gives you the authority to be a teacher and we hope this book will provide you with some strategies and thinking points to support your learning.

The book aims to guide your decision making about how to teach, based on personal and professional judgements about the needs of children, recognising their different, individual needs, what excites them and what makes them want to learn. You will become a teacher who understands children's different backgrounds, difficulties, local and personal environments, and that emotional and social development are an integral part of cognitive development. You will become a teacher who enjoys exploring learning *with* children, who fosters their imagination and curiosity, who works in partnership with children's parents and carers, who helps children to be articulate about and evaluate their learning. You will be confident in working with others to plan children's learning and to monitor it in skilful and sensitive ways. You will learn how to make professional judgements about classroom organisation and how to manage behaviour effectively.

What, exactly, are 'professional studies'?

Professional studies courses educate you to make professional judgements, based on the knowledge you have about the ways in which children learn and the things that stop them reaching their potential. This knowledge is based on your familiarity with the rich body of literature relating to child development and creating classrooms that are safe, exciting and inclusive learning environments, negotiated environments for which you and the children both take responsibility and share the excitement of learning. Your judgements are also based on a combination of what you know from your reading and the way you relate this to, and interpret it in terms of, your own experience of working with children, colleagues and parents in schools. Professional judgement is not static: it grows, develops and changes as you grow and as society changes, very much like three-dimensional chess, and a great number of factors influence teaching and learning. Above all, this book shows you how to interpret the ever-changing demands made on teachers by continually changing curriculum requirements, assessment requirements, reports and recommendations, with imagination and integrity, so that you can interpret the agendas of politicians and other stakeholders with confidence, articulate your ideas, and explain and justify your practice. There are many otherwise good teachers who cannot explain the complexity of their practice to others; this undermines their status and also prevents them analysing and developing their practice. This book aims to enable you to meet current and future government requirements within a broad and deep interpretation of the concept of 'professional studies'.

Acknowledgements

Hilary Cooper is grateful to Sally Elton-Chalcraft, who agreed to co-author the third edition of *Professional Studies in Primary Education*. They both thank the authors of the previous edition for thoroughly updating their chapters for this edition and also the many new contributors, all experts in their fields, who have contributed important new chapters, which expand the scope of the book.

SAGE would like to thank the following reviewers, whose comments have helped shape this third edition:

Caroline Mytton, Birmingham City University

Moira Brazil, University of Roehampton

Claire Norcott, Edge Hill University

Ian Luke, University of St Mark & St John

Online Resources

The third edition of *Professional Studies in Primary Education* is supported by a set of online chapter resources which extend the discussion for a number of chapters in the book.

This is available at: **https://study.sagepub.com/cooper3**

Introduction to the Third Edition

Hilary Cooper and Sally Elton-Chalcraft

Why is a third edition of *Professional Studies in Primary Education* necessary?

The central thesis of this book is that, paradoxically, the only constant in education is change, and the need to interpret changes in a professional way. So it is not surprising that, after 2 years of changes since the publication of the second edition in 2014, it is appropriate to weave these changes into a third edition. The third edition does this in the following ways.

Responses to reviewers' commendations and suggestions

The reviews of the second edition were satisfyingly positive in terms of the content, scope and style of the book. The third edition builds on the many aspects that reviewers appreciated. They found it to be consistently interesting, useful, clear and succinct. They said that they admired the ways in which it encouraged critical thinking and reflection, the ways in which philosophy and ideology was interwoven with policy and the progression through the three parts of the book.

Chapter-specific suggestions

Each chapter writer has built suggestions specific to their chapter into the third edition. For example, Chapter 3 includes a section on homework and discuses a variety of ways in which English can be taught across the curriculum. Chapter 4, on assessment, has been extensively rewritten, including new policies and ideas, such as assessment without levels and the concept of mastery. Chapter 8, on inclusion and special educational needs, has been thoroughly updated to align with the Special Educational Needs and Disability Code of Practice 2015.

New chapters

In this third edition, Chapters 3 and 4 on planning and on assessment have been extended. There is a new chapter on behaviour for learning (Chapter 9) and a wide-ranging new chapter on safeguarding (Chapter 11), as this is seen as increasingly important in schools. Chapter 15 is a new chapter, 'Fundamental British Values: Your Responsibility, to Promote or Not to Promote?', dealing with new concerns and policies. Chapter 14 has been extended to discuss teaching in post-European times and there is a new chapter on 'Language and Learning in a Multilingual World' (Chapter 12). Reviewers suggested that a chapter on research-informed practice would be a welcome addition. This ties directly into the trend towards bringing higher research literacy to teachers in schools, which is becoming a policy point with the Department for Education, promoting 'research leaders' in school who can foster an informed culture, and also the social media-driven #researchED drive for teachers to interrogate the evidence base for good practice. This is the theme of Chapter 19, 'Moving on to Master's level'.

New writers

New chapters have brought new writers, from a range of universities, who are all recognised in their respective fields. They all share the philosophy on which this book is based. We are delighted to welcome to the writing team: Ian Shirley, Sue Soan, Simon Ellis, Janet Tod, Richard Palmer, Nicky Batty, Jayne Metcalfe, Lynn Revell, Vini Lander, Vicky Duckworth and Sue Harrop. And of course we are very pleased to still be working with many of our original team, although some have now moved to new positions and institutions.

Development of our key features

Reviewers liked the reflective tasks, which ask readers to consider what they have read and relate it to their own nascent experience, the Work in School scenarios, in which students ask for advice from a mentor about a problem they encounter in school, which the mentor responds to and analyses. There were also requests for more M Level references to further reading for aspiring students. In response we have strengthened these features, with three or four reflective tasks, extended school vignettes and questions for discussion at the end of every chapter. The references to further reading all include an article in an academic journal.

Recent literature and policies

The chapters, of course, refer to post-2013 literature as well as to the many recent policy documents published since the second edition.

The structure of the book

The edition, as previously, is organised into three parts. Throughout the book cross references are made demonstrating links with other chapters. Part 1 introduces you to the philosophy that underpins the book: the range of professional issues about which teachers have to make judgements and decisions in interpreting statutory frameworks. It does so in the context of what we might call the foundations of professional studies; that is, the generic professional knowledge, skills and understanding that underpin the curriculum. These chapters outline the history of state primary education in England and of educational philosophy, and show how understanding of these areas helps you to make judgements about implementing the basic components of professional studies, planning, assessment and managing the learning environment.

Part 2 is concerned with different aspects of inclusion, the need to take into account children's varied individual needs and strategies for doing this, in order to provide equal educational opportunities.

Part 3 deals with strategies for critical thinking about educational issues and reminds you of the statutory requirements you will need to take into account in doing so. It begins with a chapter specifically focusing on the learning you can acquire while teaching in school. It concludes with a review of the increasingly sophisticated understanding you should have, after engaging with the previous chapters, and suggests networks, which will support you in continuing to develop as an imaginative, exciting and inspiring teacher.

Using the book

The three sections are essentially sequential, each deepening your thinking about the educational decisions and judgements required and how to engage with them. However, the book can be used in flexible ways. You may read a chapter before a related teaching session, in order to discuss the questions and issues it poses, on the basis of colleagues' contrasting experiences – for there are often many different and equally valid answers. Each chapter provides cross references to related material in other chapters. You may want to follow up the session by dipping into the suggestions for further reading, which will give you more information and further food for thought. You may want to skim read the whole book to 'get the feel of it', then return to specific chapters in connection with seminars or to throw light on your work in school and find ideas for discussions with teachers and mentors, or reread certain chapters when you find yourself teaching a different age group or in a different type of school. You may well find it useful to keep ongoing notes in relation to the Teachers' Standards (Table I.1 below) as evidence of your developing philosophy, reading and practice. And you may well find it helpful for your continuing professional development (CPD), in preparation for postgraduate study.

Teachers' Standards: England, Wales, Scotland, Northern Ireland

Table I.1 analyses the professional attributes addressed throughout the book. It shows how the Standards for both trainee and experienced teachers in England (DfE, 2013) can be linked to the Standards for Qualified Teacher Status in Wales (2011), the Standards for Registration in Scotland (2013) and the Professional Competences for Teaching in Northern Ireland (2009). These Standards are not discrete but are referred to throughout the book. The final column shows the pages in this book that refer to each of the Standards.

The four sets of Standards address this continuum in different ways. In England the Standards apply to all trainees and teachers, interpreted according to their role and context. In Wales the Standards referred to in the table are those for practising teachers. There are also Standards for higher level teaching assistants, and for leadership. In Scotland there are Standards for initial teacher education (ITE), for full registration as a qualified teacher (given in Table I.1) and Standards for headship. In Northern Ireland each competence statement is supported by exemplars of how it should be interpreted for ITE, induction, early professional development and CPD (see also Chapters 3 and 4).

Constructing this table was an interesting, although time-consuming exercise. Each of the English Standards in column one cross-refers with parts of statements in the other three sets of Standards. The four sets of Standards are basically homogeneous, but are developed more specifically in some cases (which accounts for a lot of the overlap). The main differences are specific references to each country's National Curriculum.

Table I.1 This table links the Teachers' Standards for England (DfE, 2013) with the Standards for Wales, Scotland and Northern Ireland, and shows the pages in this book which are related to them

Standard for trainees and teachers (DfE, 2013)	Brief description (DfE, 2013)	Practising teacher Standards GTC Wales (2011)	Qualified teacher status registration GTC Scot. (2013)	Competences for trainees and NQT teachers GTC N. Ireland (2009)	Pages in this book referring to the competence
Preamble	First concern is the education of their pupils	1. 5.			Throughout
	Are accountable for achieving the highest possible standards in work and conduct	3. 24. 26. 27.	2.1.4.	PC15	Throughout
	Act with honesty and integrity Have strong subject knowledge	16.		PC1	
	Keep their knowledge and skills as teachers up to date and are self-critical	9. 10. 15. 16.	2.4.1. 2.4.3. 3.2.	PC3i PC3ii PC11	
	Positive professional relationships	8. 28. 54.	2.1.5.	PC1 PC10	
	Work with parents (carers) in the best interests of their pupils	4. 6. 32. 39.	2.1.5. 3.3.		144–7, 158, 166
PART 1 Teaching 1 Set high expectations which inspire, motivate and challenge pupils	Establish a safe and motivating environment for pupils, rooted in mutual respect	2. 21. 40. 32. 40. 48.	2.2.1	PC19	121–2, 125–30
	Set goals which motivate and challenge pupils of all backgrounds	3. 16. 21. 24. 26. 27. 46.	2.1.4.	PC5 PC10 PC15 PC20	80, 83, 86, 89, 115, 134–5, 156

(Continued)

Table I.1 (Continued)

Standard for trainees and teachers (DfE, 2013)	Brief description (DfE, 2013)	Practising teacher Standards GTC Wales (2011)	Qualified teacher status registration GTC Scot. (2013)	Competences for trainees and NQT teachers GTC N. Ireland (2009)	Pages in this book referring to the competence
	Demonstrate consistently the positive attitudes, values and behaviour which are expected of pupils	32.	2.2.1.		95–6, 121, 131–3
Teaching 2 Promote good progress and outcomes by pupils	Be accountable for pupils' attainment and outcomes		2.3.2. 2.4.1.	PC15	
	Be aware of pupils' capabilities and their prior knowledge and plan teaching to build on these	21. 24. 26. 46.	2.1.1. 2.1.4.	PC5 PC14 PC15	79, 83–8, 295
	Guide pupils to reflect on the progress they have made and their emerging needs	5. 21. 24. 26. 36. 46.	2.1.2. 2.1.4.	PC10 PC15 PC24	88, 102, 154
	Demonstrate knowledge and understanding of how pupils learn and how this impacts on teaching	14. 15. 16.	2.1.1.	PC6	49–55, 84, 88–90, 125–9, 154, 285–9, 324, 459
	Encourage pupils to take a responsible and conscientious attitude to their own work and study	5. 21. 24. 26. 36. 46.	2.1.2. 2.1.4.	PC15	102, 109, 300–14
Teaching 3 Demonstrate good subject and curriculum knowledge	Have a secure knowledge of the relevant subject(s) and curriculum areas, foster and maintain pupils' interest in the subject and address misunderstandings	16. 21. 24. 26. 27.	2.1.1. 2.1.3. 2.4.3.	PC3ii PC15 PC25	86–8, 102
	Demonstrate a critical understanding of developments in the subject and curriculum areas and promote the value of scholarship	9. 10. 14.15. 16.	2.4.1. 2.4.3. 3.2.	PC3ii PCxi	

(Continued)

Standard for trainees and teachers (DfE, 2013)	Brief description (DfE, 2013)	Practising teacher Standards GTC Wales (2011)	Qualified teacher status registration GTC Scot. (2013)	Competences for trainees and NQT teachers GTC N. Ireland (2009)	Pages in this book referring to the competence
	Demonstrate an understanding of and take responsibility for promoting high standards of literacy, articulacy and the correct use of standard English, whatever the teachers' specialist subject	17.		PC3i	176–7, 281, 287, 290
	If teaching early reading demonstrate a clear understanding of appropriate teaching strategies	14. 17.		PC3i	176–8
Teaching 4 Plan and teach well-structured lessons	Impart knowledge and develop understanding through effective use of lesson time	21. 25. 31. 47.		PC5	122–31
	Promote a love of learning and children's intellectual curiosity	5. 16. 21. 27. 46. 53.		PC15 PC17 PC20	122–30, 154, 175–6
	Set homework and plan other out-of-class activities to consolidate and extend the knowledge and understanding pupils have acquired				88
	Reflect systematically on the effectiveness of lessons and approaches to teaching	10. 21. 24. 25.	2.3.2. 2.3.2. 2.4.1.	PC3i PC20	90–1, 384, 393
	Contribute to the design and provision of an engaging curriculum within the relevant subject area(s)	16. 21. 25. 27.	2.1.2. 2.1.3. 2.4.3. 3.3.	PC5 PC20	67–81

(Continued)

Table I.1 (Continued)

Standard for trainees and teachers (DfE, 2013)	Brief description (DfE, 2013)	Practising teacher Standards GTC Wales (2011)	Qualified teacher status registration GTC Scot. (2013)	Competences for trainees and NQT teachers GTC N. Ireland (2009)	Pages in this book referring to the competence
Teaching 5 Adapt teaching to respond to the strengths and needs of all pupils	Know when and how to differentiate properly, using approaches which enable pupils to be taught effectively	14. 15. 16. 19. 21. 24. 26. 35. 42.	2.1.1. 2.1.3. 2.1.4. 3.1.	PC6 PC8 PC9 PC15	67, 80, 86, 89, 110–11, 128, 152–3, 393, 438–9
	Have a secure understanding of how a range of factors can inhibit pupils' ability to learn and how best to overcome these	14. 15. 16. 19. 21. 24. 26. 35. 42.	2.1.1. 2.1.3. 3.1.	PC6 PC8 PC9 PC15	130, 197–200, 258–9, 284–97, 324
	Demonstrate awareness of the physical, social and intellectual development of children and how to adapt teaching to support pupils' education at different stages of development	14. 15. 16. 19. 21. 24. 26. 35. 42.	2.1.1. 2.1.2. 2.1.3. 2.1.4. 3.1.	PC6 PC8 PC9 PC15	130, 133, 154–5, 166, 236–52, 394
	Have a clear understanding of the needs of all pupils, including those with special educational needs; those of high ability; those with English as an additional language; those with disabilities; and be able to use and evaluate distinctive teaching approaches to engage and support them	14. 15. 16. 19. 21. 24. 26. 35.	2.1.1. 2.1.2. 2.1.3. 2.1.4. 3.1.	PC6 PC8 PC9 PC15 PC21	203–7, 284–97, 324
Teaching 6 Make accurate and productive use of assessment	Know and understand how to assess the relevant subject and curriculum areas, including statutory assessment requirements Make use of summative and formative assessment to secure pupils' progress	14. 16. 25. 26. 33. 34.	2.3.1.	PC24 PC25 PC26	32–3, 75, 80, 96, 98, 99, 102–3, 129

(Continued)

Standard for trainees and teachers (DfE, 2013)	Brief description (DfE, 2013)	Practising teacher Standards GTC Wales (2011)	Qualified teacher status registration GTC Scot. (2013)	Competences for trainees and NQT teachers GTC N. Ireland (2009)	Pages in this book referring to the competence
	Use relevant data to monitor progress and plan subsequent lessons	21. 25. 26. 33. 36.	2.3.1.	PC24 PC26	79, 83, 88, 98–9, 101, 102–3
	Give pupils regular feedback	5. 21. 24. 26. 33. 36. 38.	2.1.2. 2.1.4. 2.3.1.		
Teaching 7 Manage behaviour effectively	Have clear rules and routines for behaviour in classrooms and take responsibility for promoting good and courteous behaviour, both in classrooms and around the school, in accordance with the school's behaviour policy	2. 21. 40. 49.	2.2.1. 2.2.2.	PC6 PC19 PC7 PC15 PC22	131–3, 214
	Have high expectations of behaviour and establish a framework for discipline, with a range of strategies, using praise, sanctions and rewards consistently and fairly	21. 49.		PCvi PCvii PC15 PC22	222–32
	Manage classes effectively, using approaches which are appropriate to pupils' needs, in order to involve and motivate them	46.	2.1.2. 2.2.1. 2.2.2.	PC6 PC7 PC21	124–37
	Maintain good relationships with pupils, exercise appropriate authority and act decisively when necessary	2. 21.	2.2.1. 2.2.2.	PC6 PC7 PC15 PC22	
Teaching 8 Fulfil wider professional responsibilities	Make a positive contribution to the wider life and ethos of the school	7. 30.	3.3.	PC12 PC17	150–1

(Continued)

Table I.1 (Continued)

Standard for trainees and teachers (DfE, 2013)	Brief description (DfE, 2013)	Practising teacher Standards	Qualified teacher status registration	Competences for trainees and NQT teachers	Pages in this book referring to the competence
		GTC Wales (2011)	GTC Scot. (2013)	GTC N. Ireland (2009)	
	Develop effective professional relationships with colleagues, knowing how and when to draw on specialist advice and support	8. 20. 28. 32. 54.	2.1.5. 2.2.2. 2.4.2.	PC1 PC3i	156, 396, 459
	Deploy support staff effectively	8. 28. 29.	2.1.5.	PC10 PC16	147–8, 340–5, 349
	Take responsibility for improving teaching through appropriate professional development, responding to advice and feedback from colleagues	9. 10. 16.	2.4.1. 2.4.3. 3.2.	PC3i PC3ii PC10 PC11	147–8, 148–9, 181, 359–80, 393–4, 430–53, 440–1, 466–70
	Communicate effectively with parents with regard to pupils' achievements and well-being	4. 6. 39.	2.1.5. 3.3.	PC1 PC10 PC27	145–7, 151, 158, 166
PART 2 Personal and Professional Conduct	1. Treat pupils with dignity, building relationships based on mutual respect, observing proper boundaries appropriate to a teacher's professional position	2.		PC19	153, 257
	2. Safeguard pupils in accordance with statutory provisions	48.		C 1 C 9 C13 C14 C 22	141

(Continued)

Standard for trainees and teachers (DfE, 2013)	Brief description (DfE, 2013)	Practising teacher Standards GTC Wales (2011)	Qualified teacher status registration GTC Scot. (2013)	Competences for trainees and NQT teachers GTC N. Ireland (2009)	Pages in this book referring to the competence
	3. Show tolerance and respect for the rights of others				Throughout
	4. Not undermine fundamental British values, including democracy, the Rule of Law, individual liberty and mutual respect and tolerance of those with different faiths and beliefs				321–3, 340–5, 349
	5. Ensure that personal beliefs are not expressed in ways which exploit pupils' vulnerability or might lead them to break the law				321–3
	6. Have proper and professional regard for the ethos, policies and practices of the school in which they teach and maintain high standards in their attendance and punctuality		1.2.2.	C22	
	7. Have an understanding of and always act within the statutory frameworks set out in their professional duties and responsibilities	12. 13. 22.	1.2.1. 1.2.2.	C22	400–26

It is not possible here to give a detailed analysis of other differences in emphasis which distinguish them but only to point out some interesting differences. Chapter 18, on statutory professional responsibilities, includes comprehensive references to requirements for teachers in Wales, Scotland and Northern Ireland.

Theory, research and debate

The English Standards require teachers to take responsibility for their professional development, and to 'understand how children learn'. Part 3 of the English Standards stresses the importance of working within school policies and statutory frameworks and maintaining 'British values'. This contrasts significantly with the aims and aspirations of the NI Competences, which are embedded in an inspiring document, *Teaching: The Reflective Profession* (GTCNI, 2009). This stresses the importance of developing a professional identity in order to exercise professional autonomy, in a constantly changing educational context, and the importance of professional dialogue. It talks about vision and moral purpose, creativity and value-based practice. It describes teachers as characterised by concerns for the purposes and consequences of education, prepared to experiment with the unfamiliar and learn from it, by openness and wholeheartedness. Such teachers act as activist pedagogues and are experts in teaching and learning, reflective and critical problem solvers, researchers and change agents, creators of knowledge and builders of theory. The Scottish Standards refer specifically to 'relevant principles, perspectives and theories to inform professional values and practices' (1.3.1) and 'an understanding of research and its contribution to education' (1.3.2), accessing and evaluating professionally relevant literature (2.4.1), and to constructing and sustaining reasoned arguments (2.4.2) about educational matters and professional practices. The Welsh Standard 9 requires teachers to 'share and test understandings with colleagues through active involvement in professional networks and learning communities'.

Social justice and the community

The English Standards refer to making a positive contribution to the life and ethos of the school and to working with parents, while the Scottish Standards refer to a commitment to social justice (3.1) and to valuing, respecting and showing commitment to the communities in which teachers work (3.3). Professional values and personal commitment include: values of sustainability, equality and justice and demonstrating a commitment to engaging learners in real-world issues to enhance learning experiences and outcomes, and to encourage learning our way to a better future, critically examining the connections between personal and professional attitudes and beliefs, values and practices to effect improvement and, when appropriate, bringing about transformative change in practice. One of the Welsh Standards (7) refers to celebrating the contribution children and young people make in their communities.

Teaching is a complex, serious and important business. There are always some lows to overcome for all of us. But it is also satisfying and rewarding – and it is fun! For if you are not enjoying yourself, how can you expect that the children are? We hope this book will help you to always want to know more, to teach better and to enjoy your work with confidence.

References

Department for Education (DfE) (2013) *Teachers' Standards*. Available at: www.education. gov.uk.

Department for Education and Skills, Welsh Government (2011) *Revised Professional Standards for Education Practitioners in Wales*. Available at: www.cymru.gov.uk.

General Teaching Council for Northern Ireland (GTCNI) (2009) *Teaching: The Reflective Profession*. Available at: www.gtcni.org.uk.

General Teaching Council for Scotland (GTCS) (2013) *Standards for Registration*. Available at: www.gtcs.org.uk/standards.

Footnote regarding the second edition: We are grateful to Pete Boyd and Graham Hallett, authors of the material on p. 204 of the second edition, which can be found in greater detail on http:// cumbria.ac.uk/Courses/SubjectAreas/Education/Continuing ProfessionalDevelopment/ CumbriaTeacher/Firstclass/ManagingClassroomBehaviour/Home.aspx.

Part 1

INTRODUCTION TO PROFESSIONAL STUDIES

The first six chapters of this book introduce readers to the philosophy that underpins the book and establish what we might call the foundations of professional studies in primary education. The philosophy of the book aims to show that, within statutory requirements, teachers are nevertheless responsible for constantly making professional decisions and judgements in all aspects of teaching and learning, interpreted through the qualities and skills of confident professional integrity. In Part 1 you will read about the history of primary education so that you can take an objective and long-term view of the present and of future changes. You will learn, through philosophical enquiry, how to ask questions about, debate and challenge educational theories, practices and policies. And you will begin to see how there are complex decisions and judgements to make and evaluate, in planning and assessment, in creating an effective learning environment and in your interactions with children and adults in school. You will begin to develop your own educational philosophy, which will enable you to become a teacher who is capable of managing change with integrity.

1

History of Education

Susan Shaw and Ian Shirley

By the end of this chapter, you should:

- have knowledge of the education system from 1870 onwards
- have an understanding of changes in the philosophy, curriculum, management and accountability in primary schools
- be able to speculate about the future of education
- begin to form your own professional philosophy and values
- understand the need to respond to changes with professional integrity.

Introduction

In order to fully appreciate and understand the education system that will be in place once you qualify, it is necessary to have an insight into the influences and decisions that have taken place in the past to form and develop the current system of primary education (Winton and Brewer, 2014). The norm today is for all children aged 5 years to attend primary school. However, compulsory primary education in England did not begin until 1880. Before this, there were many types of formal and informal schooling. This chapter will highlight some key dates, people and events that have contributed to the current education system and the primary curriculum. It will also show how educational policy offers only a 'temporary settlement' (Ball, 1993b) in the ongoing struggle over educational reform. From Forster's 1870 Education Act to the Academies Act of 2010 and beyond, educational policy is the means by which governments seek to control state education.

This chapter considers the impact of legislation on teaching and learning (e.g. the curriculum and the effects of increasing centralisation, testing and league tables) and the advantages claimed for this legislation (i.e. the values underpinning the National Curriculum). It shows how an informed educational philosophy helps us respond to centralised changes and considers the development of new curricula.

1870: the beginning of compulsory state education

Rationale

By 1870 England was a largely industrial rather than an agricultural society. Conditions in many of the rapidly expanding cities were often very bad. Compulsory schooling was introduced, partly to provide the labour force with the basic skills and routines necessary in an industrial society and also to attempt to prevent civil unrest, which people feared as a very real possibility, considering revolutionary activity in neighbouring France.

Church and state

The Education Act of 1870, known as the 'Forster Act', laid down the requirement to establish compulsory, elementary education in England. It recognised a dual education system consisting of both voluntary denominational schools and non-denominational state schools. These were intended to supplement rather than replace schools already run by the churches, guilds and private individuals or organisations. In other countries, the church was less involved in state education but in Britain, as a result of the 1870 Act the church has continued to play a substantial part in the education of young children.

School Boards

School districts were formed throughout the country and where there was not enough educational provision for the children in a district, School Boards were formed. They set up schools that became known as Board Schools. These had to be non-denominational. The School Boards could charge a weekly fee if there were insufficient funds, but the fee was not allowed to be more than 9 pence. The School Boards had to ensure that children between the ages of 5 and 13 attended the schools in their districts and this was enforced by an Attendance Officer.

The curriculum

The curriculum in the 1870s mainly consisted of the 3 Rs (reading, writing and 'rithmetic) and religious instruction, which provided faith, nurture and moral instruction as an integral part of the school curriculum. Despite this the 3 Rs were not actually compulsory. There were some additional aspects, for example, drill and 'object lessons'. Object lessons involved the study of an artefact. Needlework was an extra for girls and carpentry an extra for boys. Her Majesty's Inspectors visited the schools to test children's skills in the '3 Rs', and teachers' payment was based on the children's attainment, that is, it was 'payment by results'.

In some respects, as we shall see, primary education remains tied to its Victorian roots. The exceptionally early start for formal schooling, the generalist primary school teacher, the separation of 'infants' and 'juniors', the focus on the basics at the expense of a broader curriculum remain and have not been seriously questioned. But the Victorian Elementary School was intended to prepare the poor for their 'station' in life rather than to broaden their opportunities.

1902–1944

There were three developments in education during this period: the Balfour Act (1902), which created Local Education Authorities (LEAs), the Fisher Act (1918), which raised the school leaving age from 12 to 14, and the Hadow Reports (1923–31), one of which recommended school transfer at 11, so creating the idea of the primary school.

Reflective task

Read *Children, their World, their Education*, Chapter 13 (Alexander, 2010), which compares the curriculum past and present. In groups, compare the curriculum in the late 1800s with the curriculum of today. Compare similarities and differences. To what extent are the external forces that influence the content of the curriculum the same or different today? If you could put together a primary curriculum, what would your priorities be?

In Chapter 15 Elton-Chalcraft, Revell and Lander propose that Victorian education policy may have influenced British education in order to suppress revolution, which was happening in neighbouring France, and to inculcate allegiance to the social order. In what way do you think contemporary school culture promotes allegiance to the dominant social order?

Post World War II: primary schools and three types of secondary school

The Butler Education Act of 1944

The tripartite system for secondary education

The education system offered primary education, secondary education and further education. The tripartite system of secondary education, implemented in the 1944 Act, offered three types of education after the age of 11: grammar schools for the most able, based on 'intelligence tests', secondary modern schools for most pupils and secondary technical schools for those perceived to have technical or scientific ability. This was intended to increase opportunities for all.

Church schools

After the 1944 Act, the Church of England still had control of most rural schools and many urban ones. The 1944 Act put church schools into two categories: 'voluntary aided' (where the church had greater control) and 'voluntary controlled' (where the LEA had greater control), and this is still the case. This control is in regard to buildings, staffing and the religious curriculum and worship.

Local Education Authorities

Primary education and secondary education became free for all children up to the age of 15. The LEAs took more responsibility and there was a rise in their status. They had to ensure that there was sufficient provision for the educational needs of pupils in their geographical area. Through the provision LEAs offered, they had to make sure that pupils had an effective education that contributed to their spiritual, moral, mental and physical development, but they were not responsible for the more detailed curriculum.

The curriculum

The Act gave head teachers, in consultation with governors, control of the school curriculum and resourcing. The Act said very little about the curriculum, apart from religious education. Teachers were left to decide what to teach and how to teach it. Religious education and collective worship were to take place in all schools, and if you worked in an aided school you could be dismissed by the governors if you did not deliver religious instruction 'efficiently and suitably'. It is quite clear at this point that there was no expectation that the national government would ever have control of the curriculum. However, it is evident that there was concern for the moral soul of the population and allegiance to the social order.

Special educational needs provision

The 1944 Act included provision for pupils with special educational needs (SEN). If pupils were deemed to be unable to profit from being educated in a mainstream school, their education had to be provided in a special school. At this time, the types and degrees of disability were named and this was the case until 1981, when it was agreed that these labels were inappropriate. (See the section on policy and practice in Chapter 8, 'Inclusion and Special Educational Needs'.)

Effects of the 1944 Education Act

The selection process, rather like Standard Attainment Tests (SATs), had an effect on primary education. The need to 'get children through' the eleven-plus had the same effect as the need to get Level 4 or 5 at age 11. There were also large classes throughout the late 1940s and 1950s and a shortage of teachers. Whole-class teaching continued and the curriculum emphasised basic literacy and numeracy: 'Writers looking back at the early curriculum saw that, in fact, the tradition derived from 1870 was still dominant' (Galton et al., 1980, p. 36). It was not until the 1960s that more formal class teaching gave way to new ideas. In 1964 the Schools Council was formed, and the partnership between LEAs, schools and universities led to more experiments with the curriculum.

The Plowden Report: a new philosophy of education?

There had not been a specific review of primary education since the Hadow report of 1931. The context of the time in which the Plowden Report (1967) was written was one of a liberal view of education and society. The emphasis of the Plowden Report could be encapsulated in the phrase 'at the heart of the educational process lies the child' (Plowden, 1967, p. 9). Plowden advocated experiential learning, increased parental involvement, universal pre-school education and opportunities for the less privileged. It highlighted firmly the need for differentiation and supported the requirement for personalisation when saying 'individual differences between children of the same age are so great that any class … must always be treated as a body of children needing individual and different attention' (Plowden, 1967, p. 25). Chapter 2 also discusses testing and the use of IQ (Intelligence Quotient) tests in eleven-plus selection tests in the 1950s and 1960s. Plowden says that they 'should not be treated as infallible predictors. Judgements which determine careers should be deferred as long as possible.' It was the Labour government of this time that almost removed all eleven-plus tests at the end of primary schooling, but since it lost the election in 1970, it failed to quite eradicate all testing at 11. There are many aspects of the Plowden Report that most primary teachers would agree with.

> One of the main educational tasks of the primary school is to build on and strengthen children's intrinsic interest in learning and lead them to learn for themselves rather than from fear of disapproval or desire for praise. (Plowden, 1967, p. 532)

The persistent acknowledgement of individual learning, flexibility in the curriculum, use of the environment, learning by discovery and the importance of the evaluation of children's progress have a certain resonance, not only with educational theory but in the philosophy of many teachers.

The Plowden Report endorsed the move away from formal class teaching to group work, projects and learning through play and creativity. Chapters of the report challenged the existing aims of primary education, classroom organisation and the curriculum, and supported 'child-centred' primary schools. It was a real attempt to enlarge the concept of primary education.

Nevertheless, most schools changed very little. The Her Majesty's Inspectors (HMI) primary survey (DES, 1978) reported that only 5 per cent of primary schools adopted exploratory approaches and three-quarters still used 'didactic' methods.

Back to basics, market forces and increasing centralisation

Economic recession led to cutbacks in educational expenditure and was partly blamed for the series of 'Black Papers' written by right-wing educationalists. The first paper was published in 1969. Specifically focusing on the 'progressive education' being developed in the primary schools, the writers challenged the figures on reading standards and accused teachers of neglecting basics and concentrating too much on informality. The years 1992 and 1998 also saw a return of the 'back to basics' theme and a desire to challenge 'progressive' ideas in education.

Her Majesty's Inspectorate 1975

In 1975 HMI began a survey of the primary curriculum. This included assessments of children's work at 7, 9 and 11. The report was not published until 1978. It criticised teachers' underestimation of children's abilities and noted the lack of specialist teachers. The questioning of teacher assessment, which later resulted in SATs, and the content of the curriculum are recurring themes for both Conservative and Labour governments and successive Secretaries of State for Education.

Callaghan's Ruskin Speech – Great Debate on Education 1976

Labour Prime Minister, James Callaghan, 'brought comfort to his Tory enemies … schools were convenient scapegoats, education a scarecrow…'. This was 'the impression conveyed by the Prime Minister' (Morris, 1988, p. 7). He argued that not just teachers and parents but also government and industry had an important part to play in formulating the aims of education.

In his historic speech, Callaghan spoke about:

- a public debate on education: employers, trade unions, parents, teachers and administrators were to make their views known
- a curriculum that paid too little attention to the basic skills of reading, writing and arithmetic
- how teachers lacked adequate professional skills, could not discipline children or teach them good manners and did not manage to instil in them the need for hard work
- the underlying reason for all this, which was that the education system was out of touch with the fundamental needs of the country.

Callaghan's speech troubled the educational waters. As Ball (2008, p. 83) notes, he called into question the wisdom of leaving educational decision making to teachers, LEAs and educational academics. His view on English education was framed by increasing financial and economic uncertainty, social unrest and a growing distrust among right-wing politicians towards post-war, welfare-state reform. This Great Debate on Education seems to have been ongoing since 1976 and consecutive governments have increasingly tightened their grip on education. Whether 'progressive education' was slowed down by James Callaghan's speech or by the next 18 years of Conservative rule and education policy is debatable.

The 1979 Education Act

Margaret Thatcher was Education Secretary before becoming Prime Minister. She overturned Labour's 1976 Act and gave back to LEAs the right to select pupils for secondary education at 11. However, comprehensive secondary education was popular and reversal did not gain the backing expected. Key to Thatcher's educational reform was the dual influence of neo-liberal and neo-conservative values. These require some explanation.

Neo-liberal policy influences sought to end state subsidy and intervention within education through 'deregulation, liberalisation and privatisation'. According to Rizvi and Lingard (2009) neo-liberal education policy emphasises competition, markets and choice as solutions to educational problems. They add that neo-liberal education policy influences what people do in education, and how people account for themselves. Winter (2012) argues that, under neo-liberalism, the discourse around education has moved from one of personal growth to one of national success within the international global market.

Neo-conservatism, sometimes called the 'New Right', concerns what constitutes official school knowledge (Apple, 2014). Some authors, such as Hill (2006), argue that neo-conservative influences imagine a glorious past of 'real knowledge' to which society may one day return. Neo-conservative influences are seen to influence curriculum choices within education, and are responsible for the emphasis on testing and accountability within school attainment.

A framework for the curriculum 1980

This was the first of a long series of reports about what the curriculum should contain: *Framework for the School Curriculum* (HMI, 1980a), *A View of the Curriculum* (HMI, 1980b), *The School Curriculum* (DES, 1981a), and Circular 6/81 (DES, 1981b). *The School Curriculum 1981* encouraged putting a high priority on English and mathematics:

> It is essential that the early skills in reading, writing and calculating should be effectively learned in primary schools, since deficiencies at this stage cannot easily be remedied later and children will face the world seriously handicapped. (DES, 1981a, para. 35)

However, schools also had to provide a 'wide range of experience, in order to stimulate the children's interest and imagination and fully to extend pupils of all abilities' (DES, 1980, p. 10). Religious education, topic work, science, art and craft, physical education, music and French were all mentioned in this report, alongside personal and social development. From 1981 to 1986, Sir Keith Joseph had responsibility for implementing education policies, right down to everyday practice.

Reflective task

In his famous talk, 'Changing Educational Paradigms', Ken Robinson (2008) discusses cultural identity and economic influences on contemporary education policy. The talk is available with animations at www.ted.com/talks/ken_robinson_changing_education_paradigms. Watch the video and consider Robinson's points in relation to your own experience of educational change.

The Curriculum from 5 to 16 (HMI, 1985)

This was a forward-looking document talking about 'areas of learning and experience'. This concept was developed in the introduction of a National Curriculum, in the Education Reform Act 1988. The curriculum of all schools had to provide pupils with the following areas of learning and experience: aesthetic and creative, human and social, linguistic and literary, mathematical, moral, physical, scientific, spiritual and technological.

Work in school

Student A: From what I have read about the history of primary education it seems to be swings and roundabouts – one step forward, one step back – teachers having to respond to constant policy changes. Am I right about this?

Mentor: It can seem like that, but there are underlying developments I think. Why don't you look at the 1967 Plowden Report? It talks about experiential learning through the environment, evaluating progress, parental involvement, differentiation and personalised learning, a

(Continued)

(Continued)

flexible curriculum and a philosophy in which the child is at the heart of educational processes. Inspectors found that it hadn't had much impact by 1978. But I suggest you note, under these headings, evidence you find of its influence in the 2013 National Curriculum and in this school today. You may be surprised.

Student B: In recent years there seems to have been increasing emphasis on reading, writing and arithmetic. I agree that these are essential skills. But I also think music, art, history – all the rest of the curriculum – are very important and that children should enjoy learning. How can I combine these beliefs?

Mentor: Well, there are two questions to think about here. First let's think of all the ways in which 'the basics' can be taught in ways the children enjoy. And also think about how you can teach literacy and maths across the curriculum. Note down some ideas to discuss before our planning meeting – and have a look at what Alexander (2010) says about primary schools being seen as happy places, which nevertheless do not neglect the 3 Rs.

Parent power

Successive governments had tried to get parents to engage with education. The neo-liberal Conservative government of the 1980s chose to cast parents as consumers and clients. The 1980 Education Act gave more power to parents. Parents were encouraged to serve on governing bodies. Thatcher's 'free-trade' ideology brought increased parental choice, which meant that parents had the right to choose their children's schools and the opportunity to appeal if their choice was not upheld. The publication of exam and text results introduced an element of market competition between schools, which later became cemented in national school comparison tables. The Warnock Report (1978) gave parents new rights in relation to SEN. LEAs identified the needs of children with learning difficulties but also had to produce 'statements' for parents on how these needs would be met. Parent power was increased in the 1984 Green Paper, *Parental Influence at School* (HMI, 1984), which reiterated the role and responsibilities of parents and the vital role parents have to play in the education system.

The 1986 Education Act

The 1986 (1) Education Act introduced the requirement that the LEAs had to give governors financial information on the financing of schools. The 1986 (2) Education

Act adopted the proposals in the 1985 White Paper, *Better Schools*, arguing yet again for breadth, balance and progression in order to achieve standards in literacy and numeracy – a close throwback to comments by HMI in 1978. *Better Schools* opened with: 'The Government will: take the lead in promoting national agreement about the purposes and the content of the curriculum …' (DES, 1985, p. 1).

The Education Reform Bill 1988

The Great Education Reform Bill (generally known as Gerbil) was seen as the most important Education Act since the 1944 Act, and aimed to give more power to schools. However, from the LEAs' point of view, it was taking power from them and giving it to the Secretary of State. Governmental power over education was wielded through the following power technologies.

A National Curriculum

The Act had significant implications for primary schools. The government proposed a common curriculum for pupils aged 5 to 16, a National Curriculum. This was a shift away from teachers deciding what was taught to central government having control. The curriculum was divided into discrete subjects and there were three core subjects (English, mathematics and science) and seven 'foundation subjects'. Prior to this, teachers wrote schemes of work they considered appropriate for their pupils.

Written by a government 'quango' of subject specialists and with a substantial content base, teachers were hardly involved in the development of the National Curriculum and felt they were deliverers of a curriculum rather than designers and pace-setters. The National Curriculum had three main aims: the school curriculum had to provide opportunities for all pupils to learn and to achieve; pupils across the country were entitled to the same broad curriculum; and the curriculum should aim to promote pupils' spiritual, moral, social and cultural development, and prepare all pupils for the opportunities, responsibilities and experiences of life (DES, 1988). Evident within government thinking at the time was a neo-conservative emphasis on high standards, basics and traditional values. Ball (1993a) describes the government's approach to National Curriculum subjects as 'restorationist' in that they sought to re-invoke a golden-age curriculum from a glorious, yet mythical, past (Ball, 1993a, p. 202). Furthermore, he argues that the approach to learning advocated by government represents a 'fossilized tradition … divorced from the here and now and from the possibility of engagement' (Ball, 1993a, p. 201).

The *Three Wise Men Report* (DES, 1992) was a government-commissioned report that emphasised the need for a return to quality in primary school pedagogy: 'Whatever the mode of curriculum organisation, the breadth, balance and consistency of the curriculum experienced by pupils must be of central concern' (DES, 1992, p. 23). The *Three Wise Men Report* was written by Robin Alexander, Jim Rose and Chris Woodhead, all of whom had a further impact on primary education beyond this document.

Assessment

Before the Education Reform Act, pupil progress was tracked by teacher assessments. The Act introduced compulsory national SATs at 7, 11 and 14. The tests were based on the 1988 Black Report produced by the National Curriculum Task Group on Assessment and Testing (TGAT). The results had to be published annually in league tables. This allowed the government to compare schools directly in terms of these data.

Local Management of Schools

Local Management of Schools (LMS), flagged in the Education Act, was not introduced until 1991. It allowed the delegation of financial and managerial responsibilities to schools. Management for the budget was the responsibility of the school and budgets were taken away from LEAs. There were some centrally held resources in the LEAs, such as curriculum advisory and support services and school library services, although these increasingly diminished during the 1990s. There were mixed views among head teachers as to whether LMS gave schools greater flexibility, but they certainly had greater responsibility. LMS might be seen as the first step in the transformation of the school leader as one concerned, not just with educational attainment, but with efficiency, educational entrepreneurialism and the commitment to government educational objectives.

Grant maintained schools

Although grammar schools were not reintroduced as part of the 1988 reforms, grant maintained (GM) schools were introduced. Schools were able to opt out of LEA control and be funded directly by central government. It was seen as a bribe to schools to encourage them to opt out, especially as they were offered additional funding. GM schools also had more control over admissions and were allowed to select up to 10 per cent of their pupils on ability, putting them at a possible advantage in terms of school league tables.

The Office for Standards in Education

The creation of the Office for Standards in Education (Ofsted) also resulted from the 1988 Education Act, although it wasn't actually set up until 1992, when it replaced visits to schools by HMI with a more rigorous inspection system. When Ofsted inspected schools, a report was to be published, and the emphasis was on inspection and not support. It came across as an antagonising system and stressful for teachers as there was naming and shaming of failing schools when they were put into 'special measures'. Chris Woodhead, one of the authors of the Three Wise Men Report, was appointed Her Majesty's Chief Inspector of Schools and Head of Ofsted in September 1994.

In-service training

As part of the reform of the teaching profession, Secretary of State Kenneth Baker introduced compulsory training days to manage the process of reform and the implementation of the National Curriculum. The training days were known as Baker Days for some time, and today, five in-service training days are included as part of the annual school calendar. The issue of teacher continuing professional development (CPD) is taken up in Chapter 16 by Boyd on 'Learning Teaching' in School', and Chapter 19 on 'Moving on to Master's Level' by Darbyshire, Harrop and Duckworth.

The National Curriculum Revised: The Dearing Report 1993

The Dearing Report made several key proposals about the National Curriculum and the changes cost an estimated £744 million. He advised that the curriculum should be slimmed down, the time given to testing should be reduced and around 20 per cent of teaching time should be freed up for use at the discretion of schools. However, the proposals were difficult to implement as the government wanted literacy and numeracy to take up 50 per cent of the timetable, leaving the other eight subjects to be squashed into the remaining 50 per cent.

'Education, education, education' 1997

'Ask me my three main priorities for government and I tell you education, education, and education' (Blair, 1996). Blair put education right at the top of the political agenda during the election of 1997. Speaking to the Labour Party conference after becoming Prime Minister in 1997, he stated: 'Our goal: to make Britain the best educated and skilled country in the world; a nation, not of a few talents, but of all the talents. And every single part of our schools' system must be modernised to achieve it' (Blair, 1997).

Gewirtz (2003) criticises New Labour's 'third-way' educational policies in that they try to balance both market and humanist values. She notes a tension between the attempt to promote educational markets, competition, privatisation and managerial processes on the one hand, while arguing for a broad educational experience, teacher professionalism, and social equity and justice on the other.

Excellence in Schools 1997

This White Paper (DfEE, 1997) pointed towards the importance of the basics and set a target of 80 per cent of all 11-year-olds to reach the 'required standard' of literacy and 75 per cent to reach the 'required standard' of numeracy by 2002.

It was proposed that class sizes should be less than 30 for 5–7-year-olds and this was adopted in the School Standards and Framework Act 1998. There was to be at least an hour a day spent on English and mathematics in primary schools and this set the scene for the literacy and numeracy strategies.

LEAs set targets for raising standards in individual schools. Governors had to publish school performance tables that showed the rate of progress pupils made against the targets set. Schools deemed 'failing' by Ofsted could not hide. LEAs could intervene in the schools, which were given 2 years to improve or they would be closed or have management changes imposed on them.

Back to basics 1998

In a speech to the National Association of Headteachers (NAH) in 1999, New Labour Prime Minister, Tony Blair, complained of low standards in education. He argued that many children failed to achieve competency in the basics of literacy and numeracy. The 'back to basics' theme returned, and schools no longer had to teach National Curriculum programmes of study in all subjects, just in the three core subjects. This set up the background for introducing the literacy and numeracy strategies.

Literacy and numeracy strategies 1998 and 1999

Both these strategies were very prescriptive, giving both the content of what had to be taught and the delivery method. These were daily lessons that, although not statutory, were often seen as mandatory. Schools had to be very brave to break the mould and deliver their own ideas of lessons and schemes for literacy and numeracy. The National

Literacy Strategy (DfEE, 1998), the National Numeracy Strategy (DfEE, 1999b) and National Learning Targets were introduced (DfEE, 1999a). The Labour government was now seen to be telling teachers how to teach, in addition to teaching the National Curriculum, which had been seen as telling them what to teach.

National Curriculum 2000

The launch of a National Curriculum Review took place in 1997. However, it was 2000 before all the changes took place. To the huge relief of teaching staff, the curriculum was slimmed down, but not without the addition of citizenship. However, whilst testing was happening at the age of 11, creativity was not top of the list in the classrooms of Years 5 and 6. The paper *Schools – Achieving Success* (DfES, 2001) proposed allowing successful primary schools to opt out of the National Curriculum and seek to develop innovation. The Foundation Stage for children aged 3–5 years was introduced and had six areas of learning. This may have influenced the thinking for the development of the curriculum in the Rose Review (DCSF, 2009).

Every Child Matters 2003

In 2003, the government published its Green Paper *Every Child Matters* (ECM) (DfES, 2003a) following the death of Victoria Climbié. The ECM agenda had five clear outcomes that schools needed to consider in the development of their curriculum. These were: to be healthy; stay safe; enjoy and achieve; make a positive contribution; and achieve economic well-being.

Excellence and Enjoyment 2003

Excellence and Enjoyment (DfES, 2003b) claims to promote excellence in teaching 'the basics' and enjoyment through the broader curriculum. The existing National Numeracy Strategy (1999) and National Literacy Strategy (1998) conflated into one document, the *Primary National Strategy* (PNS) (DfES, 2006). The PNS again aimed to promote high standards that should be achieved through a rich, varied and exciting curriculum. It aimed to build on the literacy and numeracy strategies but to give teachers more chance to take control of their teaching. There was more flexibility for schools to adopt ways of working that suited them. Testing and target setting were all part of the PNS and assessment for learning developed out of this report. The success of the PNS is a matter of debate. Boyle and Bragg (2006), for example, show how, despite the PNS, a culture of performativity and the emphasis of two core subjects has led to a further decline in the teaching of primary foundation subjects and science.

Towards a new curriculum

The Children's Plan (DCSF, 2007) announced a root and branch review of the curriculum and this was to be headed by Sir Jim Rose, another author of the so-called *Three Wise Men Report* (DES, 1992). Running concurrently with this was a review by Robin Alexander and a team of researchers, the Cambridge Primary Review (CPR). This is a more philosophical and research-based report, published as *Children, Their World, Their Education* (Alexander, 2010). Neither review became policy.

Where to next?

The CPR (Alexander, 2010) provides firm research evidence that, despite these intense pressures, primary schools are highly valued by children and parents. The CPR claims that primary schools are seen as largely happy places that consistently celebrate the positive. It suggests they do not, as some claim, neglect the 3 Rs. Furthermore, the CPR contends that 'those who regularly make this claim are either careless of the facts or are knowingly fostering calumny' (Hofkins and Northen, 2009, p. 7). The Cambridge Primary Review Trust (CPRT) continued for 10 years producing research papers and supporting local regional networks of university tutors and schools to improve learning and teaching based on sound educational research. Formally closed in 2017 the CPRT resources were relocated to the Chartered College for Teaching. See https://www.collegeofteaching.org.

Beyond 2010

The Conservative/Liberal Democrat Coalition government, elected in 2010, immediately planned changes in education: in the curriculum, in teacher education, in management of schools, in examinations at secondary level and in policies on, for example, behaviour management and SEN. The new *Teachers' Standards* (DfE, 2013a) are discussed in the introduction (p. 5). Behaviour management and SEN policies are discussed in Chapters 8 and 9.

National Curriculum 2014

Draft versions of the new National Curriculum were published for consultation in February and July 2013, accompanied by much media discussion, before the new curriculum was agreed by parliament, prior to the implementation of the final version from 2014. This requires state-funded schools and maintained schools, community special schools, voluntary aided and voluntary controlled schools to follow the statutory curriculum. This new curriculum retained the four Key Stages (5–7, 7–11, 11–14, 14–16) with English, mathematics and science as core subjects and art and design, citizenship, computing, design and technology, geography, history, music and physical education compulsory throughout the primary phase, with a foreign language at Key Stage 2. The Curriculum also requires that all state schools make provision for a daily act of collective worship, teach religious education and provide good practice in personal, social and health education. These schools, and also academies, must 'provide a balanced and broadly-based curriculum which, similar to the previous National Curriculum, promotes spiritual, moral and physical development … prepares pupils for opportunities, responsibilities in later life and makes provision for personal, social, health and economic education'. State-funded, voluntary aided, voluntary controlled and maintained schools may, in addition to the National Curriculum, include 'other subjects or topics of their choice in planning their own programmes of education' (DfE, 2013b, p. 4). However, academies and free schools are only required to offer a 'broad and balanced curriculum' (Academies Act 2010, www.legislation.gov.uk/ukpga/2010/32/section/1). All schools must publish their curriculum, by subject and academic year, online (DfE, 2013b, p. 4).

The purposes, aims and content for each subject are set out, with greater detail for the core subjects, and each subject is supported by non-statutory notes and guidance. This subsumes the necessity for supplementary strategies for English, mathematics and, for example, for citizenship. A significant difference from the previous National Curriculum is that the progression in skills and processes involved in each subject are embedded in the Purposes and Aims of Study for each subject and the Attainment Targets require pupils to know, apply and understand these skills and processes at the end of each Key Stage. This seems to make it easier for teachers to continuously plan for and monitor differentiated progress. Unlike the previous curriculum, it does not make detailed claims for an artificial notion of what progress in some subjects may consist of.

Chartered College of Teaching

The Chartered College of Teaching was formally recognised from the beginning of 2017. The Chief Executive Officer of the college, Dame Alison Peacock, was appointed in August 2016 after a very successful headship at Wroxham Primary School. She has written and spoken extensively about challenging notions of children's fixed ability through her work on Learning without Limits (Peacock, 2017). The Chartered College aims to represent the collective voice of the teaching profession, drawing on research and best practice among a professional community of peers. The aims of the College are to raise the status of the teaching profession, to guide career-long professional development, and to influence decisions about policy and practice in the future.

Initial teacher education

There is a complex array of ITE provision in England:

- ITE (traditional university-based route): where academic training takes place in university and professional practice within schools.
- School Direct (SD) ITE: professional practice takes place in schools but the academic content can be taught at school hubs by the university or at the university base; however, the cluster of schools must have a named university with whom they work in partnership. SD ITE where trainees study at university is called a 'partnership model' and those where they study away from university a 'hub model'.
- SD clusters are a group of schools, with a lead school that liaises more closely with the university than the rest of the schools in the cluster.
- The vast majority of ITE and SD trainees exit with a Postgraduate Certificate in Education (PGCE) and qualified teacher status (QTS).
- School Centred Initial Teacher Training establishments (SCITTs) are schools that have been approved by the National College of Teaching for Leadership (NCTL) to run school-centred QTS courses. Their focus is on the professional practice and not the academic element, therefore many do not offer the PGCE qualification.
- Teaching schools are 'strong schools led by strong leaders that work with others to provide high-quality training, development and support to new and experienced school staff' (NCTL, 2014). They are not to be confused with School Direct. Teaching schools may additionally lead an SD cluster but equally they may just sit within a cluster. They are often in an alliance with another school (teaching school alliance) and model outstanding practice to other schools.

The Coalition government's White Paper (2010), *The Importance of Teaching*, announced the direction of travel for training our teachers was switching from universities towards schools. However, in *Training Our Next Generation of Outstanding Teachers* (DfE, 2011) the paper states 'In the White Paper, *The Importance of Teaching*, we recognised that we have in our schools today the best generation of teachers we have ever had ...' (DfE, 2011, p. 3). The government proposals challenged how far schools and universities integrate and synthesise the learning of trainee teachers.

The House of Commons Select Committee in 2012 favoured the universities and schools working in partnership and stated that training should include 'theoretical and research elements … as in the best systems internationally' (House of Commons Education Committee, 2012, p. 32). This approach favoured by the Select Committee begins to mirror the Finnish system of training teachers; however, in addition to expecting high-quality, well qualified trainees, the Finnish system requires their teachers to achieve an MA. Therefore from this and Ofsted's inspection findings for initial teacher training (ITT) from 2008–2011 (Ofsted, 2008), where there was 47 per cent outstanding practice in higher education institutions (HEIs) provision and only 23 per cent in the school-centred partnerships or employment-based routes, at a time when 78 per cent of all teachers trained were in HEI-led provision, we might conclude that the government approach would follow the recommendations of the Select Committee (2012).

Former Education Secretary Michael Gove (2010) gave an early indication of the direction of travel in his view: 'Teaching is a craft and it is best learnt as an apprentice' (Gove, 2010), and following on from this statement, Minister for School Standards Nick Gibb (2014) placed the blame for falling standards at the door of the university providers: 'Who is to blame for our education system falling down the international rankings? The academics in the education faculties of our universities' (Gibb, 2014). In England (2016), there was major change that hit the 'complex landscape of many different routes into teaching' (Jackson and Burch, 2015, p. 1). Traditionally, teacher training centred on university-based provision that included undergraduate and post-graduate routes. Next, following on from the publication of two government circulars (DfE, 1992) a new approach to teacher training opened up known as school-centred initial teacher training (SCITT) (Furlong et al., 2000, p. 2). SCITTS provided opportunities for graduates to gain QTS. In 2012 more schools were encouraged to engage in school-led provision, working in tandem with a university or SCITT partner. The elements proposed in the government White Paper, *Education Excellence Everywhere* (DfE, 2016), threw many ITT departments, within university education faculties, into extremely uncertain times as the Conservative government laid out their plans for the next 5 years. The report states that there will be reform in the delivery of ITT and allocation of teacher training places so that ITT is delivered by 'school-led providers' and there is to be an 'increase in the proportion of ITT offered by the best schools' (DfE, 2016, p. 12).

The Department for Education (DfE) has been accused of missing its targets to fill teacher training places, which brings into question whether their current strategy of moving more training places into schools is actually working. Allocating more numbers to School Direct (a government initiative whereby teacher training is led by schools) has offered a further route into ITE, however, only 43 per cent of schools are involved in the programme (HC73, 2016). Despite the criticism by the Public Accounts Committee (2016) the allocation process for the 2017/18 intake was not significantly changed.

The direction of travel that would appear favoured by the government is the balance of power moving away from universities and into school-led training by 2020 (DfE, 2016). Carter (DfE, 2015) elevating QTS rather than the need for a PGCE has in effect challenged universities to articulate what the PGCE can offer to the trainee teacher and schools. The lifeline of evidence-based research and theoretical perspectives provides an opportunity for universities to develop a strong partnership with schools as the balance of power is deliberated within the political sphere. This changing and challenging landscape and developing routes into ITE provide an opportunity for changing practice and research in the field of ITE.

Schools

Teaching schools

Teaching Schools were planned to lead the training and professional development of teachers and head teachers, and performance-related pay was proposed. It became government policy that, by the end of the parliament, 10,000 students a year could be trained by schools that are full providers of teacher training or offer 'School Direct Places'. The School Direct strategy allows primary and secondary schools to train top graduates as teachers in the subjects they need. Placements usually last 1 year and students are eligible for a bursary of up to £20,000 a year while they train. For the School Direct salaried programme, trainees need 3 years' previous work experience and earn a salary while they train.

Teach First

Teach First is a charity, founded in 2002, which aims to train outstanding graduates to address the problems of low educational achievement in challenging circumstances. An increasing number of graduates have trained through Teach First since 2010.

Free schools

Soon after the election, groups of parents, teachers and charities were invited to submit proposals for free schools. These are all-ability state-funded schools set up in response to what local people say they want and need, in order to improve the education of their children. They are run by teachers, not Local Authorities. They have the ability to choose the length of the school day and terms, the curriculum, teachers' salaries and how they spend their money. By September 2016 there were over 400 free schools (Bolton, 2016). The National Audit Office (2017) has raised a number of issues with free school policy. These centre on duplication of provision, value for money and diversion of educational funding. Despite this, the development of the free school idea remains a government priority.

Academies

The Academies Act 2010 allowed existing schools to convert to academies, with the approval of the Education Secretary. Academies are publicly funded independent schools. They have freedom from Local Authority control to set the pay and conditions of staff, to create and deliver the curriculum and to set the length of days and terms. They receive the same funding from the Education Funding Agency as they would from an LEA but have greater freedom on how they use their budgets. 'Failing schools' were turned into academies. Some academies, often those which were failing schools, have a sponsor from, for example, a business, university, charity or faith group background. The sponsor is responsible for improving school performance by challenging traditional thinking on how schools are run and what they should be like for students. The National Audit Office has predicted that, in 2017, the number of academies will be over 6400 (see www.nao.org.uk/work-in-progress/department-for-education-converting-schools-to-academies/).

University Technical Colleges

University Technical Colleges (UTCs) were introduced to provide technical education for 14–19-year-olds. Sponsored by a local university and employers, they are intended to meet the needs of modern business.

Studio schools

These were introduced to teach 14–19-year-olds an academic and vocational curriculum in a practical way that includes experience in the workplace.

The struggle over education

In this chapter we have shown how the history of education might be seen as something of a struggle for power over and in schools, both in terms of underpinning ideology and in terms of political control. For Thatcher's Conservative government, who instigated the 1988 Education Reform Act, education reform was a struggle over left-wing, progressive and politically correct teachers, Local Authority advisers and academics (Ball, 1993b). The Education Reform Act sought to refocus education on the basics of reading, writing and mathematics, and on an appreciation of England's glorious past. For the subsequent New Labour government, education reform was concerned with the development of skills, the future workforce and the development of human capital. Under New Labour, education became part of economic policy, and a concern for England's place within the global economy (Rizvi and Lingard, 2009). Under New Labour, education reform was micro-managed as government sought to dictate both pedagogy and professional practice (Hodgson and Spours, 2013).

Current educational reform in England (at the time of writing), under the Conservative government, appears to be dominated by neo-liberal and neo-conservative ideology. The reform process is guided by a form of 'governmentality' that, at the surface level, affords greater autonomy and control to school leaders. In tandem with increased autonomy comes increased accountability in the form of school performance and output measures (Rizvi and Lingard, 2009, p. 122). Whitty (2006) argues that this process of governmentality is facilitated by a new breed of educational professionals who prioritise school performance and educational entrepreneurialism. Gewirtz (2003, pp. 2–3) argues that increased accountability and entrepreneurship are driven by a new professional morality that is central to the processes of governmentality. Furthermore, this process, which seeks to centralise control by affording schools greater autonomy and accountability, diminishes further the authoritative role of the LEA.

The struggle over education continues at many levels: between teachers and school leaders, between school leaders and LEAs, between parents and the government, between right-wing traditionalists and left-wing progressivists, between comprehensivists and grammarians. You will notice many of these struggles in the press and on social media. Ball (1993b) notes that this is an ongoing struggle, which will have no resolution. Therefore, it is difficult to predict how education will develop over the course of a career. How individuals choose to deal with this ongoing struggle depends as much on personality as it does on circumstances. However, teachers can make choices, and each has a voice. Therefore, each teacher needs to continue to reassess what they do and why they do it, and to consider their role in the struggle against injustice, exclusion and political domination (see Chapter 15 by Elton-Chalcraft, Revell and Lander on fundamental British values).

Reflective task: Perspectives on the struggle for education

In groups discuss how you think education is political:

- Consider current political issues within education.
- Consider what you think are the priorities for education.
- Consider where you think there is injustice in education.

Summary

This chapter has outlined changes in the philosophy, curriculum, organisation and accountability in primary schools, moving from the 1800s to the ideas espoused in the Plowden Report, then to more centralisation, beginning with the Education Reform Act of 1988 and the creation of education fashioned by the concept of market forces and economic growth and measured attainment. In the final section it outlined changes, since 2010, in the curriculum, teacher education and the funding of new types of schools. Against this constantly changing background, the chapter aimed to encourage readers to understand the need to develop, defend and implement robust personal and professional philosophies that will enable them to respond to changes with professional integrity.

Supplementary information on legislation, Alexander (2010), the Final Report of the Rose Review (DCSF, 2009), an overview of the implications for classroom practice of legislation described in this chapter, and an additional reflective task and bibliography can be found on the website related to this book (https://study.sagepub.com/cooper3).

Questions for discussion

- Do we need Ofsted or is there an alternative? Consider: teacher stress, cost, standards, accountability, closure of schools, improvement.
- Consider the areas of reform in the 1988 Education Reform Act: the National Curriculum, national testing at 7 and 11, league tables, religious education and collective worship, local management of school budgets

(Continued)

(Continued)

(LMS), governing bodies, Ofsted and grant maintained (GM) status. How have these had an impact on our schools over the past 20 years?
- Discuss the impact of neo-liberal and neo-conservative influences on education. Has education become a marketplace? In what way has the school curriculum become narrow? What is the impact on children's educational experience? You may find it helpful to compare how educational issues are represented in different newspapers.

Further reading

Ball, S. (2013) *The Education Debate*. Bristol: Policy Press.
In this text Ball takes a critical view of the development of contemporary education policy in England. Ball's sociological perspective examines how global influences have shaped education policy. In particular he focuses on how education reform has shaped initiatives such as parental choice, academies, free schools and the curriculum.

Chitty, C. (2014) *Education Policy in Britain*. Basingstoke: Palgrave Macmillan.
In this book Clyde Chitty examines the development of educational policy in England, beginning with the Education Act of 1944 through to the development of academies and free schools in contemporary education policy.

Clark, A. (2010) '"In-between" spaces in postwar primary schools: A micro-study of a "welfare room" (1977–1993)', *History of Education*, 39 (November): 767–78.
This very interesting article explores the ways in which, after the Second World War, architects and educationalists in the UK began to explore how learning environments could be redesigned, replacing rows of chairs and 'a yard' with spaces and objects that reflect and enhance the learning and teaching needs of children and adults. This paper focuses on how 'in-between spaces' can be used in different ways.

McCulloch, G. (2011) *The Struggle for the History of Education*. London: Routledge.
This exciting book broadens our understanding of the significance of the history of education by exploring the reasons why different groups have struggled to improve education and society at large; for example, struggling for social change, social equality and new methodologies. It argues that an education system that ignores its past is unlikely to achieve its own best future. It seeks to understand the nature of issues and trends and to assess the prospects of addressing them effectively.

Nutbrown, C. and Clough, P. (2008) *Early Childhood Education: History, Philosophy and Experience*. London: Sage.
This accessible book recognises that, with persistent policy changes, early education practitioners might have few opportunities to ask where ideas began, how practice developed and

what roots and philosophical ideas lie behind them. It gives an historical overview of the development of key ideas, biographical accounts of contributors in the fields, a comparison of their ideas and an analysis of their links with current practices.

References

Alexander, R. (ed.) (2010) *Children, Their World, Their Education: Final Report and Recommendations of the Cambridge Primary Review*. London: Routledge.

Apple, M. W. (2014) *Official Knowledge: Democratic Education in a Conservative Age*. Abingdon: Routledge.

Ball, S. J. (1993a) 'Education, majorism and "the curriculum of the dead"', *Curriculum Studies*, 1 (2): 195–214.

Ball, S. J. (1993b) 'What is policy? Texts, trajectories and toolboxes', *The Australian Journal of Education Studies*, 13 (2): 10–17.

Ball, S. J. (2008) *The Education Debate*. Bristol: Policy Press.

Blair, T. (1996) Speech to the Labour Party Annual Conference, 1 October, Brighton.

Blair, T. (1997) Speech to the Labour Party Annual Conference, 30 September, Brighton. Available at: www.prnewswire.co.uk/cgi/news/release?id=47983 (accessed 29 September 2010).

Bolton, P. (2016) 'Free school statistics: A briefing paper', House of Commons, available at: http://dera.ioe.ac.uk/22728/1/SN07033.pdf.

Boyle, B. and Bragg, J. (2006) 'A curriculum without foundation', *British Educational Research Journal*, 32 (4): 569–82.

Department for Children, Schools and Families (DCSF) (2007) *The Children's Plan*. London: DCSF.

Department for Children, Schools and Families (DCSF) (2009) *The Independent Review of the Primary Curriculum: Final Report* (The Rose Review). London: DCSF.

Department for Education (DfE) (1992) *Get Into Teaching*. London: DfE. Available at: https://getintoteaching.education.gov.uk/explore-my-options/teacher-training-routes/school-led-training/scitt (accessed 20 November 2017).

Department for Education (DfE) (2010) *White Paper 2010 The Importance of Teaching*. London: DfE. Available at: https://www.gov.uk/government/uploads/system/uploads/attachment_data/file/175429/CM-7980.pdf (accessed 23 April 2016).

Department for Education (DfE) (2011) *Training Our Next Generation of Outstanding Teachers*. London: Department for Education. Available at: https://www.gov.uk/government/uploads/system/uploads/attachment_data/file/181154/DFE-00083-2011.pdf (accessed 12 January 2012).

Department for Education (DfE) (2013a) *Teachers' Standards*, Ref. DFE-00066-2011. Available at: www.education.gov.uk.

Department for Education (DfE) (2013b) *National Curriculum: A Framework*. Available at: www.gov.uk.

Department for Education (DfE) (2015) *Carter Review of Initial teacher Training (ITT)*. London: Department for Education. Available at: https://www.gov.uk/government/uploads/system/uploads/attachment_data/file/399957/Carter_Review.pdf (accessed 20 January 2015).

Department for Education (DfE) (2016) *White Paper 2016 Educational Excellence Everywhere*. London: Department for Education. Available at: https://www.gov.uk/government/uploads/

system/uploads/attachment_data/file/508550/Educational_excellence_everywhere__print_ready_.pdf (accessed 18 March 2016).

Department for Education and Employment (DfEE) (1997) *Excellence in Schools*, White Paper. London: DfEE.

Department for Education and Employment (DfEE) (1998) *The National Literacy Strategy*. London: DfEE.

Department for Education and Employment (DfEE) (1999a) *The National Curriculum for England*. London: DfEE.

Department for Education and Employment (DfEE) (1999b) *The National Numeracy Strategy*. London: DfEE.

Department for Education and Skills (DES) (1978) *Primary Education in England: A Survey by Her Majesty's Inspectors of Schools*. London: HMSO.

Department for Education and Skills (DES) (1980) *A Framework for the School Curriculum*. London: DES.

Department for Education and Skills (DES) (1981a) *The School Curriculum*. London: DES/HMSO.

Department for Education and Skills (DES) (1981b) *Circular 6/81*. London: DES/HMSO.

Department for Education and Skills (DES) (1985) *Better Schools: A Summary*. London: DES.

Department for Education and Skills (DES) (1988) *The National Curriculum*. London: HMSO.

Department for Education and Skills (DES) (1992) *Curriculum Organisation and Classroom Practice in Primary Schools (The Three Wise Men Report)*. London: DES.

Department for Education and Skills (DfES) (2001) *Schools – Achieving Success*. London: DfES.

Department for Education and Skills (DfES) (2003a) *Every Child Matters*. London: DfES.

Department for Education and Skills (DfES) (2003b) *Excellence and Enjoyment: A Strategy for Primary Schools*. London: DfES.

Department for Education and Skills (DfES) (2006) *Primary National Strategy: Primary Framework for Literacy and Mathematics*. Available at: www.webarchives.gov.uk.

Furlong, J., Whitty, G., Whiting, C., Miles, S. and Barton, L. (2000) *Teacher Education in Transition: Re-forming Professionalism?* Buckingham: Open University Press.

Galton, M., Simon, B. and Croll, P. (1980) *Inside the Primary Classroom (The ORACLE Report)*. London: Routledge and Kegan Paul.

Gewirtz, S. (2003) *The Managerial School: Post-welfarism and Social Justice in Education*. London: Routledge.

Gibb, N. (2014) 'Teaching unions aren't the problem – universities are'. Available at: https://www.theguardian.com/commentisfree/2014/apr/23/teaching-unions-arent-problem-universities-schools-minister (accessed 12 April 2017).

Gove, M. (2010) Speech to the National College Annual Conference, Birmingham. Available at: https://www.gov.uk/government/speeches/michael-gove-to-the-national-college-annual-conference-birmingham (accessed 4 April 2016).

HC73 (2016) *Training New Teachers: Third Report of Session 2016–17*. London: House of Commons. Available at: www.publications.parliament.uk/pa/cm201617/cmselect/cmpubacc/73/73.pdf (accessed 3 June 2016).

Her Majesty's Inspectors (HMI) (1980a) *Framework for the School Curriculum*. London: HMSO.

Her Majesty's Inspectors (HMI) (1980b) *A View of the Curriculum*. London: HMSO.

Her Majesty's Inspectors (HMI) (1984) *Parental Influence at School: A New Framework for School Government in England and Wales*. London: HMSO.

Her Majesty's Inspectors (HMI) (1985) *The Curriculum from 5–16: HMI Series Curriculum Matters No. 2*. London: HMSO.

Hill, D. (2006) 'Class, neoliberal global capital, education and resistance', *Social Change*, 36 (3): 47–76.

Hodgson, A. and Spours, K. (2013) *New Labour's New Educational Agenda: Issues and Policies for Education and Training at 14+*. London: Routledge.

Hofkins, D. and Northen, S. (2009) *Introducing the Cambridge Primary Review*. Cambridge: University of Cambridge.

House of Commons Education Committee (2012) *Great Teachers: Attracting, Training and Retaining the Best. Government's Response to the Committee's Ninth Report of Session 2010–12*. London: House of Commons.

Jackson, A. and Burch, J. (2015) *School Direct, a Policy for Initial Teacher Training in England: Plotting a Principled Pedagogical Path through a Changing Landscape*. Professional Development in Education. Abingdon: Taylor and Francis.

National Audit Office (NAO) (2017) *Capital Funding for Schools*. London: The National Audit Office. Available at: https://www.nao.org.uk/wp-content/uploads/2017/02/Capital-funding-for-schools.pdf.

National College of Teaching for Leadership (NCTL) (2014) 'Teaching schools: A guide for potential applicants'. Available at: https://www.gov.uk/guidance/teaching-schools-a-guide-for-potential-applicants (accessed 2 July 2017).

Morris, M. (ed.) (1988) *Education, the Wasted Years? 1973–1986*. Lewes: Falmer.

Ofsted (Office for Standards in Education) (2008) Inspection for Initial Teacher Education 2008–11: Written Evidence Submitted by Ofsted. Available at: https://publications.parliament.uk/pa/cm201012/cmselect/cmeduc/1515/1515we28.htm (accessed 20 November 2017).

Peacock, A. (2017) Chartered college of teaching vision. Available at: https://chartered.college/vision (accessed 31 October 2017).

Plowden Report (1967) *Children and their Primary Schools. Report of the Central Advisory Council for Education (England)*. London: HMSO.

Public Accounts Committee (2016) House of Commons Committee of Public Accounts 2016. Training New Teachers. Third Report of Session 2016–17. Available at: https;//publications.parliament.uk/pa/cm201617/cmselect/cmpubacc/73/73.pdf (accessed 20 November 2017).

Qualifications and Curriculum Development Agency (QCA) (1999) *The National Curriculum: Handbook for Primary Teachers in England, Key Stages 1 and 2*. London: QCA.

Rizvi, F. and Lingard, B. (2009) *Globalizing Education Policy*. London: Routledge.

Robinson, K. (2008) *Changing Educational Paradigms*. RSA Animate, The Royal Society of Arts/Edge Lecture, London.

TGAT Report (1988) *Report of the Task Group on Assessment and Testing*. Chaired by Professor Paul Black.

Warnock Report (1978) *Report of the Committee of Enquiry into the Education of Handicapped Children and Young People*. London: HMSO.

Whitty, G. (2006) 'Education (al) research and education policy making: is conflict inevitable?' *British Educational Research Journal*, 32 (2): 159–76.

Winter, C. (2012) 'School curriculum, globalisation and the constitution of policy problems and solutions', *Journal of Education Policy*, 27 (3): 295–314.

Winton, S. and Brewer, C.A. (2014) 'People for Education: A critical policy history', *International Journal of Qualitative Studies in Education*, 27 (9): 1091–109.

2

Philosophy of Education and Theories of Learning

Hilary Cooper

By the end of this chapter, you should:

- understand the kinds of questions educational philosophers ask, how they discuss them and why it is important for you to practise engaging in the kinds of enquiries that underpin this book
- understand the relationship between educational philosophy and theories of how children learn
- have a basic understanding of key learning theories and of their implications for teaching and learning
- be aware of the contribution neuroscience is making to our understanding of learning.

Introduction

This chapter is relevant for educators in early years settings, in primary schools and beyond. You will see from Chapter 1 that, for a variety of reasons, the aims of education and the degree of political influence and central control over all dimensions of education are dynamic: they change as society changes. Teachers have had little encouragement recently to question what or how to teach. And 'primary education suffers more than its share of scare-mongering and hyperbole, not to mention deliberate myth-making' (Hofkins and Northen, 2009, p. 5). The report continues: 'Isn't it time to move on from the populism, polarisation and name-calling which for too long have supplanted real educational debate and progress? Children deserve better from the nation's leaders and shapers of opinion.' The Teachers' Standards (DfE, 2013), which apply to teachers regardless of their career stage, do not expect you to explore questions about the aims, purposes and value of education. However, they do require teachers to, 'act with honesty and integrity … and to be self-critical' (p. 7). If children's lives are not to be at the mercy of political whim, it is essential that teachers learn the skills of robust, critical evaluation, based on their reading, experience and reflection, in order to develop strong personal philosophies about what, how and why we teach children, and to interpret changes in ways which are professionally valid and have integrity. It is important to learn scepticism, and have a concern about the larger questions and a deep understanding of what we teach, to have time to reflect, research and study. This chapter aims to help you do this. First, it gives an overview of the questions philosophers have asked about education in the past, and ask currently, and shows you how to engage with them. Then it links these to theories about how children learn.

What is primary education for?

This is a fundamental philosophical question. Discussing a broad set of aims will prevent you from narrow thinking about what children can and should do. And it is essential that, having begun to discuss educational aims, through reading this chapter, you use these to shape what you do as a teacher and what the children you teach experience in the curriculum, teaching and assessment. Since the beginning of state education the 'basics' have generally been seen as central to primary education. But what is basic in the twenty-first century? How can we empower children to find meaning in their lives? Independence and empowerment are achieved through exploring, knowing, understanding and making sense, through imagination and dialogue, through constructivist approaches. And before you can educate your pupils, based on these aims, you must learn to empower yourself.

The long tradition of educational philosophy

Plato to Rousseau

Since Plato in the fifth century BCE (Before Common Era) and Aristotle in the following century, philosophers have considered the aims, processes and content of education and the relationship between education and society, and their ideas remain relevant today. Plato and Aristotle saw education as holistic, balancing the practical and theoretical. Avicenna (980–1037 CE) (in Goodman, 2005) said that children should discuss, debate and learn from each other. John Stuart Mill (1859) also wrote of the importance of contesting and defending ideas. Jean Jacques Rousseau (1762) saw education as developmental, changing in response to pupils' needs and based on learning from the environment.

Spencer to Steiner

Spencer (1851) advocated moving from concrete to abstract. Heywood Cooper (1892) championed the rights to education of women and ethnic minorities. Froebel (1895) emphasised learning through play and seeing children as the centre of their own worlds, and Montessori (1914) was confident that young children could make decisions for themselves, and that they should learn from their environments. Dewey (1916) wrote about the social and moral nature of schooling, and Steiner (1919) believed in the freedom of teachers to shape their own curriculum.

Educational philosophy over the past 50 years

As philosophies proliferated and since everyone was now entitled to education, it became necessary to examine more critically what was meant by education and what it should aim to achieve. R.S. Peters (1966, 1967) and Hirst (1965, 1974) made a major contribution to show how this might be done, through analysing concepts related to education which are often 'fuzzy' and which people may understand differently and by critically analysing and arguing about claims made for education. Peters (1967, pp. 1–23) asked, as Socrates had, questions such as: What is worth knowing? What do we mean by an educated person? Is the education system fair? Who knows best what children should learn? Is education different from training, teaching different from learning? How? These are questions that are complex and have no single answer, and in an open society they must be argued over. Peters explored such questions by asking: What do you mean by this question? How do you know? To explore these questions, we need to collect a range of different examples, drawing on our experiences and reading. Can we find some key principles, which will allow us to interpret the constantly changing demands made of us?

Using this process, Peters' (1967) conclusion to the question 'What is an educated person?' was essentially: someone who has been changed, by their knowledge and understanding, in the way they look at the world around them; has a body of principles for organising knowledge (subjects or areas of learning); can make connections between areas of knowledge; and cares about what they know and understand. But this concept of an educated person raises questions. Peters claimed that this process of conceptual analysis was free from politics and had universal significance, identifying certain values and ideals, irrespective of culture and society. Matthew Arnold (1869) had said that education should convey the best that has been thought and said. But is that still appropriate? Educational aims must be relevant to the culture, society and world in which children live, and knowing only 'the best' may not reflect their own worlds. Yet should they have access to it?

But later Peters accepted the criticisms of Dearden et al. (1972) and McIntyre (1998) that this was not the case, and that educational aims, values and methods are inevitably embedded in society and change with society. Hirst (1998) and Hirst and White (1998) agreed that Peters' analytical approach could not produce universal answers but was part of an evolving tradition, and that the process of analysis must be closely linked to practical problems. Subsequent educational philosophers, for example Rorty (1979), took a more Aristotelian approach to addressing philosophical questions, based on a conversational style and pragmatic, practical discussion of current issues.

Contemporary educational philosophers use a rich variety of approaches to examine current educational policies and questions. Self-determination or autonomy is still seen as an important educational aim, but in the context of maximising opportunities to choose, while recognising social responsibilities (Hogan, 1997; Walker, 1999; Winch, 1999). There is a growing interest in the links between political philosophy and the notion that before we ask 'What is education?', we need to say 'What are the values of this society?' For what our society values underpins discussion of educational issues such as: multiculturalism, identity, religion, inclusion, education for citizenship and for democracy, the curriculum, educational methods, organisation and assessment, the role of adults in the classroom, governance and who controls schools, education and moral practice, behaviour, and personal and social development. For example, Hirst (1974) considered what the curriculum should consist of, a continuing contentious issue. Pring (2001) explored educational issues through the lens of moral questions. Crick (2000) discussed the nature of citizenship education. Pendlebury (2005) explored feminism and education. You will learn how to engage with such questions in the following chapters of this book, particularly in Chapters 7 and 15.

How does philosophical questioning enable us to achieve our vision within changing political constraints?

Education embodies values and ideals. Most student teachers I have known have been highly motivated by a vision of the kind of teacher they want to be. They have ideas about what they think is valuable and how it might be achieved. But visions vary. For example, interviewees often talk of their aim to help children 'to be creative', 'to love art or books', 'to be independent'. But when such aims are analysed in a group they become controversial. They are all based on value judgements about what the student thinks is important, which not everyone agrees with. They involve concepts that are abstract and are understood in different ways. What exactly is meant by 'creative', 'loving books', 'independent'? When philosophical discussion becomes a habit, it enables us to take responsibility for developing our own practice with integrity. It allows us to react against outside mandates. We stop accepting simple solutions to what we know are complex problems. It stops us being knee jerk in reaction to change by enabling us to define and work towards what we value. It allows us to ask what values and beliefs underpin our work and to use these as the basis for interpreting our responses to change and refining our practice. We can set our personal goals rather than simply responding to those we are given. This constitutes professionalism. Philosophical analysis allows us to dissect slogans such as 'education for democracy', or 'citizenship', 'equal opportunities', 'learning to learn', 'collaboration'. Once we do this, we realise that such slogans are by no means self-evident or beyond criticism. (See, for example, Chapter 15, for a critique of government policy to promote fundamental British values in education.)

Reflective task

Begin to tease out your own philosophy by asking, 'What should be the aims of education in the UK today?' Then answer Peters' question: What do you mean by this? Then give any evidence from your reading and experience to support your claims. Share your list, directly or through a discussion board, with a partner or group of colleagues.

Do people disagree about any of the aims? If so, why?

Identify any aims shared by several people.

Is it possible to create a list of key principles that underpin some of the aims?

Draft the first statement of your personal philosophy of education. As you read through this book, you will add to this, modify it and add your responses to the many other philosophical discussions you will have.

Philosophy of education and learning theories

Another response to the need to provide mass education explored what is involved in the process of learning, by seeking to define systematic rules, based on the evidence of observed behaviour. In psychology, hypotheses are tested in experiments and, if confirmed to a reliable degree, suggest theories. These theories inform practice and through practice the theory is refined. All teachers can, and should, reflect on how learning theories impact on their teaching in different contexts, consider in what ways they might develop, evaluate or modify theory–practice links and share their reflections through professional discussion and professional publications (DfE, 2013, Standards 4.4, 4.5). An enormous amount of data has been accumulated about, for example, how children learn, although there is no single theory but several overlapping theories. The dominant theories over the past century were: behaviourism, in which the teacher controls the learning; constructivism, in which the teacher supports the child in constructing their own learning; and Hierarchies of Needs, which identify conditions necessary for learning to take place.

Behaviourist theories

During the first half of the twentieth century, the dominant theory about how children learn was behaviourism. The central idea is that most of human behaviour, like that of animals, is susceptible to simple, mechanistic explanation. It ignores the fact that language significantly distinguishes us from animals (Fontana, 1984).

Classical conditioning

Behaviourism begins with classical conditioning: Pavlov's finding that dogs that salivate at the sight of food (an unconditioned stimulus), when presented with food accompanied by an aural signal, learnt to salivate in response to the signal when no food was present (a conditioned stimulus). Don't we still train young children to stop talking when they hear the wind chimes, a special tune, a hand clap? But the uses for this classical conditioning are limited. (See Chapter 9 where Ellis and Tod suggest strategies for learning.)

Operant conditioning

Thorndike (1903) put a rat in a cage with a lever, which it pressed to release food. However, when the food was replaced by shocks the rat stopped pressing the lever – hence, there are responses to reward and punishment. This is known as operant conditioning because the animal (or person) has to do something, which has an associated consequence. And don't some teachers give stars or points or 'golden time' and praise to encourage good work or behaviour and 'traffic lights' to warn against, then punish, undesired work or behaviour? Don't some teachers apply Ferster and Skinner's (1957) 'different intermittent schedules of reinforcement': fixed intervals for some rewards (marbles in a jar at the end of the week), fixed ratio schedules (names on the board, four times and you stay in), varied ratio schedules that reward only after a number of positive responses and variable interval schedules (rewards given irregularly to keep the children on their toes)?

Implications of behaviourism for teaching and learning

Behaviourist theory was largely unquestioned during the first half of the last century. Teaching was seen as instructing and training, transmitting information, without understanding the connecting principles and rationale behind the information, which was often piecemeal and not necessarily considered of immediate use or intrinsic interest, but necessary to know later in life. This attitude to education was instrumental and materialistic. Since behaviourism aims to mould behaviour and depends only on observed behaviour, it is not concerned with the inner life: emotions, the child's world, relationships between pupils or teacher and pupils, ideas and concepts. It is hardly likely to change children's views, knowledge or understanding of the world or their relationships or teach them to make decisions or take responsibility. The teacher's function is to manipulate and it is difficult to see this as moral. It leads to the teacher deciding on the curriculum irrespective of children's interests and setting the pace, which aims at the middle, involves much rote learning and makes no differentiation for individual needs.

Constructivist theories

Constructivist theories explore the mental processes involved in learning. They see learning as an active process in which the learner is motivated to ask questions, based on experience, and tries to investigate the questions and find answers. Piaget, throughout his work, was the first to explore the processes of learning, generally focusing on individual children. Vygotsky and Bruner saw learning as a predominantly social activity. Their approach to learning underpins the thinking of educationalists today and, it can be argued, reflects a society which values the individual and is essentially democratic.

Jean Piaget (1896–1980)

Stage theory

Piaget's wide-ranging empirical studies make three major contributions to the enquiry into how learning takes place (Piaget and Inhelder, 1969). First, he saw learning as occurring in four main successive stages, characterised by qualitatively different thinking processes.

The *sensori-motor stage* is dominated by exploring through the senses: children like to feel things, to draw in their own dribble(!) and shake a rattle to make a noise.

The *pre-operational stage*, Piaget says, is dominated by perception and egocentricity: children are happy to talk to themselves without needing to convince others. Their thinking is dominated by what they perceive. A smaller person (or tree) is younger than a taller one. I've certainly seen children convinced that a short, middle-aged student is much younger than a taller 20-year-old. It is fascinating to try out Piaget's claims in the classroom with children of different ages. At the pre-operational stage, dominated by what children see, they think that a large empty box must be heavier than a small box containing heavy weights or that a litre of water changes in quantity when poured into a differently shaped container. But they begin to reason at the pre-operational stage, for example, to classify objects according to one characteristic, as in putting all the blue bricks together.

At the *operational stage*, learning is defined by reasoned thinking. A child can take in information from the outside world, retain it and apply it to new situations, as well as applying rules. Children can 'conserve' information, understanding that objects or sets of objects stay the same even when moved around or changing shape. A line of six counters remains six counters, when scattered; when matched one to one (correlation) they form two equal sets of three, the basis of multiplication and division, or divided into unequal sets (four and two), of addition and subtraction. They can use equal units to calculate mass, weight and volume, and classify sets into subsets, for example, sort a set of blue bricks into subsets of shape and size (class inclusion) or sort 'yellow flowers' into daffodils, dandelions, primroses. Children learn to use the word 'because' to make causal statements.

At the *formal reasoning stage*, Piaget concluded that it is possible to bear in mind and compare a number of variables, to test hypotheses systematically and to discuss ideological and abstract ideas.

Piaget: progressing through the stages

A child takes in information from experience of the environment to build schema – these are mental maps to make sense of the world (assimilation). New information is added to this map, which continues to make sense until this schema is challenged by information that does not fit into it. The child has to adjust the schema to encompass the contradictory information (accommodation). Everything in the water tray floats – but now put in the toy car. The previous rule no longer makes sense. Put some more things into the water tray to try to find a new rule – 'heavy things' sink? Children, Piaget says, try to balance the processes of applying previous knowledge and changing schema to account for new knowledge (equilibrium).

Piaget evaluated

Recent neuroscience has contested Piaget's stage theory, challenging a sequence of qualitively different kinds of thinking, which ignores the possibility of intervention and social interaction to accelerate learning (Goswami, 2015, pp. 21–2). Neuroscience suggests that children learn to think in much the same way as adults but lack the experience to make sense of what they find. This involves networks of neurons concerned with seeing, remembering and deducing, and with the social and emotional aspects of learning. And yet there is a basic logic to the progression Piaget outlined, and if you try out some of his ideas, about conservation, for example, his basic findings are reinforced. The important thing about Piaget is that he was the first person to explore the process of learning.

Lev Vygotsky (1896–1934)

Concept development and the Zone of Proximal Development

Vygotsky's empirical research (1962) emphasised the importance of social interaction and language in learning. He also explored the way in which concepts are learnt through trial and error. We saw from Piaget's work that concepts are categories of words/ideas that have something in common. There are hierarchies of concepts: concrete concepts such as chairs or tables, and higher order concepts into which they fit as subsets, such as furniture. Sometimes there are three levels with an abstract concept that cannot be visualised (e.g. gun, weapon, power or family, village, community). All language is an organisation of concepts, identifying shared properties through the use of language and trial and error. All small furry animals are dogs – until you encounter a cat. Concepts form the building blocks of thinking and are learnt through communication. This reflects the emphasis we now put on discussion in classrooms. Children support or contest each other's ideas, give examples and reasons. In this way they take each other's thinking forward and can reach levels of thinking none of them could on their own. In the early years, this process of forming categories of things that have common properties is evidenced in tiles of different colours, sizes and shapes, and hence concepts, which children can group in different ways. This activity stems directly from Vygotsky's research into concept development. He passed around tiles that differed in shape, colour and thickness, and asked participants to identify a nonsense word/a new concept that had two criteria in common, so creating, through trial and error, a new concept (e.g. thick and yellow, it is 'guk').

Vygotsky (1978) suggested that progress in thinking and in doing takes place through the 'Zone of Proximal Development' (ZPD), when a learner is supported by a 'slightly more able other' until he can complete the task independently; this underlines the current emphasis on pairs and partners in classrooms. Support might also be through differentiation in resources provided for different pupils, whether a teaching assistant, books at different levels of difficulty or mathematics apparatus. Differentiation, another strategy to promote learning by providing tasks at levels individual children can engage with, is reflected in this way. Vygotsky thought that children are not naturally motivated to learn academic subjects and that the motivation to do so comes from the environment for learning provided by the teacher and the satisfaction experienced in having learnt something in response to this.

J.S. Bruner (1915–2016)

The first of Bruner's three interacting contributions to explaining the learning process is emphasis on the importance of providing materials in a form that enables pupils to engage with what is being taught – differentiation again. Although he does not see these 'modes of representation' (1966) as entirely successive, he suggests that resources and experiences may be kinaesthetic, explored through physical engagement, iconic, presented as visual images or symbolic, diagrams, maps, mathematics and language.

Second, Bruner (1963) pointed out the need to identify the key concepts, questions and methods of answering them, which are at the heart of each discipline or subject. And, third, Bruner said that, having identified the concepts and questions at the heart of each discipline, we need to structure progression in learning the key concepts, questions and ways of answering them (the spiral curriculum, 1966), so that a child, from the very beginning, can engage with the essential questions and processes of every subject. The English National Curriculum (QCA, 1999) made a good attempt to do this. The 2014 curriculum, to its great credit, continues to focus on learning the processes of enquiry at the heart of each discipline, in increasingly complex ways.

More recently, Bruner (1986) has written about the importance of culture – beliefs, values, symbols, shared meanings and cultural narratives – in determining how individuals make sense of the world, and hence the importance of educators being aware of the thinking and diverse experiences pupils bring to bear on their learning.

Play

Piaget, Vygotsky and Bruner all extended their theories to consider the learning processes involved in play. Piaget (1951) suggested that play helps to overcome egocentrism since children may encounter conflicts of interest and so realise that others have goals and ideas too. It is a means of accommodating and assimilating reality. A child may imagine that a wooden brick is an aeroplane, 'assimilate' the brick into his existing schema of aeroplanes, seeing no problem in that its shape has no resemblance to an aeroplane, but may also role play the experience of seeing a street fire, in a serious attempt to 'accommodate' the reality of what he saw.

Vygotsky (1978) saw the Zone of Proximal Development as relevant to play, in that through play a child can achieve a level of thinking far higher than she can outside play. The child may, for example, wish to ride a horse. There is no horse so she might use a stick as a symbol for a horse and hence be able to ride. In order to separate the idea of a horse from a real horse, the child uses the stick as a 'pivot' for moving towards thought that is not constrained by situations. This releases the child from the constraints of the objective world to enter the world of ideas, imagination, interpretation and will.

Social Constructivism

Social Constructivism developed from the work of Vygotsky (1962, 1978) and Bruner (1986). It argues that an individual's learning takes place as a result of interactions and talk with others, in the family, school and wider society. We construct our knowledge and understanding of the world, both in everyday life and in school, through talk. Therefore, language plays a central role in mental development. The process is illustrated in Figure 2.1, which shows how, in talking to others, our thought and our speech overlap and so become 'verbal thought' (Figure 2.1).

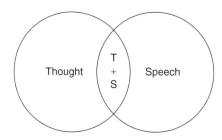

Figure 2.1   The central role of language and social contexts in developing new thinking

Vygotsky and Bruner also focus on the cultural and historical aspects of social interactions. Children acquire a rich body of knowledge through their culture, which influences their knowledge and thinking.

Implications for practice

Learning through social interaction is motivating. Teachers create learning situations in which children can talk together. They share their expertise and understanding to construct learning together. They explain, question, interpret and play an active social role in the group. Children see themselves as sense making, problem solving, assuming a part of the knowledge construction and playing an active social role in the group. Contributions that draw on their personal perspectives and experiences value cultural and other differences. Learning can be assessed by observing the part each child plays in the enquiry, their explanation of their reasoning and the competence of their participation. Studying how children create meaning gives insights into children's thinking. Siraj-Blatchford et al. (2002) in the REPEY Project (Researching Effective Pedagogy in the Early Years) analysed effective talk. They found that good curriculum knowledge as well as an understanding of child development were as vital in the early years as in later education. Recent, useful books on Social Constructivism applied to practice include Doherty and Hughes (2009), Pritchard and Woollard (2010), Pelech and Pieper (2010) and Lindon (2012).

Work in school

Student: I don't see how philosophy of education is relevant on school placement. I'm a student – just trying to meet the Standards.

Mentor: Well, education reflects society and its aims change with society. So while you are in school, talk to some experienced teachers about ways in which, in their professional experience, society, families and children have changed. Ask, how have schools responded to these changes?

Ask about changes in the statutory curriculum within their professional experience; were there any with which they disagreed? If so, were they able to adapt them in line with their personal philosophy?

Student: I'm placed in a Reception class. How can I relate the theories in this chapter more closely to my early years placement?

(Continued)

(Continued)

Mentor: Too much has been written about early years education to outline in this short chapter, but all the theorists mentioned have been very influential in developing early years practice. I suggest you look at the Reggio Emilia Approach to Education, which they use in Scotland (www.education/Scotland.gov.uk), and identify the number of theorists in this chapter who are seen as central in early years education. Then try to add some more!

Student: When I read about learning theories, I thought, surely they have been absorbed into everything we do now, so why do I need to know about these people?

Mentor: Remember that Standard 2.3 (DfE, 2013) requires you to, 'Demonstrate knowledge and understanding of how pupils learn'. This is because you need to identify the theories that underpin your practice. Otherwise you can't develop your own professional practice; you become a clone of the practice around you and of the statutory requirements, rather than interpreting theories in new contexts. Standard 2.5 says that you should encourage children to take a responsible and conscientious attitude to their work and study. Reread the second part of the chapter. How does a Social Constructivist approach help you to do this? And how does Social Constructivism and the theory of self-efficacy help you to meet Standards 1.1 and 1.2, which refer to mutual respect and to challenging pupils of all backgrounds, abilities and dispositions? I think it would be useful to annotate your planning, showing how it relates to learning theories. (Also have a look at Chapter 17, where Read supports you in reflecting on theory and practice.)

Bronfenbrenner (1917–2005)

Vygotsky and Bruner focus on the social and cultural aspects of social interactions. Bronfenbrenner (1979) developed further the importance of a child's environment in learning. He proposed an 'ecological model' of child development, in which the child is at the centre. The child affects and is affected by the settings in which s/he spends time: extended family, early care and education settings and health care and community learning sites – libraries, neighbourhoods and playgrounds. A child's development is determined by what is experienced in these settings. There needs to be communication between the settings and they need to have similar expectations. This model was very influential in the development of the Sure Start programmes introduced between 1999 and 2003, which aimed to combine family health, early years care, education and improved well-being programmes for children under 4 and their families, through integrated services, where possible in children's centres.

Bandura's theory of self-efficacy (1925–)

Bandura (1997) published his theory of 'self-efficacy', which lies at the heart of social cognitive theory. A person's attitudes, abilities and cognitive skills comprise their 'self-system' and determine the extent to which people believe that they can succeed in different situations, by planning and carrying out a course of action required to manage a situation. A person with a strong sense of self-efficacy sees challenging tasks as problems to be mastered. People with weak self-efficacy overestimate the difficulty of achieving a good result and so avoid challenging tasks, believing that they are beyond their capabilities. Teachers therefore should support those with low self-efficacy by providing tasks they can achieve, giving verbal encouragement and minimising negative stress and emotional responses.

Maslow (1908–1970)

The emphasis placed on the environment in terms of family, school and community by Vygotsky, Bruner and Bronfenbrenner, and Bandura's recognition of the significance of self-esteem are relevant to the work of Maslow, although his work stems from a behaviourist approach. His theory of a Hierarchy of Needs (1943) (see www.google.co.uk/images) raised awareness that learning is impossible until a hierarchy of basic needs is met. First, basic physiological needs such as the need for air, food, drink, shelter, warmth and sleep must be met before we can learn effectively. At the next level, security, stability, safety and order are necessary. Then come affection and relationships with family and others. If these needs are met, we can achieve, take responsibility and develop self-esteem. And when this has been achieved, we reach a level that Maslow calls 'self-actualisation'. Essentially this is self-fulfilment, the ability to be autonomous, to accept one's self and others, to be spontaneous and creative. Later, Maslow added three more categories of need: esteem needs; cognitive needs (the need for knowledge and meaning); and aesthetic needs (appreciation of beauty). Maslow's sequence of needs and his methodology and the claim that only a few people ever reach self-actualisation can be criticised. Some children certainly succeed in spite of economic, social, environmental or emotional disadvantages – but many do not. Educators have responded by providing 'nurture groups', and breakfast clubs, raising awareness of children who may lack adequate sleep or may show signs of abuse at one end of the scale, and at the other, providing opportunities for children to be independent, to treat each other with respect and to be creative.

Gardner (1943–)

Following the 1944 Education Act, selection examinations for grammar schools consisted mainly of intelligence tests – tests of reasoning, which claimed to establish each person's fixed Intelligent Quotient 'IQ'. As an alternative to this, Gardner (1983) developed a theory of multiple intelligences, which identified seven separate intelligences, beyond verbal and logical: linguistic, musical, logical/mathematical, visual/spatial, kinaesthetic, intrapersonal (our ability to understand ourselves) and interpersonal (our ability to understand others). Later (1999) he added 'naturalistic' intelligence, which combines a core ability with the way it is represented in different cultures. This theory has been seen as encouraging children's self-esteem by discovering their strengths, and also as helpful in encouraging a cross-cultural perspective of intelligence in a society with many different cultures. It is now generally accepted that intelligence is not 'fixed'. Dweck's research (1999, 2006) found that some children think their intelligence is 'fixed' and so that effort makes no difference, while others see intelligence as something malleable which be changed by effort. Dweck found that if teachers reward effort rather than performance the motivation to learn is increased.

Intra- and interpersonal skills and creativity are now seen as significantly important in learning and development. Gardner's theory led to, for example, the concept of extra support for the 'gifted and talented' in whichever area they excelled (see, for example, the plan for 'gifted and talented children' in primary schools; DCSF, 2008). Later, Gardner (2006) argued that we do not need to focus on subjects but on thinking skills that will help pupils to deal with the future: a disciplined mind, a synthesising mind, a creating mind and a 'respectful mind'. Until recently, although many teachers welcomed the value-based claims of the 'plurality of intellects', there was no evidence to prove that these different intelligences exist or that they undermine the theory of general intelligence.

For example, Visser, Ashton and Vernon (2006a, 2006b) claim that research into multiple intelligences must be rigorous (i.e. quantative). They put together a battery of tests covering the eight intelligences, and found that general intelligence ran through most of the tests. They argued that what Gardner calls intelligences are subservient to general intelligence. It is also argued that that Gardner's forms of intelligence should be called talents or abilities not intelligences. However, Gardner's response (e.g. Gardner and Moran, 2006) is that there has been much qualitative research into each of the eight intelligences with positive results and that research into multiple intelligences, to be meaningful, must be qualitative.

As professionals we must reflect critically on theories. Jumping on a bandwagon, as many schools do, can be counterproductive. (Chapters 16 and 17 develop the idea of critical reflection on practice.)

Reflective task

In groups, if possible, research the work of one of the theorists outlined above. One person can find out the biography, another more about the theory, a third the empirical research on which the theory is based. Next, through group discussion, critically analyse the theory – what are its strengths and weaknesses? (Draw on ideas from Chapter 17 to support your reflection.) Evaluate the implications for classroom practice. As a group, present your findings and views to your colleagues and invite questions and discussion.

Educational theories and neuroscience

Theories of how children learn, like philosophers' questions, change over time. Goswami (2015), in her Report, commissioned by the Cambridge Primary Review Trust (http://cprtrust.org.uk/), has collated recent research in psychology and neuroscience, which investigates how children learn. One of the Trust's priorities conforms with the aims of this book, to 'develop a pedagogy of rigour, evidence and principle rather than mere compliance'.

In some of the neuroscience research reported by the Cambridge Primary Review Trust, Goswami (2015) contests aspects of learning theory. Recent neuroscience research into progression in learning rejects Piaget's theory of a sequence of qualitatively different stages. The consensus of all the research in neuroscience is that all forms of learning for human cognition are present, in rudimentary forms from birth, that a child's brain has basically the same structures as an adult's brain, and that a child learns, cumulatively, from the home, school and general cultural environment. Neuroscience has also found that unisensory approaches, as suggested in 'learning styles' (which categorised children as having dominant learning styles, either visual, auditory or kinaesthetic), are not valid, because learning depends on neural networks distributed across multiple brain regions. Vygotsky found concept development to be essentially a process of trial and error (seeing whether new objects, feelings, etc. fit into existing concepts), whereas Goswami suggests that it may also be useful for teachers, to draw attention to the shared characteristic of the concept by direct teaching.

Other aspects of learning theories are endorsed by neuroscience. Neuroscience endorses Vygotsky's (1978) theory of Proximal Development. It supports Bruner's methods of representation (kinaesthetic, iconic, symbolic), and it confirms and develops Piaget's and Vygotsky's theories of play, finding that through perceptive and socially based cognitive learning children learn emotional reactions and deduce causes, for example, of the circumstances surrounding happiness and anger. And it reflects Theory of Mind, understanding and predicting the behaviour of others, is induced by pretend play; socio-dramatic role play gives children insights into the beliefs, desires and intentions of others, and understanding that other people are not like them. Conversations about why people behave as they do give children opportunities to argue and reflect on human behaviour.

Work in school

Student: I have noticed that some children in my class are not 'on target', as the teacher puts it, for quite a while sometimes. They may be slowly sharpening a pencil or looking out of the window. They are not 'messing around' and when they do complete their work it is often of good quality. But it worries me, when there is so much to get through, that they are so laid back. I wonder whether, because they are competent in what they do they are getting lazy. Should I 'stretch them more'? How should I get them back on task?

Mentor: Some children may well put off getting down to work for various reasons. Are they not motivated? If not, why? Is the work stimulating? Is it too easy or difficult? Are they tired or not very well? If they are young children are they being asked to sit still too often? Or are they apparently doing nothing because they are reflecting on the task and how to go about it, collecting resources, reflecting on others' ideas or identifying emotionally with a task? No one can write a poem or paint a picture on demand! First, I think you need to decide what the reason is that they are not 'on task', in order to decide how to respond appropriately.

(Continued)

Analysis

Research by Galton et al. (1980) was based on observation studies of pupils and teachers. They found that children were 'on task' only 70% of the time. During much of the rest of the time they were described as 'not concentrating', 'staring into space', 'daydreaming' or 'out of base', which was assumed to be time wasted. However Immordino-Yang et al. (2012) found a novel brain network, which suggests that emotions rely on paying attention to the inner psychological self rather than to the outer world and that the activity of this network is suppressed when people focus on implementing short-term, goal-directed tasks. This led them to wonder whether asking children to consistently focus on attention-grabbing, goal-directed tasks, without time to reflect, rest or daydream, was healthy, and in particular, whether it might hinder complex emotions and skills for engaging in abstract, personal and socio-emotional thoughts. This, they say, also has implications for the impact of urban and classroom stress. Lapses in outward attention may be due to inward focusing. Absence of play for children or for older children to dream may have negative effects on their ability to attend to tasks and to their socio-emotional well-being.

Summary

This chapter began by considering the kinds of questions educational philosophers ask and why it is important for you to engage in this process, followed by a look at developments in the methods and scope of philosophical enquiry about education over the past 50 years. The second part of the chapter focused on empirical research into the *processes* of learning and the implications for classroom practice. It concluded with an examination of the potential for neuroscience to evaluate cognitive theories of learning.

Questions for discussion

- Should the state control what teachers teach?
- Should teachers criticise their government?
- Should teaching involve 'character education'? If so, what should be taught?

(Continued)

(Continued)

- Teachers are required to promote 'British values'. According to Ofsted, British values are 'democracy; the Rule of Law; individual liberty; mutual respect for and tolerance of those with different faiths and beliefs and for those without faith', although the Inspection Handbook (2014, para. 152) omits to mention 'those of no faith'. Teachers also have a duty to monitor and report on potential extremism (July 2015). What controversial issues do these requirements raise? (See Chapter 15, where Elton-Chalcraft, Revell and Lander challenge you to respond to this government directive.)
- Think of an area of expertise you have that is not directly related to school (e.g. playing an instrument, performing a magic trick, cooking a particular dish, dancing). Write a lesson plan to show how you could teach this skill to a group of peers, using as many aspects of learning theories as possible. List the learning theories you apply and say why you used them. Present the lesson and invite your peers to identify the theories you applied.
- What are your most enjoyable experiences of learning something, in or out of school? What did they have in common? How can this inform your philosophy of teaching and learning?

Further reading

Cerriti. C. (2013) 'Building a functional multiple intelligences theory to advance educational neuroscience', *Frontiers in Psychology: Educational Psychology*, 19 December. https://doi.org/10.3389/fpsyg.2013.00950
Cerruti states that Gardiner's theory of multiple intelligences does not describe how the mind works, although educators took strongly to it, but he argues that it may be a basis for providing a scientific theory.

Immordino-Yang, M.H. (2015) *Learning and the Brain: Exploring the Implications of Affective Neuroscience*. New York and London: W.W. Norton and Company.
It is suggested, based on neuroscience, that cognition and emotion are regarded as two interrelated aspects of human functioning. From the interface between cognition and emotion the origins of creativity emerge – artistic, scientific and technological and also social creativity, which underpins moral and ethical thought.

Lewin, D., Guilherme, A. and White, M. (2016) *New Perspectives in Philosophy of Education*. London: Bloomsbury.
This book discusses ethical issues that are important in a society where education depends on grades and political issues; for example, the extent to which individuals can be brought into

the social world through education and the political importance of education at a time when policy and practice lack a substantive ground.

Noddings, N. and Brooks, L. (2017) *Teaching Controversial Issues: The Case for Critical Thinking and Moral Commitment in the Classroom*. New York: Teachers College Press.
This book focuses on critical thinking: what words mean, how words connect to convey meaning and how to consider and evaluate arguments, how to understand all perspectives and ideally find a core of shared meaning that can enable us all to work together.

Williams, K. and Williams, P. (2017) 'Lessons from a master: Montaigne's pedagogy of conversation', *Educational Philosophy and Theory*, 49 (3): 253–63.
This paper draws together strands of the pedagogy of Montaigne, and demonstrates how earlier writers can still contribute to our understanding of teaching and learning. Montaigne focuses on the need to move from the comfort zone of acquired convictions and the crucial role of conversation in creating intellectual and moral openness, which enables us to do so.

References

Arnold, M. (1869) *Culture and Anarchy* (republished, S. Collini (ed.), 1993). Cambridge: Cambridge University Press.

Bailey, R., Barrow, R., Carr, D. and McCarthy, C. (2010) *The Sage Handbook of Philosophy of Education*. London: Sage.

Bandura, A. (1997) *Self-Efficacy: The Exercise of Control*. New York: Freeman.

Bronfenbrenner, U. (1979) *The Ecology of Human Development: Experiments by Nature and Design*. Cambridge, MA: Harvard University Press.

Bruner, J.S. (1963) *The Process of Education: A Landmark in Educational Theory*. Cambridge, MA: Harvard University Press.

Bruner, J.S. (1966) *Towards a Theory of Instruction*. Cambridge, MA: Harvard University Press.

Bruner, J.S. (1986) *Actual Minds, Possible Worlds*. Cambridge, MA: Harvard University Press.

Cerruti, C. (2013) 'Building a functional multi-intelligences theory to advance educational neuroscience', *Frontiers in Psychology: Educational Psychology*, 19 December. https://doi.org/10.3389/fpsyg.2013.00950.

Cooper, A.J.H. (1892) *A Voice from the South*. Available at: www.docsouth.unc.edu.

Crick, B. (2000) *Essays on Citizenship*. London: Continuum.

Dearden, R.F., Hirst, P.H. and Peters, R.S. (eds) (1972) *Education and the Development of Reason*. London: Routledge and Kegan Paul.

Department for Children, Schools and Families (DCSF) (2009) *The Independent Review of the Primary Curriculum: Final Report*. London: DCSF.

Department for Education (DfE) (2013) *Teachers' Standards*. Available at: www.education.gov.uk.

Dewey, J. (1916) *Democracy and Education: An Introduction to the Philosophy of Education*. Available at: www.ilt.columbia.edu.

Doherty, J. and Hughes, M. (2009) *Child Development: Theory and Practice 0–11*. New York: Pearson Longman.

Dweck, C.S. (1999) *Self Theories: Their Role in Personality, Motivation and Development*. Philadelphia, PA: Psychology Press.

Dweck, C.S. (2006) *Mindset: the New Psychology of Success*. New York: Ballantine Books, Random House.

Ferster, C.B. and Skinner, B.F. (1957) *Schedules of Reinforcement*. New York: Appleton-Century-Crofts.

Fontana, D. (1984) 'Behaviourism and learning theory in education', *British Journal of Educational Psychology*, Nonagraph No. 1.

Froebel, F. (1895) *The Pedagogies of the Kindergarten*. New York: D. Appleton and Company.

Galton, M., Simon, B. and Croll, P. (1990) *Inside the Primary Classroom*. London: Routledge.

Gardner, H. (1983) *Frames of Mind: The Theory of Multiple Intelligences*. New York: Basic Books.

Gardner, H. (1999) *Intelligence Reframed: Multiple Intelligences for the 21st Century*. New York: Basic Books.

Gardner, H. (2006) *5 Minds for the Future*. Boston, MA: Harvard Business School Press.

Gardner, H. and Moran, S. (2006) 'The science of multiple intelligences theory: A response to Lynne Waterhouse', *Educational Psychologist*, 41 (4): 227–32.

Goodman, L.E. (2005) *Avicenna: Arabic Thought and Culture*. London: Routledge.

Goswami, U. (2015) *Children's Cognitive Development and Learning*. York: Cambridge Primary Review Trust. Available at: http://cprtrust.org.uk/wp-content/uploads/2015/02/COMPLETE-REPORT-Goswami-Childrens-Cognitive-Development-and-Learning.pdf.

Hirst, P.H. (1965) 'Liberal education and the nature of knowledge', in R.D. Archambault (ed.), *Philosophical Analysis and Education*. London: Routledge and Kegan Paul (republished 2010, pp. 76–95).

Hirst, P.H. (1974) *Knowledge and the Curriculum: A Collection of Philosophical Essays*. London: Routledge and Kegan Paul.

Hirst, P.H. (1998) 'Philosophy of education: The evolution of a discipline', in G. Haydn (ed.), *50 Years of Philosophy of Education*. London: London University, Institute of Education. pp. 194–98.

Hirst, P.H. and White, P. (eds) (1998) *Philosophy of Education: Major Themes in the Analytical Tradition*. London: Routledge.

Hofkins, D. and Northen, S. (eds) (2009) *Introducing the Cambridge Primary Review*. Cambridge: University of Cambridge, Faculty of Education. Available at: www.primaryreview.org.uk.

Hogan, P.J. (1997) 'The politics of identity and the epiphanies of learning', in W. Carr (ed.), *The Routledge Falmer Reader in Philosophy of Education*. London: Routledge. pp. 83–96.

Immordino-Yang, M.H., Christodoulou, J.A. and Singh, V. (2012) 'Rest is not idleness: Implications of the brain's default mode for human development and education', *Perspectives on Psychological Science*, 7: 4352–64.

Lewin, D., Guilherme, A. and White, M. (2016) *New Perspectives in Philosophy of Education*. London: Bloomsbury.

Lindon, J. (2012) *Understanding Child Development 0–8 years: Linking Theory and Practice*. London: Hodder Education.

Maslow, A. (1943) 'A theory of human motivation', *Psychological Review*, 50 (4): 370–96.

McIntyre, A. (1998) 'An Interview with Giovanna Borradori', in K. Knight (ed.), *The McIntyre Reader*. Cambridge: Polity Press. pp. 255–66.

Mill, J.S. (1859) *On Liberty*. Charleston, SC: Forgotten Books (republished 2008).

Montessori, M. (1914) *Dr. Montessori's Own Handbook*. Mineola, NY: Dover Publications (republished 2005).

Pelech, J. and Pieper, G.W. (2010) *The Comprehensive Handbook of Constructivist Teaching: From Theory to Practice*. Greenwich, CT: Information Age Publishing.

Pendlebury, S. (2005) 'Feminism, epistemology and education', in W. Carr (ed.), *The Routledge Falmer Reader in Philosophy of Education*. London: Routledge. pp. 50–62.

Peters, R.S. (1966) *Ethics and Education*. London: Allen and Unwin.

Peters, R.S. (ed.) (1967) The *Concept of Education*. London: Routledge and Kegan Paul.

Piaget, J. (1951) *Play, Dreams and Imitation in Early Childhood*. London: Routledge.

Piaget, J. and Inhelder, B. (1969) *The Psychology of the Child*. London: Perseus Books.

Pring, R. (2001) 'Education as a moral practice', *Journal of Moral Education*, 30 (2): 101–12.

Pritchard, A. and Woollard, J. (2010) *Psychology for the Classroom: Constructivism and Social Learning*. London: Routledge.

Qualifications and Curriculum Authority (QCA) (1999) *The National Curriculum: Handbook for Primary Teachers in England*. Available at: www.nationalarchives.gov.uk.

Rorty, R. (1979) *Philosophy and the Mirror of Nature*. Princeton, NJ: Princeton University Press.

Rousseau, J.J. (1762) *Emile*. Available at: www.gutenberg.org/ebooks/5427.

Siraj-Blatchford, I., Sylva, K., Muttock, S., Gilden, R. and Bell, D. (2002) *Researching Effective Pedagogy in the Early Years* (Research Report 356). Annesley: Department for Education and Skills. Available at: www.ioe.ac.uk/_research_report.pdf.

Spencer, H. (1851) *Essays on Education and Kindred Subjects*. Available at: www. gutenberg. org/files/16510/16510-h/16510-h.htm.

Steiner, R. (1919) *The Renewal of Education*. Available at: www.ebook3000.com.

Thorndike, E.L. (1903) *Educational Psychology*. New York: The Science Press.

Visser, B.A., Ashton, M.C. and Vernon, P.A. (2006a) 'Beyond g: Putting multiple intelligences theory to the test', *Intelligence*, 34 (5): 487–502.

Visser, B.A., Ashton, M.C. and Vernon, P.A. (2006b) 'g and the measurement of multiple intelligences', *Intelligence*, 34 (5): 487-502.

Vygotsky, L.S. (1962) *Thought and Language*. Trans. E. Hanfmann and G. Vakar. Cambridge, MA: MIT Press.

Vygotsky, L.S. (1978) *Mind in Society: The Development of Higher Psychological Processes*. Cambridge, MA: Harvard University Press.

Walker, J.C. (1999) 'Self-determination as an educational aim', in R. Marples (ed.), *The Aims of Education*. London: Routledge. pp. 112–23.

Winch, C. (1999) 'Autonomy as an educational aim', in R. Marples (ed.), *The Aims of Education*. London: Routledge. pp. 74–84.

3

Short-, Medium- and Long-term Planning

Kim Harris and Suzanne Lowe

By the end of this chapter, you should be able to:

- identify the teaching and learning priorities for your school context and make an informed, positive contribution to curriculum development
- confidently plan to provide learners with engaging and meaningful learning experiences that motivate, promote understanding and development of skills
- demonstrate a clear understanding of the relationship between planning and assessment.

Introduction

This chapter addresses the following Teachers' Standards (DfE, 2013a), which apply to trainees and teachers across all Key Stages:

Standard 1 Set high expectations which inspire, motivate and challenge pupils.

Standard 2 Promote good progress and outcomes by pupils.

Standard 3 Demonstrate good subject and curriculum knowledge.

Standard 4 Plan and teach well-structured lessons.

Statutory curricula are dynamic and change to meet new needs and with new governments. This chapter introduces you to ways in which schools and teachers translate national requirements (DfE, 2013a) into whole-school plans for their school, and develop medium-term plans from the long-term plans and use these to plan lessons on a weekly and daily basis. Planning is integrally related to assessment, so that sequences of work continuously build on pupils' previous knowledge. This chapter examines the decisions involved in planning and some of the controversial aspects of the process, thus illustrating that teaching is 'a complex engagement with children' (John, 2006). Constructivist theory, put very simply, indicates that children build their knowledge through extending their prior understanding. Piaget (1953) found that when new knowledge is presented it needs to be assimilated, using what the child already knows. If this information does not fit into prior knowledge, adaptations need to be made and accommodated to form new knowledge. Early years education, particularly, is based around providing stimulating opportunities for children to construct their own learning, through a range of experiences, many of which are 'play' based. Children are given the opportunity to choose from the range of experiences available and to repeat an experience while it has interest for them. Planning is therefore concerned with listening to the interests of the children, assessment of their prior learning, and then providing opportunities for the children to challenge and develop their understanding.

Effective planning contributes to every area of teaching and learning including:

- Behaviour management – if pupils are bored or frustrated this may have an impact on their attitude to learning and behaviour in the classroom; therefore, planning activities appropriate for the abilities of the class is essential.
- Learning environment – integrating display into planning enables teachers to utilise additional resources to support children's learning and independence. This may be in the form of word banks, number lines or grids, topic-based information or interactive exhibitions.
- Motivation – if planned activities are not meaningful and/or inspiring children may not willingly participate, therefore knowing what interests the children and incorporating this in your planning is essential.
- Inclusion – all children's needs should be considered so that they do not feel isolated or excluded from the lesson content. This is a challenging area for teachers to manage because of the range of issues that may be present, from academic ability to aspects of health and well-being.

There is a range of approaches to planning. This chapter aims to meet students' beginning needs and give a firm foundation for further development, while being mindful that 'for some, the encounter holds creative possibilities; for others, it is a brick wall of bewilderment and anxiety' (John, 2006, p. 483).

The examples below illustrate the impact different government priorities can have on teaching and learning in the classroom, particularly on the curriculum content and how it is organised. A focus on different curricular agenda can help us to understand how education priorities are developed. Although the examples given present a narrow view, in terms of global priorities, they show how, since devolution within the UK, different countries have different values and ways of implementing these.

Scotland: 'Curriculum for Excellence'

The Scottish Curriculum for Excellence aims to ensure that all children and young people in Scotland develop the attributes, knowledge and skills they will need to flourish in life, learning and work: 'The knowledge, skills and attributes learners will develop will allow them to demonstrate four key capacities – to be successful learners, confident individuals, responsible citizens and effective contributors' (www.gov.scot/Topics/Education/Schools/curriculum).

The National Curriculum in England, statutory from 2014

The 2014 National Curriculum is the result of the Coalition government's consultation on how best to meet the educational needs of children. It states that:

Every state-funded school must offer a curriculum, which is balanced and broadly based and which:

- promotes the spiritual, moral, cultural, mental and physical development of pupils at the school and of society, and
- prepares pupils at the school for the opportunities, responsibilities and experiences of later life. (DfE, 2013b); https://www.gov.uk/government/publications/national-curriculum-in-england-framework-for-key-stages-1-to-4/the-national-curriculum-in-england-framework-for-key-stages-1-to-4

The latest version of the National Curriculum specifies the aims, purposes and content for English, mathematics, science, art and design, citizenship, computing, design and technology, geography, history, music and physical education for each Key Stage, with the introduction of a foreign language at Key Stage 2. It is worth noting that free schools and academies do not have to follow the National Curriculum.

A Curriculum for Wales – a curriculum for life

The Welsh Curriculum 3–13 identifies skills for each subject and the range of contexts, opportunities and activities through which these should be assessed. A new curriculum is currently being designed that will be implemented in 2018. The Welsh Curriculum includes a requirement for the teaching of the Welsh language to all pupils:

> The four purposes will be at the heart of our new curriculum.
>
> - Ambitious capable learners
> - Healthy, confident individuals
> - Enterprising, creative contributors
> - Ethical, informed citizens[1]

Planning for learning: Levels of planning

The statutory curriculum is mediated and interpreted at different levels. The statutory curriculum and policies are translated into a whole-school curriculum plan and then further broken down into school policies.

Whole-school plan

Whatever the statutory content, schools must translate it into whole-school plans for their school. The whole-school curriculum plan is developed from national requirements and the school ethos and priorities. This is usually organised in Key Stages/age phases and is often referred to as the 'long-term plan'. In this you can observe the cyclical 'spiral' nature of the curriculum, with subjects being revisited throughout a child's time in school. Also, cross-curricular links or themes can be identified, and the long-term plan ensures that all areas of the curriculum are taught at appropriate times and in relevant detail across the age phases. For example, looking at the National Curriculum (DfE, 2013b) requirement to teach 'significant people in British history' at Key Stage 1 teachers may decide to teach about optional examples given in the curriculum: Queen Victoria, Christopher Columbus, Rosa Parkes or Mary Seacole. These may be selected for good reasons. But has thought been given to the locality of the school, available resources and the personal skills, interest areas and knowledge of

---

1 http://gov.wales/docs/dcells/publications/151021-a-curriculum-for-wales-a-curriculum-for-life-en.pdf; http://learning.gov.wales/?lang=en

the teaching team? It is also possible to respond to the enthusiasms and interests of the children in your class, although this is more normally at lesson level than for longer-term planning.

Different approaches to the curriculum

School ethos and philosophy

All schools have individual mission statements and aims, and the values and attitudes stated are the underlying principles on which all activity in the school is built. There are many ways that curriculum expectations can be met and the decisions taken by a school, based on their mission statement and aims, can have a significant impact on the overall ethos. This individual philosophy is what makes every school different, so that when you walk in you get the 'feel' of the school from the environment (displays, welcome, orderliness, learning conversations) around you. As a student, you need to adapt to this as quickly as possible, although when you are a member of the teaching team you will be able to contribute to the ethos and to the development of the whole-school curriculum plan and policies. While subject content, and possibly how much time should be dedicated to individual subjects are set by government policy, the way that these are organised is the responsibility of school leaders and staff. This discussion explores some of the issues facing teachers today. How to teach areas of the curriculum can be dependent on teachers' own philosophical beliefs concerning how children learn or on school approaches to learning and ethos. Changes to the curriculum at national level will resonate with some teachers and not with others.

Single subject or linked subjects

Schools can choose to teach each subject separately or link several together. However, to teach all subjects in a discrete (subject-specific) way can sometimes introduce seemingly rigid boundaries between content, making it difficult for children to see the commonality between subjects. In the real world we learn experientially and the distinctions between subjects tend to be blurred, making learning meaningful and intrinsically motivating. Therefore, enabling children to learn more naturally, rather than planning disjointed learning blocks, would seem to be highly advantageous in today's classrooms. In addition, depending on the number of subjects included in the curriculum, it may be difficult to teach all of them every week. Some schools choose to focus on particular foundation subjects in specific terms rather than teaching them all year to accommodate this difficulty.

Cross-curricular approach

Some schools redress the balance by using a cross-curricular approach rather than always teaching through discrete subjects. In using a cross-curricular approach it is important to ensure that there is breadth across the curriculum and that all the necessary curriculum objectives are taught. In an effective cross-curricular lesson there will be shared emphasis on the learning outcomes from different subject areas. Barnes (2011, p. 259) explains how effective units of work may also include opportunities for children to use creative approaches to applying the learning to new situations, thus allowing the teacher (and child) to assess how well the learning has been understood.

Themes

Many schools use 'themes' to link subjects under an umbrella context. Lessons can be taught using either a subject-discrete or a cross-curricular approach. The choice depends on what knowledge, skills or understanding is intended to be developed, and teacher judgement about how the children will best be able to learn this. The chosen theme may be taught in a variety of ways, for example, one day per week for several weeks, or it may be fully timetabled with all lessons linked to the theme. One of the key advantages of a thematic approach is that, as for cross-curricular lessons, it is thought to be a more contextually-based approach to learning, by encouraging children to make connections between different areas of learning. In addition, many believe that this promotes deep learning and supports transference of skills, knowledge and understanding between the areas of learning. A concern in some schools is that children may not naturally transfer the skills learnt in one subject, say literacy, into other subject areas. Conversely, some teachers believe that depth of subject knowledge can only be taught through discrete subject teaching and are concerned that a surface approach to the curriculum may be the result of a thematic approach.

The Mantle of the Expert

The 'Mantle of the Expert' (O'Neill, 2015, pp.109–46) is another approach to teaching and learning that some schools find helpful in enabling children to take ownership of their learning. Children in a class work as a business or take on a project whereby they identify the key areas they want to develop. The teacher works as a facilitator to guide pupils to devise programmes of action, for example, conservation projects, so that they can take ownership and lead their own learning. While many of the curriculum areas can be included in this approach there can be challenges related to making sure core skills are explicitly taught, so skilled planning across the curriculum is essential. Another possible approach is Philosophy for Children (P4C), which has a key focus on enquiry and questioning as the basis of lessons. James Nottingham (2013) discusses strategies for the development of P4C through the ASK approach (attitudes, skills and knowledge).

Areas of learning

The Independent Review of the Primary Curriculum (IRPC) (DCSF, 2009) suggested an approach to making cross-curricular links that is still relevant and could enable whole-school curriculum planning through restructuring of the curriculum into six 'areas of learning':

- understanding the arts
- understanding English, communication and languages
- historical, geographical and social understanding
- mathematical understanding
- understanding physical development, health and well-being
- scientific and technological understanding.

'The areas of learning capture the essential knowledge, key skills and understanding that children need to develop as they progress through their primary years' (QCDA, 2010, p. 16). These 'areas of learning' may be a useful place to start when considering combining subjects in your lesson planning. While the Rose Review proposal outlined 'a design for the curriculum which promotes challenging subject teaching alongside equally challenging cross-curricular studies' (p. 4) it also 'insisted that literacy, numeracy and ICT must be prioritised' (p. 6). An additional emphasis was placed on the importance of talk, as Rose considered the 'prime skills of speaking and listening to be essential in their own right and crucial for learning to read, write, to be numerate and, indeed, to be successful in virtually all of the learning children undertake at school and elsewhere' (p. 6).

The Cambridge Primary Review

The Cambridge Primary Review (Alexander, 2010) made suggestions about the interpretation of the primary curriculum based on extensive research undertaken between 2006 and 2009. The investigation took into account the views of the general public on primary education including suggested changes, as well as carrying out 31 research reports investigating ten key themes. Suggestions included that the National Curriculum should take up just 70 per cent of teaching time with a locally set 'community curriculum' for the remaining 30 per cent. The curriculum should comprise eight 'domains': arts and creativity; citizenship and ethics; faith and belief; language, oracy and literacy; mathematics; physical and emotional health; place and time; science and technology. In addition teaching and learning should be situated in the local area as much as possible, particularly the community curriculum.

Reflective task

Consider your personal views on this issue of subject-based teaching versus theme-based and cross-curricular teaching. Are these *values*-based judgements? Are they linked to how much worth we apportion to each subject? Do you believe it is necessary to prioritise basic skills over the arts and humanities? In your experience so far what do you believe to be the 'best' approach? Why? What strategies do you have to address the potential issues? What do you consider may be the benefits of using 'the locality' to promote and inspire learning? What potential difficulties may arise?

The way forward?

It is worth considering that the Rose Review and the Cambridge Primary Review proposed a reorganisation of the curriculum into areas or domains rather than maintaining a separate subject-specific focus. Whatever the curriculum, and acknowledging that change is likely to occur throughout a teacher's career, it is likely that schools and teachers will increasingly need to make decisions about how different curricular areas can be linked in meaningful ways. There are many opinions on and rationales for this (Barnes, 2011; Rowley and Cooper, 2009). One suggestion might be some units of work 'blocked' and taught intensively over a short period of time, for example. Another consideration could be the extent to which the local community and expert visitors could be utilised to enhance children's learning within a thematic curriculum. Some schools have worked with local archaeologists, for example, or with a local firm of architects, builders, the National Trust, a theatre, or with a children's writer, ballet dancer, artist or musician – even fashion designers. What contribution can parents or grandparents make to a wider and more diverse curriculum? Even within the constraints of recent years, many schools have developed exciting curricular opportunities, so be brave and 'think outside the box'. It is possible and important to interpret changes in statutory requirements mediated by your own professional philosophy; this chapter will give you strategies for doing this, in terms of planning and assessing what is taught and learnt, with confidence.

There is an ongoing tension related to the prioritisation of literacy and numeracy above other areas of the curriculum, with some teachers believing it is important for children's education to focus on core subjects and others believing that core skills can be taught contextually through other subjects.

Applying your philosophy to mediate statutory requirements

Epistemology is the branch of philosophy concerned with different ways of knowing and considering what are the most valid ways of knowing. How can we get beyond our personal opinions to something we can feel has validity? Some things we know because they are based on reason. Other things we know from experience. We think we know how children learn based first on reason, on what we have learnt from research and from the authoritative experience of others about learning. In addition, we have our empirical knowledge: what we observe about the children in our classrooms. We develop our personal educational philosophy based on a combination of what we learn from scholarly authorities and our personal experience. We may therefore find ourselves in agreement with the current prevailing ideology of education, or at times find ourselves teaching in ways that we fundamentally believe to be misinformed. It is vital that we adopt the view presented by Pollard:

> Professional ideologies are always likely to remain strong among teachers – they represent commitments, ideals and interests. Reflective teachers should be open-minded enough to constructively critique their own beliefs, as well as those of others. (Pollard, 2008, p. 94)

Work in school

The following discussion takes place during a staff meeting:

Amy: I prefer to teach my literacy skills when the children are learning other subjects so they have a context. So, this week we are looking at the structure of newspaper reports and writing up our activities in groups to make a report for Year 2, to let them know about what happens in Year 3, when they come to visit.

(Continued)

Andrew:	No, I prefer to teach the skills separately. How can you tell how much each child understands about the newspaper features? Once we have learnt the skills in literacy then we use them in history to write about the Ancient Egyptians.
Amy:	If I do it that way I don't feel I have enough time to give quality teaching to all the subjects. I find a more thematic approach works better for me.
Barbara:	But how do you make sure you plan for all the individual needs? In my class, some children prefer the 'joined up' thematic approach but others really seem to thrive when they can focus on one subject at a time. So, I plan from knowing my children, their prior knowledge, and then what I am to teach is tailored to that. So, sometimes I plan to teach in a theme, sometimes not.

This discussion explores some of the issues facing teachers today. How to teach areas of the curriculum can be dependent on teachers' own philosophical beliefs concerning how children learn or on school approaches to learning and ethos. Changes to the curriculum at national level will resonate with some teachers and not with others. Planning a successful learning experience then depends on the children, the teacher, the school, and its community, all within the context of a wider curriculum.

Long-term plan

Table 3.1 shows how a long-term plan for a Year 4 class based on the new National Curriculum (DfE, 2013b) might look.

The 2013 curriculum requires children to learn about electricity in Year 1 (electric lights), Year 4 (circuits) and Year 6 (circuits, voltage and symbols). This illustrates the spiral nature of the curriculum, with subjects being revisited to 'build' on prior knowledge and allow for consolidation of learning through experience. After each unit of work has been taught, teachers would make a 'summative' assessment to ascertain the level of individual understanding. Formative assessment is used regularly to inform planning and support learning.

Table 3.1 Example of a Year 4 long-term plan

Year 4/ Curriculum area	Autumn 1	Autumn 2	Spring 1	Spring 2	Summer 1	Summer 2
Science	Living things	Animals, including humans	States of matter	Sound	Electricity	Choice
History	Britain's settlement by Anglo-Saxons and Scots	Depth study of Anglo-Saxon art and culture			Earliest civilisations: Mayan	Ancient Greece
Geography					Similarities and differences between own region and …	
					United Kingdom and a region in Europe	
Citizenship	Understand political system of the UK and how citizens participate in democratic government					
Art		Great artists	Sketch book recording of observations		Drawing and painting	
Computing/ design and technology	Design and write programs			D/T design/ make/ evaluate a game		D/T cooking and nutrition: cook a series of healthy savoury dishes
Music	Compose music for play related to Christmas concert	Play composition Prepare for performance	Choice		Choice	
Physical education	Dance – basic skills	Gym		Swimming	Games; adventure camp	Athletics
Foreign language (French)	Portraits		Les Quatre Amis		Ça pousse! On y va	

Reflective task

Some of the areas lend themselves to a cross-curricular approach and would be taught in this way. Examine the long-term plan in Table 3.1 to see which lessons you would teach using this approach. For example, explain how you might combine sound in science and music, art with history, design and technology with geography or dance and music.

Medium-term plan

To help deliver specific areas of the curriculum, the whole-school long-term plan is organised into medium-term plans, which are targeted at specific year groups and often for a specific term, half-term or 'unit' periods. The long-term plan can be delivered in cross-curricular themes or subject-specific chunks or a mixture of the two, as decided by the school management team to best meet the learning needs of the children. Barnes (2007, p. 184) states that

> A medium-term plan should show the proposed relationship between key questions and attention to specific subject-based skills and knowledge. It must show progression towards a questioning stance and the development of ever-deeper understanding.

Many schools plan in teams or in subject groups in order to share their knowledge and experience. The medium-term plan (unit of work) should also show when assessment is to take place and begin to make clear the differentiation strategies to be used across the 'unit of work'. These should include a range of approaches to assessment, to enable all learners to demonstrate their successful learning. We shall discuss differentiation and assessment later in the chapter and in Chapter 4.

Weekly plans

Short-term plans are often called 'weekly plans'. From these an individual lesson plan can be constructed. These are necessary to ensure that all areas of the curriculum are taught effectively and in adequate depth to enable children to learn. Although weekly plans are meant to outline specific activities and sessions throughout the week, they need to be flexible, so that you can respond to changes, in order to extend children's learning.

The Process of Mediation from National Curriculum to weekly plan

The different levels of mediation/interpretation at each level are shown in Figure 3.1.

The National Centre for Excellence in the Teaching of Mathematics (NCETM) illustrates the development of planning for maths using the useful structure outlined below. This can be applied in any subject area, and the principles can also be applied in thematic approaches to planning.

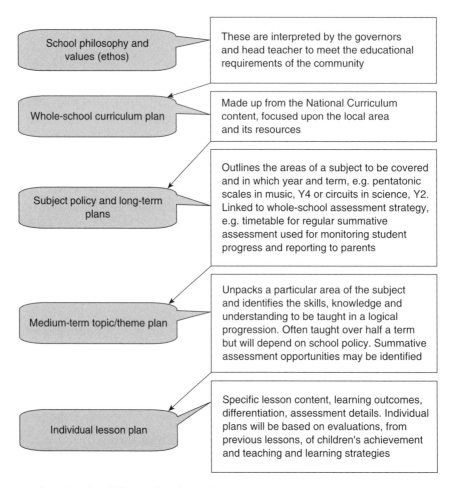

Figure 3.1   Showing the different levels of planning and the stages at which teachers can interpret the statutory curriculum and policies to reflect the philosophy of the school and teachers

Features of effective practice

An effective structure for curriculum planning shows how mathematics is planned for at the long-, medium- and short-term level. Effective planning:
   Has a long-term plan (planning for progression) which:

- clearly states an expected pathway of progression across the Key Stage
- breaks down the Key Stage progression into a yearly plan
- reflects the school's vision and national priorities.

Has a medium-term plan (structuring the planning of units) which:

- links clearly to the long-term plan
- makes clear what is to be taught and when
- is based on prior attainment, not what year group the pupils are in
- contains differentiated teaching objectives addressing process as well as content
- gives clear links to rich and interesting activities and resources
- indicates teaching approaches which will engage and interest the pupils
- contains a schedule for various assessment items in line with school policy
- reflects the school's vision and national priorities.

Has a short-term plan (lesson planning) which:

- links clearly to the medium-term plan
- makes clear what is to be taught
- encourages the teacher to plan a sequence of lessons rather than 'standalones'
- gives guidance for a range of teaching approaches to be used within the sequence of lessons
- indicates key vocabulary that might be barriers to learning
- gives guidance to support teachers to plan in more detail the approaches and resources which will engage and interest the students
- gives guidance for assessment activities and strategies, for example, probing questions, self- and peer assessment opportunities
- gives examples of ways in which learning can be taken beyond the classroom, for example, consolidation, extension, application, historical links
- offers prompts for reflecting on and evaluating the lesson in order to inform/ review the planned next steps for this unit
- reflects the school's vision. (https://www.ncetm.org.uk/resources/21510)

Key questions you may ask

We now look at some key questions that you may have as a student teacher:

1. 'What MUST I get right when I'm writing a lesson plan?'

Five key things are:

*   Know what children have previously done, and whether they remember and understand this.
*   Know exactly what you want children to achieve and have a target that reflects this.
*   Plan for inclusion, for example, differentiation.
*   Know what resources are available.
*   Plan and manage the length of each stage of a lesson and what you and any other adults in the classroom will be doing at each stage.

2. 'How can I plan for differentiation?'

This is an essential question to ask in order to have both a child-centred and a focused approach to learning and teaching. It indicates that you recognise that per-sonalisation and differentiation are necessary in each effective lesson. You need to learn how to set the correct level of challenge for individual children. The Teachers' Standards (DfE, 2013a) require you to 'set goals that stretch and challenge pupils of all backgrounds, abilities and dispositions' (Standard 1.2). There are lots of ways you can begin to do this. For example:

*   Know the children well and understand what their interests are and how they learn most effectively.
*   Plan based on your assessment of the previous lesson.
*   Ask the class questions at the beginning of, during and at the end of a lesson to gauge different levels of understanding. (Formative assessment)
*   Observe children working and listen to them talking to each other. Talk to them about their work.
*   Consider using 'choice and challenge' – allowing children to choose from three levels of difficulty depending on their self-evaluation. (Peacock, 2016, pp. 117–188)

Always plan extensions for those who may not be sufficiently challenged, although these should include opportunities to deepen children's skills, knowledge and under-standing, and should not just be more of the main lesson content. Get to know and take into account children's different personalities, interests and backgrounds, including cultural backgrounds, their language levels and any special educational needs, and consider what will motivate and interest different children (Standard 5, DfE, 2013a).

In many subjects, for example, in art or history, you can design open activities that children can respond to at their own levels. Or you can give children the choice of working at the level of challenge they want to try … using labels such as hot/spicy, medium or mild (or curry types vindaloo, dhansak, korma).

For some activities ask children to work in pairs or groups of mixed abilities so that they can support and extend each other.

3. 'I don't know much about this so I'm having trouble finding ideas for activities which will fit the learning objective. Where can I find ideas? I don't have enough time to research this thoroughly.'

Standard 3 (DfE, 2013a) expects you to 'have a secure knowledge of the relevant subjects of the curriculum', but this isn't acquired overnight! You increasingly consolidate your subject knowledge over time through your own research, with the support of colleagues or through continuing professional development (CPD) opportunities.

The internet can be a useful resource, both websites for teachers and those that are not specifically educational. Websites for art galleries or museums, for example, can stimulate informed creative thinking – see, for instance, the National Gallery's Take One Picture at www.takeonepicture.org.uk/ – or books of course, including those for children. And don't be afraid to ask other students and experienced teachers, particularly subject leaders – they will appreciate your request for ideas. Are there visitors with expertise in this subject who might be invited to work with you: archaeologists, musicians, artists, parents, local businesses? Are there resources in the local history or archive library, or a local museum with an education department?

There are often many opportunities for collaborative planning practice in schools and students have said that they have learnt many good strategies in this way, for example, through children devising the lesson focus, cross-curricular teaching, interactive lessons, learn-apply-experiment or learning outside.

4. 'I have learned, at university, that I should take initiatives in my planning, but when I have been in school the teachers expect me to rely on their planning methods, which I don't really agree with. In one school differentiation was frowned upon and in another I was criticised for responding to a surprise opportunity that arose during a lesson rather than sticking to my lesson plan. Yet we are assessed on our ability to do these things. This has caused tensions with my mentor and not done my self-esteem much good!'

It is important, whether a student or teacher in a school, that you take time to read the policies and understand their expectations. All schools have a range of policies that outline their approach to teaching and learning, as well as health and safety and safeguarding. Having discussions with mentors and teachers about lesson planning and how this is done helps to develop positive relationships and avoid misunderstandings.

The research of Hattie (2012) shows that the greatest benefits to all involved come from:

- increased experience in schools observing a range of teachers
- planning for a wider range of children
- being part of the community of teachers
- having dialogue related to planning.

As John (2006) has said:

> It seems that greater exposure to teaching challenges the novices to see planning and preparation less as an unalterable event and more as a concept associated with unpredictability, flexibility, and creativity. It was as if the student teachers were seeing planning as the glue that held the various pieces of learning and teaching together and the linear format, despite being a course requirement, was largely superfluous to their needs as teachers. (p. 489)

What are the children going to learn or what am I going to teach?

Planning and assessment or assessment and planning, which comes first? There is no definitive answer. It is like the proverbial 'chicken and egg'. Many beginning teachers become involved in what they need to teach rather than focusing on what the children will learn. If governments continue to define prescriptive and crowded curricula, teachers may be led to 'covering' the objectives, for example, 'delivering the literacy objectives' rather than fostering a love of literature, or focusing on 'facts' to be learnt rather than the excitement of enquiry-based learning. It is worth considering who the lesson plan is for when deciding how much content needs to be included. Obviously observed lessons need to be very detailed so that the observer can follow your thinking process and you can demonstrate your knowledge of the children, pedagogical content knowledge (PCK) and your ability to plan a satisfying and complete learning experience at the correct level. Lesson planning in general needs to contain as much information as is necessary to enable learning to occur and so that you can teach with confidence.

When planning the beginning of a new topic it is helpful to start from the big picture, share the overall goal, show children where they are going and then break it down into manageable steps. Successful athletes use a positive mental attitude technique where they visualise themselves achieving their goal and this can be used with children. What will it feel like and look like to be successful? How will they know? It is also important, as a teacher, to know what you are aiming for, what skills, knowledge and understanding you want children to learn, how you will get there and how you will know that the children have learned. From this it is clear that teaching and assessment are cyclical and dependent on each other. Skemp (1979) states that learning is either innate or taught, formal or informal, and very often, although teachers think they are teaching something, the messages that children receive are not necessarily what was intended. In order to learn, children need to classify new information and then relate it to what they already know. How the new information is explained will have an impact on what is understood and how it is used. For example, a trumpet could be described as: a very loud instrument, a coiled brass cylindrical pipe with valves and a mouthpiece or something you use in an orchestra. All of these descriptions are correct but do not necessarily support learning what a trumpet is. Therefore, understanding definitions and explanations depends on prior experience and fitting new knowledge into what is already known. The percentage of new knowledge taught in lessons can be anything between 50 per cent and 90 per cent depending of the complexity of the subject matter (Hattie, 2012; Allison and Tharby, 2015). This finding suggests that lesson content needs to be carefully monitored in terms of challenge so that key messages are understood and added to previous knowledge but pupils are not bored or frustrated. Allison and Tharby (2015, p. 42) advocate that challenge should be set 'just outside their comfort zone', which concurs with Vygotsky's ideas on the Zone of Proximal Development (ZPD) where children, with support, work above the level that they could cope with alone. This needs careful management, resilience and perseverance (Dweck, 2012) on the part of the children and is reliant on the classroom ethos established by the teacher. It is essential that teachers model problem solving methods by showing children how they deal with challenges without giving up.

Two factors are essential to ensure the best pupil outcomes and these are content knowledge and quality of instruction (Allison and Tharby, 2015, p. 5). In addition, 'expert teaching requires:

- Challenge – so that students have high expectations of what they can achieve
- Explanation – so that students acquire new knowledge and skills
- Modelling – so that students know how to apply the knowledge and skills

- Questioning – so that students are made to think hard with breadth, depth and accuracy
- Feedback – so that students can evaluate and further develop their knowledge and skills'.

(Allison and Tharby, 2015, p. 7)

This leads us to consider, what is knowledge?
Kinds of knowledge

Biggs (2003, pp. 41–3) gives a theoretical analysis of the kinds of knowing that can result from the need to 'get through the prescribed curriculum' and the kind of knowing that changes the way we tackle problems and look at life, leading to learning which is deep and transformative:

- Demonstrating what you know, without necessarily understanding it (declarative or propositional knowledge) – for example, rote learning, repeating times tables, delivering the curriculum, learning that 'area' is length times breadth.
- Using such knowledge to solve problems ('functioning knowledge') – for example, planning a class party, solving problems in maths or science, applying your formula for area in a context.
- Knowing what comes next in a sequence without understanding why (procedural knowledge) – for example, following through a series of lessons as outlined in a 'scheme' or unit as written, or knowing that after area comes teaching of volume.
- Using what you know in order to make informed judgements, which is by far the most important kind ('conditional knowledge') – for example, you know the area of carpet needed for your classroom, but now you consider the use of the room, the children and alternative solutions.

It is useful to know whether the process or the product of a learning episode is of greatest importance. Is the correct answer most critical as in learning times tables or the method through which it is achieved? These issues are part of the planning process in that they will indicate what should be the focus of your attention during the lesson and what should be left until a later date. Stobart (2014) discusses the importance of Pedagogical Content Knowledge (PCK) in that, although it is necessary to have secure subject knowledge, knowing how to share this in a clear and logical manner is equally significant. Stobart (2014) discusses layers of learning, building one upon the other in order to reach an end goal, knowing what you want children to achieve and what it will look like is a key part of this process. A study carried out by

Lui and Bonner (2016) found that when marking children's work strong conceptual knowledge enabled in-service and pre-service teachers to be more accurate in their marking than those who worked at a procedural level. This demonstrates that, while it is important to know the sequence of learning, having a deep conceptual understanding of the subject being taught is necessary in order to enable the children to progress effectively. When planning lessons a deep understanding of the subject content and a knowledge of how to break it down into manageable chunks are essential. We have all seen comedy programmes where the lead character is talking to a foreigner who does not understand, and rather than find a different way to approach the problem merely shouts louder. The ability to recognise where misconceptions or misunderstandings may occur and develop a range of strategies to deal with these in a timely and sensitive manner is the skill of an excellent teacher.

Planning for learning

Individual lesson plans

Each school will have a particular approach to the individual lesson plan with a preferred proforma. Your initial teacher education (ITE) provider may also have a recommended format. So rather than confuse you with a table to be completed, we thought it more important to identify the key elements that should be included in an individual lesson plan.

General information

- year (e.g. 4)
- class – number of students, may be wanted in gender numbers, that is, male and female
- teacher
- time of lesson and duration.

Lesson-specific information

- Title of lesson (usually taken from medium-term plan).
- Intended Learning Outcomes (ILOs) and assessment criteria.
- Previous assessment information (if any is available).
- Current assessment opportunities and strategies.
- Activities – should be linked to the learning outcomes and the assessment, the more aligned with each other these are, the better the learning opportunities.

Fautley and Savage (2013) suggest that these should be in the form of learning episodes with timings so that learning can move through several stages during the lesson. This is a good strategy for inexperienced teachers but lessons very rarely go as planned, so ongoing evaluation and flexibility are also required.

- Differentiation – what strategies will be utilised? This should include reference to any school support plans for children with special educational needs and disability (SEND) or strategies for specified children, though some activities may be better differentiated by outcome.
- Groupings – these may be based on partners, mixed-ability or friendship or ability. There are good reasons for any of these groupings, but it is essential to be clear about why you have chosen a particular grouping for a particular activity and do not keep the same groups all the time. Consider why you might decide on different grouping for different activities.
- Key vocabulary – this is very important and should include any new language you want children to use in the lesson as well as consolidating previously taught vocabulary.
- Key questions – adding key questions to your lesson plan is a good idea so that you don't forget your focus during the lesson.
- Possible misconceptions – this includes possible issues that may occur within the new subject content being taught but also any misconceptions that were noticed in previous lessons so that they can be dealt with before moving on.
- Resources, including staff (other adults) – having resources ready and available well beforehand enables you to prepare properly for the beginning of the lesson. Sharing planning, including your expectations, with additional adults in the classroom means that you will all be working towards the same goal. This is especially important if particular strategies or procedures need to be followed including aspects of health and safety.
- Plenary – or a series of mini-plenaries, to correct misunderstandings, consolidate learning or introduce next learning steps.

Once you are familiar with the needs and abilities of your class and the intricacies of planning for learning, then it is possible, and enjoyable, to move to less structured/ linear approaches. It is important to note that experienced teachers may seem to have minimal planning but this is usually because a large amount of the information has been 'internalised', much akin to the skills needed in driving a car.

Intended Learning Outcomes (ILOs)

Teachers use the statutory curriculum and national strategies to devise ILOs for each lesson. These are then shared with the class, sometimes in the form of 'We Are

Learning To…' (WALT) or child-friendly notices. From these and the discussion that follows, 'Success Criteria', which may be called 'What I'm Looking For' (WILF), can be constructed. This is called constructive alignment and is the explicit connection between what is to be learnt and what you will be assessing. As each child is an individual, how they will learn and be able to demonstrate this learning may be evidenced differently. ILOs are critical to successful learning and form the basis of the content of the lesson. It is easy to make the mistake of finding an interesting activity and then deciding what your ILO will be, but it is much more effective to identify the ILO and then design a relevant activity. By doing this you will make sure that you are teaching what you think you are and that children's needs will be met. Bloom's taxonomy can support the planning of ILOs but an additional model that may be of assistance is the 'Structure of Observed Learning Outcomes' (SOLO) (Biggs and Collis, 1982), which outlines five levels of language associated with the quality of children's work. Although it is similar to Bloom's Taxonomy there are differences, as Bloom's Taxonomy describes a learner's behaviour but SOLO describes their quality of thinking. This may seem to be a very subtle difference but both Hattie (2014) and Stobart (2014) advocate the value of SOLO as a means of making judgements about children's understanding and learning.

According to Biggs and Collis (1982), SOLO is ordered into five stages, which build progressively.

The five stages are:

- Prestructural – children do not understand at all or incorrectly.
- Unistructural – they can understand one particular aspect.
- Multistructural – they understand several pieces of information but do not necessarily make connections between them.
- Relational – children can connect several pieces of knowledge and explain how they are connected.
- Extended abstract – they can use their knowledge beyond the immediate problem in a new situation and can generalise to other areas of learning.

The first two stages relate to surface learning through the ability to memorise facts and the last three to deep learning demonstrating developing conceptual knowledge and understanding. Examples of how different schools have used Bloom's Taxonomy and SOLO Taxonomy to support planning and assessment can be found at https://www.gov.uk/government/uploads/system/uploads/attachment_data/file/349266/beyond-levels-alternative-assessment-approaches-developed-by-teaching-schools.pdf.

The ILOs may be differentiated for ability groups within the class, and consequently there will be a similar number of differentiated success criteria. Personalisation of approach to enable individualised learning is perhaps too idealistic a goal for every teacher in every lesson, if it is the teacher who has the 'control' and determines what is learnt. However, through self-determination and personalisation of the success criteria, children can be encouraged to be involved in the lesson outcomes. This does come with a caveat though. Whilst children perceived to be 'gifted and talented' and those confident in the curriculum area in question may relish this 'challenge', there may be some children whose self-esteem is too poor for them to believe they can achieve in any way. Giving this group of children the opportunity to set realistic, attainable yet high standards may take some encouragement and support, until they become comfortable and confident in this area. Good planning based on prior knowledge (from assessment) will ensure allocation of the correct resources (including staff) to support the children in their early steps until they become more confident in this approach. A useful approach may be through adding a context to the lesson by presenting a 'This Is Because...' (TIBS) aspect to help children understand how the knowledge and/or skills they have learnt in the lesson may be of wider use. This could also be linked with an aspect of children's prior experience and learning.

Homework

The Teachers' Standards (Standard 4) requires teachers to 'set homework and plan out-of-class activities to extend the knowledge and understanding pupils have acquired'. Careful consideration needs to be given to what kind of homework is set and why. Bearing in mind that Standard 4 also requires teachers to 'promote a love of learning and children's intellectual curiosity', many primary schools expect children to at least undertake reading, literacy and/or mathematics tasks at home. The amount increases with age, and the frequency is variable, although weekly spelling homework and daily reading are still fairly common. Some teachers and many parents believe that homework is a useful extension to the school day and if parents are supportive then this may well be the case. However, limited space at home, insufficient backup from adults and limited access to computers must be taken into consideration (Alexander, 2010, pp. 83–4).

Thought needs to be given to the content of the homework. Is it to be carried out independently by the child, or with the support of their parents or carers? Do they have the support of parents and carers and the necessary equipment at home to be able to complete the homework successfully?

When work is returned, judgements need to be made about how much the child has understood independently and how much they may have been supported. For this reason, it is important to have additional evidence of learning by the child before conclusions are reached about their understanding and achievement.

Differentiation

Planning should include 'differentiation'. This is the term used to explain when the teaching and learning are specifically targeted and made different, to meet the needs of all children within the class. This will include varied aspects of education: learning, social, emotional and any physical needs. In any classroom of children there will be a range of abilities; whether this is linked with understanding of concepts, skill levels or factual knowledge, for example, for children for whom English is an additional language (EAL), or who have physical, social or emotional barriers to learning. Because of this expected range of abilities (for want of better terminology), which may well alter for individual children across the curriculum, teachers should aim to plan specifically to support children to succeed at the differentiated levels.

In addition to this there are children who require a more individualised approach to their learning, which may involve an Individual Education Plan or development plan to meet their specific needs. Additional staffing and resources to support these children in their development and learning may be available depending on the severity of their needs.

Teachers will need to use their thorough understanding of whichever statutory curriculum requirements apply underlying principles with regard to inclusion and their knowledge of the strengths and needs of the individual child to plan with a flexible approach. This approach will in no way involve reduced expectations of achievement, rather a personalised approach with each child achieving appropriately.

Reflective task

Consider a class of children you have worked with at some point of your ITE so far. Can you identify a spread of abilities? What strategies did you and the class teacher use to remove any barriers to learning and help all children to achieve? How were these identified in your planning?

Strategies you may have noticed could include grouping (classroom organisation), support, outcome, task or resource. If so, make notes about how well you feel these worked for the child, the teacher, other children.

Logically, as planning involves many aspects to ensure inclusion and achievement by all, then assessment must also be varied and differentiated in approach to allow all children to demonstrate their strengths. As Wearmouth (2009) puts it, 'Students' sense of themselves as having the potential to be effective in the community of practice of learners may be constructed and/or constrained by the forms of assessment that are used with them' (p. 93).

Remember, you cannot plan effectively without reference to previous assessment and you must include opportunities for assessment throughout the lessons you plan.

Lesson evaluations

These should focus first on the learning and then on the teaching, leading to an end product that informs the next planned teaching (Standard 4, DfE, 2013a). A further area to consider is children's attitudes to, and enjoyment of, the learning. These are professional judgements that will both support teacher knowledge of an individual child and inform future planning decisions.

Case study

Sometimes a surprise event can help you rethink your teaching strategy, such as in the following example. In a music lesson with a Year 4 class of 20 boys and nine girls, the children were listening to Saint-Saëns' *The Carnival of the Animals*, identifying how the musical elements combined to create the effect and help us relate this to particular animals. The children used language to describe how the music represented the animals, and described the mental images the music evoked. Partway through the lesson the 'surprise' happened: a group of boys asked if they could dance to illustrate the movement of the animals, in addition to describing the musical elements that contributed to the effect of the music. The assumptions this teacher made when planning had not included the boys wishing to dance. The children's desire to respond this way impacted on future planning to include more opportunities for dance.

An evaluation of each lesson taught will support the teacher's knowledge through identifying children who have achieved the learning objectives, those children who have achieved more than expected and those who have yet to fully achieve the ILOs, as well as any children who have misconceptions that will need to be addressed. Teachers will also evaluate how children responded to the teaching strategies used and which learning strategies children relied upon.

Resources, learning environment and classroom management are also areas for consideration due to the impact they have on a lesson. It is important also to obtain feedback on your teaching from the children; for example, with young children through drawing or role play, by consulting a focus group of children you perceive to be having problems, or by pupils commenting on an aspect of their learning through analysing a video of a lesson.

Purposeful lesson evaluations and record keeping are useful tools to aid memory and impact upon future planning. Therefore, they need to be 'user-friendly'. In most situations, making annotations on the planning sheet is an acceptable form of record keeping for day-to-day evaluation. This should be clear and specific to aid planning for the next appropriate lesson.

Teachers and schools have differing methods for recording children's achievement through records of progress and attainment; it is usually the medium-term end of unit summative assessments that go to build up this record.

Reflective task

When next on placement ask your school for a copy of the long-term plan and a subject-specific or themed medium-term plan and then try to see how an individual lesson you have observed (or taught) fits into the big picture. Evaluate the lesson to identify the strategies needed to teach the next lesson to the same class. Which misconceptions need to be corrected? What will the gifted and talented children learn? How will you differentiate appropriately?

Summary

This chapter began with an overview of the statutory curriculum, then discussed different ways in which it may be structured, as single subjects or through cross-curricular approaches, the value judgements involved and the impact of changing government priorities on these decisions. The English National Curriculum (DfE, 2013b) and its rationale was compared with the curricula for Scotland and Wales, and with previous recommendations (DCSF, 2009) and the Cambridge Primary Review (Alexander, 2010). We considered the many decisions that teachers must make in order to mediate national requirements at the levels of long-term, whole-school planning, medium-term planning, daily planning and lesson planning. The importance of integrating planning and assessment in a cyclical way, at all levels, was emphasised and is developed in Chapter 4. Finally, the process of needing to reflect on teachers' planning and on children's learning was explained in order that both may be taken forward.

Questions for discussion

Refer to the *National Curriculum: A Framework* (DfE, 2013b)

- It was said (p. 64) that teachers' planning involves 'listening to the children'. Discuss ways in which this can be done, based on the planning guidance above, within the statutory curriculum.
- Consider ways in which you aim to make your teaching and children's learning inspiring.
- Discuss ways in which planning for different subjects in the new curriculum can begin with the locality, as advised in the Cambridge Primary Review (Alexander, 2010) and how this could link with the National Curriculum subject content.
- Differentiation: reflect on how you have differentiated for a particular child; how might you have done this better?

Further reading

Barnes, J. (2015) *Cross-Curricular Learning 3–14*, third edn. London: Sage.
Clear discussion related to planning and teaching through a cross-curricular and thematic approach. There are strong links to creativity and research-based pedagogy throughout. Chapter 11 is focused on planning for cross-curricular activity.

Fautley, M. and Savage, J. (2013) *Lesson Planning for Effective Learning*. Oxford: Oxford University Press.
This book gives excellent planning advice by combining theoretical perspectives and best practice in a readable format.

Hattie, J. (2012) *Visible Learning for Teachers*. Abingdon: Routledge.
Pages 39–76 focus on preparing the lesson. Key points focus on the importance of planning with other teachers and the necessity of knowing the children in a holistic way. Pages 51–3 consider issues related to challenge, commitment, confidence and conceptual knowledge.

John, P.D. (2006) 'Lesson planning and the student teacher: Re-thinking the dominant model', *Journal of Curriculum Studies*, 384: 483–98.
John considers the role of lesson planning in ITE. He raises interesting points related to a range of models of lesson planning and focuses on the importance of dialogue in planning for student teacher development.

Nottingham, J. (2013) *Encouraging Learning*. Abingdon: Routledge.
This book is a key text for supporting the development of your personal philosophy of planning. It is research-based and begins from the focus of what is important … the learning and the individual child.

Terhart, E. (2011) 'Has John Hattie really found the holy grail of research on teaching? An extended review of visible learning', *Journal of Curriculum Studies*, 433: 425–38.
A review of the research of John Hattie, this article is both interesting and provides a challenge to consider multiple perspectives on any one area of research.

References

Alexander, R. (2010) *Children, their World, their Education: Final Report and Recommendations of the Cambridge Primary Review*. London: Routledge.
Allison, S. and Tharby, A. (2015) *Making Every Lesson Count*. Carmarthen: Crown House Publishing.
Barnes, J. (2007) *Cross-Curricular Learning 3–14*. London: Sage.
Barnes, J. (2011) *Cross-Curricular Learning 3–14*, second edn. London: Sage.
Biggs, J. (2003) *Teaching for Quality Learning at University: What the Student Does*. Society for Research into Higher Education. Buckingham: HRE and Open University Press.
Biggs, J. and Collis, K. (1982) *Evaluating the Quality of Learning: The Solo Taxonomy: Structure of the Observed Learning Outcome*. New York: Academic Press.
Department for Children, Schools and Families (DCSF) (2009) *Independent Review of the Primary Curriculum*. Available at: www.webarchive national archives.gov.uk.
Department for Education (DfE) (2013a) *Teachers' Standards*. Available at: www.education.gov.uk/.
Department for Education (DfE) (2013b) *National Curriculum: A Framework*. Available at: www.education.gov.uk.
Dweck, C. (2012) *Mindset: How You Can Fulfil Your Potential*. London: Robinson.
Hattie, J. (2012) *Visible Learning for Teachers*. Abingdon: Routledge.
Hattie, J. (2014) *Visible Learning and the Science of How We Learn*. London: Sage.
Fautley, M. and Savage, J. (2013) *Lesson Planning for Effective Learning*. Oxford: Oxford University Press.
John, P.D. (2006) 'Lesson planning and the student teacher: Re-thinking the dominant model', *Journal of Curriculum Studies*, 384: 483–98.
Lui, A. and Bonner, S (2016) 'Preservice and inservice teachers' knowledge, beliefs, and instructional planning in primary school mathematics', *Teaching and Teacher Education*, 56(May): 1–13.
National College for Teaching and Leadership (NCTL) (2014) *Beyond Levels: Alternative Assessment Approaches Developed by Teaching Schools*. Crown Copyright. Available at: https://www.gov.uk/government/uploads/system/uploads/attachment_data/file/349266/beyond-levels-alternative-assessment-approaches-developed-by-teaching-schools.pdf.

Nottingham, J. (2013) *Encouraging Learning*. Abingdon: Routledge.

O'Neill, C. (2015) *Dorothy Heathcote on Education and Drama*. Abingdon: Routledge.

Peacock, A. (2016) *Assessing for Learning Without Limits*. Oxford: Oxford University Press.

Piaget, J. (1953*) The Origin of Intelligence in the Child* (republished 1997, *Origin of Intelligence in the Child, Selected Works Vol. 3*). Vol.111. London: Routledge.

Pollard, A. (2008) *Reflective Teaching*, third edn. London: Continuum.

Qualifications and Curriculum Development Agency (QCDA) (2010) *The National Curriculum Primary Handbook*. London: QCDA.

Rowley, C. and Cooper, H. (eds) (2009) *Cross-Curricular Approaches to Teaching and Learning*. London: Sage.

Skemp, R. (1979) *Intelligence, Learning and Action*. Chichester: John Wiley and Sons.

Stobart, G. (2014) *The Expert Learner*. Berkshire: Open University Press.

Wearmouth, J. (2009) *A Beginning Teacher's Guide to Special Educational Needs*. Maidenhead: Open University Press.

4

Assessment

Kim Harris and Suzanne Lowe

By the end of this chapter, you should be able to:

- make assessment choices and decisions with confidence
- use a wide range of assessment strategies to inform future planning, develop learning and independence
- understand the wider implications of assessment within primary education contexts.

Introduction

What is assessment?

Assessment is a means of identifying what skills, knowledge and understanding children have learnt, either before, during or after a period of teaching. All schools must have a clear assessment framework in place and must adhere to the statutory assessment arrangements outlined by government policy. Skilful assessment linked to learning is essential to enable effective teaching throughout the Foundation Stage and Key Stages. The central purpose of assessment is 'to promote good progress and outcomes for pupils' and, as a teacher, it is you who is accountable for 'their attainment, progress and outcomes' (Teachers' Standard 2, DfE, 2013). Assessment is an integral part of teaching and learning but tends to be one of the most difficult areas for student teachers to master. As effective teachers, we aim to use professional judgement, informed by evidence, to assess children's abilities, in order to construct a bridge between teaching and learning to enable progression to take place. An important point to remember is that learning and teaching are complex; the act of teaching does not necessarily mean that children will learn but equally children do not need to be assessed in order for learning to take place. Assessment is simply the means of measuring and quantifying the learning that has taken place. The previous chapter on planning outlined the importance of using assessment to inform future planning. This chapter explores ways in which this may be done particularly within the more flexible context of the 2014 National Curriculum assessment strategy.

Types of assessment

Different types of assessment generate data or evidence that can be used for different purposes and for different audiences. The main approaches to assessment broadly fall into two categories, formative assessment and summative assessment, although it is possible to use summative assessment strategies to produce data that have formative value. The differences depend on the way that they are applied and who the information is for. Teachers' Standard 6 (DfE, 2013) refers to 'making accurate and productive use of assessment' by demonstrating secure subject knowledge, choosing appropriate assessment tools, providing evidence and using data to monitor progress and through effective feedback. This overarching Standard encompasses both forms of assessment including data collected informally in the classroom and formally for external use. Although there are a wide range of different assessment strategies and approaches nothing is as important as knowing the children well, both as pupils and as people: 'The quality of the relationship that a student has with you is likely to be an important factor in that student's well-being' (Hattie, 2014, p.18). Taking that idea forward, if children feel safe and secure within the classroom environment they will be more relaxed and open to effective teaching and any assessments carried out will have greater validity.

Assessment contributes to and derives from effective planning. Any activities planned for children should be assessed either formally or informally in order to support and extend children's learning. Different types of assessment each have different advantages and disadvantages. It is important to consider who the assessment is for and this will inform the type of assessment chosen.

Is the assessment for:

- The children, to inform future learning? This could be through teacher, peer or self-assessment to identify their own developing needs. Comments need to be age-appropriate, timely and shared in a format that the children can understand, for example, annotating their work, verbal feedback. Targets need to be clearly shared and related to learning intentions as well as checked to make sure that learning has taken place. There is no point writing effective comments in books if they are going to be ignored. Children will only value comments if teachers also value them by following them up.
- Parents, to let them know how their children are doing? Partnership between schools, teachers and parents is an important area to develop in order to support children's learning both in and out of school. There is a legal requirement for an annual written report for parents but many schools supply more. Parents' evenings or open days are a good opportunity for verbal reporting. There is often informal feedback given to parents at the end of the school day particularly for younger children.
- Yourself, the class teacher, to inform your future planning, to inform your reporting to parents, to identify specific difficulties in individual children or to support special educational needs (SEN) provision? This could take a variety of formats, although most schools have an assessment policy that will stipulate the minimum requirements expected and also outline strategies for best practice.
- The school, to meet the requirements of the School Development Plan, to benchmark school performance against other schools locally and nationally and also to make sure that pupils are making appropriate progress and meeting expected attainment in order to facilitate inter-school transfer?
- Government agencies, for statistical information whereby they can measure the impact of policy making through standardised summative assessment and develop league tables? Many schools use online data collection programs to self-evaluate their performance internally and against external measures to support school improvement. In addition, school performance analysis from such programs can be used by Ofsted to inform their pre-inspection briefings with schools.

The planning, teaching and assessment cycle

Regardless of the assessment strategy adopted by schools a clear connection between planning, teaching, assessment and recording is essential in order to effectively manage and extend children's learning. Figure 4.1 outlines the planning, teaching and

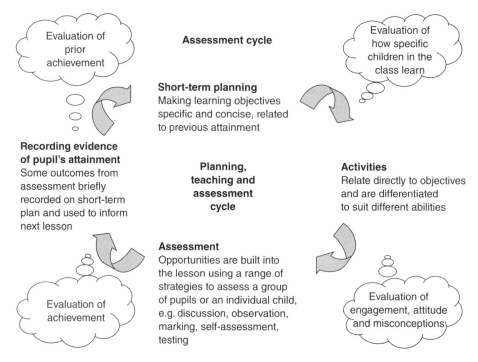

Figure 4.1   shows the assessment cycle, with explanation of how the key parts of the planned lesson fit together

assessment cycle at the heart of effective teaching. Good planning for children's individual needs is dependent on knowing 'where they are in their learning' so that challenge can be incorporated into activities alongside appropriate scaffolding. Therefore, accurate and detailed assessment and recording are key elements of good teaching in order to identify next steps in learning, misconceptions to be addressed and effective differentiation. Linking teaching to an ongoing cycle of learning and assessment is an effective way of implementing Teachers' Standard 6 (DfE, 2013), which states that teachers must 'use relevant data to monitor progress, set targets and plan subsequent lessons'.

Summative assessment

Teachers' Standard 6 (DfE, 2013) requires teachers to make 'summative assessments to secure pupils' progress'. In Key Stage 1 and 2, assessment at the end of a theme, topic or unit of work is generally summative, giving an indication of how much a child has learnt through studying that area. This form of quantitative data can be used to produce evidence that children have met particular learning objectives or can help to identify individual or group difficulties within the class. Records could include tick sheets linked to learning objectives, portfolios, multiple choice tests or grouping children according to guiding statements. For example: some children/ most children/a few children will........... and highlighting children's names. If schools need support to plan their whole-school assessment process, there is a range of online assessment schemes on the market that they can buy into, although it is important to be aware of the need to keep children's data safe. For children in the early years foundation stage summative assessment is in the form of the early years foundation stage profile, which contains a set of criteria to be reached by the end of the Foundation Stage of schooling.

Summative assessment through national tests

The Teachers' Standard 6 (DfE, 2013) requires teachers 'to know and understand how to assess using statutory assessments requirements'. Since 1991 national summative assessments (Standard Assessment Tests, SATs) have taken place at the end of Key Stages 1 and 2 in England and Wales. They have been adapted and continue to be updated over time, currently at Key Stage 1 these tests are not formal and are assessed by class teachers. In addition to the Key Stage 1 tests in English and mathematics there is also a phonics screening check carried out towards the end of Year 1. The Key Stage 2 SATs, however, are still formal written tests and are externally marked, although teacher assessments (TAs) in mathematics, reading, writing and science are also carried out to give a broader picture of children's attainment. The results, which are reported to schools, Local Authorities and parents, form league tables that are published by the government every year and are used as part of the Ofsted process to measure the efficacy of teaching and learning in schools. The SATs in England are currently limited to the curricular areas of English and mathematics, however science SATs sampling takes place in alternate years. A sample of schools is chosen to undertake Key Stage 2 science tests, which are not necessarily written but can be in the form of experiments or investigations.

Alexander (2010, p. 498) believes that,

> While the assessment of literacy and numeracy is essential, a broader, more innovative approach to summative assessment is needed if children's achievements and attainments across the curriculum are to be properly recognised and parents, teachers and children themselves are to have the vital information they need to guide subsequent decisions and choices.

Arguments against national standardised assessments include the view that they could be interpreted to identify weak or ineffective teaching rather than supporting children's learning. A further limitation associated with externally marked summative assessment is that they tend to be dependent upon pencil and paper methods of assessing, where the focus is on how literate a child is rather than being a true reflection of the child's ability in the subject under test. The questions that can be asked in this form of testing and external marking may lead to narrow answers limited to factual knowledge or short answers that need good examination technique to complete well, although work has been done in an attempt to mitigate this. In addition, testing has a limited impact on the identification of skills and attitudes such as flexibility, resourcefulness, resilience or team work, all of which contribute to the ability to learn independently and meet the unknown challenges of work in the future.

As there is a level of accountability through this process many children, parents and teachers can feel an unnecessary degree of 'stress'. A search of the internet will quickly show that there are numerous websites aimed at parents and devoted to strategies for relieving SATs stress for children in Year 6. Other criticisms suggest that testing on a particular day can disadvantage children who are ill or have had some sort of upset that affected their performance at a specific time. In this case, formative assessment is essential in order to develop an overview of each child over a longer period of time.

Many secondary schools throughout England carry out further testing for Year 7 children, which they argue can give a more accurate assessment of children's ability than the SATs. Perhaps one solution is to make several wider stroke summative assessments across the broad curriculum, at the end of a topic or unit of study, either as a result of cumulative formative assessments or by assessing a product resulting from the topic or unit. For example, by making a summative statement about a book or file of work on the topic, a piece of drama that has drawn on what is learnt in a history topic, a series of art using different techniques or a musical composition resulting from a sequence of lessons. A further consideration when assessing is to what extent a teacher can assess a child's enjoyment or attitude to a piece of art or music, dance or drama. It is possible through observation, discussion, photographs or videos to understand how much a child is enjoying what they are learning and discover their attitude to it through self- or peer evaluation of their work. Summative methods of assessment would be unlikely to give the same depth of response, demonstrating how important it is to identify the correct assessment tool for each individual purpose.

Statutory assessment arrangements in Scotland and Wales

It is important to mention here that since devolution there are differences in the statutory assessment arrangements in England, Scotland and Wales. Schools in Scotland follow the 'Curriculum for Excellence' which 'aims to achieve a transformation in education in Scotland by providing a coherent, more flexible and enriched curriculum from 3 to 18' (www.gov.scot/Topics/Education/Schools/curriculum).

Assessment in Scottish primary schools is carried out continuously throughout a child's schooling at appropriate times, which are identified and managed by the teacher, according to individual needs. Scottish teachers are supported by a new national resource – the National Assessment Resource (NAR) – which provides examples to ensure consistent standards and illustrations of children's work to clarify expectations at each level (www.gov.scot/Topics/Education/Schools/curriculum/assessment).

In Wales the curriculum is organised into Foundation Phase 3–7, Key Stage 2 and Key Stage 3/4. Baseline assessments are administered in the Foundation Phase across four of the Foundation Phase Areas of Learning and teachers are required carry out an End of Foundation Phase assessment in three of the Areas of Learning. Statutory assessment in Key Stage 2 is in the form of National Reading and Numeracy tests for children in Years 2–9, as well as end of Key Stage Teacher Assessments in English, Welsh or Welsh second language and mathematics. There are resources available to support teachers in their judgements (http://learning.gov.wales/?skip=1&lang=en).

Diagnostic assessment

Diagnostic assessment is a useful tool in helping to find out what children already know before starting a new topic. Effective planning of learning intentions is dependent on an accurate understanding of children's knowledge, skills and understanding in the subjects being taught. This could be done through a spider diagram either individually or in small groups, for example, 'What do you know about forces?' Children can then develop their diagram and this can be assessed to enable the teacher to know at what point in the topic to begin teaching and in order to support appropriate progression for different abilities. This form of assessment can also help to identify children who have particular strengths due to external influences. Many children have extensive knowledge of a variety of different subjects such as science, music, art, geography or history because of the interests or occupations of their parents. Alternatively, this form of assessment could be used to identify specific difficulties that individual children are experiencing in order to develop a teaching strategy to ensure appropriate progress is made. Diagnostic assessment can also be used to identify individual SEN but in this case the focus is on identifying strengths and weaknesses rather than previous knowledge. Stobart (2014) suggests that educational assessment has much in common with medical practice in that the teacher needs to listen carefully to children's answers in order to be able to diagnose conceptual understanding and identify next steps. He argues that listening is a key skill for teachers to develop, although in many instances this is limited to asking factual questions rather than specifically planning opportunities for children to give in-depth answers that can then be scrutinised and unpicked (Stobart, 2014). This approach may necessitate a change in classroom ethos where children are encouraged to be risk takers and active learners rather than passive recipients of facts. Teachers need to develop cognitive complexity, encompassing a wide range of pedagogical knowledge, subject knowledge and experience in the field in order to be effective practitioners 'in action' (Schön, 1987). In other words, teacher expertise depends on 'expert diagnostic decision making' through the use of previous experience, secure subject knowledge, and the ability to identify different solutions and consider different options before deciding on the best course of action (Stobart, 2014, p. 107).

Diagnostic assessment can also be used to provide evidence of pupil progress through the use of a Cold (blue paper) task, before a period of teaching and a Hot (pink paper) task carried out after a period of teaching. This strategy is particularly applicable to writing activities but could be used in any subject as a means of demonstrating progression throughout a period of learning.

Formative assessment

Teachers' Standard 6 (DfE, 2013) requires that teachers must make 'formative assessments to secure pupils' progress'. Formative assessment has been shown to be most valuable for children's learning because of its potential to empower each learner to recognise where they are in their learning, where they need to go next and how they are going to get there. This type of ongoing, and in the moment, assessment provides a broad overview of a child's achievement over a period of time. It generally focuses on the whole child and includes both academic and pastoral aspects, enabling teachers to identify children's personal interests and ways of learning. Formative assessment 'is not a test or a tool but a process with the potential to support learning beyond school years by developing learning strategies which individuals may rely on across their entire life-span' (Clark, 2012, p. 217). Recording methods include observation, targeted and insightful questioning, pieces of work, self-assessment, peer assessment or a combination of these.

Teachers' Standard 6 (DfE, 2013) states that teachers must 'give pupils regular feedback, both orally and through accurate marking and encourage pupils to respond to the feedback'. Effective formative assessment is highly dependent on the quality of interactions and emotional connections between the teacher and the children and the children and their peers. Hargreaves (2013) discusses the importance of relationships between teachers and pupils concluding that 'both parties must reflect, converse and make changes' in order to encourage autonomous learning. The crucial message here is that teachers need to have an excellent understanding of their pupils both personally and academically to ensure that they are motivated and appropriately challenged in order to progress in their learning. Black and Wiliam (1998) state that 'the dialogue between pupils and a teacher should be thoughtful, reflective, focused to evoke and explore understanding, and conducted so that all pupils have an opportunity to think and express their ideas' (Black and Wiliam, 1998, p. 144). A key difference from other forms of assessment is the engagement of the children with the assessment process. Harrison and Howard (2009) emphasise this point by saying that 'What is paramount in this process is the children realising that their thinking is valued by their teacher, so that they are encouraged to discuss their understanding and misunderstandings openly' (Harrison and Howard, 2009, p. 9). Learning is an emotive business, which concerns the whole child and centres on children's self-esteem and their ability to take risks. Dweck (2012) calls this 'Growth Mindset', whereby children have the belief that they can overcome obstacles to learning through perseverance and an understanding that intelligence is not fixed but malleable and improved by practice. Ipsative assessment strategies can help to reinforce children's self-belief by enabling them to self-evaluate against their own previous performance to measure their personal progress and development. Through the use of metacognitive strategies children can learn more effectively because they are able to understand what they know, what they don't know and how they learn best. By making learning more explicit, teachers can improve motivation through the use of next-steps teaching and enabling children to set their own achievable targets.

Assessment is about teachers noticing minute shifts in children's conceptual understanding by listening carefully to their responses and using their observations to inform and enhance planned learning opportunities: 'Creating an environment in which children can safely share, question and explore their emerging understanding provides a rich context for assessment' (Peacock, 2016, p. 19). The impact of this process is the children's ability to recognise their development within a nurturing environment, celebrate their individual achievements and identify next goals for themselves as they become self-regulatory.

Reflective task

Consider the relationships and ethos of your classroom:

- How do you encourage the children to take risks and learn from their mistakes?
- What assessment strategies support this?
- How can you incorporate these ideas into your planning?

Assessment without levels

Following the implementation of the 2014 National Curriculum schools have been given the freedom to devise their own assessment strategies using teacher assessment and statutory end of Key Stage assessments against Age Related Expectations (AREs). A specific change has been the implementation of 'assessment without levels' (DfE, 2015), which has presented schools with some choices in relation to what, how and when they will assess their pupils. The rationale behind the initiative centres on more flexibility for schools to design their own assessment frameworks so that depth and breadth of understanding can be enhanced and gaps in learning can be identified and addressed more effectively. The overarching aim is that 'schools should be free to develop an approach to assessment which aligns with their curriculum and works for their pupils and staff' (DfE, 2015). While the arguments for giving schools more autonomy and flexibility in their assessment processes using teachers' professional judgement are commendable, this is situated within a framework of greater accountability, parental choice and marketisation (Pratt, 2016).

Hunter (2016) likens the current role of school leadership to that of football managers: 'Accountability is high and very public' (Hunter, 2016, p. 20). Not only do schools assess pupil progress at the end of the early years foundation stage, Key Stage 1 and Key Stage 2 in the form of statutory testing, children's performance is also measured within and across years and these data are linked to teacher performance making progression a high stakes activity. Certainly, providing evidence through supporting data has become highly important for teachers, therefore 'they have to make what they do more visible, in order that it becomes measurable' (Pratt, 2016, p. 896). In addition children's work, or more importantly evidence of children's work, has become not only of value in order to provide effective feedback to support learning, but also 'to be "used by" or even "used on", teachers in order to drive changes in school outcomes' (Pratt, 2016, p. 896). Pratt argues that assessment data, as well as being a means to measure children's progression, have also to some extent become a commodity through which teachers can justify their practice.

The responsibility for the development of approaches to monitoring and recording of assessment and how these will be applied has created both challenges and opportunities for schools. A key challenge has been the development of a whole-school approach to assessment so that pupil progression can be mapped across year groups and consistency of expectations is maintained throughout the school. The whole-school approach is described in the box below. Hunter (2016) discusses the challenging conversations that she and her staff had concerning progression and how this could be evidenced.

They were so used to telling me if that child had … moved a sub-level that they were quite at sea deciding if acceptable progress had been made now the old measure had been removed. It hit me between the eyes that we were so reliant, me included, in summing up progress in terms of average point scores (APS) that we started to forget to talk naturally about progress in terms of work in books and what children could now do that they couldn't do before. (Hunter, 2016, p. 35)

The whole-school approach

At the whole-school level there needs to be a coherent approach to sharing the progress made by students. Crucially, this information needs to be easily understood by the students themselves, as well as by parents/carers and other stakeholders. As the assessment model will be different for each school, it is also important that there is clear communication about the mechanisms for determining and tracking student progress as well as the ways in which assessment will be used to inform future learning. https://www.nfer.ac.uk/publications/GTGA01/GTGA01.pdf

Black and Wiliam's (1998) research into assessment led to the development of 'assessment for learning' (AfL) and, although the research was undertaken 20 years ago, the arguments made resonate strongly in assessment without levels. Black and Wiliam found that the use of strategies including sustained, relevant feedback, and peer and self-assessment improved the learning of the pupils involved. They argued that the use of feedback should be kept separate from grades or levels because most children would simply take note of their level but not necessarily read the accompanying feedback to improve their work further. Children's independent learning could be enhanced by sharing specific information about their work so that the purpose of marking was not for teachers to tell children what they had done right or wrong but was developmental, enabling them to understand how they could improve.

Although this has not been an easy journey for some schools, it has also provided opportunities for teachers, and school teams, to challenge and re-evaluate their own beliefs and attitudes to assessment in order to design an assessment system that is effective for their pupils and themselves. The National Foundation for Educational Research has published a document, *Refocusing Assessment* (2017), that 'provides a framework for school leaders and department heads to plan a coherent whole school approach to assessment that will support the learning of each and every student'.

Although this publication is aimed at Key Stage 3, the questions asked in order to begin the whole-school policy process are extremely relevant to subject leaders in primary settings.

A framework for planning a whole-school approach

Five key questions for all departments

Use these questions as a starting point to discuss your department's approach to assessment and how this contributes to the whole-school assessment policy.

1.   What does it mean to be a successful student in this subject?

     - What is the purpose of our subject?
     - What does it mean to be a good mathematician/musician/historian, etc?
     - Is this what we are preparing students for?
     - What are the core knowledge and skills required for success?

2.   What is the purpose of assessment in our subject?

     - Why do we assess?
     - Who is assessment for?

3.   What does progress look like in our subject?

     - How do we know when a student is making progress?
     - How might progress vary over time?

4.   How can progress be assessed most effectively in our subject?

     - Which assessment techniques work best in our subject?
     - How successfully do we use formative assessment approaches?
     - How can formative and summative assessment work together to ensure effective assessment for learning?
     - How do we benchmark/quality assure our assessment practices?

5.   How do the assessment practices in our department contribute to/work with whole-school policy?

https://www.nfer.ac.uk/publications/GTGA01/GTGA01.pdf

Questioning

Questioning should not be used only as a pedagogical tool but also as a deliberate way for the teacher to find out what students know, understand and are able to do. Good questioning should cause children to think hard but is also a valuable method to find out what children know in order to inform your planning. However, many examples of questioning in the classroom consist of short closed questions rather than provide opportunities for children to investigate, reason and speculate on complex questions or extend their cognitive understanding.

Questioning from the teacher can be 'open', wherein the pupil can give explanation and detail in the answer, or 'closed', wherein the expected response is generally limited to factual knowledge and is correct or incorrect. Questions can be targeted towards specific children or groups during a lesson, for the teacher to assess ongoing understanding and engagement, or can be used at the start or end of a lesson to review learning and check for misconceptions. There is a further level of questioning that needs flexibility in planning and this involves 'enquiry-based learning' with questions generated by children. Often, they will suggest areas for research or discovery, or ask questions for clarification when they are motivated and engaged in the tasks at hand. This may originate with something they have learnt during the lesson or outside school. It can be difficult to assess imagination and enquiry, yet these are key skills within society and should be encouraged. Good subject knowledge is essential to support learning, however, often children do not need to be told the answer to their questions, they need to be taught how to find the answer and how to weigh the validity of the answers they have found. In order to extend children's ability to debate and discuss it is sometimes good to use a statement to engage their interest rather than a question, for example, 'Woodlice only eat wood'. Children would then need to find a way to prove or disprove the statement. It is important to be specific when replying to children's answers to your questions: don't just move on, probe for a deeper engagement with the misconception, for example, 'Why did they think that?' Good questioning means there is less opportunity for children to get it right by accident. Teachers need to plan questions in advance and give children time to answer before intervening. Hattie (2012) found that the largest percentage of talk in the classroom is done by teachers, who ask between 200 and 300 questions a day, the majority of which require factual answers or are related to classroom procedures rather than initiating discussion or posing higher order questions. In addition, most pupil answers involve no more than three words and take less than five seconds to complete. Effective teacher/pupil interactions are crucial in developing thinking skills and deep rather than surface learning. Therefore, Stobart (2014) argues that classroom discussions should resemble a basketball game rather than a ping-pong match, whereby ideas are passed from person to person around the room instead of simply being monopolised by two players. It is easy for teachers to gravitate to those children who have their hands up because they are confident that they will have a sensible answer to the question, but this approach can also alienate those children who are less forthcoming or lack self-confidence. The 'basketball' strategy aims to transform classroom discussions from passive activities in which most children do not participate to active learning opportunities shared by all, but also enables the teacher to model higher order questions so that children can develop their own skills in a supportive environment. The language of questioning and development of higher order thinking skills is of paramount importance in encouraging deep rather than surface learning and should be explicitly taught through demonstration rather than implicitly suggested. Other effective strategies include pair-share, giving children time to formulate and test their answers before sharing them with a wider audience, which can support the less confident or quieter members of the class. In addition, using individual whiteboards can give teachers the opportunity to see all answers in order to quickly assess pupil understanding and address misconceptions before they become embedded. Children do not need to be right all of the time to learn but they do need to have opportunities to learn from their mistakes and this should ideally be through discussion and collaboration with their teacher. Children's incorrect answers can give an insight into not only what they do not know but also what they do know. For example, a child may give the wrong answer to a calculation but by asking further questions may explain the correct process. This is invaluable information for planning next steps and addressing an error that may be common for more children. Some teachers find responding to children's mistakes difficult, particularly in whole-class situations, but they are opportunities for real learning to take place and therefore should be explored in a sensitive manner and resolved or picked up at a later date. Stobart (2014) argues that the real work of school is talk, allowing children time to explain what they mean before being interrupted; therefore, teachers need to develop effective listening skills as well as effective questioning skills.

Finally, not only should teachers be effective questioners but also children should be encouraged to develop their own questions so that they can be active participants in their learning leading to greater motivation. Providing opportunities for children to pose questions on 'Wonder Walls' or in small groups based on an overarching topic can enable teachers to tap into their interests and plan topics that children will want to engage in.

New Bloom's Taxonomy (Table 4.1) clearly shows the hierarchy of questioning language from remembering to creating. The original Bloom's Taxonomy (1956) was devised to be a tool to support the development of exam questions but has changed over time to become a much more useful instrument because of the use of verbs. Try to devise questions that enable children to be challenged and engaged rather than simply remembering facts. Use the table below to devise learning outcomes, success criteria and questions for children of different abilities around the same theme or topic.

Reflective task

- Choose a subject or topic you will be teaching. Use Table 4.1 to design learning objectives and set related success criteria at different levels.
- Compose some questions that you could ask to assess what children know, can do and understand related to the topic.

Table 4.1   Based on New Bloom's Taxonomy (http://maasd.edublogs.org/files/2012/04/BloomsVerbs-24dwzts.png)

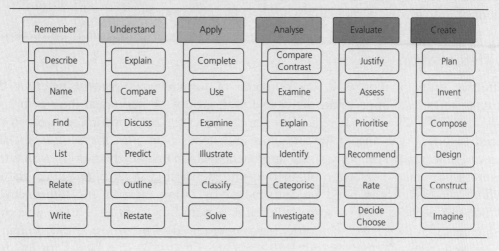

Remember	Understand	Apply	Analyse	Evaluate	Create
Describe	Explain	Complete	Compare Contrast	Justify	Plan
Name	Compare	Use	Examine	Assess	Invent
Find	Discuss	Examine	Explain	Prioritise	Compose
List	Predict	Illustrate	Identify	Recommend	Design
Relate	Outline	Classify	Categorise	Rate	Construct
Write	Restate	Solve	Investigate	Decide Choose	Imagine

Transference of skills, knowledge, understanding and personal development

Teachers need to engage in ongoing formative assessment to allow and encourage transference of knowledge and skills across subjects and topic areas to enhance children's development of skills, knowledge and understanding. For example, children collaborating in a music activity not only learn about music but also learn to collaborate and develop social skills. These skills are generic and transferable into other areas of the curriculum and crucial to their future success as adults. So, teachers need to be aware of the attainment of each child not only in skills, knowledge and understanding across the curriculum domains, but also in relation to their personal development. This will ensure that assessment of each child's strengths and areas for development takes into account both their social skills and generic skills across the curriculum. This holistic approach will help them to reach their full potential. Consider being more creative with assessment tasks especially when teaching cross-curricular topics.

Transferring knowledge into different contexts consolidates learning and enables children to apply what they already know. Sometimes rather than starting the lesson with a learning objective, teach the lesson and then ask the children to tell you what the objective was. This will allow you to see if the children have learnt what you intended and how effective the lesson was.

Although cross-curricular learning has benefits for children in making links between previous and new learning, there can be challenges in relation to assessment of individuals, particularly when working in groups.

Differentiation

Effective differentiation is a key outcome of formative assessment whereby the teacher can create appropriate activities for all groups of learners at their own level and stage of ability. This is related to Standard 5 (DfE, 2013), which focuses on the need to 'adapt teaching to the strengths and needs of pupils, knowing when and how to differentiate properly, using approaches which enable children to learn effectively'. Differentiation is often planned as an extension task, an open-ended activity where children are assessed by outcome or by doing more of the same activity, which can be perceived by some children as a punishment rather than an acknowledgement that they have achieved what was required of them. Good differentiation is derived from effective formative assessment so that tasks can be set for children that challenge and extend their learning, thereby creating a motivated and inspired classroom environment. If teachers do not have an in-depth understanding of the abilities of the children in their class they cannot plan relevant activities to enable appropriate progression. Vygotsky (1978) developed the idea of a 'Zone of Proximal Development' (ZPD), which identifies the gap between what children can do alone and what they are able to do with support from an adult or peer. By differentiating appropriately teachers can access this learning opportunity by grouping children or deploying teaching assistants effectively to provide the optimum environment for learning. Another challenge when considering differentiation is that children may be put into ability groups for literacy and numeracy but stay in the same groups for other subjects. This means that children who may have particular strengths in art but have difficulty in literacy, for example, may be working within art at a level where they are not challenged or motivated because of this mismatch of activity. Gardner's (1993, 1999) work on multiple intelligences suggests that there are nine different types of intelligence; it is the job of the teacher to notice what children are enthused by so that they can plan lessons to develop those interests.

An alternative view of differentiation is shared by Swann et al. (2012) whereby children are given choices regarding the work that they attempt based on their own assessment of their ability to complete the task. This can be very empowering for children because they are trusted to make a considered selection based on their own perceptions of ability rather than through differentiated groupings allocated by the teacher. This is an example of a much more holistic method of teaching and learning and, while there are challenges in managing children who do not choose realistically, the strategy can raise the 'glass ceiling' for those who are perhaps not motivated to challenge themselves to their limits because of their perception of the ability group they are in.

Mastery Learning

Mastery Learning can be described as advanced performance above expectations or a particular teaching and learning strategy whereby topics are broken down into small units in order to provide a logical sequence of learning, and depth of understanding is more important than the speed of learning. The Department for Education (DfE) *Final Report of the Commission on Assessment without Levels* (2015) states that mastery is 'something which every child can aspire to and every teacher should promote. It is concerned with deep, secure learning for all, with extension for more able students rather than acceleration' (DfE, 2015, p. 17) In contrast to differentiation this form of teaching assumes that all children can learn the same content as long as they are supported appropriately. It would seem that the most important aspect to be considered is how the activity is introduced and what developmental steps are planned so that learning can take place. Effective learning is therefore critically dependent on the subject knowledge, pedagogical understanding, planning and inspiration of the teacher. Mastery Learning must be carefully planned through a series of small stages that are frequently monitored using assessment for learning strategies so that all children make progress. Children who are working below the level of the rest of the class are supported with intervention strategies, and children working above are given tasks that deepen and extend learning in the topic rather than moving on to something new. In order to assess Mastery Learning it is important to develop problem solving activities that encourage deep thinking so that children can apply what they know to different contexts and applications. Aspects of Bloom's Taxonomy (1956) discussed earlier in this chapter could be helpful in order to identify appropriate learning objectives that enable children to demonstrate their skills, knowledge and understanding in the subject areas taught.

Formative assessment throughout each lesson

Ongoing evaluation of the learning *throughout a lesson* is vital. The use of questioning and observation to collate an accurate picture of children's (or a child's) depth of understanding related to the learning outcomes will be needed to inform your teaching. This could be done through adding a mini-plenary to redirect or extend class learning, through specific questioning or teaching to correct a misconception, or through adding a resource to support learning. Good lesson planning based on accurate assessment and evaluations, coupled with secure subject knowledge, is necessary to facilitate effective learning. They allow the teacher to be flexible in response to the needs of the children and to have confidence in a range of teaching strategies that are best suited to the group of children being taught. Teaching a well-structured lesson and reflecting systematically on the effectiveness of the lesson and approaches to teaching it are essential aspects of effective formative assessment, as stated in Standard 4 (DfE, 2013). (See also Chapter 17 on reflecting effectively.)

Effective feedback

Giving effective feedback to children about their work can be a challenging area of practice. If children are praised for their intelligence they are less likely to be motivated than those praised for their perseverance or effort (Dweck, 2012). Rather than writing fixed statements regarding what was right or wrong about the piece of work, it is much more productive to focus on the learning process through questions, to prompt thoughtful responses and encourage independent self-assessment. Eriksson et al. (2016) categorised different types of feedback used by teachers through observing lessons in four primary school classrooms with children aged 7–9 years old. Their research highlighted the complexity of communications in the classroom and they identified five main feedback strategies that teachers used. These were:

- Expecting – relating to teachers' expectations of task difficulty and the abilities of their pupils.
- Emotionally responding – praising pupils, being disappointed about work produced or behaviour or comforting in order to raise self-esteem.
- Normalising – sharing reasons why a pupil may not perform according to expectation because of external or internal influences outside the pupil's control, for example, 'that task is a bit tricky'.
- Steering – this can be through confirming, correcting, implanting or piloting but overall is used to guide pupils to the 'right answer'.
- Deliberating – encouraging analysis, discussion or evaluation around a problem or issue.

These categories showed that teacher feedback affected not only academic performance but also social behaviour and was contextual and situated within each specific classroom. (See also Chapter 9, where Ellis and Tod discuss behaviour for learning.) Individual children were given different feedback depending on the teacher's perception of their academic or social needs at the time, indicating a high level of skill and knowledge about each child. This demonstrates why teaching is such a complex activity and why we never stop learning or working towards excellent practice.

Effective feedback needs to be carefully timed and formative rather than quantitative: children want to know how they can improve their work. Having clear, easily understood learning intentions can support this for the child and the teacher when assessing. Very often less is more in terms of feedback. If every small mistake is identified it can be very daunting; choose the most important areas to focus on and work on those before moving to the next target. Try to make sure that feedback is given when it is deserved and not for small things that would be expected anyway. In this way, your praise will be valued by the children and sought after because they will know that you are sincere.

Work in school

Student 1:   On every school placement I have a different age group. I know this is good experience, but how do I know what is appropriate for children of different ages?

Mentor: The National Curriculum in England Framework document (2014) outlines the statutory Age Related Expectations (AREs) for each year group in core subjects and end of Key Stage expectations for foundation subjects. This will be the starting point for schools to devise their whole-school assessment grid or plan. The planning ILOs will be aligned with the assessment and so should all be age-appropriate. As there is more flexibility related to subject content for each year group it is possible to use learning objectives (AREs) from previous or later years depending on the topics being taught and/or the abilities of the children.

The fine-tuning comes with practice, just by assessing more and more work and also by speaking to experienced teachers about it as well as attending assessment tutorials on placements, or moderation meetings with other staff.

Student 2:   How do I know that the children in my class have made progress?

Mentor: This can be monitored for your class through the use of continuous formative and summative assessment such as children's work, formal questioning strategies and 'hot and cold tasks' at the beginning and end of periods of teaching (see the diagnostic assessment on p. 101 for more information). In addition, you could include the children's peer or self-assessment of progress in your assessment strategy, particularly when assessing progress in foundation subjects. Questions could be completed in a personal progress book or sheet for each child at the end of a period of teaching asking: 'What have I learnt? How have I used my learning? What am I proud of? What do I need to do next?' This would give you an alternative method to find out how children feel about their learning, important in terms of resilience, and whether it is consolidated and secure. It is also a useful piece of evidence to share with parents. Schools also hold pupil progress interviews across year groups, whole schools and across cluster schools where teachers can discuss and compare progress being made by the children they teach.

(Continued)

Many schools choose to design and use assessment grids or rubrics specific to the needs of classes or individuals in their school as identified through analysis of past assessment. The most effective assessment grids will be designed through teacher collaboration and will involve the concept of a continuum which will show progression for the individual and allow for monitoring of this. Effective assessment grids will address the breadth of learning and account for different foci. The continuous sampling of work showing a child's meeting of the range of skills, knowledge and their understanding will develop an extensive evidenced picture of the child's progression. This can then be used to show parents, or other stakeholders, perhaps governors and for Ofsted. Assessment grids that are created through collaboration promote sharing of expertise and experience across the school staff team, in line with the research of Hattie (2012). To ensure effective learning this allows for moderation, shared understanding of expectations and standards, and has a quality assurance base. Assessment grids based on success criteria and the input of the children also promote high expectations as all staff and children know the incremental steps for improvement, and thus these can be used for self-, peer and teacher assessment.

Sometimes illustrated rubrics, particularly in cross-curricular work, are very useful in allowing children to see what the next increment 'looks like' and can therefore promote self-regulation, and challenge setting for children.

Student 3: How do I find time and maintain consistency?

Mentor: Useful strategies include using Post-it® notes, or a small notebook, to jot your observations through the day's lessons. Using photographs to supply evidence, especially for children working below expected levels of attainment. Using teaching assistants' notes alongside your own notes to gather evidence. Holding regular moderation meetings to ensure parity and maintain quality assurance. Making effective use of self- and peer assessment, based on children understanding the success criteria. It is important to remember that assessment is a dialogue between child and teacher, not simply identifying what is correct or incorrect, rather identifying next steps.

There is no need for the teacher to assess every child in every lesson, however you should ensure you make brief notes related to which children have exceeded, or not met, the ILOs to inform your planning for any following lessons so you can plan for the appropriate level of challenge.

(Continued)

(Continued)

Student 4:   What kind of records should I keep?

Mentor: This is very much related to the record keeping and tracking systems that your school uses, although many teachers also keep their own records for their personal use.

The simplest form of recording is a tick sheet with children's names down one side and the learning objectives or success criteria across the top. This is a quick way to assess the whole class but doesn't always give you much information about what the children were thinking or their learning processes. Using a triangle icon – one line shows they were there, the second shows they completed the task, the third shows they understood it – or using a red/amber/green coding system is a more sophisticated way of tracking achievement because it can be updated over time.

Many teachers add an extra box at the end or down the side of their lesson plans so that they can record particular children's responses throughout the lesson and use these to adapt future planning. An additional way to record children's achievement throughout the lesson is to ask the teaching assistants to make records about the children they work with. If this strategy is to work effectively it is important that you spend time with the teaching assistant before the lesson explaining what the learning outcomes are and what kinds of comments you would like – 'good work!' will not tell you anything about the child's achievement.

You could stick a grid to the inside front cover of each child's exercise book allowing spaces for the date, activity, learning objective or success criteria, and a section for formative comments and next steps/targets to be addressed next time.

An index box or an Excel file on the computer would enable you to make informal notes relating to pastoral matters such as personal issues, particular interests or additional information about the children that could have a bearing on their learning. Make sure that this is kept confidential and kept securely if it contains sensitive information. When you are writing reports, this type of information is invaluable to demonstrate to parents that you know their children well because you know what interests them and what their particular passions are.

Many schools are now buying computer programs to support record keeping.

These are just a few ideas, there are many more but the important point is that assessment should be informative, manageable, ongoing and specific in order to be effective.

Assessing the concepts, methods of enquiry, knowledge and understanding of each subject

We said in our introduction that there are challenges and opportunities related to assessment in the 2014 National Curriculum and that schools will need to engage in curriculum and assessment development in ways they have not previously needed to. For the core subjects, English, mathematics and science, there is non-statutory guidance on what a pattern of progression in learning might be, but in other subjects assessment is based on 'knowing, applying and understanding the matters, skills and processes specified in the programme of study'. In some ways this is liberating; it has been argued that progression in the skills of historical enquiry or in art, for example, is too complex, dependent on variables and lacking in research-based evidence to define. However, given the time constraints on ITT programmes, in recent years, for the acquisition of subject knowledge, it is arguable whether new teachers will feel confident to plan for progression in thinking across the curriculum without considerable professional development (CPD) opportunities in place.

Summary

One of the challenges in writing Chapters 3 and 4 is the integrated nature of planning and assessment. We have tried to show how good planning is based on meaningful assessment and that accurate assessment comes through good planning. To avoid confusion, we have perhaps reinforced the separation of the two areas in your mind although we believe assessment and planning to be intricately linked. Certainly, if you look at the Teachers' Standards that assessment is related to at the beginning of the chapter you will begin to realise how it permeates through all teaching and learning activities.

The complexity of planning and assessment practice is linked to the discussion we had earlier on kinds of knowledge. You can know the facts of what to do and how to do it, you can know the sequence, but effective planning and assessment will only come when you have reached the point of 'conditional knowledge' allowing you to make informed judgements. What is important is that you become an expert on the children you teach so that you can make a real difference to their education, aspirations and ultimately their future careers.

The following chapter will show the importance of classroom organisation and the learning environment in promoting children's learning.

Discussion questions

In Chapter 3 we asked you to consider your own philosophy of learning and teaching and how this may impact upon your planning.

- Now consider how this will impact on your assessment methods. Discuss with your colleagues.
- How does the creativity agenda fit with planning and assessment? How can you be creative in a subject-based curriculum? Is teaching in this way more or less 'creative' than teaching through themes?

Further reading

Alexander, R. (2010) *Children, Their World, Their Education*. London: Routledge.
Chapter 16 gives a thorough overview of assessment practices in primary schools. Pages 83–4 highlight some of the complexities involved in the homework debate.

Goodhew, G. (2005) *Meeting the Needs of Gifted and Talented Students*. London: Network Continuum.
For ITE generalist students and educators it is a useful resource to focus on an aspect of inclusive practice termed 'a bit of a Cinderella' by Goodhew in the introduction. From the necessary discussion relating to the difficulty in coming to a definitive definition of the terms 'gifted', 'talented' and 'exceptionally able', Goodhew uses a variety of sources to develop shared understanding for the purpose of the book, examining a variety of perspectives. Perhaps the most relevant chapter in relation to planning and assessment is Chapter 4, which discusses classroom practices.

Johnson, S. (2012) *Assessing Learning in the Primary Classroom*. Abingdon: Routledge.
This book gives a very good overview of assessment including statutory assessment, recording and reporting, and how this links to international perspectives.

Peacock, A. (2016) *Assessment for Learning without Levels*. Oxford: Oxford University Press.
This book follows the successful *Creating Learning without Limits* (Swann et al., 2012), and shares a range of strategies for the development of a whole-school approach to assessment and assessment strategies to motivate and support pupil progress.

References

Alexander, R. (2010) *Children, Their World, Their Education, Final Report and Recommendations of the Cambridge Primary Review*. London: Routledge.
Black, P.J. and Wiliam, D. (1998) *Inside the Black Box*. London: King's College London School of Education.

Bloom, B.S. (ed.), Englehart, M.D., Furst, E.J., Hill, W.H. and Krathwhol, D.R. (1956) *Taxonomy of Educational Objectives: The Classification of Educational Goals. Handbook 1: Cognitive Domain*. New York: David McKay.

Clark, I. (2012) 'Formative assessment: Assessment is for self-regulated learning', *Educational Psychology Review*, 24: 205–49.

Department for Education (DfE) (2013) *Teachers' Standards*. Available at: www.education.gov.uk.

Department for Education (DfE) (2015) *Final Report of the Commission of Assessment without Levels*. Crown Copyright. Available at: https://www.gov.uk/government/uploads/system/uploads/attachment_data/file/483058/Commission_on_Assessment_Without_Levels_-_report.pdf.

Dweck, C. (2012) *Mindset: How You Can Fulfil Your Potential*. London: Robinson.

Eriksson, E., Bjorklund Boistrup, L. and Thornberg, R. (2016) 'A categorisation of teacher feedback in the classroom: A field study on feedback based on routine classroom assessment in primary school', *Research Papers in Education*. Available at: http://dx.doi.org/10.1080/02671522.2016.1225787.

Gardner, H. (1993) *Frames of Mind: The Theory of Multiple Intelligences*, second edn. London: Fontana Press.

Gardner, H. (1999) *Intelligences Reframed: Multiple Intelligences for the 21st Century*. New York: Basic Books.

Hargreaves, E. (2013) 'Inquiring into children's experiences of teacher feedback: Reconceptualising assessment for learning', *Oxford Review of Education*, 39 (2): 229–46.

Harrison, C. and Howard, S. (2009) *Inside the Primary Black Box*. London: GL Assessment.

Hattie. J. (2012) *Visible Learning for Teachers*. Abingdon: Routledge.

Hattie, J. (2014) *Visible Learning and Science of How We Learn*. Abingdon: Routledge.

Hunter, S. (2016) *Life after Levels*. London: Sage.

National Foundation for Educational Research (2017) *Refocusing Assessment*. Available at: https://www.nfer.ac.uk/publications/GTGA01/GTGA01.pdf.

Peacock, A. (2016) *Assessment for Learning without Levels*. Oxford: Oxford University Press.

Pratt, N. (2016) 'Neoliberalism and the (internal) marketisation of primary school assessment in England', *British Educational Research Journal*, 42 (5): 890–905.

Schön, D. (1987) *Educating the Reflective Practitioner*. San Francisco, CA: Jossey-Bass.

Stobart, G. (2014) *The Expert Learner*. Oxford: Oxford University Press.

Swann, M., Peacock, A., Hart, S. and Drummond, S.J. (2012) *Creating Learning without Limits*. Oxford: Oxford University Press.

Vygotsky, L. (1978) *Mind in Society: The Development of Higher Psychological Processes*. Cambridge, MA: Harvard University Press.

Scotland

Assessment for Curriculum for Excellence
www.gov.scot/Topics/Education/Schools/curriculum
www.gov.scot/Topics/Education/Schools/curriculum/assessment

Wales

Learning Wales: raising standards together
http://learning.gov.wales/?skip=1&lang=en

Websites

National Centre for Excellence in the Teaching of Mathematics

https://www.ncetm.org.uk/search?q=assessment

New Bloom's Taxonomy

http://maasd.edublogs.org/files/2012/04/BloomsVerbs-24dwzts.png

Assessing without levels – DfE

https://www.gov.uk/government/uploads/system/uploads/attachment_data/file/483058/
  Commission_on_Assessment_Without_Levels_-_report.pdf

https://www.gov.uk/government/uploads/system/uploads/attachment_data/file/304602/
  Assessment_Principles.pdf

5

Classroom Organisation and the Learning Environment

Jan Ashbridge and Jo Josephidou

By the end of this chapter, you should be able to:

- discuss the key factors to consider when providing for an appropriate learning environment
- consider how theory and research impact on how the learning environment is designed
- reflect critically on learning environments you have observed on placement and question assumed practice
- examine how your own values and attitudes as a teacher can impact on the learning environment and the children's learning.

Introduction

Teachers' Standard 1 (DfE, 2013a) requires that teachers set up learning environments for their pupils that are safe, stimulating and rooted in mutual respect, where positive attitudes, values and behaviour are promoted. But learning environments are complex and creating them involves making many sensitive decisions. In the early years, practitioners will use the terminology 'Enabling Environment' (DfE, 2014, p. 6) to describe a learning environment where children feel safe, supported and able to work and play independently – an environment that Malaguzzi (1920–1994) would describe as 'a third teacher'. Malaguzzi took it for granted that 'the environment is the third educator, the other two being the teachers assigned to each group of children' (Smidt, 2013, p. 100). Interestingly, although mentioned at length in the early years foundation stage framework, the learning environment and classroom organisation is not mentioned in the current *National Curriculum in England* (DfE, 2013b). The document does discuss supporting the learning of children with additional needs and barriers to learning by asking teachers to take these into account in their planning (DfE, 2013b, p. 8). This is undoubtedly important but is certainly not the whole story.

This chapter will explore why the learning environment is so important, regardless of the age of the child. It begins by discussing a common classroom scenario in order to explore the reasons why learning environments are complex, significant and shaped by a teacher's personal educational philosophy. As Kelly notes 'How you organise your classroom depends on how you believe children will learn in your classroom' (2014, p. 170). Constructivist learning theories are drawn on to suggest starting points for creating effective learning environments that promote independence, social skills, self-esteem, positive attitudes to learning and give children a sense of ownership of their environment (Tomlinson, 2015).

Different perceptions of the learning environment

The child's voice

'It's in-time!'

The bell goes and it's time to go into school but first I need to line up. If I'm really quick then I can get to the front. I make it in time but then Sally pushes ahead of me and stands on my toe. I dig her in the ribs with my elbow just as Mrs Jones is coming around the corner to collect us. Oh no, trouble again before I've even got into the classroom. I hate hanging my coat up because everyone pushes and the coat pegs are too near together. I get trampled on so I try to hang back until everyone has finished. Trouble again, I'm late.

'It's register time!'

I sit on the carpet quickly but then I realise that my name has been put on the amber traffic light and I'm really worried. Am I going to miss playtime? If I sit really still and listen, Mrs Jones will put my name back on green but then I feel the cold, hard floor digging into my bottom and I realise that the Velcro on my left shoe has stuck to the carpet. I'm concentrating so hard on sitting still so the Velcro doesn't make a noise that I miss my name being called and I'm in trouble again.

'It's handwriting time'

Once register is finished it's handwriting time. I'm on the Yellow table. Books are ready in the middle of the table and the pencils are sharpened in the yellow pot. I try to get comfortable on my chair because I know I am not allowed to get up until the big hand is on the six. Oh no, I should have gone for a wee when I was hanging my coat up. I know I have to look at the handwriting display and practise the letters on the yellow balloon. My teacher calls it being in-de-pen-dent. Red group have to practise the cursive letters on the red balloon. Mrs Smith always comes to help Yellow table but she calls the letters different names to Mrs Jones and I get a bit confused. Zainab gets a sticker because she is holding her pencil beautifully. Sometimes, near the holidays, we are allowed to play in the role play area and with the sand and water. The holidays seem a long way off.

The teacher's voice
'Going into class'

The bell is about to go. Time to go and get the children in from the playground. You'd think by Year 2 they could make a straight line. Look at Sally, she's always at the front standing so smartly, having the maturity to ignore the little boy, Karim, behind her who's trying to push in front. I'm so glad we line them up; it makes it so much easier. I have worked very hard on training the children to make them independent and most of them manage to sort themselves out quickly and come back to the classroom to sit quietly on the carpet. They know my expectations.

'Taking the register'

Karim is back 3 minutes after everyone else. I won't tell him off because I don't want to lower his self-esteem but I quietly get up and move his name from the green traffic light to the amber. The children sit beautifully for register and show really good listening. Everyone sitting still, all eyes towards me. I don't have to remind them, I just have to point to the good listening checklist on the wall.

'Handwriting practice'

It's good to start the morning off with handwriting because they can all get on with it quietly whilst I hear readers. To make sure they can be independent I have prepared all the resources and put them out ready on the table for the children. The activity is carefully differentiated and all children know what level they are working at. My colour-coding system works a treat. I have directed Mrs Smith to Yellow table today as they need an extra bit of input. Those who finish quickly will get 15 minutes to choose a free activity.

Reflective task

Read the above scenarios and note down the key themes and issues where mis-matches in perceptions are apparent:

- What has the environment taught the child?
- What does the teacher believe the environment is teaching the child?
- How does the environment do this?

Use the grid below to observe and reflect on the way that children respond to the environment and routine in the classroom.

Aspect of the environment or routine	Possible teacher's intention	Impact on the child	Possible reason for response	Reflection

---

The importance of the learning environment

The learning environment is a complex and ever-changing place. It is a physical area with resources and furniture and has to fit in children and adults comfortably. It is an emotional environment too, where people form relationships, learn rules and develop attitudes, beliefs and values relating to themselves, each other and the world they live in. It is a place where children not only learn the curriculum, but also begin to understand their strengths, weaknesses and how they measure up to the others around them. Boundaries are set and particular behaviours are expected. It is not only where children learn but also where children learn to learn. It is vital then to give much consideration to the way that it looks, feels and operates from a range of perspectives.

Organising the learning environment

The learning environment of the classroom is first and foremost a place where effective learning needs to take place with a minimum of fuss (Delceva-Dizdarevik, 2014, p. 52). A key characteristic of this is where clear aims are agreed and teaching is purposeful. Theories of cognitive development tell us that for children to learn effectively they need to be actively involved in their learning: creating and constructing new knowledge in ways that are meaningful to them. It stands to reason, therefore, that the environment in which they are to do this must reflect their ways of learning and their individual needs. It must allow them to develop the skills they need to become independent learners and also to interact with the environment and resources, as well as with each other, in ways that make constructing knowledge purposeful and motivating. In order for this to happen, children need to be seen as central to the learning process, not only in planning but also in the creation, organisation and management of the learning environment.

The scenario – analysis

Let us take the scenario above and consider what the teacher was trying to achieve. She is aiming to make the children in her class as independent as possible. She has done this through ensuring that the children know what is expected of them, ensuring that all necessary resources are easily accessible and that carefully differentiated work is provided along with additional adult support for those who may need it. The children are able to complete the activity with the minimum of fuss and noise. She aims to make them aware that their behaviour affects others and that they should respect the right of those others to be able to get on quietly. The clear ability grouping and the associated classroom display support this. She has set up the environment to enable the children to be able to learn by themselves.

Constructivist theories, classroom organisation and the learning environment
Exploration and stimulating experiences

What do theories of cognitive development have to tell us about the learning environment and how can they shed light on what happens in the scenario above? If we take the work of Piaget, we can see that his influential ideas about children needing developmentally appropriate activities are reflected in many classrooms, especially in Foundation Stage and Key Stage 1, although the same principles, differently interpreted, apply in any primary classroom. Piaget believed that the environment and children's interactions with it and within it are the key to children's learning and it is through engagement and exploration of real, concrete experiences that they are able to learn and develop their understanding. Piaget felt it was important for children to have stimulating activities, opportunities for symbolic play and an environment to actively explore (Daly et al., 2006; Kelly, 2014, p. 171). We can see that despite the teacher's good intentions, these opportunities are not offered and perhaps the learning needs of the children are not being met.

Social interaction and talk

Vygotsky focused more on the role of the adult in guiding children's learning. He also saw how important social interactions and language were to children's intellectual development. His work has influenced teachers and encouraged them to provide children with a challenging environment and activities. Such activities provide opportunities to work alongside adults and more knowledgeable others, including peers, to extend their understanding within the 'Zone of Proximal Development'. More recent research has also stressed the importance of children developing effective communication skills with a broad cross-curricular vocabulary. This ability to articulate their thoughts helps them to make links in their learning and therefore their thinking (Daly et al., 2006; Kelly, 2014, p. 171).

Planning for exploration and talk

In the situation described above, although the children are grouped together, social interaction between the group or between groups is not encouraged; nor does the task given to the children encourage constructive talk. The way that teachers organise the physical environment (tables, chairs, etc.) sends out messages to the children about what kind of activities they are likely to be engaged in. Where children are all sitting looking at the front, they expect that the teacher will be talking to them and that they will be expected to focus their attention there and that any activity will probably be of an individual nature. When children are sitting around a table together, it appears that a more social and collaborative way of learning is expected and children will interact. It appears in the example above that there is a mismatch between the organisation of the classroom and the task given to the children. Social grouping is a valuable tool for teachers in supporting learning but it is very often used simply for convenience as a seating arrangement (Moyles, 1992, p. 18). Conflicting messages such as this can be avoided by keeping the environment flexible and making the organisation match the task.

Effective adult interventions

In our scenario, the children on the Yellow table have access to a teaching assistant. She is available to scaffold the children's learning, helping them to achieve with support what they could not do unaided. This idea, first introduced by Wood et al. (1976), requires the adult to match their interventions to the needs of the individual child and decide what sort of support is necessary (Doherty and Hughes, 2009, p. 270).

Effective groupings

Vygotsky's model of social constructivism may best be played out when children are seated in mixed-ability groups. This provides opportunities for 'less academically confident' children to work within their Zone of Proximal Development, having input from a more knowledgeable other. More confident learners who take on this role of more knowledgeable other can, therefore, both consolidate and articulate their learning. Gnadinger (2008) demonstrates in her research that peer collaboration is an effective learning strategy for children. In addition, other research has shown that higher achieving children who work in ability groups actually have their potential limited rather than enhanced, as they 'develop a crystallized view of their ability which may lead them to avoid challenges which are necessary for effective learning' (Dweck and Legget, 1988, cited in MacIntyre and Ireson, 2002, p. 250). Dweck (2008) distinguishes between two types of pupils: those with a 'growth mindset' and those with a 'fixed mindset':

> In the fixed-mindset world, students worry about making mistakes. They see making mistakes as a sign of low ability. They also worry about effort and view it in the same way – as a sign of low ability. They believe that if they have high ability they shouldn't need any effort. These are both terrible beliefs because mistakes and effort are integral parts of learning. Because students with fixed mindsets make them into things to be avoided, they actually stand in the way of learning. In fact, research in psychology indicates that the main thing that distinguishes people who go to the top of their fields and make great creative contribution from their equally able peers is the effort they put in. The fixed mindset cannot take people to that level. (p. 56)

Elsewhere she highlights learning environments where 'teachers praise the learning process rather than the students' ability, convey the joy of tackling challenging learning tasks, and highlight progress and effort' (Dweck, 2010, p. 20), saying that 'Students who are nurtured in such classrooms will have the values and tools that breed lifelong success' (2010, p. 20). In a 'post-assessment levels' world these ideas are beginning to take more hold in our primary classrooms and there are lively debates and strongly held views on both sides, more of which later.

Moving around

All that we know about children's cognitive development tells us that active learning and problem solving approaches can be beneficial. They enable children to engage with their learning in individual ways depending on their preferred way of learning and thinking. Active learning involves problem solving and this requires children to move around, talk, collaborate and gather resources. Any environment for learning needs to facilitate these approaches and teachers need to be sure they know the children well enough to be able to anticipate these needs and reflect them in the organisation of the classroom.

Displays and 'institutional body language' (Dadzie, 2000)

Is the learning environment *stimulating*? Elton-Chalcraft and Mills (2015) discuss how to make both teaching and the learning environment challenging with reference to their 'phunometre scale'. Is the learning environment *inclusive* with displays representing all types of people and family make ups (see Chapter 14 where Warner and Elton-Chalcraft discuss Stella Dadzie's concept of 'institutional body language') to guard against racism, sexism and so on, instead promoting equality and diversity.

Reflective task

Consider the information above and your own experiences of classroom environments. What do you think a classroom for children of a given age needs to look like, in order to support children's learning as described? How might your use of the learning environment be reflected in your planning?

Encouraging independence and autonomy in the learning environment

Return to the scenario

Classroom layout and organisation

Let us return to the scenario. Consider for a moment what messages the classroom layout and organisation are giving to the child:

- How does he think that the class teacher wants him (Karim) to use the environment?
- How does he think that the teacher views learning?

- How independently is he able to think and learn in this environment?
- What skills is he learning?
- What do you think the teacher's priority was for his learning?

Classroom organisation reflects your educational philosophy

Waterson (2003) claims that the classroom needs to reflect the way in which an individual teacher intends to organise and teach the children. It sends messages to the children about how they are going to learn and what their part in that learning is likely to be.

Much of what often happens in primary classrooms is directed through print in the form of worksheets, PowerPoint slides and lots of written recording. These are quite individual acts that do not necessarily develop children's critical thinking skills or their creativity – skills that are required if children are going to become independent and autonomous learners (Bowles and Gintis, 1976). If we as teachers have abandoned the notion of the child as a 'tabula rasa' or 'empty vessel' (Kehily, 2010, p. 5) onto which we transmit relevant knowledge, then surely as class teachers we should be encouraging those skills which enable the children to think for themselves and therefore to take some control over their own learning.

How much better is it not only to teach children, but also to ensure that our learning environment encourages the consolidation of skills such as information processing, reasoning, enquiry, creative thinking, [and] evaluation? We want to plan for and provide as many opportunities as possible for children to develop skills of meta-cognition, the ability to think about thinking (Goswami, 2008, p. 295). If the children's learning is determined by how much we as teachers allow them to learn, then how limited will their learning be?

Encouraging independence

What do children actually need in order for them to become independent learners? A good place for teachers to start is by overtly giving children the permission to learn in this way. Delceva-Dizdarevik (2014, p. 52) notes that the classroom is an environment where it is the children as well as the teacher who need to have agency and involvement. Even so, the skills required for independent learning do not develop by themselves; the teacher is needed to provide structure and support.

Children need to be clear about what they are learning and how they are able to engage with this learning. If aims and objectives are shared clearly and reinforced through displays and resources, ambiguity is avoided and children are then able to focus on the task in hand. Teachers' own beliefs and attitudes about learning are thrown into stark relief at this point. Alexander asserts that classroom organisation is really just 'the framework within which the acts and interactions central to teaching and learning take place' (Alexander, 1989, cited in Moyles, 1992, p. 11). The objectives that teachers choose, the way they are shared and the ways that teachers expect children to engage with that learning, will influence the ability of the children to work in independent and autonomous ways just as much as the physical environment.

Teachers who believe that knowledge is a 'public discipline' (Kendall-Seatter, 2005, p. 97) will create a classroom where the interactions and the environment focus on transmission of knowledge, whereas if knowledge is seen as being 'a fluid act of interpretation' (Kendall-Seatter, 2005, p. 97), a very different ethos pervades. Autonomous and independent learners have control and ownership over their learning. This needs to be supported by and negotiated with the teacher, who will use classroom interactions and the environment to encourage collaborative working and more meaningful contexts for learning.

Organisation of resources and classroom layout

If this is to succeed, the emotional and physical environment must be equally supportive. Resources must be easily identifiable, relevant and available, as well as flexible enough for the children to use them in the way that they need to. The physical layout of the room also needs to be flexible enough for children to work in ways that are appropriate for the task in hand. Planned opportunities for paired and group work, along with careful differentiation of tasks, are required in order to build up the skills to enable children to learn with and from each other and their environment.

The scenario again

In our scenario, the teacher believes that she is enabling independence, and within the context and purpose of this particular task, it could be argued that she is. The learning for the session is explicit to the children but it is tightly controlled by the teacher, illustrating nicely Fang's point (1996) that there is often a lack of consistency between what teachers think they are doing and what is actually happening. If this is representative of other teaching and learning interactions within this classroom, then children become at risk of 'learned helplessness'. The theory of 'learned helplessness' is fully discussed in Peterson et al. (1993). Essentially it refers to a child who has repeatedly experienced failure and therefore gives up trying to achieve. It may also occur if children are not encouraged to think for themselves. They may become accustomed to accepting extrinsic motivation and organisation and unable to succeed without it. They do not have the necessary strategies. The teacher in our situation has created an environment where children have little need to be independent: they are lined up, sat down, moved to tables and given a specific task with specific resources. It is all organised and done for them. This teacher believes it is for the benefit of the children but in reality it could have more to do with convenience for herself. Children do not have to consider others or the effect of their behaviour as they are closely monitored. It is perhaps for this reason that in the only part of the scenario where the children are not under the direct supervision of the teacher, in the cloakroom, there is a breakdown of order. Children have not been helped to think independently and behave autonomously. These skills enable children to be resilient, to tolerate and adapt to new and different ideas and experiences, and to stay engaged with things that are outside their comfort zone.

Reflective task

Think about a classroom that you have spent time in. Make notes on:

- the routines
- the types of tasks
- the resources used and the ways they were organised
- the physical layout used in the classroom.

Put these into two columns – those that supported independence and autonomy and those that hindered it. How can you ensure that your learning environment encourages those skills that support independence and autonomy?

Supporting positive behaviour through the learning environment

Disruptive behaviour, whether low-level or with greater impact, will of course always hinder effective learning, so it is important to consider how our learning environment may help the children to choose appropriate behaviours that enable all to make good academic progress. (See Ellis and Tod, Chapter 9, for a more detailed discussion of behaviour for learning.) Ecological psychologists note that the learning environment is important for children and that it can affect their behaviour (Bronfenbrenner, 1979; Gump, 1987; Pointon and Kersher, 2000, cited in Pollard, 2008). Learning dispositions can be influenced by the environment: 'creating a positive climate' has been highlighted as a 'prime characteristic of quality teachers' (Muijs and Reynolds, 2011, p. 128). An environment that is scruffy and untidy will not be respected by the children. If it is dull or cold, they will not be happy about being there. If it is cluttered, it can make children feel stressed and overwhelmed, whereas a tidy, organised environment can help children to feel calm and positive, ready to learn in a place where there is a perception of order and structure (Cowley, 2006). This can be achieved through carefully organised stations or areas of provision so children know how, and where, to access equipment. Signs, labels and displays will help to clarify these areas. Interactive displays are an effective learning tool, which, alongside the use of music, sound and light, can encourage interest and focus engagement with the environment.

A sense of ownership

Learning environments are places where a complicated mix of factors come together – local community values, parental expectations, religious values, children and their attitudes, and so on. McNamara and Moreton (1997), cited in Kendall-Seatter (2005), showed that where children were actively engaged in their classroom, a higher level of involvement was ensured and shared ownership, shared values and mutual respect were fostered.

Looking at the scenario, Karim did not seem to feel any sense of ownership over the environment he was in. He was not involved in setting it up nor does it appear to consider the ways in which he needs to behave in order to learn effectively. Some classrooms are still sterile laboratories where the children are fenced in by table arrangements and discouraged from moving from their places unless it is a key transition time. Everything is put in front of them – paper, pencil and books – so that they have to make few decisions or interactions with peers and adults.

Depending on the teacher's philosophy, personal preference, the age of the children and the type of learning, classrooms may be like a workshop, a bustling busy place with children moving between different areas, collecting resources independently, sometimes standing, sometimes sitting, sometimes even working on the floor. Sometimes it may look messy – workshops are full of very busy, productive people. Sometimes they are quiet and reflective places where children are playing with ideas and are facilitated in discussion and problem solving through well-planned, motivating activities. This may look calm and well-ordered. It is important to remember that activity and engagement is not only or exclusively a physical thing: it is also to do with thought and positive intellectual engagement. Our learning environment needs to be stimulating, well-ordered and accessible in ways that all children can recognise. This positive engagement, in whatever form it is manifested, appears to be the key to encouraging appropriate behaviours. Teachers' Standard 7 (DfE, 2013a) explicitly links the learning environment to positive behaviour and makes clear the importance of teachers taking into account the ways that children engage and interact with it. Ellis and Tod (2014) believe that 'an inevitable feature of ... professional standards is that they largely reflect what the teacher will be doing rather than the pupil's response to it' (p. 2). Here there is an opportunity to redress that balance and support the children in developing positive behaviours for learning through well-planned organisation of the learning environment created with the children for specific purposes.

Evaluating engagement with the environment

As teachers, how can we tell if children are able to engage with an environment? Do the children sit still for too long? Are they uncomfortable? Do children know what is expected of them? Are instructions clear? Can they get the resources they need? What should they do if they finish the set task? What strategies can they use if they get stuck? Are they bored? Is the work too easy or too hard? Can they make decisions about their learning? Are they able to choose how to approach a task? Can they talk to their peers about their learning? (See Chapter 17, where Read suggests some ways to reflect deeply on your teaching and the children's learning.)

The scenario

Let us consider the scenario again. The child knows that he is expected to sit still for quite some time. He is also aware that he finds this difficult. Ouvry (2000, p. 23) asserts that 'the most advanced level of movement is the ability to stay totally still, which requires entire muscle groups to work in cooperation with balance and posture'. The struggle to do as he knows he should requires him to concentrate on the issue of staying still and, as a result, he misses other information. What is he engaged with? At all points, he is trying very hard to behave and this has a detrimental impact on his ability to engage with the learning he is being presented with. The teacher's perception of his behaviour is very different to his own desire to behave appropriately within the constraints of the environment she has created. How could the teacher have set the environment up differently to enable a more positive experience for this child? Muijs and Reynolds (2011) highlight how 'teaching and learning in school need to be adapted to the needs and developmental levels of pupils' (p. 115). They stress boys' preferences for 'active learning styles' and how they 'may not react well to prolonged periods of having to sit still and listen' (p. 115), suggesting that the teacher introduces short periods of physical activity within the teaching and learning sequence.

Creating a work-centred atmosphere

Where the teacher creates a work-centred atmosphere, classes tend to behave better (Docking, 2002). There is, however, a wide range of advice and research about how this is best achieved. Plowden (The Plowden Report, 1967) advised teachers to put children in mixed-ability groups in order to promote active, problem solving discussion. Later studies showed that although teachers grouped children, they were usually directed to work individually. The group situation but individualised nature of the task meant that children were often found to be off task and talking inappropriately (Whedall and Glynn, 1989). In 1995, a study by Hastings and Schwieso found that primary children concentrated better in rows, where disruptive children were less distracted. There was no eye contact to disturb them and the better they behaved, the more positive reinforcement came from the teacher. So are rows the answer? Probably as primary teachers, something inside us recoils at the idea! Why is this? Could it be that we really do believe that children learn better in a social environment and that our training tells us that it cannot be right that teachers' requirements for conformity and rules should override the child's need for 'understanding and engagement in high quality learning tasks' (Holt, 1982, cited in Pollard, 2008, p. 309). We need, therefore, to be challenged to provide a flexible environment where the needs of the children, the classroom, the tasks and experiences, groupings, levels of challenge, boundaries and routines, and expectations all come together to support children's positive behaviour. A challenge indeed!

Work in school

Student: I feel as if, all the time, I'm having to deal with a whole range of behaviours. For example, children are constantly getting up out of their seats, or they're shouting out, distracting others... It's wearing me down me down. I feel that I'm just trying to stay on top of behaviour issues. I'm really worried that I'm not teaching them much, but they've got to learn to behave first, haven't they?

Mentor: It is important to have good behaviour in the classroom: children can't learn easily if they are distracted or distracting. Have you observed any particular behaviour skills some of the children need to learn?

(Continued)

Student: Well, for example, if I've asked a group to – say – put things into sets that belong together, and explained this very clearly, some start arguing about how to do it, others don't seem to want to do it – it's very frustrating...

Mentor: So what positive behaviours do they need to learn?

Student: They need to learn to how to collaborate, how to talk to each other, how to talk and listen to each other, to take turns, give everyone a chance and not be bossy...

Mentor: And these skills need to be taught – constantly. So how can you help them to learn these skills?

Student: Maybe I could sit with this group for a bit – encourage those who make a good contribution, explain, listen, when the activity is going well ask them why they are working so well together. Yes, I see what you mean about *learning* positive behaviour skills. It's quite complex really...

Mentor: Good. I think you will find Ellis and Todd (2014, p. 12, and also Chapter 9, this volume) really helpful. They talk about how to help children who need to learn to feel confident, independent, responsible. The thing to remember is, 'how can I help this child to do something?', then you won't have to tell her not to do something all the time!

Analysis

Although the student's approach to managing behaviour is behaviourist, she also asks the children to work together in a group, to make sets 'of things that belong together'. The section on constructivist learning theories in Chapter 1 shows the need to develop some children's self-confidence, to enable them to participate (Bandura), and that learning to work together is not just important for social development but also essential for cognitive development (Vygotsky).

Encouraging self-esteem and emotional development through the learning environment

Few would disagree that the learning environment may also have a powerful impact on the child's self-esteem and emotional development. Without a doubt, the class teacher in the above scenario will have spent many long hours planning and resourcing her delivery of the curriculum, but one wonders how much time was spent planning the hidden curriculum and how to 'manipulate the environment' (Child, 1997, p. 265) to offer opportunities to make the children feel valued, safe and that they have a contribution to make.

Case study

Karim's low self-esteem was reinforced by the seating arrangements, the use of wall displays and his observation of rewarded behaviours. Teachers are fond of using and applying the label of low self-esteem and may take up a one-woman/man crusade to help re-educate parents or offer strategies to develop self-esteem in the home, but how do we know that Karim did not arrive at school aged 4 ready to conquer the world and it is actually school that has taught him he is failing?

Our understanding of brain development informs us that a child under stress is unable to learn effectively. If you reread his perception of the scenario, you will note that there were many issues for Karim in his environment that were sources of stress for him and that could have prevented him from learning. Sometimes empathetic teachers or teaching assistants will recognise stress issues for children but may inadvertently impact on their achievement and therefore self-esteem even more by removing challenge from tasks they are required to do and encouraging the 'learned helplessness' we have already made reference to. Kendall-Seatter (2005) speaks of the necessity to provide environments that are 'low-stress–high-challenge' (p. 59) to ensure achievement for all children regardless of ability.

Karim's concerns will not just be with how his teacher perceives and values him; the opinions of his peers will also be of great importance to his positive self-esteem. The 'ripple' effect (Jacques and Hyland, 2003, p. 161) set into motion by the classroom teacher as she sets up the learning environment to reflect her own values and beliefs about learning and children will continue until all children included in that environment cannot help but be influenced by them. There will be a shared, if unspoken, understanding that some children are failing, whilst others are successful and will always continue to be so. The failing children, the 'Karims' of this world, may feel they are powerless to move from the level in the

(Continued)

hierarchy they have been assigned by the learning environment, the teacher and their peers, and it is then, once they have decided there is no point any longer in trying, that disaffection may set in. If, on the other hand, the ripple that the teacher, through the environment, sets in motion is an inclusive one that demonstrates that all children are valued for the unique and individual talents and attributes they bring, all children will see themselves as learners regardless of their ability. Muijs and Reynolds (2011) remind us that 'teachers should emphasize pupils' successes rather than their failures' and that 'Pupils should be encouraged to strive for their own personal best, rather than … constantly comparing their results with those of their classmates' (p. 187).

Children's perceptions of their place in society

The environment will dominate children's understanding of their own role and place in society regardless of the teacher's discourse. This is why, as classroom teachers, it is so important to get it right and leave nothing to chance. We may feel we have a group of learners, but in reality we have a group of individuals (Kendall-Seatter, 2005, p. 62).

Work in school

'Teachers often find themselves in a gap between their ideals of teaching and classroom management and the harsh … reality of everyday classroom life' (Salkovsky and Romi, 2015, p. 56).

'It's hard when you're a student teacher because you have to follow the class teacher's ways of doing things even if you don't agree…'

'When you're busy in the classroom doing all the practical stuff with the children you haven't got time to think about all the theories we've looked at during uni sessions – it can leave you thinking "What's the point?!"'

How will you apply your learning from this chapter to your school placement when you may feel as a student teacher you can have limited impact on how the learning environment is set up? Look back at the bullet points on p. 121 and then reflect on the last time you were in a school setting:

(Continued)

(Continued)

- What small changes could you have made to the learning environment that would have impacted on the children's learning and well-being? Make sure you can provide an appropriate rationale for your decisions.
- Consider Piaget and Vygotsky's work, highlighted on pp. 124–6. What opportunities were there to (i) 'actively explore', (ii) 'socially interact' and (iii) work with or be 'a more knowledgeable other'. How could you extend these opportunities?

Summary

For effective learning to take place, the environment needs to be flexible enough to be created around the needs of children. However loud the teacher's voice may be, the environment will always be able to shout louder, declaring to every child in the class the values and attitudes of that teacher. Children pick up these subliminal signals, adapting their behaviour accordingly where possible to fit into the requirements of their environment. Our challenge to you, whatever your level of experience, is to think hard about your underpinning values and attitudes towards teaching and learning, and to create, within the limitations with which you find yourself working, an environment that will demonstrate to the children what you truly believe learning is.

Questions for discussion

- Children's voices: how might teachers find out how children feel about and respond to the learning environments they provide?
- How might children at each Key Stage be involved in creating their own learning environment?
- How might learning in the classroom be linked to learning outside the classroom at Key Stage 1? At Key Stage 2?
- What might your ideal learning environment at either Key Stage be like? What might be the constraints in creating this environment?

Further reading

Hayes, B., Hindle, S. and Withington, P. (2007) 'Strategies for developing positive behaviour management: Teacher behaviour outcomes and attitudes to the change process', *Educational Psychology in Practice*, 23 (2): 161–75. EBSCOhost [online]. Available at http://web.b.ebscohost.com.
This paper looks at the impact on pupil behaviour caused by a more positive approach and attitude by the teaching staff. It considers how important teachers' words and attitudes are in changing difficult behaviour displayed by children.

Hewitt, D. (2008) *Understanding Effective Learning: Strategies for the Classroom*. Maidenhead: Open University Press.
This book explores these important concepts by examining learning in a range of classroom settings and drawing on evidence from teachers and pupils, through interviews and observations. The focus is two-fold: to understand learning in the classroom, and to develop practices that will support learning.

Roffey, S. (2010) *Changing Behaviour in Schools*. London: Sage.
Taking a holistic approach to working with students, the author provides examples of effective strategies for encouraging pro-social and collaborative behaviour in the classroom, the school and the wider community. Chapters look at the importance of the social and emotional aspects of learning, and ways to facilitate change.

Skinner, D. (2010) *Effective Teaching and Learning in Practice*. London: Continuum.
Based on excellent summaries of recent research on teaching and learning, this book presents a clear framework around which teachers can build their classroom practice. It provides an excellent starting point for new entrants to the profession as well as a source of reflection for their more experienced colleagues.

References

Alexander, R. (1992) *Policy and Practice in Primary Education*. London: Routledge.
Alexander, R. (ed.) (2010) *Children, Their World, Their Education: Final Report of the Cambridge Primary Review*. London: Routledge.
Bowles, S. and Gintis, H. (1976) *Schooling in Capitalist America*. London: Routledge and Kegan Paul.
Bronfenbrenner, U. (1979) *The Ecology of Human Development*. Cambridge, MA: Harvard University Press.
Child, D. (ed.) (1997) *Psychology and the Teacher*, sixth edn. London: Continuum.
Cowley, S. (2006) *Getting the Buggers to Behave*, third edn. London: Continuum.
Dadzie, S. (2000) *Toolkit for Tackling Racism in Schools*. Stoke-on-Trent: Trentham Books.

Daly, M., Byers, E. and Taylor, W. (2006) *Understanding Early Years Theory in Practice*. Oxford: Heinemann.

Delceva-Dizdarevik, J. (2014) 'Classroom management', *International Journal of Cognitive Research in Science, Engineering and Education*, 2 (1): 51–5.

Department for Education (DfE) (2013a) *Teachers' Standards* (DFE-00066-2011). Available at: www.gov.uk/government/collections/teachers-standards.

Department for Education (DfE) (2013b) *The National Curriculum in England: Key Stages 1 and 2 Framework Document*. Available at: www.gov.uk/government/publications.

Department for Education (DfE) (2014) *Statutory Framework for the Early Years Foundation Stage*. Available at www.gov.uk/government/publications.

Docking, J. (2002) *Managing Behaviour in the Primary School*, third edn. London: David Fulton.

Doherty, J. and Hughes, M. (2009) *Child Development: Theory and Practice 0–11*. Harlow: Pearson.

Dweck, C. (2008) 'Mindsets: How praise is harming youth and what can be done about it', *School Library Media Activities Monthly*, 24(5): 55–8.

Dweck, C. (2010) 'Even geniuses work hard', *Educational Leadership*, 68 (1): 16–20.

Elton-Chalcraft, S. and Mills, K. (2015) 'Measuring challenge, fun and sterility on a "phuno-metre" scale: Evaluating creative teaching and learning with children and their student teachers in the primary school', *Education 3-13*, 43 (5). Available at: www.tandfonline.com/doi/abs/10.1080/03004279.2013.822904.

Ellis, S., and Tod, J. (2014) *Promoting Behaviour for Learning in the Classroom*. Abingdon: Routledge

Fang, Z. (1996) 'A review of research on teachers' beliefs and practices', *Educational Research*, 38 (1): 47–65.

Gnadinger, C. (2008) 'Peer-mediated instruction: Assisted performance in the primary class-room', *Teachers and Teaching*, 14 (2): 129–42.

Goswami, U. (2008) *Cognitive Development: The Learning Brain*. Hove: Psychology Press.

Gump, P. (1987) 'School and classroom environments', in I. Altman and J.F. Wohlwill (eds), *Handbook of Environmental Psychology*. New York: Plenum Press. pp. 131–74.

Hastings, N. and Schwieso, J. (1995) 'Tasks and tables: The effects of seating arrangements on task engagement in primary classrooms', *Educational Research*, 37 (3): 279–91.

Jacques, K. and Hyland, R. (2003) *Professional Studies: Primary Phase*. Exeter: Learning Matters.

Kehily, M. (ed.) (2010) *An Introduction to Childhood Studies*, second edn. Maidenhead: McGraw-Hill.

Kelly, P. (2014) 'Organising your classroom for learning', in T. Cremin and J. Arthur (eds), *Learning To Teach in the Primary School*, pp.118–28. Abingdon: Routledge.

Kendall-Seatter, S. (2005) *Primary Professional Studies: Reflective Reader*. Exeter: Learning Matters.

MacIntyre, H. and Ireson, J. (2002) 'Within-class ability grouping: Placement of pupils in groups and self-concept', *British Educational Research Journal*, 28 (2): 249–63.

McNamara, S. and Moreton, G. (1997) *Understanding Differentiation*. London: Taylor and Francis.

Moyles, J. (1992) *Organising for Learning in the Primary Classroom*. Maidenhead: Open University Press.

Muijs, R.D. and Reynolds, D. (2011) *Effective Teaching: Evidence and Practice*. London: Sage.

Ouvry, M. (2000) *Exercising Muscles and Minds*. London: The Early Years Network.

Peterson, C., Maier, S.F. and Seligman, M.E.P. (1993) *Learned Helplessness: A Theory for the Age of Personal Control*. Oxford: Oxford University Press.

Plowden Report (1967) *Children and their Primary Schools: A Report of the Central Advisory Council for Education (England)*. London: HMSO.

Pollard, A. (2008) *Reflective Teaching: Evidence-informed Professional Practice*, third edn. London: Continuum.

Salkovsky, M. and Romi, S. (2015) 'Teachers coping styles and factors inhibiting teachers' preferred classroom management practice', *Teaching and Teacher Education*, 48: 56–65.

Smidt, S. (2013) *Introducing Malaguzzi: Exploring the Life and Work of Reggio Emilia's Founding Father*. London: Routledge.

Tomlinson, C.A. (2015) 'Teaching for excellence in academically diverse classrooms', *Society*, 52 (3): 203–9.

Waterson, A. (2003) 'Managing the classroom for learning', in K. Jacques and R. Hyland (eds), *Professional Studies: Primary Phase*. Exeter: Learning Matters. pp. 74–85.

Whedall, K. and Glynn, T. (1989) *Effective Classroom Learning: A Behavioural Interactionist Approach to Teaching*. Oxford: Basil Blackwell.

Wood, D., Bruner, J. and Ross, G. (1976) 'The role of tutoring in problem solving', *Journal of Child Psychology and Psychiatry*, 17: 89–100.

6

The Role of the Teacher and Other Adults

Jan Ashbridge and Jo Josephidou

By the end of this chapter, you should be able to:

- discuss the many roles of the teacher in the education and care of children
- examine how teachers work with other adults within and beyond the classroom to develop effective practice that will impact on children's achievement
- consider how positive relationships between adults and children can impact on their learning
- reflect critically on the values and philosophies you hold regarding the education of children.

Introduction

The best early years practice focuses on the importance of 'positive relationships' to lay the foundations of successful learning for young children. Once these children make the transition to Key Stage 1 and then later Key Stage 2, it is vital that these 'positive relationships' are maintained to ensure that these transitions are smooth and supportive for each child. But what is your role in the establishing and maintaining of these 'positive relationships' as a classroom teacher? The first part of this chapter will ask you to consider some of the people you will need to develop positive relationships with and how this might be achieved. Then the second part of the chapter will use metaphors to consider the many other dimensions of the teacher's role: supporting the development of the whole child, facilitating and scaffolding learning, pastoral care, inspiring learners and coordinating all these roles; see Chapter 16 where Boyd discusses teacher identity. This chapter reflects Standard 8 (DfE, 2013), which refers to the importance of making a positive contribution to the life of the school, developing effective professional relationships with colleagues, deploying staff effectively and communicating well with parents with regard to their children's achievements and well-being.

Reflective task

Imagine yourself in your first classroom with your first class of children. Take a mental photograph of the picture this creates in your head. Now describe this image to a peer.
  Describe the following:

- What are you doing?
- What are the children doing?
- Is there anyone else in the classroom?
- What are they doing?

It will be interesting to see whether the image you have described has changed by the end of this chapter.

Teachers are a cog in a much bigger mechanism. It is easy to focus only on the cogs immediately around us, where it is obvious how they affect our work and how we affect them. Understanding the bigger picture is a key way of beginning to grasp the main issues in partnership working and avoiding the appearance of a 'muddled system of education and care' (Penn, 2008, p. 193).

Reflective task

Who are we in partnership with?

In small groups, write down on separate sticky notes all the different professionals who might be working alongside a teacher in their work and who may influence their practice. What different ways can you find in which to group them? By role? By sphere of influence? By the immediacy of their impact on the teacher's work?

On a large sheet of paper, draw the teacher in the middle – can you organise your sticky notes around them? Who seems nearest, who seems less important?

This activity should have illustrated the number of people that teachers work with. A study of roles and responsibilities (adapted from Siraj-Blatchford et al., 2002, p. 7) found the following roles and responsibilities in today's primary schools:

- teaching assistant (and equivalent learning support assistant, nursery nurse, therapist)
- pupil welfare workers (education welfare officer, home–school liaison officer, learning mentor, nurse and welfare assistant)
- technical and specialist staff (information and communication technology (ICT) network manager, ICT technician, librarian, science technician, technology technician)
- other pupil support staff (bilingual support officer, cover supervisor, escort, language assistant, midday assistant, midday supervisor)
- facilities staff (cleaner, cook, other catering staff)
- administrative staff (administrator, finance officer, office manager, secretary, personal assistant to the head teacher)
- site staff (caretaker and premises manager).

This list is considerably extended when we add colleagues within the school and the community and multi-agency working.

Let us now examine some of these key partnerships for the classroom teacher.

Working with others: the teacher as partner

Partnership with parents and carers

Perhaps the key partnership teachers must engage in is with parents and carers. Parents are statutorily responsible for their child's education, are legally entitled to state a

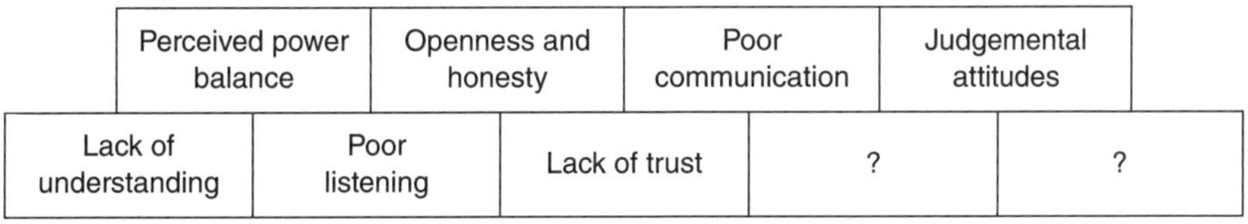

Perceived power balance	Openness and honesty	Poor communication	Judgemental attitudes	
Lack of understanding	Poor listening	Lack of trust	?	?

Figure 6.1 Stumbling blocks

preference for a particular school and have a legal right to parental representation on the governing body. As a result of this, they are major stakeholders in children's education and are able to influence school policy. This responsibility is shared, as when a child is at school teachers are *in loco parentis* and have a common-law duty to promote children's safety and well-being as well as their education (Children Act 1989).

What might be some of the stumbling blocks to effective partnership with parents? Figure 6.1 here suggests possible barriers to successful school–parent relationships. Parents know their children better than the teacher ever can. They are the children's first educators and have vital information on what the children enjoy, how they learn, etc. Most learning happens outside school (Dean, 2000, p. 140), and this needs to be recognised and valued by those within the school too.

Opportunities to share information with parents

Teachers can usually think of many ways to share information with parents. Before the first, nervously anticipated 'parents' evening', you may have met many of the parents informally at the beginning or end of the school day. You may have written notes to them about school events or out-of-school visits. You may have been encouraged to invite them to a meeting at the beginning of term to introduce yourself, explain what the children are going to be learning about and why, and to discuss how they may like to be involved. If you have managed initial encounters with parents in a friendly and professional way, this will be a good basis for meeting them on more formal occasions to discuss their children's progress. Some schools invite parents to meetings to learn more about how the school teaches, for example, reading or mathematics, so that they can be more involved in their children's learning. But this is not a partnership if you do not also learn from the parents: 'For partnerships to be truly collaborative … learning must be part of the experience for all involved' (Loughrey and Woods, 2010, p. 85).

Opportunities for parents to share information with teachers

Even confident parents may feel threatened by meeting a teacher to discuss their child's progress, attitudes, social skills and behaviour. Less confident parents may have had poor experiences of school themselves and feel insecure or alternatively confrontational. How might parents feel about sharing family information with a teacher? How can you help parents to feel confident in telling you about their children? What might you want to know, and why?

Parents' contributions to school life

There may be many reasons why parents seem reluctant to get involved with school life and it is not necessarily because 'they can't be bothered' or that they don't care about their child's progress: Desforges and Abouchaar (2003, p. 6) suggest that 'the extent and form of parental involvement is strongly influenced by factors such as family social class, maternal level of education, material deprivation, maternal psycho-social health and single parent status'.

A key aspect of your role as classroom teacher is to build strong professional relationships with parents so that you can encourage them to contribute to the life of the school, because there is a wealth of research to indicate that parental involvement will impact on the achievement of their child. How can parents contribute to the life of the school? Through your formal and informal communications with parents, you may find that they have special expertise, through their work or their interests, which would enrich an aspect of your teaching. Some parents are eager to 'help in class'. Could there be difficulties in welcoming this and, if so, how could they be resolved? Some parents may have little English. How might you involve them in helping in school? How might you make parents from different cultural backgrounds feel included in school life?

Reflective task

In pairs: one person thinks of a child they have taught who was finding school difficult in some ways. The partner, in role as the class teacher, needs to find out why. Role play a meeting between parent and teacher. Share what you both know and feel about the child and agree how you can work together to support her. Then share your thoughts about the difficulties encountered and how well both partners negotiated them. Share the role play with others. Compile a list of ways in which you might work in partnership with parents to support a child.

This relationship has considerable influence over the way parents feel able to support their children's learning, resulting in a shared purpose, understanding and belonging for all (Dean, 2000, p. 151). Also see Chapter 12 where Conteh discusses supporting learners with English as an additional language (EAL), and Chapter 14 where Warner and Elton-Chalcraft reflect on ethnicity.

Social events with teachers and parents

Partnerships can be strengthened by situations in which parents and teachers work together on a more equal footing to support the school. One head teacher set up a number of projects more enterprising than the 'school fete', themed dance evenings and fancy dress parties, although these were greatly enjoyed. The projects included a school garden, the construction of an 'adventure fort' and a pet shed. Children, teachers and parents worked together on these projects. The fort project was particularly successful in involving dads, some of whom did not live at home. Loughrey and Woods (2010) describe a creative project involving children, parents, teachers and artists that impacted positively on all those involved in an area of great poverty where previous attempts at engaging parents had been unsuccessful.

True partnerships with parents cannot flourish where respect and power are not equal. Home–school communication is a complex process in which 'issues of control and power are present and shape the forms of communication'. However, when effective communication with parents is achieved, 'the contribution that parents make to their child's learning is often rich and varied' (Alexander, 2010, p. 81).

Partnership with teaching assistants

The same skills are required to work alongside the other adults in the classroom. Teaching assistants (TAs) and other support staff often have a slightly different relationship with children and families and can, therefore, add another perspective to planning and to supporting children's needs, although it is fair to say that the TA's role has changed considerably over the past few years and is shifting to include work that would previously only have been carried out by teachers, such as teaching, planning and assessment (Mackenzie, 2011). Involving them and using their knowledge and experience can ensure more effective learning outcomes for the children and can create a more responsive and motivated team approach in the classroom.

It was the intention that the considerable increase in teaching assistants and other support staff between 2003 and 2006, as a result of 'workforce reform', should strengthen teaching and learning, by using the full potential of teaching assistants, allowing them to take on wider and deeper roles, and allowing schools to focus on the individual needs of every child. However, TAs can feel that their role in the classroom is ambiguous and at times not clearly defined. In Mackenzie's research (2011) TAs voice their confusion over the 'lack of clarity' about their role and she signposts other research which shows that teachers and TAs often have very different perspectives on their role in the classroom.

How to work with TAs in ways that will realise these opportunities involves decisions about how best to use their expertise in ways that meet the needs of the children in your class, and the ability to forge mutually supportive relationships. Don't forget that the research shows that 'TAs very often have a strong commitment to their work' (Mackenzie, 2011, p. 65). It is essential that teachers include TAs in planning, monitoring and assessment, medium-term, weekly and daily, and this requires time. They also need to be clear about what their role is within what the teacher is planning, with an individual, a group or the whole class and how they are going to monitor and assess this. Reflect on how one of Mackenzie's TA interviewees discusses the tension of working with a class teacher:

> I never get lesson plans. You've got to think on your feet, you've got to adapt material when you don't even know what they're doing. You have to listen to what the teacher is teaching the class so that you understand everything. But at the same time you are meant to be out of the class changing all the materials. You don't get any time to change or adapt things. (2011, p. 67)

They may have particular areas of curriculum expertise to contribute, in art, or music or dance, for example. But the most important aspect of working effectively with your TA is to develop a mutually supportive relationship so that you enjoy working together. Bear in mind that working collaboratively with your TA is not a simple matter, but when you persevere and have the determination to make it work, you, as class teacher, your TA and the children will benefit greatly. Another of Mackenzie's interviewees noted how she enjoyed working with teachers who were: 'fair, firm, adapting the curriculum, understanding the needs of the classroom, making sure that the kids love you and empowering them so that they become active learners' (2011, p. 67).

Partnership with other teachers

A school is a community, a collaborative, inclusive community for learning. This community creates and conveys values, attitudes and purposes. Relationships between teachers and the ways in which they behave have an important impact on the ethos of that community. They are models that children notice. A positive and mutually agreed and shared whole-school philosophy, shared values, mutual respect and support are a powerful, formative influence on children and on the community. Whole-school policies and planning contribute to the school ethos.

Within schools, there are teams that must work effectively with each other and the school community: management teams, curriculum leaders, special educational needs coordinators (SENCOs), year group teams, Key Stage teams. And there is evidence that if all these groups work effectively, this has an impact on all aspects of children's learning.

Partner with local schools

In rural areas particularly, schools work in local clusters to share resources and expertise and to support each other. It is important that they work together cooperatively rather than submit to government encouragement of competition.

Partner with global colleagues

Many teachers also think that it is important to develop the global dimension of education and liaise with teachers and schools in other countries and continents. This demands sensitivity, for example, when resources and opportunities are unequal.

Working in partnership with professionals in other agencies
Primary Care Trusts

From 2001–2013 Primary Care Trusts (PCTs) worked with families, children and schools. Teachers therefore worked with the PCT services such as: disabled children's teams, child development teams, health visitors, health education programmes, occupational therapists, speech therapists, physiotherapists, community parent schemes and children's mental health teams.

These multi-agency teams were set up in partnership with schools in 2002 to promote well-being, positive behaviour and attendance, and to raise attainment through early intervention. The PCTs were abolished in 2013.

The 2004 Children Act

In 2003 the *Every Child Matters* initiative was introduced. This became part of the Children Act 2004. It was intended to secure the well-being of all children and in particular those in danger of abuse. Local Authorities were to provide 'joined up' education and care services with multi-agency cooperation. Schools were to work with health care agencies, social services, family law and criminal justice agencies, and services concerned with the arts, recreation and sports. These include public, private and voluntary agencies.

Children's trust boards

In 2007 the government announced that children's trust boards would be set up. These were to consist of representatives from schools and the other integrated services, and would be held responsible for child protection measures.

Implications for teacher as partner

It has been complex to manage multi-agency work and some schools have been criticised for lack of involvement, but where it has been successful children and parents have benefited. It has been suggested that agencies should liaise with clusters of schools. However multi-agency work develops in the future, its success will depend on teachers being prepared to work with other professionals and to share information and expertise.

Extended schools

Extended schools were created to provide all children with access to a variety of clubs and sports, and adults with access to education classes and parenting support. The aim was that by 2010 all children would have access to an extended school. Teachers are not required to contribute to extended schools, but may choose to.

Partnership and the community

'To establish itself as a thriving cultural and communal site should be the principal aim of every school' (Alexander, 2010, p. 500). The community of the school – its pupils and their families, and often the school staff – is part of the wider community. So the wider curriculum needs to gain meaning by starting with that community, its geography, its history, its opportunities for creating art, music, drama and all kinds of writing related to the community and the people who lived and live there.

Children need to learn about citizenship through taking an interest in and contributing to their community. This might involve discussing a proposed development, making suggestions to the town council about changes they would like to see, attending council meetings, becoming aware of sustainability and environmental issues, contributing to a display in the local library (if there still is one) or presenting a performance at an old people's home.

Parents can contribute in all sorts of ways. One Year 1 class had a 'teddy museum'. Children brought in their teddy bears and wrote brief information labels. Parents did the same with their teddies. In another school, in groups, children from each Key Stage 2 class were helped by parents to prepare a lunch related to a theme they were learning about, then invited a member of the community, perhaps a librarian or nurse or police officer to share their lunch. Parents may demonstrate skills or hobbies or talk about their interests or working day.

People from local businesses can enrich the curriculum in all sorts of ways, perhaps inviting children to make a positive contribution: making designs for a new flower bed in the park, or a new building in town, or a new recipe for the sandwich bar. Alexander (2010, p. 276) suggests that community–curriculum partnerships should be convened by the Local Authority, including representatives from schools and the community and experts in contributory disciplines, and involving consultation with children. This community curriculum would include elements agreed collectively by the schools, with each school responding in ways that build on and respect the lives of their children.

Having discussed the role of the teacher as partner, let us now consider the multifaceted role of the teacher through the use of metaphors. Hattingh and de Kock (2008) cite Inbar's research (1996), which highlighted that student teachers naturally used metaphors when discussing their role. His research pinpointed 7042 such metaphors in use. In this part of the chapter we will ask you to consider only five:

- teacher as signpost
- teacher as magician
- teacher as gardener
- teacher as bridge
- teacher as superhero.

By considering the role of the teacher in this way, we are hopeful you will reflect on your present perceptions of how you see yourself as a teacher and how you can impact on the achievement and well-being of those children you teach.

The developing child: teacher as signpost

Children's learning is often seen as a journey. Children move along a path from the early years, through the primary school and on to high school and beyond. Along the way they develop, they grow, they learn. Careful planning ensures that the children's itinerary takes them to visit a variety of different places and experience a range of situations.

The teacher's role here is perceived to be to lead and manage the curriculum at a number of different levels and in a variety of ways. As seen in the previous chapter, the environment and its careful management and use is key to effective learning and teaching. Children need to be kept safe, resources organised and accessible, and social interactions, groups and tasks carefully considered and appropriately employed.

It is interesting here to note who is making the decisions about these issues. Many of these management decisions are taken for the benefit of the adult. The image of a signpost offers us a slightly different perception of the role of the teacher. It is one where some of the control over decisions about learning is given to the children. They are able to indicate a choice of where they want their learning to go, how they want to engage with it and how much time they need to master it. It is still very much about moving children on and supporting their progress, but with a key difference: the children are more involved in the direction their learning may take them.

In order to be able to respond appropriately to children in this situation, teachers need to understand that 'teaching and learning [are] a continuous unfolding of related knowledge, skills and understanding' (Hayes, 2004, p. 151). We cannot simply give children complete free choice over what and how they learn. We need to have an overview. Continuity of learning is 'achieved when there is a discernable thread of knowledge, skills and understanding' that runs through different learning experiences (Hayes, 2004, p. 151). Aiming for this will enable us to be effective signposts, allowing children to progress smoothly along their learning journey.

Facilitating learning: teacher as magician

Magic moments

Sometimes the classroom teacher glimpses small nuggets of gold when a child grasps and articulates a concept in a way the teacher had not considered before. Or a group of children display a skill or ability beyond that same teacher's expectation. Or the wisdom of children as opposed to the knowledge of adults is allowed to take centre stage so that the classroom becomes a real learning community. By being the catalyst, the facilitator of all these events, the teacher could be forgiven at times for feeling as if they were a magician, an alchemist, a producer of gold.

Catering for individual differences

The teacher as magician is there to do the seemingly impossible – to facilitate learning for all. The successful teacher will do this by being very clear about the individual learning needs of the children. Some children learn more effectively by having their learning introduced in small steps, while others like to view the bigger picture and proceed from there. The wise teacher will not seek to impose strategies that may not work for all children and will not succumb to the flawed opinion that because they themselves learnt successfully in one way then so will all children. Some children will disengage much more quickly than others so the teacher as magician will seek to captivate their attention for as long as possible by creating an exciting learning environment, rich with stimulating and purposeful activities and opportunities to succeed.

A learning community

The teacher as magician will be clear about learning outcomes, will know that at the end of the show the white rabbit has to come out of the hat, but at the same time will read her audience and be flexible about how this outcome is achieved. Audience participation is encouraged because by fostering interaction between teacher and children, and children and children, the effective teacher is aware that a learning community is being constructed that everyone can both contribute to and learn from. Talk and questioning are used to extend learning rather than as a focus for 'guess what is in the teacher's head' type activities.

Transformative learning

It could be argued that indeed the analogy of the magician does stand up as a description of the teacher. Just as the magician can change the silk handkerchief into the white rabbit, so can the class teacher bring about real transformation and change. On the other hand, just as the magician's feat is an illusion of change, so too can the education system support the illusion of change by the introduction of strategies and the massaging and analysis of statistics and data, teaching to tests that inflate key assessment results rather than deliver any lasting change, growth in knowledge and skills or transformation. Just as the magician puts on a show to bring a real sense of wonder and excitement to his audience, so too does the classroom teacher, at times, draw her audience in, sometimes to entertain, sometimes to enthral, at other times to turn the mundane and simple into spectacles worthy of the children's attention.

Pastoral care: teacher as gardener

We cannot afford to ignore the social and emotional development of children. Children who are happy at school, who share good relationships with both adults and peers in that environment, are children who will make good progress academically. So this is why we turn now to the analogy of the teacher as gardener, carefully considering and providing the best possible environment and conditions for the children to thrive and grow in all areas of their development.

Praise

Teacher praise has always been an effective motivator for children, though Child (1997, p. 119) reminds us that it must be used carefully if it is to have any impact otherwise it can become meaningless and limiting. Moyles too warns us to be careful about how we offer it: 'praise may appear to make children work harder, but what was the cause of any reluctance to do so in the first place?' (2001, p. 69). Instead, many would argue that appropriate behaviours should be considered the norm, not something to be rewarded, and that the present fashion for acknowledging teacher pleasure through the constant bestowing of certificates and stickers actually decreases children's intrinsic motivations and undermines them as learners (see Ellis and Tod, Chapter 9, and also Hymer and Gershon, 2014).

Lifelong learners

Teachers who are aware that their role is much more than a transmission of knowledge will work hard to plan for resilient lifelong learners who are enthusiastic about learning because they know they have the freedom to make mistakes, seeing mistakes as necessary stepping stones on the way to academic success (see Chapter 5 by Ashbridge and Josephidou, and also Dweck, 2006). They will look to provide opportunities for children to build on and demonstrate their strengths rather than focusing on the child's weaknesses within the rigid framework of assessment 'where the threat to self-esteem is ever present' (Cockburn and Handscomb, 2006, p. 45).

Fostering independence

The teacher is an expert at asking questions of the children but it may be pertinent for her to ask herself about how it feels to be a learner in the classroom environment she has created. Do the children feel quite dependent on the teacher for their learning or are they confident enough and skilled enough to see and use their peers 'as a resource' (Moyles, 2001, p. 13)? Children who are strong and healthy, not just physically and cognitively but also emotionally resilient, need the correct conditions or learning environment to grow and thrive.

Scaffolding learning: teacher as bridge

Teachers are curriculum makers. They take their detailed knowledge of the frameworks and statutory expectations of children, combine this with an understanding of children's needs, their development and their current skills and understandings and create an environment with meaningful and challenging learning experiences for all. This professional responsibility means that we are ultimately accountable for the learning situations that we create for the children in our class and for the children's responses to these in terms of learning and progress. Teachers are constantly using their professional judgement but must be able to justify their decisions.

Progressing learning

A bridge is something that gets you from one side of a gap of some kind to the other. As classroom teachers, we aim to support children as they travel from their current knowledge to concepts and skills as yet unknown and unexplored but perhaps anticipated and eagerly awaited. In supporting children from one side of this gap to the other, we need to have our eyes fixed firmly on the connection, the learning itself and on the process of connecting. To get this right, we must return again to theories of cognitive development. These can give us an insight into the way that children make connections and what we can do to make these as strong as possible. In this way, we can interpret the curriculum in appropriate ways for specific groups of children.

Siraj-Blatchford et al. (2002) argue that it is this bringing together of children and adult in a learning situation that enables co-construction of knowledge where both are engaged and involved. Their research showed that where adults and children were engaged together in these 'sustained shared thinking interactions' (Siraj-Blatchford et al., 2002, p. 10), a high level of intellectual challenge enabled children to make good progress in their learning.

Interventions

It would seem, therefore, that we support children's learning and their interpretation of what they are experiencing through careful scaffolding and sensitive yet challenging adult interventions. These interventions, which are designed to make connections between existing understanding and new knowledge, form part of a complicated process. On their own, children may not be able to make these connections or could make inaccurate ones. Enabling children to bridge this gap will lead to 'principled understanding' (Edwards and Mercer, 1987, p. 95, cited in Myhill et al., 2006, p. 87), where children make deep, meaningful, conceptual connections in their learning.

Listening to children's voices

The challenge for the teacher is to enable and support all children to make these connections when each child has a 'uniqueness and individuality of … prior knowledge … that has to be incorporated into a classroom setting' (Myhill et al., 2006, p. 85). The answer seems to lie in listening to children and their thoughts and ideas rather than more formal recapping of previous curriculum coverage and relating this to a current learning focus that narrows children's thinking rather than provoking 'speculation and extend[ing] imagination' (Siraj-Blatchford et al., 2002, p. 47). The types of questions used by teachers are instrumental in helping children to truly explore their prior knowledge and also to share their understanding and begin to construct an extended understanding together.

The inspiring teacher: teacher as superhero

Modelling

Children's media are full of superheroes. They are enthralled by characters with super powers and look up to champions of good over evil. For many primary school children, their teacher can be a superhero figure. When trainee teachers are asked to consider how they perceive the role of the teacher, they will often use the term 'role model', but what exactly are they implying by their use of this phrase? Certainly, the idea of modelling is a key theme that runs through issues surrounding effective teaching and learning at primary level. The effective teacher models a range of skills, from how to solve mathematical problems to how to deal with conflict in the playground, and then supports the child in their own interpretation of this modelling until finally the child has the confidence and is ready to use these skills independently. This view of children and their 'guided participation' (Rogoff, cited in Penn, 2008, p. 49) mirrors practices in cultures across the world where the child is viewed as competent and ready to learn skilled adult activity, and also links with the work of Bruner and Vygotsky already discussed in Chapter 2. The effective teacher may also feel that not only is their role one of modelling for children but also for other adults working in the classroom and, at times, parents and other teaching colleagues. We can disseminate excellent practice by allowing others to observe us at work, by the way the learning environment we have created speaks of our values and expectations and by articulating clearly and explicitly why we have chosen to adopt certain strategies and philosophies.

The metaphor of the superhero was chosen because this is a powerful, inspirational figure, a defender of children who will ensure that their learning needs are at the forefront of everything the teacher does. However, it is important to recognise that these same children are strong, competent individuals who need an advocate to fight their corner rather than a rescuer to come and save them.

Work in school

Scenario 1

Student: I'm there to teach lessons – surely it is up to the teaching assistants to do all the caring stuff!

Mentor: Oh dear! Surely you aren't saying that you don't care about the children! You and the teaching assistant work as partners in supporting children's learning. And both teaching and learning involve both cognitive and affective dimensions. As their teacher you are an important person in a child's life; it is important that children know you care about them as 'a whole child' for them to succeed as learners. Think about the teachers you responded best to when you were at school.

Student: Mmm... I remember Mrs McQueen. She knew I was sad when my auntie and uncle went to live in Canada. She found Canada for me in a children's atlas, and we looked for pictures, so I could find out what it was like. She helped me make cards for them and when they wrote back she read the letter to the class and everyone used to ask me about them. Not like Miss Barber. When my mum was in hospital Miss Barber didn't even ask me how she was. I got very tearful...

Mentor: Mrs McQueen sounds a very good teacher.

Student: Yes I got on really well in her class ... so yes ... I'd never really thought about *why* I got on so well...

Scenario 2

Student: I find it really hard when I have to tell people who are older and more experienced than me what to do – you know like teaching assistants, I feel like I'm being rude.

(Continued)

(Continued)

Mentor:	You aren't the only student to feel like this. But it is important that you demonstrate that you can plan effectively for other adults in the classroom. This is quite natural because as a young adult, with limited experience in the classroom, you feel uncomfortable directing those not only older but much more competent in working with the children. Remember though what Mackenzie (2011) found out in her research – these are highly committed professionals who have an expectation that you will share your planning and direct them so that they can do their jobs properly. If you do not do this effectively you are impacting on their job satisfaction.

Scenario 3

Student:	I try very hard to engage with parents but they don't seem to want to know.
Mentor:	As a young professional you need to consider objectively why they might not seem bothered. We have talked about some of the reasons, but other things you may want to reflect on are your body language and your 'teacher presence'. If you are in the class as a student teacher, it is normal that parents will prefer to engage with the class teacher, after all they will be the ones picking up the pieces when you have left! But explain to your class teacher that you would like the opportunity to chat to parents and that you need to demonstrate that you have experience of relating to parents. For example, at home time or in the morning a parent will be pleased to share news about a good piece of work their child has completed. At the beginning and end of the day, be a visible presence in the playground, this will help you build up your confidence in relating to parents and let both them and their children know that you care.
Analysis:	Theories underpinning the mentor's advice
Scenario 1:	In Chapter 1 the section on Maslow shows the importance of affectionate relationships in effective learning.
Scenarios 2 and 3:	Bronfenbrenner (Chapter 1) shows how children are influenced by their learning experiences in different settings, and so how important it is that there is communication both between different adults in school and also between home and school.

Summary: teacher as conductor

As we have explored, the role of the teacher is complex and multifaceted. It requires partnership with a wide variety of others. We need to have excellent knowledge of child development and subject knowledge. We must understand how to facilitate learning, how to scaffold learning, how to nurture the whole child, how to inspire. At some points, we can feel like a conductor, orchestrating children's learning experiences, their responses, the curriculum, resources, routines and other adults. This wider view is important as it ensures that we can pull all this together into a holistic, coherent experience, with each child expressing themselves and performing positively.

Questions for discussion

- For many children, their socio-economic circumstances are a barrier to learning. In what ways can a school 'make a difference' in spite of this?
- It has been suggested that children should have specialist subject teachers rather than generalist class teachers in the primary school. Do you agree?
- In most European countries, subject knowledge is included in the field of professional studies but there is less emphasis on pedagogy. What are the advantages and disadvantages of this?
- It has been said that multi-agency working and classroom assistants are a threat to teachers' professionalism. Do you agree?

Further reading

Eaude, T. (2011) *Thinking Through Pedagogy for Primary and Early Years*. Exeter: Learning Matters.
This user-friendly text encourages readers to consider how children learn, and how teachers can best support their learning. It begins by asking 'what is pedagogy?' and goes on to examine the wider context, including how language and education impact on pedagogy.

Loughrey, D. and Woods, C. (2010) 'Sparking the imagination: Creative experts working collaboratively with children, teachers and parents to enhance educational opportunities', *Support for Learning*, 25 (2): 81–90.
A case study that describes effective and powerful collaborative working between children, teachers, parents and artists.

Mackenzie, S. (2011) '"Yes, but…": Rhetoric, reality and resistance in teaching assistants' experiences of inclusive education', *Support for Learning*, 26 (2): 64–71.
This interesting piece of research will give you a real insight into TAs' perspectives.

Muijs, D. and Reynolds, D. (2017) *Effective Teaching*, fourth edn. London: Sage.
This book encompasses the latest research on effective teaching and learning. Appropriate for all age groups, it provides a comprehensive overview of what is now a large body of knowledge on effective teaching.

Pritchard, A. and Woollard, J. (2010) *Psychology for the Classroom: Constructivism and Social Learning*. London: Routledge.
A discussion of interactive approaches to teaching, this book provides a background to research in constructivist and social learning theory, offering a broad and practical analysis that focuses on contemporary issues and strategies, including the use of e-learning and multimedia.

References

Alexander, R. (ed.) (2010) *Children, their World, their Education: Final Report and Recommendations of the Cambridge Primary Review*. London: Routledge.
Child, D. (1997) *Psychology and the Teacher*, sixth edn. London: Continuum.
Cockburn, A. and Handscomb, G. (2006) *Teaching Children 3 to 11*, second edn. London: Paul Chapman Publishing.
Dean, J. (2000) *Improving Children's Learning*. London: Routledge.
Department for Education (DfE) (2013) *Teachers' Standards*. Available at: https://www.gov.uk.
Desforges, C. and Abouchaar, A. (2003) *The Impact of Parental Support and Family Education on Pupil Achievements and Adjustment: A Literature Review*. Research Report No. 433. Nottingham: DfES.
Dweck, C. (2006) *Mindset: the New Psychology of Success*. New York: Random House.
Hattingh, A. and de Kock, D.M. (2008) 'Perceptions of teacher roles in an experience-rich teacher education programme', *Innovations in Education and Teaching International*, 45 (4): 321–32.
Hayes, D. (2004) *Foundations of Primary Teaching*, third edn. London: David Fulton.
Hymer, B. and Gershon, M. (2014) *Growth Mindset Pocket Book*. Alresford: Teachers' Pocket Books.
Loughrey, D. and Woods, C. (2010) 'Sparking the imagination: Creative experts working collaboratively with children, teachers and parents to enhance educational opportunities', *Support for Learning*, 25(2): 81–90.
Mackenzie, S. (2011) '"Yes, But…": Rhetoric, reality and resistance in teaching assistants' experiences of inclusive education', *Support for Learning*, 26 (2): 64–71.
Moyles, J. (2001) *Organising for Learning in the Primary Classroom*. Maidenhead: Open University Press.
Myhill, D., Jones, S. and Hopper, R. (2006) *Talking, Listening, Learning: Effective Talk in the Primary Classroom*. Maidenhead: Open University Press.
Penn, H. (2008) *Understanding Early Childhood: Issues and Controversies*, second edn. Maidenhead: McGraw-Hill.
Siraj-Blatchford, I., Sylva, K., Muttock, S., Gilden, R. and Bell, D. (2002) *Researching Effective Pedagogy in the Early Years*. Nottingham: DfES.

Part 2

INCLUSIVE DIMENSIONS OF PROFESSIONAL STUDIES

In Part 1 you were introduced to the philosophy underpinning this book and to the broad foundations of Professional Studies: planning and assessment, classroom organisation and ethos and the significance of relationships with children and adults. Part 2 builds on these foundations by focusing on a range of themes which have in common the concept of inclusion – the need to take into account children's individual needs. These depend on children's levels of ability and maturation, social, cultural and ethnic backgrounds, and personal and social development.

You will consider the different personal, social and cognitive needs of 3- to 5-year-olds when they first join the school community, how to manage children's behaviours in ways which enable them to maximize the learning opportunities school offers, how to nurture their personal and social growth, how to help them to keep safe in the different contexts they encounter, and how to live and learn happily in our multi-cultural society.

You will consider inclusive teaching and learning strategies which will enable you to provide children with equal opportunities to learn and to meet their potential. And you will realise that each of these themes involves informed value judgements about how best to proceed.

7

Reflective Practice in the Early Years: Provision for 3- to 5- Year-Olds in School

Lin Savage and Anne Renwick

By the end of this chapter, you should:

- have an informed understanding of controversial issues related to teaching 3- to 5-year-olds in schools
- have some understanding of the importance of the play-based curriculum and how to protect it in mixed-age classes, the importance of creative and innovative practice and how to develop this
- have some understanding of the importance of developmentally appropriate approaches to teaching 3- to 5-year-olds and of how to do this
- have some understanding of theories underpinning the teaching of 3- to 5-year-olds
- understand some international perspectives on early years education.

Introduction

This chapter will focus on issues related to teaching children aged 3–5 in the school context. It will address several controversial issues such as school starting age, the entitlement to a play-based curriculum and different pedagogical approaches to early reading. The chapter will focus on the need for early years foundation stage (EYFS) teachers to develop an evidence-based personal philosophy and to use this to develop innovative and creative teaching practice, which extends young children's learning in a manner appropriate to their age and stage of development.

Through reflective, enquiry-based activities, readers will be encouraged to consider issues particular to teaching young children, including how to protect the entitlement to a play-based curriculum for children in the EYFS and in mixed-age classes. Some consideration of the Teachers' Standards (DfE, 2012a) and their interpretation and application for teachers of children aged 3–5 will be included. Theoretical models and international perspectives will be drawn upon to encourage a consideration of education in the wider context.

Some challenges and issues

The variety of early years contexts

Provision for children under 5 has undergone major changes in the past two decades. Supporting parents into work to enhance family finances has become a political priority for successive governments (DfES, 2004). The introduction of nursery vouchers in 1997 and the merger of education and care settings have resulted in a range of contexts available for children in the early years, prior to beginning statutory school. Providing an affordable childcare service has resulted in a growth in private nursery provision, which incorporates education for 3–4-year-olds. A range of childcare qualifications, including initially Early Years Professional Status and, more recently, Early Years Teacher, have been developed alongside the EYFS and Birth to Three documents in an attempt to ensure quality provision. These changes in the wider context of early years provision have impacted on EYFS classes in schools. Parents now have a wider choice of provision, often with flexible availability in terms of number of days and length of hours available each day. Younger children are offered free hours in private nurseries and school EYFS classes can be under pressure to accept younger children, sometimes as young as 2 years old, who require a very different environment and learning style from the typical 3- to 5-year-old. Nursery providers in schools may feel pressured to prioritise practice that supports parents to aid their working life rather than providing hours, organisation and practice more centred on the child, or in line with primary school classes in the school. School teachers who work with under 5s may feel that their identity is eroded by the confusing array of early years practitioner qualifications. Within schools various different methods of organising EYFS children are adopted, there may be a separate nursery class and Reception class, for example, or an EYFS unit with children from 3–5 sharing space and staff. In some schools there may be no provision for children in the nursery year of the EYFS, and in small village schools EYFS children are often taught in mixed-age classes with other children in Key Stage 1. All of these different contexts have particular challenges and demands for planning and providing suitable learning experiences for EYFS children. School leaders may not be trained in the EYFS and unaware of the crucial elements of play and scaffolding critical thinking in imaginative contexts so vital to early development (Goswami, 2015). Some school leaders are happy to appoint teachers to work in the EYFS who may not have been trained in educating the youngest children and lack the crucial understanding of child development and how young children learn.

Reflective task

Consider the following three scenarios and the particular advantages and challenges to providing good practice for all EYFS children in each:

1. School A has a nursery class with 10 full-time places (9am till 3.30pm) plus 15 part-time morning places (9am till 12.00) and 15 afternoon places (12.30pm till 3.30pm). Additionally there are two Reception classes; children enter Reception from the school nursery and five different private pre-school providers in the area.
2. School B has an EYFS unit with 50 children aged 3 to 5. Reception and nursery children share the same space and staff.
3. School C is a small village school, eight Reception age children are taught with six Year 1 and eight Year 2 children.

Settling children

As the leader of the first class in a child's education, the EYFS teacher has particular challenges and issues to consider. Children arrive at school having had a variety of diverse experiences prior to beginning school in nursery or Reception. While an EYFS class is likely to include many children who have had some nursery or pre-school experiences, it is possible that some children will be leaving their home and family for their first experience of the wider world. Settling children successfully at the beginning of their school life is a skill many student teachers do not get an opportunity to practise in training, but it is a crucial aspect of the EYFS teacher's role, and can heavily influence a child's attitude to school and disposition for learning.

The chances of a child's successful adjustment to school can be increased by the adoption of certain transition strategies, such as home visits, familiarisation with the buildings and close communication with parents throughout the process (Fabian and Dunlop, 2002). Margetts (2002) has noted that children who have difficulties adjusting to school in the early days are more likely to experience difficulties in adjustment throughout their schooling; this reinforces the responsibilities of the teacher in this crucial period.

Dealing with differences in maturation

Additionally, in this age range the 11-month gap between a September- and August-born child can amount to approximately a quarter of the child's life span, and developmental stages of individual children can be extremely varied. The only way to deal with this wide spectrum of experience and development is to start where the children are. The EYFS teacher will need to be skilled in observation and child development in order to begin to make sense of the range of experiences of each specific group of children, and to learn about their abilities, needs and motivations in order to plan appropriate learning experiences.

Good practice includes:

* practitioners with a sound knowledge of child development
* regular use of a variety of observation approaches, used to build individual profiles of children
* observation used to inform planning of appropriately matched learning experiences.

The importance of relating to parents and carers

Relationships with parents and carers are an important aspect of the EYFS teacher's work. There is a rare opportunity, while the children are young and brought to school, to have daily contact with parents and carers. This can create the climate for forming the all-important relationship between home and school that will hopefully last throughout the child's primary education. Research (Desforges, 2003; Sammons et al., 2007) indicates that parents and home learning have the most significant impact on children's attainment, and understanding and working with parents is, therefore, a central concern for EYFS teachers and one that was emphasised in the 2012 *Review of the Early Years Foundation Stage* (Tickell, 2011).

In addition to the possible anxieties of children adapting to new surroundings, the EYFS teacher has, also, to be mindful of the feelings and views of the child's parents. There are occasions when difficult separations are not only about the child's needs: some parents can require significant support during the early days and weeks of leaving their children at school. Parents' preoccupations and anxieties in these early days are often focused on school dinners, toileting behaviours and social aspects of transition, and EYFS teachers need to recognise the significance of the child's holistic experience of the school environment and be versed in communicating sensitively with parents about children's learning in its widest sense.

Good practice includes:

- offering home visits to meet families in their own environment
- clear and user-friendly information packs
- planning for parents to stay and settle children
- use of a noticeboard for informing parents
- allocating time to listen to parents.

A meeting of cultures

In trying to analyse the specific issues inherent in the challenges and issues for 3- to 5-year-old children and teachers, it can be useful to analyse the various cultural perspectives impacting on the EYFS class experience. The child's first encounter with school life involves the meeting of a number of cultures that may be typified by different values and beliefs, different traditions, behaviours and rules.

At least three specific cultures meet and impact on the EYFS-age child: the culture of the home, what we will refer to as the culture of 'early years provision' and the culture of the primary school. Of course, there are also additional cultures impacting on the child's situation such as the community and national cultural influences, but in this chapter, the three cultures outlined above will provide the focus for reflection and analysis (see Chapter 12, where Conteh discusses English as an additional language (EAL) learners, and Chapter 14, where Warner and Elton-Chalcraft discuss race and ethnicity issues).

The culture of the home

Children's home lives will, of course, vary considerably, but some significant generic aspects of home life might be:

- family traditions and routines
- cultural and religious identity
- the amount and quality of attention from key adults
- relationships with older or younger siblings
- the home environment – the amount and quality of space, familiarity and ownership of space and key objects (e.g. own room, toys, cup, plate, etc.)
- freedoms (e.g. to sleep, eat, drink when they need to).

It can be too easy to underestimate the impact of arriving in a building that is completely unfamiliar and unlike 'home'. This has been brought to the attention of the authors on many occasions, for example, when children look around the room wide-eyed and ask 'Where's your bed?' or emerge from the school toilets having washed their hair.

Fabian (2002) refers to this experience for the child in terms of a 'physical discontinuity', which, in transition, is accompanied by 'social discontinuity' as the child adjusts to different key adults and larger social groups of children.

The culture informing early years provision

In this section, we refer to the culture informing early years provision that has developed in England over the past two centuries, stemming from the work of early pioneers such as Susan Isaacs and Margaret McMillan, and informed by seminal research such as *Researching Effective Pedagogy in the Early Years* (Siraj-Blatchford et al., 2002) and *Effective Provision of Pre-School Education* (Sylva et al., 2003). The early years community has a strong body of researchers, writers and practitioners with a well-researched and deep-seated set of principles. This was endorsed in the 2011 Tickell review of the EYFS and continues to inform the current statutory EYFS Framework (DfE, 2017), as it has influenced the ethos and documents of the past decade and includes:

- commitment to a curriculum, which starts from observations of the child rather than specific curriculum content to be taught
- providing a curriculum that uses play as a vehicle for planning meaningful learning experiences
- planning a curriculum appropriate for the child's developmental stage
- a focus on active learning, which deepens conceptual understanding
- the equal importance of all areas of learning when planning learning experiences
- the centrality of partnership with parents and families
- an emphasis on using the environment to facilitate learning, including the outdoors
- a balance between adult-led and child-initiated activity
- the interlinked nature of education and care
- routines such as small group times with key workers, snack time, singing and story sessions.

Children's experiences of early years provision before entering the EYFS will reflect the principles outlined above in varying degrees as quality varies. The EYFS (DCSF, 2008) and its current revision (DfE, 2017) applies to children until the end of their

EYFS year and should be the guiding ethos for the EYFS teacher. In some classes, particularly those working with children in the Reception year of the EYFS, this is not evident in practice.

A report published in 2004 by the Association of Teachers and Lecturers, entitled *Inside the Foundation Stage: Recreating the Reception Year*, concluded:

> There is a demonstrable gap between the quality of children's experiences in the Reception classes in our sample, the *second year* of the Foundation Stage, and the quality of their experiences in the *first year* of the Foundation stage in our best nurseries and family centres as highlighted in other research, e.g. Bertram *et al.* 2002; Whalley 1994. (Adams et al., 2004, p. 19)

What constitutes good practice in the Reception year has recently become an area of focus and some contention with the publication of the Teaching Schools Council report on effective primary school teaching (2016), which emphasises preparation for Year 1. The report has been criticised by the early years community for the lack of early years expertise in its authors and the small sample of schools (https://www.early-education. org.uk/press-release/early-years-experts-challenge-recommendation-review-reception). The Early Excellence organisation has now launched its own review of the Reception year intending to collect data from a wider and more varied audience (http://early excellence.com/hundredreview/), *The Hundred Review* (Early Excellence Centre for Inspirational Learning, 2017).

Reflective task

Summarise the main findings of the Cambridge Primary Review Trust report *Children's Cognitive Development and Learning* (Goswami, 2015).
   http://cprtrust.org.uk/wp-content/uploads/2015/02/COMPLETE-REPORT-Goswami-Childrens-Cognitive-Development-and-Learning.pdf
   How would you explain the key points of this report to:

- a Key Stage 2 colleague
- a parent
- a health or other integrated services practitioner?

What would be the key points you would want to communicate to each of these people? Role play a conversation in order to extract key points.
   What are the main recommendations of this report? How would they inform your practice, particularly with children in the Reception year of the EYFS?

The culture of the primary school

Here we consider the culture of the wider primary school and some of its principles, traditions and routines in order to raise awareness of some of the tensions, which can have an impact on EYFS-age children and their teachers, and which are currently particularly pertinent to current divisions regarding Reception class practice.

The statutory documentation for the primary curriculum in England is the National Curriculum (DfE, 2013). As in early years provision the ethos of primary schools can differ considerably, but external factors have impacted on the culture of the English primary school with certain generic consequences.

Some features of the primary school culture include:

- a curriculum presented in discrete subjects
- a curriculum focus on subject knowledge and content
- priority given to core subjects (English, mathematics, science)
- the statutory programmes of study and historical impact of the primary strategies
- standard assessment tasks that inform school league tables
- routines such as assembly, undressing and dressing for physical education (PE), playtimes, school dinners.

Practice in EYFS classes can vary a great deal and we have found it useful in explaining and analysing this with regard to the cultural perspectives model outlined above. In different schools, the meeting of the cultures outlined above will favour some cultural perspectives and associated values more than others, and practice will reflect the dominant ethos.

The Early Years Curriculum Group (EYCG), a nationally recognised group of early years specialists, identified a number of factors that have placed constraints upon the adoption of the early years ethos in EYFS classes (EYCG, 2002).

These factors include:

- the false assumption that the earlier children learn something, the more high achieving they will later become
- fear of the inspection process, which has resulted in a strong emphasis on literacy and numeracy targets
- the top-down pressure of Year 2 Standard Attainment Tests (SATs), which has created inappropriate expectations about early success in particular aspects of literacy and numeracy
- confusion about the principles of early years pedagogy, and an erosion of the practitioner's commitment to the importance of play as a vehicle for learning. (Adams et al., 2004, p. 12)

Reflective task

Consider an EYFS class in a school you are familiar with. To what extent do the three cultures outlined above impact on practice? Draw a diagram representing the interplay of the three cultures outlined in this chapter and the dominant influences in an EYFS class you have experienced.

In mixed-age classes, the pressure to pursue the primary school values and routines is even stronger than with a straight EYFS class. This has been resisted by some teachers who have planned for Key Stage 1 children using some of the principles of early years provision. Attempts to bring the primary provision closer to the early years culture have been made, with the introduction of the Continuing Learning Journey (QCA, 2005) training and, to some extent, the primary curriculum (2009), which reconfigured discrete subjects into areas of learning. England has not been as successful in this as Wales, where the Foundation Phase refers to the 3–7 age phase. The imposition of daily phonics sessions suggested in the *Letters and Sounds* (DCSF, 2007) document discussed below has been the precursor of a shift towards a more formal and traditional approach for primary school teaching, as can be seen in the current National Curriculum (DfE, 2013). Synthesising the child-centred early years ethos with the increasing subject knowledge content requirements of the current primary curriculum poses a challenge for teachers working in mixed-age classes.

Good practice for children in mixed-age classes includes:

- using active learning and play-based activities inside and out to deliver the 5–7 curriculum, including tasks differentiated to provide the full range of challenge
- expecting older children to work independently at times and interacting with younger children in child-initiated play situations
- planning mixed-age group work for some curriculum delivery.

Reflective task

Consider the Qualified Teacher Status Standards (QTS, 2012) (available at https://www.gov.uk/government/publications/teachers-standards).

(Continued)

(Continued)

In 2013 the Early Years Teacher Qualification was introduced for graduates working with children from birth to 3 in non-maintained settings. Compare and contrast the early years Teaching Standards (available at https://www.gov.uk/government/uploads/system/uploads/attachment_data/file/211646/Early_Years_Teachers_Standards.pdf) with the standards for QTS. Analyse the extent to which both sets of standards, including the language adopted, reflect the early years ethos and training needs of an early years teacher, and particularly an EYFS teacher.

Would you like to amend the standards for the early years workforce in any way in the light of this comparison?

School starting age: international comparisons

The statutory age at which a child begins formal schooling varies across the world and has become an area of controversy within the UK. Even within the UK, there are differences, with children in Northern Ireland beginning at 4, while England, Scotland and Wales have official statutory starting ages of 5, though many begin school at 4. In most other European countries, age 6 or 7 is the norm (Sharp, 2002). Debate and discussion centre around the quality of the provision accessed by these young children and its appropriateness for their age and stage of development. In those countries with a later school starting date, most children will have access to some form of pre-school provision in a nursery or kindergarten.

The formality, structure, expectations and demands on the children, of each country's curriculum, whether prescribed or not, vary considerably. When comparing England with the rest of Europe and indeed other countries around the world, it becomes apparent that as a society we impose a statutory curriculum and assessment process on our children at a younger age than most (Bertram and Pascal, 2002; Pascal et al., 2013). However, in international comparisons of later achievement, UK children do not perform significantly better than those starting school at 6 or 7 (OECD PISA, 2015).

The reviews of the primary curriculum (Rose, 2009; Alexander, 2010) have only served to fuel the debate. While Rose suggested an earlier school starting age of 4, Alexander proposed 6 as a more appropriate starting age, saying that anxiety focuses on the fact that, at the age of 5, against the grain of evidence, expert opinion and international practice, children in England leave behind their active, play-based learning and embark on a formal, subject-based curriculum. For many, this process begins at 4. The report continues to say that there is overwhelming evidence that children of this age need structured play, talk and interaction with others, and that this is particularly true for children from disadvantaged homes. (For the key recommendations of the Cambridge Review, see Alexander, 2010, p. 491.) Yet the Labour (1997–2010) government's commendable investment in the early years collided with its 'standards agenda' and downward pressure from Key Stage 1 and 2. It could be suggested that formal schooling at too early an age has been counterproductive, with children from poor homes continuing to be outperformed by their classmates (Save the Children, 2012), as well as the disappointing performance of the UK in international league tables (OECD PISA: 274).

In England, one of the key findings from a review of international research and policy on the issue of relative age highlights that 'pupils who are younger in the year group (known as "Summer borns" in the UK) do less well in attainment tests, are more frequently identified as having special educational needs and are more frequently referred to psychiatric services' (Sharp et al., 2009).

The Coalition government (2010–15) and the current Conservative government (2015 to date), while allowing more flexibility for summer-born children's school starting ages (DfE, 2014), have reinforced and confirmed the focus on early formal schooling, through an emphasis on school readiness and encouraging baseline assessment of children on entry to school (Tickell, 2011; Ofsted, 2014; DfE, 2015).

There has been much concern expressed nationally and internationally regarding the schoolification of children and the pressures of formal schooling at an early age (House, 2011; Save Childhood Movement, 2013; Too Much Too Soon Campaign, 2013).

Sue Palmer has been drawing our attention to wider issues related to childhood in the twenty-first century and the 'dangers' children face in the modern world. Poor diet, lack of exercise and the dangers of television and computers, to name a few of her concerns, are all impacting on the quality of childhood (Palmer, 2015).

A United Nations International Children's Emergency Fund report (UNICEF, 2007) assessed the well-being of children and young people in 21 industrialised countries and gave the UK the lowest ranking. This shocking result provided impetus for improvements to be the focus for those in both education and government. The report of 2013 placed the UK at 16th out of 29 countries and indicated that 'the UK has moved up the league table, but there is still a way to go to be near where we should be' (UNICEF Office of Research, 2013). The most recent report, *Fairness for Children* (UNICEF Office of Research, 2016) focuses on comparisons related to inequality and, while the UK is 7th with regard to income, it only manages 25th for education, 19th for health and 20th for life satisfaction, placing the UK 14th in an average rank across all dimensions of inequality.

The Good Childhood Report was a landmark report for the Children's Society, looking at the condition of childhood in the UK, drawing our attention to the higher levels of child poverty and lower levels of well-being experienced by children in the UK compared with their counterparts in Europe (Layard and Dunn, 2009). Subsequent reports from the Children's Society continue to document the issues and offer suggestions for improvement for policy makers (The Children's Society, 2016).

With children in the UK attending school from the age of 4 and among the youngest in Europe, there are significant implications and responsibilities for the EYFS teacher to ensure that the children's needs are appropriately met and that they are prepared for the pressures of the modern world. While protecting children from real risks, we must be careful to ensure that we do not produce children who are 'wrapped in cotton wool' with little resilience or ability to cope in the modern world (Gill, 2009; Solly, 2015).

Creative and innovative practice, based on first-hand experience, which enables children's self-esteem as well as social and emotional learning to develop and thrive, must be key.

The world-renowned preschools of Reggio Emilia in Northern Europe, the Forest Schools of Scandinavian countries, Te Whāriki, the curriculum of New Zealand and, more recently, the Finnish school system, with their emphasis on the social and creative needs of young children, have all influenced the development of recent practice within the UK.

Good practice includes:

- planning for children's developmental needs, abilities and interests, whatever the setting
- using the curriculum in a flexible way to ensure that children's needs and interests are met
- practitioners who use their developing knowledge of the experiences from other countries to extend their own thinking and allow this to impact on the experiences they plan for children
- challenging our own thinking about the needs and interests of children
- allowing children to take the lead – this requires a confidence and underpinning understanding of child development
- listening to children, verbally and through observation, in order to create an environment that allows for creativity.

The importance of a play-based curriculum

Play, indoors and outside, is generally recognised by early years practitioners to be of crucial importance. It is well researched, documented and part of early years pedagogy. High involvement levels and the maximising of learning through child-initiated experiences are supported though the work of Ferre Laevers (2005). The statutory curricula have placed high importance on using play as the means through which children learn. The original EYFS document (DCSF, 2008) included 'Play and Exploration' as one of the key commitments within the learning and development theme and recognised its importance: 'Children's play reflects their wide-ranging and varied interests and preoccupations. In their play children learn at their highest level. Play with peers is important for children's development.' The revised and current EYFS documents (DfE, 2012a, 2014, 2017) describe 'playing and exploring' as one of the three 'characteristics of effective teaching and learning' for children of this age. Alongside 'active learning' and 'creating and thinking critically' play is recognised as an important way in which children learn. In planning for children's learning and development, EYFS teachers are required to ensure that this is translated into practice. Further guidance is available in *Development Matters in the Early Years Foundation Stage*, non-statutory guidance material supporting practitioners in implementing the statutory requirements of the EYFS (Early Education, 2012). Recent research reinforces the need to support children's learning through play and active learning inside and outdoors (Goswami, 2015), with the development of positive interactions that support children's independent play and thinking (Fisher, 2016).

International influences, referred to above, reinforce the role of play and follow the interests of children in order to maximise learning.

The well-trained early years teacher will recognise its importance in delivering all areas of the curriculum and resist those top-down pressures associated with a concentration on literacy and numeracy. At the beginning of their school career, before they have acquired the formal skills of reading and writing drawn upon by so many primary lessons, the EYFS requires a pedagogy of its own that builds on what children can do and develops fundamental skills in a meaningful context. The process of planning meaningful learning experiences that cannot, by their nature, rely on the skills of reading and writing, which have not as yet been fully mastered, presents a challenge to many trainee and experienced teachers.

It must also be recognised that children require a balance of child- and adult-initiated experiences in order for their learning to be maximised (Siraj-Blatchford et al., 2002; Sylva et al., 2003). There are skills and concepts that need to be taught directly to children, through the support of a knowledgeable adult who has provided a suitable environment to support learning through play, while at the same time scaffolding children's learning in an appropriate way. Interactions in a well-organised and planned learning environment are essential. 'Sustained shared thinking' occurs when two or more individuals 'work together' in an intellectual way to solve a problem, clarify a concept, evaluate an activity, extend a narrative, etc. 'Both parties must contribute to the thinking and it must develop and extend the understanding' (Sylva et al., 2003). This concept requires highly skilled adults to support children in an appropriate way (Ofsted, 2015). The challenge for EYFS teachers, and perhaps particularly when working in a mixed-age class, is to enable staff members to contribute to these interactions within the areas of continuous provision. An emphasis only on direct teaching to small groups, or the whole class, will miss the opportunities for spontaneous interactions at the most relevant time for the child. In mixed-age classes, it can be all too tempting to allocate support for the EYFS children to those least qualified, or in some cases to volunteers. Challenges to provide an appropriate play-based curriculum, indoors and outside, may also include the lack of resources and the size of the space available to many EYFS classes. Where there is no access to an outdoor area enabling continuous free flow of movement in both environments, teachers must think creatively in order to meet the need for daily access to an outdoor environment (White, 2011). Developments in brain research reinforce the importance of movement to support cognitive development and should not be underestimated (Daly and O'Connor, 2015; Goswami, 2015).

Good practice includes:

• a well-planned, organised and resourced environment – indoors and outside – appropriate to the developmental needs of children
• practitioners who plan to extend and widen children's experiences, while enabling children to follow their own interests
• practitioners who engage, extend and develop creativity and critical thinking across the curriculum, allowing children to be independent in a safe, yet challenging environment.

Early reading

Children bring a variety of early reading experiences to the EYFS class in school. Some children may have few books in the home, while others have a whole 'library' of books in their bedrooms. Whatever their home circumstances, most children will have some experience of print in the environment, on television or a computer screen, and those attending nursery or pre-school will have accessed books in these settings. Learning to read is a complex process and can be challenging for those with little prior experience of books or a secure language base on which to build.

The most appropriate age and method through which to teach children to read has long been a subject for heated debate. To date, there is no significant research that suggests that starting reading earlier produces long-term benefits (Suggate, 2009) and, as suggested above, those countries who have later school starting ages do not suffer significantly in terms of reading competence – quite the opposite (Ofsted, 2003). Following the *Independent Review of the Teaching of Early Reading* (Rose, 2006), teachers are currently strongly encouraged to adopt a 'synthetic phonics' approach and use the 'simple view of reading'. This approach can be used inappropriately, to introduce children to formal reading before they are developmentally ready, detracting from children's enjoyment of reading and adding to the pressures of formal schooling at too early an age (House, 2011; Save Childhood Movement, 2013; Too Much Too Soon Campaign, 2013).

EYFS staff with weighty responsibility for the introduction of children to statutory education, and in particular for the teaching of early reading, must be mindful that this experience can significantly impact on children's lifelong attitude to school.

Introducing children to fundamental skills is a complex process and it can be too easy for young children to feel like a failure before they even begin Key Stage 1. Pace and appropriateness of delivery are crucial, and differentiation for different stages of child development is imperative.

As Rose (2006) suggests: 'the introduction of phonic work should always be a matter for principled, professional judgement based on structured observations and assessments of children's capabilities'. Parents want their children to succeed in school and can unwittingly communicate unrealistic expectations to young children of their potential achievements, 'now they are at big school'. Following a pilot in 2011, the introduction of a Year 1 phonics screening check has increased potential top-down pressures on schools, to introduce children to reading as soon as possible so they will perform well in the check (DfE, 2012b).

EYFS staff should ensure that 'best practice for beginner readers provides them with a rich curriculum that fosters all four interdependent strands of language: speaking, listening, reading and writing' (Rose, 2006).

Good practice includes:

- teachers who protect children from the pressures of 'learning to read' before they are developmentally ready to do so
- a stimulating environment with an attractive reading area, containing a wide variety of reading materials, as well as books, story sacks and materials for storytelling
- adults who model the reading process and engage children in enjoyable reading experiences, including 'talk' about books and stories.

Different curricula will come and go but good practice will continue to require a focus on child development and provision that is appropriate for individual children.

Work in school

Early years students and practitioners are often in the minority in school situations and find it difficult to access information and reassurance on aspects of good quality early years provision.

These are some of the questions students frequently ask us.

Play

Student: I have 30 children in my early years foundation stage class. I don't know how I can support them all to follow their own interests.

Mentor: If the classroom is organised into areas of well-resourced continuous provision, then children can follow their own interests on a daily basis, accessing the areas and resources they need. The child or group of children who are interested in a birthday or wedding experienced by one of the group, for example, can be given access to the resources to support their role play.

Children can be grouped for larger projects, according to their interest in a particular idea, event or theme. This may need to involve adults planning with the children, on an outing or visit, for example.

Reading

Student: We are told that children should practise their developing reading and writing skills independently, but I'm not sure how I can encourage them to do this.

Mentor: Children do need to be directly taught certain knowledge and skills, which the teacher plans for according to the ability and needs of individuals and groups of children. However, children then need to be able to practise independently, in an interactive way that allows them to follow their own interests and needs. Reading and writing resources available to children in areas of provision around the classroom enable children to then use the skills they have been taught in play scenarios, thus reinforcing and developing them. Children's involvement in their self-chosen activities is generally at a much higher level than during teacher-initiated activities and you will see that this allows a deeper level of learning.

(Continued)

Formative assessment

Student: How can I manage the formative assessment process? The problem always seems to be: how can I treat so many children as individuals? I understand how important this is but – how can I realistically do this?

Mentor: Formative assessment should be an integral part of everyday planning as, unless you know what the children can do, you will be unable to plan their next steps. In adult-led learning experiences you should decide how you are going to assess learning. Sometimes this may be possible by annotating a piece of writing, a drawing or model after the session. Ephemeral objects can be photographed and the photo annotated. Often you will need to make observation notes during an activity, as it will be the children's comments that reveal what they know and any misconceptions. It is also important to record observation notes in children's free flow play as it is in this context that they will demonstrate conceptual knowledge, skills and information that they have assimilated. A notebook or Post-its® are suitable methods of recording. They are working documents so you can develop your own abbreviations for speed and it is important to train all adults working in the classroom to undertake formative assessment. They will need some training from you on what to look for and how to record it, but the pay off will be worth the time spent. Frequency and the detail included in observations will vary depending on your focus at any one time and the children you may wish to target. Recording significant achievements will enable next steps in children's learning to be planned and act as evidence for summative assessment. Sharing these with children and parents will enhance the process.

Balance of adult- and child-led activities

Student: How can I convince my primary colleagues of the importance of child-initiated learning? I think this is essential but I find it difficult to explain this to people who have more experience than I have. I don't want them to think I'm being impertinent.

(Continued)

(Continued)

Mentor: Well it's not a simple process of 'either/or'. Explain that *Researching Effective Pedagogy in the Early Years* (*REPEY*; Siraj-Blatchford et al., 2002) has underlined the importance of both learning activities involving direct teaching and free flow play situations in a well-designed learning environment. Planned learning experiences give children the opportunity to learn specific skills, concepts and knowledge planned by the teacher to ensure curriculum coverage and differentiated to meet children's specific needs informed by formative assessment. This is complemented by children's free flow play. Children's motivation in this context will be high and they will rehearse skills and knowledge recently gained as well as exploring concepts and following their own lines of thought and creativity. In both contexts the important consideration is the quality of the learning experiences provided and the skill of the adult in developing critical thinking skills with sensitive and challenging adult interventions.

We argue that effective pedagogy in the early years involves a balance of the first two approaches, both the kind of interaction traditionally associated with the term 'teaching', and also the provision of instructive learning environments and routines. We argue that where young children have freely chosen to play within an instructive learning environment, adult interventions may be especially effective. (Siraj-Blatchford et al., 2002, p. 12)

For more information on all the issues above refer to the *REPEY* (Siraj-Blatchford et al., 2002) report on organisation (p. 12).

Developing an evidence-based philosophy

Earlier in this chapter, we used a cultural perspectives approach to consider differences in ethos that underpin practice variations in EYFS classes. EYFS teachers can approach their role with more confidence and clarity if they have considered their own values and beliefs and how these will influence the ethos, guiding principles, behaviours and rules they wish to adopt with EYFS-age children.

It is important to inform a personal philosophy with evidence in order to support practice with rigour. There is a wealth of existing research on matters related to aspects of provision for children of 3–5 years of age in England. Additionally, a range of research from other countries can provide an interesting comparative view (Bertram and Pascal, 2002). Some starting points to engage with this research can be found in the reference list below.

Classroom teachers are increasingly completing their own classroom research, in order to inform their philosophy and improve quality of experience for young children. Taking the 'teacher as researcher' approach in your EYFS class will enhance your own understanding of the issues particular to your context. The Centre for the Use of Research and Evidence in Education (CUREE) produces materials to support practitioners in developing evidence-based practice.

Reflective task

List some of the important values and beliefs that will guide your personal philosophy when working with EYFS-aged children. Can you give any examples of when you have applied any of your beliefs or values in practice, or seen them applied? Did this confirm your philosophy?

Summary

In this chapter, we have introduced the reader to some of the controversial issues related to teaching 3– to 5-year-olds in EYFS classes in school. This included the tensions between formal and play-based learning and the importance of protecting an active approach to learning for children in mixed-age classes.

For young children to develop a positive disposition to school, their experience in the classroom needs to be exciting and inspiring. The EYFS teacher requires creative and innovative approaches to retain children's motivation and interest. Well-matched learning events, tailored to children's developmental achievements, are essential and this requires a sound knowledge of child development. The wealth of existing research can be drawn upon to develop an evidence base to underpin practice. Inspiration can be gained from the study of international perspectives on early years education.

The website related to this book gives further suggestions for web-based activities and reading (https://study.sagepub.com/cooper3).

Questions for discussion

- What training do you think would support potential EYFS teachers to induct new children into school?
- Consider the relevant research referred to above regarding school starting ages. What age do you believe is most appropriate for children to start formal schooling?
- How can we promote a lifelong love of reading? What strategies should teachers deploy in order to develop enjoyment as well as skills in early reading?
- How would you organise the environment in a mixed-age class to support active and play-based learning?
- It has been identified that the development of thinking skills is an area that needs further development in early years provision (Siraj-Blatchford et al., 2002). This has been underlined as vital in the report published by the Cambridge Review Trust (Goswami, 2015). What would you do in your own classroom to ensure the engagement of children in experiences that promote critical thinking?

Further reading

Fisher, J. (2011) 'Building on the early years foundation stage: Developing good practice for transition into Key Stage 1', *Early Years: An International Journal of Research and Development*, 31 (1): 31–42. doi: 10.1080/09575146.2010.512557.
Early years foundation stage staff need to consider the importance of transition into Key Stage 1.

House, R. (2011) *Too Much, Too Soon? Early Learning and the Erosion of Childhood*. Stroud: Hawthorn Press.
Discussion from a range of highly respected educators related to the issue of early learning and the erosion of childhood.

Melhuish, E. (2010) 'Why children, parents and home learning are important', in K. Sylva, E. Melhuish, P. Sammons, I. Siraj-Blatchford and B. Taggart (eds), *Early Childhood Matters: Evidence from the Effective Pre-school and Primary Education Project*. London: Routledge. pp. 95–114.
This research emphasises the impact of home and parental interest in supporting children's achievements at school and will support early years practitioners in understanding the importance of their work with parents.

Moylett, H. and Stewart, N. (2012) *Understanding the Revised Early Years Foundation Stage.* London: Early Education, the British Association for Early Childhood Education.
A useful overview of the issues involved in delivering the early years foundation stage.

Pugh, G. and Duffy, B. (eds) (2013) *Contemporary Issues in the Early Years*, sixth edition. London: Sage.
This book includes chapters written by several leading authors on current issues related to policy and research, practice and the workforce, and provides a sound insight into important influences on the current field of early years work.

Other recommended texts

Linked to topics of interest, the following readings have been chosen because the authors are among the leading experts in the field.

Generic issues affecting early years provision

Brooker, L., Rogers, S., Ellis, D., Hallet, E. and Robert-Holmes, G. (2010) *Practitioners' Experiences of the EYFS*. London: DfE.

Garrick, R., Bath, C., Dunn, K., Maconochie H., Willis, B. and Wolstenholme, C. (2010) *Children's Experiences of the Early Years Foundation Stage*. London: DfE.

Goswami, U. (2015) *Children's Cognitive Development and Learning*. York: Cambridge Primary Review Trust.

Office for Standards in Education (Ofsted) (2011) *The Impact of the Early Years Foundation Stage (EYFS)*. London: Ofsted.

Sylva, K., Melhuish, E., Sammons, P., Siraj-Blatchford, I. and Taggart, B. (2008) *Final Report from the Primary Phase: Pre-school, School, and Family Influences on Children's Development during Key Stage 2 (Age 7–11), Effective Pre-School and Primary Education 3–11 Project (EPPE 3–11)*. Research Report DCSF RR061. London: DCSF.

Sylva, K., Melhuish, E., Sammons, P., Siraj-Blatchford, I. and Taggart, B. (2014) *Students' Educational and Developmental Outcomes at Age 16: Effective Pre-school, Primary and Secondary Education (EPPSE 3-16) Project*. Report DFE-RR354. London: DfE.

Sylva, K., Melhuish, E., Sammons, P., Siraj, I. and Taggart, B. (2015) *Effective Pre-school, Primary and Secondary Education Project (EPPSE 3-16+): How Pre-school*

Influences Children and Young People's Attainment and Developmental Outcomes Over Time. Research Brief. London: DfE.

Parents and home influences

Department for Children, Schools and Families (DCSF) (2008) *Parents as Partners in Early Learning Project (PPEL)*. London: DCSF.

Whalley, M. (2007*) Involving Parents in their Children's Learning*. London: Sage.
Pen Green Children's Centre has completed some seminal work in teaching parents about child development and developing parents as partners in their children's learning. This book explains the work with parents in detail.

A play-based curriculum

Bilton, H. (2010) *Outdoor Learning in the Early Years*. Abingdon: Routledge.
A useful book to support setting up and extending outside provision and developing outdoor learning.

Brooker, L. and Edwards, S. (eds) (2010) *Engaging Play*. Maidenhead: McGraw-Hill.

Bruce, T. (2004) *Developing Learning in Early Childhood (0–8)*. London: Sage.
This book includes practical ideas for supporting early active learning experiences.

Fisher, J. (2016) *Interacting or Interfering? Improving Interactions in the Early Years*. Milton Keynes: Open University Press.

Goddard Blythe, S. (2005) *The Well-balanced Child*. Stroud: Hawthorn Press.

Goswami, U. (2015) *Children's Cognitive Development and Learning*. York: Cambridge Primary Review Trust.

Lindon, J. (2011) *Too Safe for Their Own Good? Helping Children Learn about Risk and Lifeskills*. London: NCB.
Reading this book will help you to consider your own position with regard to balancing risk and challenge in children's lives.

Moyles, J. (1989) *Just Playing?* Maidenhead: Open University Press.
This book will help you to pursue the ideas introduced above about the value of play. It includes sections on play and progress to aid record keeping and the tracking of children's learning.

Outdoor play and Forest Schools

The following texts provide a rich source of information around the justification for learning outside and the development of a Forest School approach in early years.

Bilton, H. (2010) *Outdoor Play in the Early Years: Management and Innovation.* London: David Fulton.

Daly, A. and O'Connor, A. (2015) *Understanding Physical Development: Linking Bodies and Minds.* London: Routledge.

Knight, S. (2011) *Risk and Adventure in Early Years Outdoor Play: Learning from Forest Schools.* London: Sage.

Knight, S. (2013) *Forest Schools and Outdoor Learning in the Early Years*, second edn. London: Sage.

Knight, S. (2013) *Forest School for All.* London: Sage

Ouvry, M. (2003) *Exercising Muscles and Minds: Outdoor Play and the Early Years Curriculum.* London: Jessica Kingsley.

Solly, K.S. (2015) *Risk, Challenge and Adventure in the Early Years: A Practical Guide to Exploring and Extending Learning Outdoors.* Abingdon: Routledge.

Tovey, H. (2007) *Playing Outdoors: Spaces and Places, Risk and Challenge.* Maidenhead: Open University Press.

White, J. (2011) *Outdoor Provision in the Early Years.* London: Sage.

Early literacy

Bayley, R. and Palmer, S. (2008) *Foundations of Literacy*, third edn. London: Continuum Books.
A practical book full of inspired ideas for planning literacy in the early years.

Whitehead, M. (2010) *Language and Literacy in the Early Years 0–7.* London: Sage.
This book gives both a theoretical and practical perspective on teaching literacy for enjoyment, across the full early years age range.

Additional websites

Foundation Years website: www.foundationyears.org.uk

Gov.uk early years website:

https://www.gov.uk/government/publications/early-years-foundation-stage-frame-work--2

https://www.gov.uk/topic/schools-colleges-childrens-services/early-years

References

Adams, S., Alexander, E., Drummond, M.J. and Moyles, J. (2004) *Inside the Early Years Foundation Stage: Recreating the Early Years Foundation Stage Year*. London: Association of Teachers and Lecturers.

Alexander, R. (ed.) (2010) *Children, their World, their Education: Final Report and Recommendations of the Cambridge Primary Review*. Abingdon: Routledge.

Bertram, T. and Pascal C. (2002) *Early Years Education: An International Perspective*. Birmingham: Centre for Research in Early Childhood.

Daly, A. and O'Connor, A. (2015) *Understanding Physical Development: Linking Bodies and Minds*. London: Routledge.

Department for Children, Schools and Families (DCSF) (2007) *Letters and Sounds*. London: DCSF.

Department for Children, Schools and Families (DCSF) (2008) *Early Years Foundation Stage*. London: DCSF.

Department for Education (DfE) (2012a) *Revised Statutory Framework for the Early Years Foundation Stage*. London: DfE.

Department for Education (DfE) (2012b) 'Phonics screening check'. Available at: https://www.gov.uk/government/collections/phonics-screening-check-administration.

Department for Education (DfE) (2013) *The National Curriculum in England: Key Stages 1 and 2 Framework Document*. Available at: www.gov.uk/government/publications.

Department for Education (DfE) (2014) 'Admission of summerborn in school'. Available at: https://www.gov.uk/government/publications/summer-born-children-school-admission.

Department for Education (DfE) (2015) 'Reception baseline assessment'. Available at: https://www.gov.uk/guidance/reception-baseline-assessment-guide-to-signing-up-your-school.

Department for Education (DfE) (2017) *Statutory Framework for the Early Years Foundation Stage: Setting the Standards for Learning, Development and Care for Children from Birth to Five*. London: DfE.

Department for Education and Skills (DfES) (2004) *Choice for Parents, the Best Start for Children: A Ten Year Strategy for Childcare*. London: HMSO.

Desforges, C. (2003) *The Impact of Parental Involvement, Parental Support and Family Education on Pupil Achievements and Adjustment: A Literature Review*. Research Report RR433. London: DfES.

Early Education, the British Association for Early Childhood Education (2012) *Development Matters in the Early Years Foundation Stage*. London: BAECE. Available at: www.foundation years.org.uk/files/2012/03/Development-Matters-FINAL-PRINT-AMENDED.pdf.

Early Excellence Centre for Inspirational Learning (2017) *The Hundred Review of Reception Practice*. Available at http://earlyexcellence.com/wp-content/uploads/2017/05/EX_TheHundredReview_Report_.pdf (accessed 17 November 2017).

Early Years Curriculum Group (EYCG) (2002) *Onwards and Upwards: Building on the Early Years Foundation Stage*. Oxford: Early Years Curriculum Group.

Fabian, H. (2002) *Children Starting School*. London: David Fulton.

Fabian, H. and Dunlop, A.W. (2002) *Transitions in the Early Years: Debating Continuity and Progression for Children in Early Education*. London: RoutledgeFalmer.

Fisher, J. (2016) *Interacting or Interfering? Improving Interactions in the Early Years*. Milton Keynes: Open University Press.

Gill, T. (2009) *No Fear: Growing Up in a Risk Averse Society*. London: Calouste Gulbenkian Foundation.

Goswami, U. (2015) *Children's Cognitive Development and Learning*. York: Cambridge Primary Review Trust.

House, R. (2011) *Too Much, Too Soon? Early Learning and the Erosion of Childhood*. Stroud: Hawthorn Press.

Laevers, F. (ed.) (2005) *Well-being and Involvement in Care Settings: A Process-oriented Self-evaluation Instrument*. Leuven: Research Centre for Experiential Education, Leuven University.

Layard, R. and Dunn, J. (2009) *The Good Childhood*. London: Penguin Books.

Margetts, K. (2002) 'Early transition and adjustment and children's adjustment after six years of schooling', *European Early Childhood Education Research Journal*, 17(3): 309–24.

OECD PISA (2015) Organisation for Economic Cooperation and Development Programme for International Student Assessment. Available at https://www.oecd.org/pisa/pisa-2015-results-in-focus.pdf (accessed 17 November 2017).

Office for Standards in Education Publications (2003) *The Education of Six-Year-Olds in England, Denmark and Finland; An International Comparative Study*. Available at: www.educationengland.org.uk/documents/pdfs/2003-ofsted-six-year-olds-comparative.pdf

Office for Standards in Education (Ofsted) (2014) *Are You Ready? Good Practice in School Readiness*. London: Ofsted.

Office for Standards in Education (Ofsted) (2015) *Teaching and Play in the Early Years. A Good Practice Survey to Explore Perceptions of Teaching and Play in the Early Years*. London: Ofsted.

Palmer, S. (2015) *Toxic Childhood: How the Modern World is Damaging Our Children and What We Can Do About it*. London: Orion.

Pascal C., Bertram, T., Delaney, S. and Nelson, C. (2013) *A Comparison of International Childcare Systems*. Birmingham: Centre for Research in Early Childhood.

Qualifications and Curriculum Authority (QCA) (2005) *Continuing the Learning Journey*. London: QCA.

Rose, J. (2006) *Independent Review of the Teaching of Early Reading*. London: DfES.

Rose, J. (2009) *Independent Review of the Primary Curriculum: Final Report*. London: DCSF.

Sammons, P., Sylva, K., Melhuish, E, Siraj-Blackford, I, Taggart, B., Grabbe, Y. and Barreau, S. (2007) *Summary Report: Influences on Children's Attainment and Progress in Key Stage 2: Cognitive Outcomes in Year 5: Effective Pre-school and Primary Education 3–11 Project (EPPE 3–11)*. Research Report RR828. London: DfES.

Save Childhood Movement (2013) 'About the movement'. Available at: www.savechildhood.net/about-the-movement/.

Save the Children (2012) *Closing the Achievement Gap in England's Secondary Schools*. London: Save the Children.

Sharp, C. (2002) *School Starting Age: European Policy and Recent Research*. Slough: NFER.

Sharp, C., George, N., Sargent, C., O'Donnell, S. and Heron, M. (2009) *International Thematic Probe: The Influence of Relative Age on Learner Attainment and Development.* Slough: NFER.

Siraj-Blatchford, I., Sylva, K., Muttocks, S., Gilden, R. and Bell, D. (2002) *Researching Effective Pedagogy in the Early Years (REPEY).* Nottingham: DfES.

Solly, K.S. (2015) *Risk, Challenge and Adventure in the Early Years: A Practical Guide to Exploring and Extending Learning Outdoors.* Abingdon: Routledge

Suggate, S.P. (2009) 'School entry age and reading achievement', *International Journal of Educational Research*, 48 (3): 151–61.

Sylva, K., Melhuish, E., Sammons, P., Siraj-Blatchford, I. and Taggart, B. (2003) *Effective Provision of Pre-School Education (EPPE).* Nottingham: DfES.

Teaching Schools Council (2016) *Effective Primary Teaching Practice Report 2016.* Available at: www.tscouncil.org.uk/resources/effective-primary-teaching-practice-2016/.

The Children's Society (2016) *The Good Childhood Report.* Available at: www.childrenssociety. org.uk/what-we-do/research/well-being.

Tickell, C. (2011) *The Early Years: Foundations for Life, Health and Learning.* London: DfE. Available at: https://www.gov.uk/government/uploads/system/uploads/attachment_data/file/180919/DFE-00177-2011.pdf.

Too Much Too Soon Campaign (2013) 'About the campaign'. Available at: www.toomuch-toosoon.org/about.html.

United Nations International Children's Emergency Fund (UNICEF) (2007) *Child Poverty in Perspective: An Overview of Child Well-being in Rich Countries. Innocenti Report Card 7.* Florence: UNICEF Innocenti Research Centre.

United Nations International Children's Emergency Fund (UNICEF) Office of Research (2013) *Child Well-being in Rich Countries: A Comparative Overview, Innocenti Report Card 11.* Florence: UNICEF Office of Research.

United Nations International Children's Emergency Fund (UNICEF) Office of Research (2016) *Fairness for Children. A League Table of Inequality in Child Well-Being in Rich Countries, Innocenti Report Card 13.* Florence: UNICEF Office of Research.

Whalley, M. (1994) *Learning to Be Strong.* London: Hodder and Stoughton.

White, J. (2011) *Outdoor Provision in the Early Years.* London: Sage.

Websites

Centre for the Use of Research and Evidence in Education (CUREE): www.curee.co.uk/

Forest Schools: www.forestschools.com/

OECD: www.oecd.org/home/

Programme for International Student Assessment (PISA): www.oecd.org/pisa/

Reggio Emilia: http://zerosei.comune.re.it/inter/reggiochildren.htm

Te Whāriki: www.educate.ece.govt.nz/learning/curriculumAndLearning/TeWhariki.aspx

The Children's Society: www.childrenssociety.org.uk, *Good Childhood Report 2016*

www.childrenssociety.org.uk/sites/default/files/pcr090_mainreport_web.pdf

UNICEF UK Office of Research Innocenti Report Card 11 2013: *Child Well-being in Rich Countries*:

A comparative overview: https://353ld710iigr2n4po7k4kgvv-wpengine.netdna-ssl.com/wp-content/uploads/2013/04/FINAL_RC11-ENG-LORES-fnl2.pdf

UNICEF UK Office of Research Innocenti Report Card 12 2014: *Children of the Recession: The Impact of the Economic Crisis on Child Well-Being in Rich Countries*: https://www.unicef-irc.org/publications/pdf/rc12-eng-web.pdf

UNICEF UK Office of Research Innocenti Report Card 13 2016: *Fairness for Children: A League Table of Inequality in Child Well-Being in Rich Countries*: https://www.unicef-irc.org/publications/pdf/RC13_eng.pdf

8

Inclusion and Special Educational Needs

Sue Soan

By the end of this chapter you should:

- have developed your own views and beliefs about inclusion, inclusive education and special educational needs
- have an understanding of how the inclusion and special educational needs agendas in the United Kingdom and in England in particular have evolved
- be able to demonstrate your knowledge and understanding of the current *Special Educational Needs and Disability Code of Practice: 0–25 Years* (DfE and DoH, 2015) (England)
- be confident to begin to implement in a classroom your responsibilities as stated in the *Special Educational Needs and Disability Code of Practice: 0–25 Years* (DfE and DoH, 2015) (England).

Introduction

This chapter will focus on issues relating to the areas of special educational needs (SEN) and inclusion. Commencing with an overview detailing how and why SEN legislation and practice have evolved into their current forms the chapter will define and explore the concept of inclusion and critically analyse the development of inclusive education in England from the mid-1990s. The disparities between ideology and practice will also be considered in relation to the impact these can have on teachers who make daily decisions for the children they teach. These discussions intend to help you begin to develop your own views and beliefs about these complex issues.

The next section of this chapter will detail information about England's current special educational needs and disability (SEND) legislation and policy, and provide you with an underpinning knowledge of how, as a primary school teacher, you are expected to meet the needs of pupils with special educational needs. You will be encouraged throughout the chapter to reflect on and consider issues relating to SEN, inclusion and inclusive education through reflective tasks, school-based scenarios and discussion questions to help you gain your own understanding of these issues.

An overview of SEN since the late 1970s–2014 in England and Wales

Although post 1990 influences are vital to understand it is important to acknowledge the significant role that the Warnock Report (DES, 1978), the 1981 Education Act (DfES, 1981) and the 1988 Education Act (DES, 1988) and the subsequent introduction of the National Curriculum (DfES/QCA, 1989) had on developing the education of children with SEN more in line with ideologies of equity and social justice (see Chapter 1 (Shaw and Shirley), which discusses the history of education policy and practice).

The Warnock Report (DES, 1978) was a significant catalyst of change and has had a long standing impact on policy and practice, notably moving terminology away from a purely medical to what the Committee felt was a more social model of disability, with the introduction of the term *special educational needs (SEN)* instead of the use of 'within child' deficient labels such as 'handicapped' and 'cripple'. The report stated that where and whenever possible children should be educated in a mainstream setting (as long as it was not to the detriment of other children and the child's additional needs could be met), encouraging to some extent both integration and inclusion over segregated provision. Interestingly, it is also this report that offered the frequently quoted statistic that the population of children with SEN is one in five pupils (20 per cent) (Armstrong and Squires, 2012), with 18 per cent of these attending mainstream schools and 2 per cent educated in special schools.

The 1981 Education Act quickly implemented the findings from the Warnock Report and it was this that introduced the Statement of Special Educational Needs and also made the teacher in the classroom responsible for both identifying and providing for those children with SEN (DES, 1981, section 5c). The Act also made Local Authorities responsible for both carrying out assessments and writing the Statements of SEN and providing the additional and different resources, whilst also giving parents the right to appeal against the decisions about their child's Statement of SEN.

Although the 1988 Education Reform Act (DES, 1988), and the subsequent introduction of the National Curriculum (DfES/QCA, 1989), was not specifically about pupils with SEN, it did have some unintended consequences that impacted on them quite specifically. As Squires (2012, p. 15) highlights, these consequences included:

- the ability of children to move between mainstream and special schools with greater ease because all were following the same curriculum
- the 'return to "Payments by Results" scenario for children with SEN' because of the introduction of quasi-market forces (parental choice of schools for their children) and the introduction of Standard Attainment Tests (SATs) (driving up standards agenda)
- the move to Office for Standards in Education (Ofsted) inspections, which at the time judged the individual ability of teachers, presenting a greater challenge to have pupils with either emotional, social or behavioural needs in their classes.

Table 8.1 Segregation to inclusion

Segregation	A totally separate special school for children with special educational needs where children's difficulties are considered 'within-child' and follow the deficit/medical model of disability.
Integration	A system where a child with a special educational need can be integrated into a mainstream if they can fit into the school: the child in this instance has to fit into the system already in place.
	Three points to remember are:
	1. The focus remains on the child's 'deficit' (medical model).
	2. The child is provided with support to access the curriculum and the school environment that is already in place.
	3. The child has to fit into the system in place (Soan, 2004, p. 7).
Inclusion	Inclusion has its roots in the social model of disability and is a process not a fixed state. Originally based on place (i.e. special versus mainstream school) inclusion is now seen in a much broader way than just SEN and placement. Thomas describes inclusion as now being 'a three dimensional terrain that now incorporates a more extensive spectrum of concerns and discourses about the benefits that come from valuing diversity' (Thomas, 2013, p. 474). There is still no single definition that everyone agrees on.
Inclusive education	This now refers to the education of all children and there are current arguments that suggest inclusive education has to be further developed 'on knowledge of the damaging consequences of inequality, relative poverty and contrastive judgment in schools. [That] inclusive education policy and practice has to build more firmly and conspicuously on knowledge about the benefits of social connection, communities of learning and social capital' (Thomas, 2013, p. 474). Florian and Linklater (2010, p. 385) also recognise however that to achieve this, teachers have to be able to enhance all children's learning and not just attainment and curriculum outcomes.
Full inclusion	Some educationalists, such as Booth (Booth et al., 2000), see full inclusion as the goal to achieve. Hodkinson (2016, p. 93) describes it as where 'all children should be educated together in terms of location, need, curriculum and attitudes, with no tolerance of or justification for the maintenance of a separate segregated system of education'.

Thus, it is perhaps not surprising that by the end of the 1980s integrated provision did not make significant changes to the education provision of children with SEN. Nevertheless, in hindsight, a bridge between segregation and inclusive education, some suggest, was achieved (Hodkinson, 2016). Also there was a shift in ideology and policy from segregation to integration, with easier movement between special and mainstream schools (Table 8.1).

Segregation to inclusion

The 1990s saw the 1993 Education Act (part III) require the first Code of Practice for children with SEN to be written. This Code of Practice, which came into effect on 1 September 1994, set out a five-stage assessment approach as guidance in an effort to help schools and Local Authorities 'match provision to need' (DfE, 1994, p. ii). Local Education Authorities (LEAs), schools, health services and social services all had to have regard to the Code when working with children with SEN. The areas of need identified as requiring special educational provision were:

• learning difficulties
• specific learning difficulties (e.g. dyslexia)
• emotional and behavioural difficulties (EBD)
• physical difficulties
• sensory impairments (hearing and visual difficulties)
• speech and language difficulties
• (some) medical conditions.

The special educational needs coordinator (SENCO) role was specifically mentioned, as was working with other professionals (cooperation), partnership with parents and involving the child in their assessment and provision. It is also interesting to note that apart from changes to the format of sentences and age groups the definition of SEN has not been amended since this original Code of Practice (DfE, 1994) (Table 8.2).

Then in 1997 *Excellence for All Children* was published and this gave governmental support (New Labour, 1997–2010) to the inclusion agenda encouraging mainstream schools to meet the needs of all pupils (DfEE, 1997). Operational forms of commitment to inclusion were strengthened by the New Labour government as the twenty-first century began. In 2001 the Education Act of 1996 was amended by 'The Special Educational Needs and Disability Act' (SENDA) (HMSO, 2001) and enabled the transformation of the statutory framework into a positive endorsement of inclusion. The publication of guidance such as *Inclusive Schooling: Children with Special Educational Needs* (DfES, 2001a) and the revised *Special Educational Needs Code of*

Table 8.2 Definition of special educational needs (England and Wales)

A child has special educational needs if he or she has a *learning difficulty* that calls for *special educational provision* to be made for him or her.

A child has a *learning difficulty* if he or she:

(a) has a significantly greater difficulty in learning than the majority of children of the same age
(b) has a disability that either prevents or hinders the child from making use of educational facilities of a kind provided for children of the same age in schools within the area of the Local Education Authority
(c) is under 5 and falls within the definition at (a) or (b) above or would do if special educational provision was not made for the child.

A child must not be regarded as having a learning difficulty solely because the language or form of language of the home is different from the language in which he or she is or will be taught.

Special educational provision means:

(a) for a child over 2, educational provision that is additional to, or otherwise different from, the educational provision made generally for children of the child's age in maintained schools, other than special schools, in the area
(b) for a child under 2, educational provision of any kind.

(Education Act, 1993, Section 156) (DfE, 1994, p. 5)

Practice (DfES, 2001b) was quick to follow, with the latter replacing the original Code of Practice (DfE, 1994).

The revised *Special Educational Needs Code of Practice* (DfES, 2001b) moved further away from the medical model of assessment towards its policy of inclusion. It focused on four much broader areas of need:

- cognition and learning
- communication and interaction
- behavioural, emotional and social development
- sensory and/or physical.

It also replaced the original Code's five stages of assessment with an SEN graduated approach of assessment and provision for children:

- *School Action (class teacher and SENCO input and support)*
- *School Action Plus (class teacher, SENCO and external specialist input and support (when evidence suggested it was necessary))*
- *Statement of Special Educational Needs (LEA commissioned a multi-professional assessment to aid decision making); if successful a Statement of SEN would be accompanied by additional support originally.*

Like its predecessor however this revised Code of Practice continued to emphasise the importance of pupil voice, of parental involvement, of multi-professional working and of every child's rights to a broad, balanced and relevant curriculum. The results of the developed practice from the 2001 Special Educational Needs Code of Practice (DfES, 2001b) were not as expected however, and by the second half of the decade the government knew things had to change.

So what happened and why?

Alongside the introduction of this revised SEN Code of Practice teachers and schools were expected to ensure that most children attained the national attainment level for their SATs at the end of Key Stage 2 as part of the government's Standards' Agenda. Therefore, when pupils did not make adequate progress they were quite frequently considered to have an SEN and placed on the SEN register. They were then often moved from School Action to School Action Plus and through to statutory assessment quite quickly with the desire to gain additional funding. This additional funding would then frequently be used to employ teaching assistants to support a specific child either in a classroom, or to run intervention programmes outside of the classroom, enabling the teacher to focus on those who could/would achieve expected levels of attainment. It can therefore be suggested that an additional consequence of the ever-growing number of teaching assistants was that many teachers started to lose their skills of differentiation and being able to adapt their teaching methods for children with SEN. Therefore, also if this suggestion is correct it could have led to teachers being reliant on teaching assistant support in the classroom and hence the need for additional funding grew even more. Indeed, an increase in the number of teaching assistants from 103,600 to 181,600 (57 per cent rise) in a matter of 7 years, between 2002 and 2009, could be considered evidence to support the above suggestion (Squires, 2012). Also between 2000 and 2012 there was an increase in the number of pupils placed on the SEN register at School Action or School Action Plus in mainstream schools, fluctuating between 15 per cent and 19 per cent (DfE, 2013; Webster, 2015).

The government recognised that the link between the identification of SEN (School Action and School Action Plus), statutory assessment and funding was actually causing schools to try to gain this additional funding by focusing on poor teaching outcomes. This is termed a perverse incentive and was one that focused on teaching failure rather than on the improvement of teaching to prevent failure (Squires, 2012). Without doubt it also worked against the New Labour government's inclusion policy and efforts to develop inclusive education.

Table 8.3   List of some of the special educational needs reports, reviews and legislation published between 2004 and 2011

Year	Publication	Focus
2004	*Removing Barriers to Achievement* (DfES, 2004)	This guidance focused on helping teachers plan and teach pupils with SEN – supporting the cutting down of bureaucracy
2006	*House of Commons Education and Skills Committee* (2006)	This report explicitly stated that the SEN system was struggling to remain 'fit for purpose' (House of Commons, 2006: 12)
2008	*The Bercow Report* (DCSF, 2008b)	Reported on findings from a review of services across England with speech, language and communication needs
2008	*The Education (Special Educational Needs Coordinators) Regulations* (HMSO, 2008)	SENCOs were now required to: a) be a qualified teacher b) work at the school where they are SENCO c) complete an induction period
2008–2010	*The Inclusion Development Programme* (DCSF, 2008a, 2008b, 2009, 2010)	This was an online continuing professional development (CPD) programme: a) dyslexia (2008) b) speech, language and communication needs (2008) c) supporting children on the autistic spectrum d) supporting children with emotional and behavioural difficulties (2010)
2009	*The Lamb Inquiry* (DCSF, 2009)	This inquiry looked at parental confidence in the SEN assessment process
2009	*The Education Special Educational Needs Coordinators (England) (Amended) Regulations* (HMSO, 2009)	This amendment stated that every new SENCO had to complete the Master's level 'National Award for Special Educational Needs Coordination' by the end of their third year in post
2010	*The SALT Review* (DCSF, 2010a)	This looked at the supply of teachers working with children with severe learning difficulties and profound and multiple learning difficulties
2010	*Special Educational Needs and Disability Review: A Statement is Not Enough* (Ofsted, 2010)	This review looked at how the current legislation and SEN assessment process served children with an SEN
2010	*Breaking the Link between Special Educational Needs and Low Attainment* (DCSF, 2010b)	High expectations for all
2010	*Improving Parental Confidence in the Special Educational Needs System: An Implementation Plan* (DCSF, 2010c)	Valuing parental involvement in the SEN assessment system
2011	Green Paper *Support and Aspiration: A New Approach to Special Educational Needs and Disability. A Consultation* (DfE, 2011)	This consultation paper set out the new Coalition government's proposals regarding the help children with SEN and/or disabilities should receive

Thus, a plethora of reports and guidance material aimed at supporting and increasing the skills of class teachers in working with pupils with SEN were published between 2004 until the Green Paper *Support and Aspiration: A New Approach to Special Educational Needs and Disability. A Consultation* (DfE, 2011) (Table 8.3).

The last two documents in Table 8.3 were published after a change of government in 2010 which saw a shift in educational policy. The Green Paper, for example, did not even attempt to define inclusion and wanted to remove the 'bias' towards inclusion. In fact, this document reverted to the definition of 'integration' in which inclusion refers solely to providing all children with SEN a place in mainstream school. The government was also concerned about the increasing identification of children with SEN – 'Since 2000, the proportion of pupils with SEN in mainstream schools has changed from 21.9% to 16.6% in 2003, up to 18.9% in 2007, then 20.7% in 2010' (Webster, 2015, p. 993) – and most significantly wanted to overhaul the whole SEN system as they believed it was no longer fit for purpose.

As a consequence of this government's change in direction for education policy new Teachers' Standards (2012) were started in September 2012 (DfE, 2013) with 5.2, 5.3 and 5.4 being the most relevant for working with children with an SEN. A new National Curriculum for England and Wales (DfE, 2014) was introduced in 2014 with a view to enabling teachers to adapt their teaching so that they could meet the needs of all their pupils. The Department for Education also revised the inclusion statement reaffirming that every school had a duty to enable full access and participation in all their teaching, learning and social activities for all children. Thus, the government decided to make key changes to the SEN system as part of its major legislative reform, the Children and Families Act 2014, which received Royal Assent on 13 March 2014. The Parliamentary Under-Secretary of State for Children and Families, Edward Timpson, said:

> Enquiries and reviews of SEN provision … have identified that the current system is complex, bewildering and adversarial. The evidence points to an assessment process which is inefficient, bureaucratic and costly, as well as insufficiently child-centred or user-friendly. (Perry, 2014, p. 333)

In England

The current SEND Code of Practice: 0–25 (DfE and DoH, 2015)

As we have heard previously 2014 saw the introduction of the current *Special Educational Needs and Disability Code of Practice: 0–25 Years* (DfE and DoH, 2014). Published on 11 June 2014 there were only a couple of months for schools and particularly SENCOs to prepare for its implementation on 1 September and as such there was very little time for workforce training. With such speed it was not surprising that on 29 January 2015 changes were made to the Code of Practice relating to those young people in youth custody, with implementation for 1 April 2015. This is the current Code of Practice you will need to implement in your classrooms, but by the time the fourth edition of this book is published there may be another version! However, this current 2015 Code of Practice is now 292 pages long and as such only the main issues relating to schools will be introduced here. So what are the significant aspects of this legislation and what does this mean for teachers and other professionals working in educational settings? First, the current SEND Code of Practice: 0–25 (DfE and DoH, 2015) (referred to as the Code from now on) clearly states that every mainstream school including academies, maintained nursery schools, 16–19 academies, alternative provision academies and Pupil Referral Units (PRUs) *must* identify, address and provide the support that pupils with SEN require (Section 6.2). Schools should also 'ensure that children and young people with SEN engage in the activities of the school alongside pupils who do not have SEN' (Section 6.2). The focus of all of this work is on pupil outcomes and not on the amount or type of provision pupils access, and this is a significant change in approach for many schools.

Broad areas of need

This 2015 Code provides greater detail concerning the areas of need to previous Codes and it has recognised areas of growing concern and level of incidence, naming for the first time, for example, attachment disorder and mental health needs. The current 2015 Code also does not include 'behaviour' in the description of an area of need, recognising that 'behaviour' is often a response to another cause such as speech and language needs or autism.

The four broad areas of need in the current Code are:

- communication and interaction
- cognition and learning
- social, emotional and mental health difficulties
- sensory and/or physical needs.

The graduated approach

The current Code also seeks to promote 'a common approach to identifying, assessing and providing support for all children's SEN' (Hodkinson, 2016, p. 127). School

Action and School Action Plus, and the Statement of Special Educational Needs, have been replaced in this Code by a graduated approach (SEN support), where schools provide a continuum of provision identified through regular assessment and review. It is also important to note that the Code states very clearly that the 'identification of SEN should be built into the overall approach to monitoring the progress and development of all pupils' (Section 6.5) and not a separate system.

The class teacher is at the heart of this approach, providing a high-quality differentiated curriculum that enables the different learning needs of pupils to be met in the classroom. However, the early identification of SEN is seen in the Code as essential for the lifelong outcomes for children and, therefore, as soon as schools assess that a child is not making adequate progress they are expected to provide the pupil with something that is 'additional' or 'different from' that which is usually provided. This might or might not lead to the pupil being considered to have an SEN. If the pupil continues not to make the expected progress schools should 'take action to remove barriers to learning' and that 'should take the form of a four-part cycle through which earlier decisions and actions are revisited, refined and revised' (Section 6.44) to secure good outcomes.

The four-part cycle in the current Code of Practice (DfE and DoH, 2015) is:

- *Assess*: The class teacher (with the SENCO) analyses the pupil's needs.
- *Plan*: Parents *must* be told if a pupil is to be provided with SEN support. Outcomes are decided and then the support and interventions are agreed in order to achieve the outcomes.
- *Do*: The class teacher should be responsible for the pupil, and his/her progress at all times, including when they work with teaching assistants or other professionals (Section 6.52).
- *Review*: The support and interventions should be reviewed and evaluated and include the views of the pupil and parents/carers.

Schools can also involve specialists at any point to support pupils with SEN with the agreement of parents of course. The Local Offer (which is the responsibility of the LEA) should set out what services are available in the local area and how they can be accessed. If, after all efforts have been tried within this school-based approach, the pupil is still not making adequate progress, the school or parents can then request an Education, Health and Care (EHC) needs (multi-disciplinary) assessment by the LEA. If successful the pupil will be given an EHC plan, which holds the same level of legal status as the previous Statement of Special Educational Needs. This has to be reviewed annually and be focused on outcomes rather than on provision.

Other significant factors included in the Code are:

- The participation of children in decision making has been given greater importance.
- The participation of parents in decision making has also been given greater emphasis.
- There is a stronger focus on high aspirations and outcomes.
- Close cooperation between education, health and social care is required through joint planning and commissioning of services.
- There is a greater focus on transitions and especially successful transitions to adulthood.

The transitions to this Code's new requirements are still being implemented and so its success in underpinning what the government called its major reform programme remains to be seen.

Reflective task

Reflect on the changes that SEN policy and practice has seen since the introduction of the current SEND Code of Practice: 0–25 (DfE and DoH, 2015).

Do you think they have helped children who have SEN and their families, or not? Think of three positive changes that the SEN system has enabled and three that you feel have not been positive. Share your views with a colleague and discuss what you think have been the most significant factors in determining the direction of SEN policy and then practice.

Do you think 'special educational need' is still a useful term or has it become outdated and needs to be contested? Indeed, could it even be 'damaging' (Kilburn and Mills, 2014, p. 168)?

Inclusion: what is it?

Alongside much of the literature, guidance and legislation already discussed above about SEN, inclusion has frequently been mentioned and referred to either because of its presence, or in more recent years its absence. However, it is not unusual to see in a school prospectus or on school websites today the claim that a school is 'an inclusive school', but what does that actually mean?

Reflective task

A) Using your current experience and also your knowledge of the literature and policy, how would you describe inclusion as you see it in practice in schools in England today?
B) Does this view differ from what you really feel 'inclusion' and 'inclusive education' in schools should be like?

Draw a table illustrating the factors that are the same between (A) and (B) and the differences. Reflect on what you see. Does this help you think of ways you might be able to enhance inclusion in the schools you teach in?
   Also consider:

- What might hinder you in developing your practice?
- How might you be able to make changes, especially if you are new to a school?
- Are there new ideas you could introduce or suggest implementing to improve parental partnership or pupil voice in particular?

Although inclusion was not a new ideology (it has its origins in the 1800s) it was in the 1990s that it began to gain what can be considered 'high status and acquired international currency within the UK's educational and social policy initiatives' (Hodkinson, 2016, p. 88). From the 1950s until the 1990s integration and then inclusion (Oliver, 1996) were focused mainly on the educational segregation of the 'disabled community' from mainstream/regular schools (locational inclusion), and on those with SEN.

The Salamanca Agreement (UNESCO, 1994, p. 3) also promoted 'enabling schools to serve all children, particularly those with special educational needs', and this was followed 6 years later by the Dakar Agreement (UNESCO, 2000, p. 71), which challenged countries to achieve 'total inclusion of children with special needs in the mainstream schools' by 2015. Thus, here you can see that for some inclusion is a process that is linked to the goal of 'full inclusion' (Hodkinson, 2016) (Table 8.1).

As signed up members of the Salamanca and Dakar Agreements, the UK's New Labour government in 1997 and in 2000 (DfES/QCA, 1989, p. 12) at least at face value committed itself to the ideology of inclusion. However, their definitions were still based on locational inclusion and on the medical model where the language of deficit was used, encouraging tolerance not inclusion (Hodkinson, 2016). Their definitions of inclusion were also confused and ambivalent, and its policies and practices showed that they felt inclusion in practice had its limitations.

Work in school

Student: My mentor in school always uses labels about children with an SEN in my class. When we discuss the different learning needs of individual children she often uses phrases such as 'Oh … is one of your SEN children', or ' You know he's autistic'. I'm really uncomfortable about this, especially as I feel expectations of these children are not as high as they should be. What should I do? Can I say anything?

Mentor: First, I'm pleased that you have identified this as a difficulty for you. This shows me that you are trying to ensure that you have really high expectations for all the pupils in your class. I suggest that you speak with the SENCO about how you are feeling to see if there is anything that can be done at the school level. You can, of course, model what you feel to be more appropriate ways of talking and thinking about the pupils with SEN. A 'drip' effect might have an impact, especially if you can show that these pupils can achieve and make progress.

Analysis

The language used in school is full of acronyms and abbreviations and it can be said that unfortunately many teachers do not actually think about how they are saying things and hence the impact on both their practice and thinking and thus on pupils. Since the adoption of the term 'special educational needs' in the Warnock Report (DES, 1978) the medical model and deficit use of language has been discouraged in schools and in society in England in general. It is important, however, still to monitor ourselves at all times to ensure that we don't abbreviate terms inappropriately or label children who have a learning need using deficit/medical language. Using scenarios from charities and national SEN organisations can help model and highlight the negative impact of the use of such terminology.

Reflective task

Kingston and Price (2012, p. 219) write that 'promoting equality and being inclusive requires us to be open to change and prepared to challenge the stereotypes and discriminatory views we may hold, as well as those of other practitioners and those found in society more broadly'.

Do you ever hear the following words or terms used? What do they mean to you and are they an inclusive way of talking about children?

SEN children   disabled   special children   dyslexic

Impaired   handicapped   autistic

Write down your responses to these and then discuss them in small groups. These terms can be undoubtedly emotive and your responses based on your values, but how might they impact on the way educators think about the needs of individual/groups of learners? Also remember that terms reflect the thinking of the time (i.e. policies) and of different cultures and countries. These are important factors that need to be considered when working with pupils and families from different cultures and countries.

Now take a look at the words and terms below? How do they differ from those above? Which do you prefer? Why? Spend a few minutes thinking about this by yourself before discussing in a group.

Children with a special educational need   differently abled pupils with dyslexia

pupils with autism   additional or different need

Internationally (USA and Canada) in the 1990s some researchers saw the importance of being able to operationalise inclusion and they started to talk about 'authentic inclusion' (Ferguson, 1995) and develop models of inclusive education in an effort to be able to think about the characteristics that would be seen in an inclusive classroom.

In the UK in the first years of the twenty-first century definitions of inclusion equally began to portray more frequently a universal principle, where inclusion was seen 'as an active, not passive process' (Corbett, 2001, p. 55) and where 'inclusive education' celebrates difference (Corbett and Slee, 2000). For some, inclusion, as we have noted above, is only achieved when there is full inclusion, but for others full inclusion was and still is seen as unrealistic, especially for children with severe and complex needs, with emotional, sensory and behavioural needs, attachment disorder or who have experienced great trauma. Warnock (2005, p. 1), for example, stated that special schools offer a 'more productive and creative interpretation of the ideal of inclusive education for all' where children who would find mainstream school challenging can have their learning needs met.

It must also be recognised that in the past 20 years or so in the UK inclusive education and inclusion have become controlled by a focus on standards, accountability and a market-based ideology where the commodity of knowledge is delivered and assessed and 'quality controlled' by Ofsted (Kilburn and Mills, 2014, p. 175). Also because of the focus on assessment 'results' and accountability, schools have had to be more concerned about their reputations and financial viability, and this is perhaps a greater issue more recently than previously as the range of education provision has expanded and an element of competition has also entered the 'market'. Are these possible reasons why some schools became and may still be 'wary of accepting children whose low attainment and discipline may affect others' learning by depressing examination and SAT scores' (Fredrickson and Cline, 2002, p. 67) and thus act(ed) as barriers to inclusion and inclusive education? Can, or should, as Ofsted (2000) suggested, inclusion be determined by either the standards agenda or measures of accountability? Thus, we see that there have been many different ways of defining inclusion and inclusive education, but by 2014 Glazzard's definition of inclusion could be said to be one that was, and I would suggest still is, broadly acknowledged (if not always accepted) by those working within education in the UK:

> Inclusion represents a proactive stance. It challenges educational settings to make adaptations and adjustments to cater for the needs of diverse learners. The purpose of inclusion is to provide all learners with equality of educational opportunity and this right is guaranteed through equality legislation. (Glazzard, 2014, p. 40)

Inclusive practice

The SEND Code of Practice: 0–25 (DfE and DoH, 2015) says that if a child does not have an EHC plan they *must* be educated in a mainstream setting (except in specific circumstances). However, for children with an EHC plan parents can state their preference for a special school, which is sometimes agreed, but not always depending on budgetary constraints and need. So is this different from previous government views?

Interestingly national statistics show that there has been a significant decrease in pupils with SEN without a Statement of Special Educational Need or EHC plan in schools since 2010. National statistics state:

Across all schools, the number of pupils with special educational needs has fallen from 1,301,445 in 2015 to 1,228,785 in 2016. 14.4% of pupils had special educational needs in 2016, a fall from 15.4% in 2015.

This reduction is due to the decline in the number and percentage of pupils with special educational needs without a statement or EHC plan. This has declined in each of the past six years, falling from 18.3% of pupils in 2010 to 11.6% in 2016.

However, the percentage of children attending special schools has risen:

The percentage of pupils with a statement or EHC plan attending maintained special schools has gradually increased each year. In 2010, 38.2% of pupils with statements attended maintained special schools and this has increased to 42.9% of pupils with statements or EHC plans in 2016. The percentage of pupils with statements or EHC plans attending independent schools has also increased between 2010 and 2016, from 4.2% to 5.7%.

Also:

The percentage of pupils with special educational needs in primary academies is 13.4%, the same as the overall percentage of pupils with special educational needs in all state-funded primary schools. The percentage of pupils in primary academies with a statement or EHC plan is the same as the overall percentage for all state-funded primary schools (1.3% for primary schools).

(DfE, 2016; https://www.gov.uk/government/uploads/system/uploads/attachment_data/file/539158/SFR29_2016_Main_Text.pdf, accessed 18 April 2017)

Reflective task

Having read the section about the SEND Code of Practice: 0–25 (DfE and DoH, 2015) and the most recent SEN national statistics, do you feel we are moving towards a fully inclusive education system or not?

Review and reflect on the answers you gave in Reflective Task 2. Have your views changed in any way and if so why? Do you think you are/can be an inclusive teacher and, if so, what are the implications for you? Do you now think a school can really say they are an 'inclusive school' or is there a more appropriate term or phrase? Discuss your answers and reasons for these answers in pairs or small groups.

Work in school

Student: I have two teaching assistants who work in my class with me. Both of them feel that they should spend their time withdrawing children in small group interventions or 1:1 support. This involves about a third of the class. I don't know what the pupils are doing when they are not in the classroom as the programmes are agreed with the SENCO. I also therefore cannot make any links for the children between what they do in class and what they do elsewhere. I am finding this very difficult, but don't know how I can change things because I don't want to upset the teaching assistants or the SENCO.

Mentor: This is a difficult issue and clearly the school has a policy of withdrawing pupils with SEN for additional intervention work. I suggest that you go and speak with the SENCO, saying that you would like to know more about what the children on the SEN register are actually doing. Perhaps also you might be able to ask for some time to meet with the teaching assistants and to discuss what they do.

Analysis

There has been much research during the past decade that has questioned the impact of teaching assistants on pupils' progress (Blatchford et al., 2009). However, in 2010, Farrell et al. reviewed a number of studies which showed that as long as the teaching assistants received training and appropriate support, their impact on pupils' academic attainments could be positive. More recently the SEND Code of Practice (DfE and DoH, 2015) has clearly stated that teachers are responsible and accountable for their pupils' learning whether they are with another professional or in a different space. Thus, you can ask if there is time available to meet with the teaching assistants so that you can find out what the pupils are focusing on and how well they are making progress.

Also the views of the pupils themselves are really important when deciding on what provision they should receive and when (Woolfson et al., 2007). Hopefully regular school pupil reviews and the requirement for class teachers to use tools such as provision mapping to monitor the progress and success of interventions, will also aid you in establishing your role in making decisions for the children with SEN. These changes are still relatively new, but are becoming established ways to identify effective ways of working.

Conclusion

This chapter has explained how special needs education has evolved and helped you to apply your knowledge and understanding of the current Code of Practice in the classroom in ways that reflect your own philosophy of inclusion.

Questions for discussion

1. Brahm Norwich (2008) has argued that the term 'special educational needs' (SEN) is both damaging and outdated as it has led to the negative labelling of children, is not defined sufficiently and has even expanded SEN into something different and 'outside of' the rest of school life. Do you agree or disagree with these views?
2. Why do you think the government has put the class teacher at the heart of the graduated approach? What do you think they might hope to achieve by requiring teachers to gain mixed-ability teaching skills?
3. Consider the latest national statistics which state that the percentage of pupils provided with SEN support using the graduated approach (and previously School Action/School Action Plus) has declined quite significantly in recent years. Why do you think this is and what does it tell you about the link between accountability, policy and practice?
4. What do you feel are the most important things to learn about teaching pupils with SEN when you are still gaining your qualifications?

Further reading

Mulholland, M. and O'Connor, U. (2016) 'Collaborative classroom practice for inclusion: Perspectives of classroom teachers and learning support/resource teachers', *International Journal of Inclusive Education*, March: 1–14.
As you will undoubtedly already understand, how professionals work together in a classroom is vital to ensure that they are actually helping pupils learn more effectively. This article will provide you with a range of perspectives to consider.

Robinson, D. (2017) 'Effective inclusive teacher education for special educational needs and disabilities: Some more thoughts on the way forward', *Teaching and Teacher Education*, 61: 164–78.
This very recent article will help you reflect on your own experiences and how they might have influenced your thinking about working with pupils with SEN and disabilities. It will also propose ways forward for teacher education that you might like to reflect on.

Thomas, G. (2013) 'A review of thinking and research about inclusive education policy, with suggestions for a new kind of inclusive thinking', *British Educational Research Journal*, 39 (3): 473–90.

This article will provide you with a further way to think about inclusive education and the way forward.

Webster, R. (2015) 'The classroom experiences of pupils with special educational needs in mainstream primary schools – 1976–2012: What do data from systematic observation studies reveal about pupils' educational experiences over time?', *British Educational Research Journal*, 41 (6): 992–1009.

In this article you will be able to engage with how pupils have experienced being seen as children with SEN since the late 1970s.

References

Armstrong, D. and Squires, G. (2012) (eds) *Contemporary Issues in Special Educational Needs*. Maidenhead: Open University Press/McGraw-Hill Education.

Blatchford, P., Bassett, P., Brown, P., Martin, C., Russell, A. and Webster, R. (2009) *Deployment and Impact of Support Staff Project*. Research Report RB148. London: DCSF.

Booth, T., Ainscow, M., Black-Hawkins, K., Vaughan, M. and Shaw, L. (2000) *Index for Inclusion*. Bristol: Centre for Studies on Inclusive Education.

Corbett, J. (2001) 'Teaching approaches which support inclusive education: A connective pedagogy', *British Journal of Special Education*, 28 (2): 55–59.

Corbett, J. and Slee, R. (2000) 'An international conversation on inclusive education', in F. Armstrong, D. Armstrong and L. Barton (eds), *Inclusive Education: Policy, Contexts and Comparative Perspectives* (pp.133–146). London: David Fulton.

Davis, J.M. (2011) *Integrated Children's Services*. London: Sage.

Department for Children, Schools and Families (DCSF) (2008a) *The Bercow Report*. Available at: http://webarchive.nationalarchives.gov.uk/20130401151715/https:/www.education.gov.uk/publications/standard/publicationdetail/page1/DCSF-00632-2008 (accessed 17 April 2017).

Department for Children, Schools and Families (DCSF) (2008b) *The Bercow Report: A Review of Services for Children and Young People 10-19 with Speech Language and Communication Needs*. Annesley: DCSF.

Department for Children, Schools and Families (DCSF) (2009) *The Lamb Inquiry: Special Educational Needs and Parental Confidence*. Annesley: DCSF. Available at: http://webarchive.nationalarchives.gov.uk/20100202100434/dcsf.gov.uk/lambinquiry/ (accessed 17 April 2017).

Department for Children, Schools and Families (DCSF) (2010a) *The SALT Review*. Available at: http://webarchive.nationalarchives.gov.uk/tna/+/ and www.dcsf.gov.uk/saltreview/downloads/SaltReportRevisedFinal.pdf (accessed 17 April 2017).

Department for Children, Schools and Families (DCSF) (2010b) *Breaking the Link between Special Educational Needs and Low Attainment*. Annesley: DCSF.

Department for Children, Schools and Families (DCSF) (2010c) *Improving Parental Confidence in the Special Educational Needs System: An Implementation Plan*. Annesley: DCSF.

Department for Education (DfE) (1994) *Code of Practice on the Identification and Assessment of Pupils with Special Educational Needs*. London: DfE.

Department for Education (DfE) (2010) *The Inclusion Development Programme*. Available at: http://webarchive.nationalarchives.gov.uk/20110202093118/http:/nationalstrategies. standards.dcsf.gov.uk/search/inclusion/results/nav:46335 (accessed 17 April 2017).

Department for Education (DfE) (2011) *Support and Aspiration: A New Approach to Special Educational Needs and Disability – A Consultation (The Green Paper)*. London: DfE.

Department for Education (DfE) (2013) *Children with Special Educational Needs: An Analysis – 2013*. Available at: https://www.gov.uk/government/statistics/children-with-special-educational-needs-an-analysis-2013 (accessed 17 April 2017).

Department for Education (DfE) (2014) *Children and Families Act*. London: HMSO.

Department for Education (DfE) (2016) National Statistics: *Special Educational Needs in England*, January 2016. Available at: https://www.gov.uk/government/uploads/system/uploads/attachment_data/file/539158/SFR29_2016_Main_Text.pdf (accessed 18 April 2017).

Department for Education and Employment (DfEE) (1997) *Excellence for All Children: Meeting Special Educational Needs*. London: DfEE.

Department for Education (DfE) and Department of Health (DoH) (2014) *Special Educational Needs and Disability Code of Practice: 0–25 Years*. London: DfE.

Department for Education (DfE) and Department of Health (DoH) (January 2015) *Special Educational Needs and Disability Code of Practice: 0–25 Years*. London: DfE.

Department for Education and Skills (DfES) (1981) *Education Act 1981*. London: HMSO.

Department for Education and Skills/Qualifications and Curriculum Authority (DfES/QCA) (1989) *The National Curriculum*. London: HMSO.

Department for Education and Skills (DfES) (2001a) *Inclusive Schooling: Children with Special Educational Needs*. London: DfES.

Department for Education and Skills (DfES) (2001b) *Special Educational Needs Code of Practice*. Nottingham: DfES.

Department for Education and Skills (DfES) (2004) *Removing Barriers to Achievement*. London: DfES.

Department of Education and Science (DES) (1978) *Special Educational Needs: Report of the Committee of Enquiry into the Education of Handicapped Children and Young People (The Warnock Report)*. London: HMSO.

Department of Education and Science (DES) (1981) *1981 Education Act: Chapter 60*. London: HMSO.

Department of Education and Science (DES) (1988) *The Education Reform Act, 1988*. London: HMSO.

Farrell, P., Alborz, A., Howes, A. and Pearson, D. (2010) 'The impact of teaching assistants on improving pupils' academic achievement in mainstream schools: A review of the literature', *Educational Review*, 62 (4): 435–48.

Ferguson, D.L. (1995) 'The real challenge of inclusion: Confessions of a "rabid inclusionist"', *Phi Delta Kappan*, 77 (1): 281–7.

Florian, L. and Linklater, H. (2010) 'Preparing teachers for inclusive education: Using inclusive pedagogy to enhance "teaching and learning for all"', *Cambridge Journal of Education*, 40: 369–86.

Frederickson, N. and Cline, T. (2002) *Special Educational Needs, Inclusion and Diversity.* Maidenhead: Open University Press.

Glazzard, J. (2014) 'The standards agenda: Reflections of a special educational needs co-ordinator', *Support for Learning*, 29 (1): 39–53.

HMSO (2001) *The Special Educational Needs and Disability Act (SENDA).* London: HMSO.

HMSO (2008) *The Education (Special Educational Needs Coordinators) Regulations.* Available at: www.legislation.gov.uk/uksi/2008/2945/contents/made (accessed 17 April 2017).

HMSO (2009) *The Education Special Educational Needs Coordinators (England) (Amended) Regulations (2009 No. 1387).* Available at: www.legislation.gov.uk/uksi/2009/1387/made (accessed 17 April 2017).

Hodkinson, A. (2016) *Key Issues in Special Educational Needs and Inclusion*, second edn. London: Sage.

House of Commons (2006) *Education and Skills Committee, Special Educational Needs, third report of the session 2005-6, Vol 1.* Available at: https://publications.parliament.uk/pa/cm200506/cmselect/cmeduski/478/478i.pdf (accessed 4 September 2017).

Kilburn, V. and Mills, K. (2014) 'Inclusion and special educational needs', in H. Cooper (ed.), *Professional Studies in Primary Education*, second edn (pp.164–189). London: Sage.

Kingston, D. and Price, M. (2012) 'Promoting equality and inclusion', in N. Edmond and M. Price (eds), *Integrated Working with Children and Young People* (p.217). London: Sage.

Lipsky, D.K. and Gartner, A. (1997) *Inclusion and School Reform: Transforming America's Classroom.* Baltimore, MD: Paul H. Brookes.

Norwich, B. (2008) 'What future for special schools and inclusion? Conceptual and professional perspectives', *British Journal of Special Education*, 35 (3): 136–43.

Office for Standards in Education (Ofsted) (2000) *Evaluating Educational Inclusion: Guidance for Inspectors and Schools.* London: Ofsted.

Office for Standards in Education (Ofsted) (2010) *The Special Educational Needs and Disability Review: A Statement is Not Enough.* Manchester: Crown Copyright.

Oliver, M. (1996) 'Defining impairment and disability: Issues at stake', in C. Barnes and G. Mercer (eds), *Exploring the Divide: Illness and Disability.* Available at http://disability-studies.leeds.ac.uk/files/library/Mercer-explorin-the-divide-CONTENTS.pdf

Perry, J. (2014) 'England: SEND measures – implementation', *British Journal of Special Education*, 41 (3): 330–7.

Soan, S. (2004) (ed.) *Additional Educational Needs: Inclusive Approaches to Teaching.* London: David Fulton Publishers.

Squires, G. (2012) 'Historical and socio-political agendas around defining and including children with special educational needs', in D. Armstrong and G. Squires (eds), *Contemporary Issues in Special Educational Needs.* Maidenhead: Open University Press/McGraw-Hill Education. pp. 9–24.

Thomas, G. (2013) 'A new kind of inclusive thinking in education policy', *British Educational Research Journal*, 39 (3): 473–90.

United Nations Educational, Scientific and Cultural Organization (UNESCO) (1994) *The Salamanca Statement and Framework for Action on Special Needs Education*. Salamanca: UNESCO. Available at: www.unesco.org/education.pdf/SALAMA_E.PDF (accessed 18 April 2017).

United Nations Educational, Scientific and Cultural Organization (UNESCO) (2000) *The Dakar Framework for Action. Education for All: Meeting Our Collective Commitments*. Paris: UNESCO.

Warnock, M. (2005) *Special Educational Needs: A New Look*. London: Philosophy of Education Society of Great Britain.

Webster, R. (2015) 'The classroom experiences of pupils with special educational needs in mainstream primary schools – 1976–2012. What do data from systematic observation studies reveal about pupils' educational experiences over time?', *British Educational Research Journal*, 41 (6): 992–1009.

Woolfson, R., Harker, M., Lowe, D., Shield, M. and Mackintosh, H. (2007) 'Consulting with children and young people who have disabilities: Views of accessibility to education', *British Journal of Special Education*, 34 (1): 40–9.

9

Behaviour for Learning

Simon Ellis and Janet Tod

By the end of this chapter, you should:

- have an understanding of the difference between a focus on behaviour management and a focus on behaviour for learning
- be able to select and evaluate behaviour management strategies based on compatibility with the principles of the behaviour for learning approach
- have an awareness of the expectations contained in national policy and guidance on behaviour in schools
- have considered some generic behaviour management strategies and how these might be used within a least to most intrusive approach.

Introduction

The term 'behaviour management' is an established part of the discourse on behaviour in schools, appearing no less than 19 times in the Steer Report (DfES, 2005) and five times in the Department for Children, Schools and Families guidance document *School Discipline and Pupil-Behaviour Policies* (DCSF, 2009). Current guidance for head teachers and school staff on behaviour and discipline in schools (DfE, 2016), reiterating advice from the Steer Report (DfES, 2005), identifies a consistent approach to behaviour management as the first of ten 'key aspects of school practice that, when effective, contribute to improving the quality of pupil behaviour' (DfE, 2016, p. 5). Though the current professional standards (DfE, 2013, p. 8) do not use the term, they do require teachers to 'manage behaviour effectively'. Additional guidance intended to improve teacher training in relation to behaviour set out to describe 'the knowledge, skills and understanding that trainees will need in order to be able to manage their pupils' behaviour'. An internet search using the term 'behaviour management' will produce a plethora of texts and websites on the subject, as well as numerous consultants and training providers. The phrase has a respectable, quasi-professional tone and its provenance is rarely explored. This chapter invites you to critically consider the limitations of a focus on behaviour management when narrowly construed to mean a set of methods used to establish and maintain control over children's behaviour. It encourages a focus on the purpose and outcomes of behaviour management, defined as the promotion of effective learning behaviours. Learning behaviours can be thought of as those behaviours necessary for effective learning in a group setting such as the classroom. Adopting this perspective, the chapter considers national policy and guidance on behaviour in schools, explores some generic behaviour management systems and techniques, and examines the teacher's role in influencing the social, emotional and curricular factors that contribute to the development of children's learning behaviour.

What is the behaviour for learning approach?

The behaviour for learning approach (Ellis and Tod, 2009, 2015) offers an alternative way of thinking about children's behaviour that seeks to reduce perceptions that 'promoting learning' and 'managing behaviour' are separate issues (Powell and Tod, 2004). It is underpinned by the conceptual framework depicted in Figure 9.1.

The conceptual framework can be used in a variety of ways but, in thinking about day-to-day practice, it can be understood in terms of some simple principles. Essentially the behaviours children exhibit in the classroom – which, from the teacher's perspective, may be considered either positive or negative – result from an interaction between social, emotional and cognitive factors. As the following Reflective Task explores, the rationale behind this conceptual framework is likely to be familiar to most, if not all, readers through their own experiences as learners.

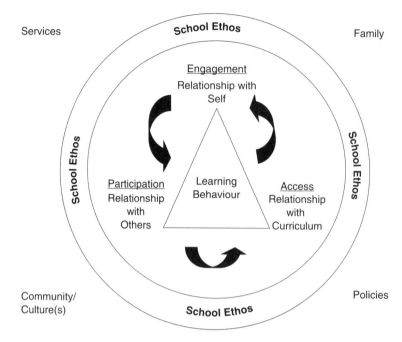

Figure 9.1   The behaviour for learning conceptual framework (adapted from Powell and Tod, 2004)

Reflective task

Think about your own learning at school and recall a lesson in which you behaved well – or, if you prefer, one in which you did not behave so well.

- How interested and capable were you in the subject being taught?
- How well did you get on with your teacher and peers in the class?
- How were you feeling emotionally in this specific lesson?

The factors explored in the preceding Reflective Task reflect, respectively, the three behaviour for learning relationships. These are:

- relationship with the curriculum (predominantly cognitive)
- relationship with others (predominantly social)
- relationship with self (predominantly emotional).

We use the term 'relationship' to reflect the dynamic reciprocity that is inherent in curricular, social and personal experiences. To illustrate what we mean by this, if we return to your recollections from your own schooldays, you can probably recall that your interest in the subject, how well you got on with your teacher and peers in the class and how you felt emotionally were influenced by factors such as:

- the way the particular teacher presented the lesson
- the types of tasks and activities set by the teacher
- your perception of how the teacher viewed you as a learner and as a person
- how the teacher related to you and your classmates
- who you were with when you were learning.

Therefore, although you are likely to have brought to your school-based learning various influencing skills, dispositions and previous experiences, your interest in the subject, how well you got on with your teacher and peers in the class, and how you felt emotionally were also influenced, for better or worse, by a range of contextual variables. The behaviour for learning approach does not leave the interaction between these elements to chance. The class teacher aims to be aware of the effect on the child's behaviour of these variables, and to work positively with them to foster the development of learning behaviour. Care would be taken to avoid any practice that would have a predictable negative impact on either the three relationships or the development of learning behaviour.

Reflective task

Think about a child whom you consider to be a well-behaved, effective learner and respond to these points:

- Describe their general ability as a learner and response (attitude and behaviour) when taking part in learning activities. What are they good at, what do they struggle with, what is their progress like?
- Describe how they present socially. How do they present when taking part in group work? What are their interactions with adults and their peers like? How do they cope with the social demands of the setting?

(Continued)

(Continued)

- Describe how they present emotionally. How do they respond when presented with unfamiliar or difficult tasks? Do they appear confident? How well do they manage strong emotions? What do you think their self-esteem is like?

Now repeat the activity but this time thinking about a child whose behaviour causes you concern.

The three bullet points reflect the three behaviour for learning relationships. The task illustrates that the behaviour for learning approach is not based on a deficit model. The three relationships are relevant to well-behaved, effective learners, as well as those whose behaviour causes concern. When tackling this activity from the perspective of a child whose behaviour causes concern you might have found that simply thinking about how they present in the three relationship areas triggered some ideas about strategies and approaches you could employ to bring about positive changes.

How does behaviour for learning differ from behaviour management?

Behaviour management is usually based on primarily verbal strategies used by the teacher to either reinforce positive behaviour or correct unwanted behaviour. The teacher will also have access to rewards and sanctions to use alongside these verbal strategies. The Teachers' Standards require teachers to 'establish a framework for discipline with a range of strategies, using praise, sanctions and rewards consistently and fairly' (DfE, 2013, p. 12). Though there is recognition of the need to reinforce positive behaviour, the purpose of behaviour management – as the name suggests – is the management of behaviour. This can encourage a focus on the elimination or reduction of unwanted behaviours and a corresponding emphasis on the acquisition of strategies and approaches that might achieve this. This can lead to a narrow and superficial focus on strategies and sanctions to use when this behaviour occurs, together with other strategies and rewards to be employed when it is not occurring. As Figure 9.2 illustrates, the behaviour for learning approach adopts a different perspective, based on a focus on the behaviours the teacher is seeking to promote.

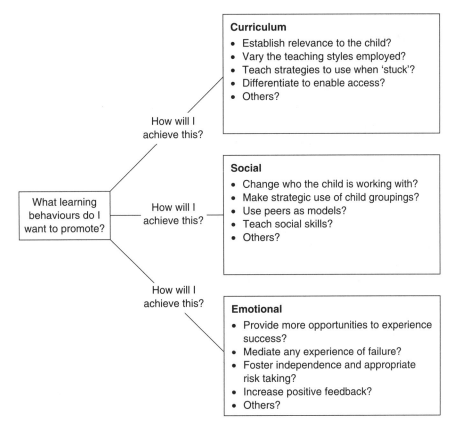

Curriculum
- Establish relevance to the child?
- Vary the teaching styles employed?
- Teach strategies to use when 'stuck'?
- Differentiate to enable access?
- Others?

How will I achieve this?

Social
- Change who the child is working with?
- Make strategic use of child groupings?
- Use peers as models?
- Teach social skills?
- Others?

What learning behaviours do I want to promote?

How will I achieve this?

How will I achieve this?

Emotional
- Provide more opportunities to experience success?
- Mediate any experience of failure?
- Foster independence and appropriate risk taking?
- Increase positive feedback?
- Others?

Figure 9.2 The behaviour for learning perspective

The examples in Figure 9.2 are, of course, generic in nature and are by no means exhaustive, but serve to illustrate that when we begin to focus on the learning behaviours we want to promote, it can encourage thinking about a broad range of strategies the teacher can employ that extends beyond those we would typically categorise as behaviour management. However, the suggestion is not that 'knowledge of generic behaviour management systems and techniques' (TA, 2012, p. 1) is unnecessary. We view the typical strategies associated with behaviour management as tools a teacher would draw on, selected from the far broader array of other professional tools at their disposal that have the potential to promote the behaviours necessary for effective learning in the classroom. Reflecting this perspective, the remainder of this chapter seeks to address the question of how a school's behaviour policy and the teacher's class-based behaviour management strategies can be used to support the promotion of learning behaviour and the associated behaviour for learning relationships.

Reflective task

Think of a child whose behaviour causes you concern. Specify in observable terms what it is they do (or do not do) that causes concern. If you find you have focused on a disposition, such as limited motivation or a lack of resilience, still try to identify the behaviours the child actually exhibits that have led you to highlight this as the concern.

Now identify one or more learning behaviours that you want to develop. For the purposes of this activity you can think of a learning behaviour simply as a positive behaviour that you wish to see the child exhibit. For example, if the concerning behaviour was 'calling out' you might identify 'uses the agreed class methods to ask a question or make a verbal contribution' as the positive behaviour to develop. Review your ideas, reflecting on these points:

- The learning behaviour should be positively expressed.
- It may simply be the opposite of the unwanted behaviour.
- It may be a behaviour that is incompatible with the problem behaviour (i.e. if the child exhibited this behaviour they would not be exhibiting the problem behaviour).
- It should be possible to identify assessable indicators of the learning behaviour's development.
- If you have selected a disposition (e.g. confidence, resilience) you should be able to identify some behaviours that would indicate its development.

The role of the school's behaviour policy in promoting learning behaviour

A school's behaviour policy is a key document in defining a whole-school approach to managing behaviour. The requirement for schools to have a behaviour policy is firmly established in legislation (e.g. the Education Act 1997; the School Standards and Framework Act 1998; the Education and Inspections Act 2006).

Although changing national policy and guidance inevitably influences aspects of the content, a typical school behaviour policy is likely to cover these broad areas:

- A statement of the principles that underpin the policy.
- A code of conduct for pupils setting out the expectations of behaviour.

- Promoting and rewarding good behaviour.
- Addressing poor behaviour through the use of disciplinary sanctions.
- Arrangements for monitoring and reviewing the policy.

In considering the contribution of the school's behaviour policy to the promotion of learning behaviour, the first basic principle is that any practice or approach set out in the policy should not be to the detriment of any of the three behaviour for learning relationships. For example, a sanction that contained an element that a child may find humiliating or embarrassing would risk impacting on relationship with self. Similarly, though 'the setting of written tasks as punishments, such as writing lines or an essay' is an example sanction in current government guidance (DfE, 2016, p. 8), we would question whether constructing writing as a sanction risks undermining the child's relationship with this element of the curriculum. Viewed from this perspective, it is interesting that this advice remains, while the suggested sanction of 'extra physical activity such as running around a playing field' that appeared in an earlier version (DfE, 2014, p. 8) was removed after pressure from members of the sporting community (e.g. Jude, 2014) and others due to concern over the portrayal of sport and exercise as a punishment.

Moving beyond the principle of simply protecting the three relationships, aligning behaviour policies more closely with the behaviour for learning conceptual framework requires greater emphasis to be placed on how individuals might experience and interpret the specified practices and approaches employed. The central purpose of a school's behaviour policy is to promote good behaviour and discourage poor behaviour among the majority. If evaluated against this purpose, most schools' policies are likely to be successful. However, children have a purpose for their behaviour. They may, for example, engage in disruptive behaviour in order to impress their peer group, divert attention from the fact that they do not know how to 'get on with their work' or to confirm a lack of belief in themselves. Differing purposes mean that not all children will automatically respond in the anticipated manner to systems and practices designed for the school population as a whole. This is not indicative of a weakness of the behaviour policy. Rather it signals that for the particular individual there is a need to better understand and address the cognitive, social and emotional components influencing the current behaviour. Effective schools will use quantitative and qualitative data on children's responses to systems and practices as an indicator of the need for this further assessment.

Work in school

Study one

Student: I don't know what to try next with Martin. He is taking up all my time with his behaviour. I am constantly having to go to him, verbally correct his behaviour or issue a sanction. I can't understand it. I'm sure he can't like continually being corrected or receiving sanctions. I thought he was attention seeking. I remembered some input we had on the course about needing to view this as attention needing and to ensure attention was provided when he was exhibiting positive behaviour. I've tried this. I've increased the amount of praise I give, trying to adhere to the principle of at least five positives for every negative (DCSF, 2009). I'm tactically ignoring negative behaviour to ensure I'm not giving attention at these times. I've set up an individualised reward system so that I can support the praise with a tangible reward. If anything he's worse. When I do reward him he often follows this with a behaviour that means I have little option but to verbally correct him or impose a sanction. It's like he's just throwing it back in my face.

Mentor: It's certainly true that increasing positive feedback can work for a lot of children. Most children want to achieve, feel valued and experience some autonomy (McLean, 2009), and positive feedback can contribute positively to two out of the three of these. I think the problem in Martin's case may be that your initial hypothesis was wrong. If the behaviour is due to attention needing then an approach underpinned by the basic behaviourist principle of positively reinforcing required behaviours with something the individual finds rewarding – in Martin's case, your attention – is a sound approach. The problem is when this is not the reason for the behaviour. I don't know Martin, but have you considered that his behaviour might be based on a desire to avoid the task? It might be that he has low self-esteem and behaviours that lead to him avoiding the task, even if this incurs reprimands and sanctions, fulfil a valuable purpose. They may protect him from the sense of failure that he may experience if he attempts the task but gets it wrong. But I'm just guessing: as I said I don't know Martin. Could it be developmental? Are you sure the learning behaviours you want to see from Martin are reasonable expectations based on his stage of development?

(Continued)

Analysis

The student teacher's approach often represents the default response when a child exhibits problematic behaviour. The problems occur if the explanation we apply is faulty. If the child has the required learning behaviours in their repertoire or, if not, is developmentally ready to be taught them, then the rewards systems can work well in providing extrinsic motivation to demonstrate these more often. In Martin's case the teacher's assumption was that he had the required behaviours in his repertoire, but the attention he received for his negative behaviour was a stronger motivator. As the tutor suggests, there may be alternative explanations to consider. Table 9.1 takes some common behaviours and links them with possible explanations to illustrate how strategy choice might be affected.

Table 9.1 Links between causal explanations for behaviour and strategy selection (adapted from Ellis and Tod, 2015)

Frequently observed behaviour	Possible explanation for the child's behaviour	Possible action
Shouting out and distracting others	The child is getting more attention by being off task	Consistently reward on-task behaviour
Keeps looking around and asking questions	The child thinks they are unable to do the task	Work with the child to reappraise the task, identify what parts of the task they can do or need help to do
Does not start the task – uses strategies to avoid starting	The child fears failure	Work to increase the child's experience of success, e.g. offer increased adult or peer support so that success is assured. Work at whole-class level to develop understanding of how to make positive use of mistakes/errors
Makes noises, does not stay in seat, does not respond to or comply with requests	The child's behaviour is consistent with that allowed in their home environment. Other children in the family may run around a lot at home or be left unsupervised in the street	Clarify the behaviours you want to see. Build on the positives, emphasise existing behaviour management strategies, model/teach skills. Possibly involve in a nurture group or social skills group. Work with parents and pastoral colleagues
Does not direct attention to the task set, short attention span, keeps asking questions, fidgeting	Perhaps the child has a learning difficulty, e.g. attention deficit hyperactivity disorder (ADHD) and/or a language difficulty	Seek advice from the special educational needs coordinator (SENCO), personalise learning (e.g. instructions, pace of work, more opportunities for kinaesthetic learning), emphasise existing class behaviour management (e.g. behavioural expectations made clear, rule reminders, use of extrinsic rewards)
Not listening, wandering about, playing aimlessly with pen/pencil	This may be due to overall developmental delay – the child may not be ready to work independently. There may be an underlying sensory difficulty and/or language difficulty	Seek advice from the SENCO. Consider a possible need for allocation of additional adult support; set more suitable learning challenges

A framework for managing behaviour: rules, rewards and sanctions

The Teachers' Standards require teachers to 'establish a framework for discipline with a range of strategies, using praise, sanctions and rewards consistently and fairly' and 'have clear rules and routines for behaviour in classrooms' (DfE, 2013, p. 12). In behaviour for learning terms, this framework should contribute to the establishment of a stable, safe and predictable environment where all children are encouraged to develop a positive relationship with the curriculum, themselves and others.

Rules

As the Elton Report (DfES, 1989) noted, it is advisable to frame rules positively. There are three main reasons for this:

1. A positively expressed rule provides information on the expected behaviour.
2. If we tell someone *not* to think of something, they will probably, at least momentarily, think of that thing. If children are going to momentarily think of something, then it would be better that it was the required behaviour. The rule might therefore be 'We use respectful language' rather than 'Do not swear'.
3. A positively expressed rule helps a teacher to frame their correction positively because they only need to formulate a sentence around the wording of the rule.

From a behaviour for learning perspective, positively phrased rules reflect the principle of keeping a focus on those behaviours that are necessary for learning in a school environment. Rules should be few in number and restricted to those that protect the rights of all members of the class, including the teacher and other adults. For younger children in particular, a photograph or cartoon illustrating the rule being followed can be helpful alongside the written version.

Rewards and sanctions

Current government guidance states that 'Schools should have in place a range of options and rewards to reinforce and praise good behaviour, and clear sanctions for those who do not comply with the school's behaviour policy' (DfE, 2016, p. 8). Depending on how they are used, rewards can play an important role in promoting learning behaviour. The teacher can use a reward, coupled with the type of descriptive positive feedback covered later in this chapter, to reinforce emerging learning behaviours. The potential for this positive recognition to also contribute to the development of a more positive relationship with self is perhaps more obvious, but it might also improve the child's relationship with others in terms of the teacher–pupil relationship or relationship with the curriculum if the learning behaviour exhibited relates to a particular curricular activity or task. Sanctions, in the traditional form of responding to misbehaviour by doing something to the child that we believe they will dislike, offer little potential to promote positive learning behaviours. The development of learning behaviour is often left to chance, based on the principle that discouragement of the unwanted behaviour will lead to positive learning behaviours being exhibited instead (behaviourist theories are described in Chapter 2). This perspective does not take sufficient account of two key points:

- The original behaviour was serving a purpose for the child and they may just substitute another unhelpful behaviour to fulfil the same need.
- The alternative behaviours may need to be taught. It cannot be assumed that these are currently within the child's repertoire.

Within the behaviour for learning approach, sanctions need to be seen for what they are: a means by which the school can demonstrate its disapproval that *may* have a deterrent effect on the individual and on others. This is not intended as a pejorative comment – pragmatically sanctions are necessary to allow staff to feel supported, for children to recognise that there are consequences and to maintain parental confidence.

Though rewards do offer some potential, the limitations of rewards and sanctions in promoting learning behaviour need to be recognised. The rewards available are a prediction of what a typical child might experience as positively reinforcing; the sanctions are a prediction of what a typical child might experience as aversive. As previously discussed in relation to behaviour policies, the behaviour for learning approach requires us to take into account individual interpretations. This can explain why some children do not respond in the predicted manner. The reasons behind some children's differing interpretation and response to rewards and sanctions may include the following:

- What as adults we consider to be rewarding may not be experienced as such by the child. Being singled out for praise, for example, may be embarrassing for some children and consequently they may exhibit less of the behaviour that gained the reward.
- What as adults we consider to be aversive may not be experienced as such by the child. For example, receiving negative attention from an adult may be experienced as preferable to receiving none.
- The child's view of the person giving a reward or sanction may influence its impact. The reward or sanction may mean more or less to the individual depending on

whether they like or respect this person. Children may also have a perception of the rewarder's or sanctioner's view of them. Therefore personal relationships are important.

- The child's reflection upon the experience of being rewarded or sanctioned is likely to influence their response. They may interpret a reward as undeserved or patronising, or view a sanction as unfair.
- There may be many other rewarding or punishing factors present besides those the teacher is controlling. For example, while the teacher may use ignoring as a response to attention seeking behaviour, it may be the attention of peers that is more important to the child.
- Rewards and sanctions are reliant on the child having the required behaviour in their repertoire. Some children may not have reached this point developmentally; others may not have learnt this behaviour and it may require teaching. Just as with a difficulty in learning, there is a need to ask ourselves whether the child knows what to do, knows how to do it and has had enough practice at doing it before 'we simply ascribe dubious motivation and rush into rewards and punishments' (Faupel et al., 1998, p. 8).
- The current behaviour may be serving a purpose for the individual that means it is too valuable to relinquish for a reward or sanction. An example might be a child who fears failure and misbehaves to avoid starting a task, thus protecting their relationship with self.

For most children, thoughtful application of rewards and sanctions in line with the school's behaviour policy will be sufficient in at least setting the scene for, even if not directly promoting, the development of learning behaviour. The teacher will endeavour to make use of rewards and sanctions in a way that ideally enhances but, at the very least, does not carry a predictable risk of impacting negatively on the three behaviour for learning relationships. For some children it may be necessary to try to understand the different interpretation that they are making in order to understand and address why they are not responding in the anticipated way to rewards and sanctions. This can be done through careful observation over a period of time, as well as talking to them about their behaviour in order to gain some insight. Just as we might talk about personalising or differentiating learning, we sometimes have to respond differently to individuals in relation to behaviour.

Providing positive feedback on behaviour

Positive verbal feedback is often referred to as praise (e.g. DfE, 2013, 2016; TA, 2012). Within the behaviour for learning approach, praise is conceptualised as the provision of verbal encouragement that is focused on the learning behaviours exhibited. It can be thought of as the provision for the child of feedback on their behavioural performance. For this reason, our preference is for the term 'positive feedback' rather than 'praise'. When a tangible reward is given, we would always expect positive feedback to accompany it so that the child still receives information on their performance. Drawing on recommendations from Brophy (1981), we would stress the following key points when using positive feedback to promote the development of learning behaviour:

- Feedback to individuals is provided within the context of a whole-class approach where desirable learning behaviours are known, explicitly referred to and regularly reinforced.
- The feedback should be phrased so that it is descriptive, providing information to the child on the learning behaviour they have exhibited that has drawn this positive attention. In the case of public positive feedback, this also allows other members of the class to hear information about the desirable learning behaviours.
- The feedback can be purely descriptive (e.g. 'John, I can see you are sitting up ready to listen') but if there is an evaluative element (e.g. 'Well done') it should form only a small proportion of the message.
- Using just an evaluative element ('Good', 'Fantastic', 'Well done') without a descriptive component misses an opportunity to convey information about the desired learning behaviours.
- Positive feedback needs to be available for effort, improvement and achievements in both learning and behaviour.
- Within the positive feedback, any reference to the reasons for success should relate to factors the child can influence (e.g. their effort, sustained attention to the task) on future occasions.
- Positive feedback should not be 'overblown' – remembering basic equipment is worthy of positive acknowledgement (e.g. 'Good to see you've remembered your ...') but more than this may be experienced as patronising or insincere.

As adults we may assume positive feedback to be, as its name suggests, a positive experience for the child. The underlying principle is that, if a required behaviour is positively reinforced by something that the child finds rewarding, they will be more likely to exhibit that behaviour again in the future. If this is a major purpose of providing positive feedback, then it makes sense to attempt to deliver any positive comment in a form that the child prefers and is likely to experience positively. Some children, for example, may prefer private positive feedback rather than more public recognition. Others may find it difficult to accept comments they perceive to be praise. Such children may benefit from a more depersonalised approach. For example, as an alternative to singling out an individual, a teacher could say, 'This group's worked well together. I liked the way you all took turns using the equipment. That's good collaboration'. Or 'I'm pleased to see everyone on this table's settled down and got their equipment out'. The hope would be that the individual child would make the connection themself that this positive comment applied to them as much as the others.

Positive correction

Positive correction refers to the approach of framing interactions with children regarding misbehaviour positively, so that the focus is on the required learning behaviour. For example, we might say 'Daniel, facing this way' rather than 'Daniel, stop turning round'. Framing corrections in terms of the required behaviours helps to keep the atmosphere of the classroom positive, unlike the frequent use of statements beginning or containing 'don't', 'no' or 'stop'. If we accept the Elton Report finding that 'schools with a negative atmosphere will suffer more from bad behaviour than those with a positive one' (DfES, 1989, p. 89), there is an obvious rationale to this approach. At the level of an individual child's experience and the general climate for learning, the classroom can become a negative environment if the air is filled with a continual stream of negatively expressed messages, even if they are directed towards other children.

Despite in its annual reports consistently reporting that behaviour was good or better in the vast majority of schools, in 2014 the Office for Standards in Education (Ofsted) published a report highlighting the impact of low-level misbehaviour (Ofsted, 2014). It attempted to quantify this impact in terms of the amount of learning time lost. The report provides an indication of the main types of behaviours identified by teachers in all types and phases of school surveyed. These were:

- talking and chatting
- disturbing other children
- calling out
- not getting on with work
- fidgeting or fiddling with equipment
- not having the correct equipment
- purposely making noise to gain attention

- answering back or questioning instructions
- using mobile devices
- swinging on chairs.

There were differences between the phases. Common problems identified by primary teachers were calling out, disturbing other children and fidgeting with equipment. Though reducing such behaviours through a range of proactive measures is a realistic aim, eliminating them completely is not (DfES, 1989). These behaviours represent predictable occurrences and it makes sense to plan forms of positive correction to use in these situations. Framing corrections positively requires thought and practice because it may not be intuitive. Taking the example of the child who calls out, the natural teacher reaction might be to say, 'Don't call out' or, if this is a regular occurrence and the source of some frustration, even, 'Don't call out. How many times do I have to tell you?' Positively framed alternatives as a response to this predictable occurrence include:

- 'Hands up without calling out, thanks ...'
- 'Remember our class rule for asking questions.'
- 'Hands up so I can see your voice.'
- 'I can hear questions; I can't see hands up.'
- 'I get concerned when several of you call out. We end up not able to hear anyone. I'd like you to remember to put your hands up.'

These examples are based on suggestions from Rogers (2011), who has, over many years (e.g. Rogers, 1990, 1997), written on the subject of behaviour management, placing particular emphasis on teacher language. From a behaviour for learning perspective, it is necessary to recognise that these interactions with children occur within the context of a relationship and will also be experienced and interpreted by the child as an individual. Consequently, the interaction cannot be reduced to the level of a script that a teacher follows. As a reader looking at these suggestions, it is likely that you will have a reaction to them based on imagining both yourself saying them and the children you work with hearing them. For example, you may not feel you could deliver the line 'Hands up so I can see your voice' credibly because it does not fit with your style and personality as a teacher. For some children, such as those on the autism spectrum, this line might be problematic because it does not make sense when a literal interpretation is applied. The fourth example, 'I can hear questions; I can't see hands up', is also problematic in this respect. Its strength is that it is depersonalised – it does not target anyone specifically – but it does require that children understand it beyond its literal level as a descriptive statement and recognise the implication that they should put their hands up rather than call out. The strength of the fifth example, is that it is in the form of an 'I' statement. In other words, it starts by describing the effect on the teacher and the wider effect on others. While there is a lot to commend this type of statement, the potential problem is the length. There may be some children who, for a variety of reasons, including their age and stage of development, cannot cope with the amount of words in this instruction. Thinking about positive correction strategies from a behaviour for learning perspective requires the teacher to select strategies based on how these are likely to be interpreted and experienced by the child.

Though positive correction should be the focus, the suggestion is not that adults should never say 'no'. For young children in particular, it may be appropriate to respond to more serious behaviours with a clear, brief message such as 'No, we don't throw the toys' or 'No, we don't hit people'. On the occasions when this is necessary it will be more effective in an environment where positive correction is generally used and it is not just one of the many 'No' messages the child hears.

Reflective task

Select two or three behaviours from the list provided by Ofsted (2014) shown above or choose some that are more relevant to your setting. For each one, identify what you would say to the child, ensuring this adheres to the principles of positive correction described in this section of the chapter.

Central to the behaviour for learning perspective on behaviour management is the principle that the teacher's role is to promote learning. The adoption of a 'least to most intrusive' approach to the use of behaviour management strategies reflects this principle. This simply means that the teacher should start with the lowest level of intervention necessary to refocus the child on their learning. Strategies such as tactical ignoring or a non-verbal signal would represent a low level of intrusion. It is unlikely anyone else in the class would even notice that the strategy was being used. A simple directive statement (e.g. 'John, sitting down now, thanks') or a reminder of a rule (e.g. 'Sarah, remember our rule for asking questions') moves a little further up the scale as the teacher is taking a brief moment out from promoting learning to manage behaviour and the comment will be heard by other children. At the most intrusive end of the scale we might locate the imposition of a sanction or exit from the class.

Reflective task

Think about the range of strategies and approaches you typically use or have seen other teachers use when misbehaviour is occurring and needs to be addressed. Record these in summary form, ideally on separate pieces of paper. Arrange these strategies and approaches in a 'least to most' intrusive order.

Typically, the ordering of some of these will be debatable and factors such as tone of voice might also affect where you place the strategy. The precise order is not important; you are simply trying to capture a general progression from least to most intrusive.

Work in school

Student: I'm really struggling to maintain an appropriate noise level in the classroom. My problem is that I just can't seem to identify where this originates from. If I knew I could follow the steps set out in the school's behaviour policy. Last week I tried the technique of writing on the board 'Whole-class detention – 1 minute'. As the noise persisted I added minutes. Eventually some pupils noticed and started to 'shush' the others. By the time I'd reached '10 minutes' on the board the class was quiet so this seemed to work. It meant I had to give up 10 minutes of my lunch time to keep them in but it's probably worth it.

Mentor: I can understand your frustration. Most behaviour management techniques do rely on being able to identify the right person and in a situation like this where you can't it becomes very difficult. However, I do have some concerns about this approach. It does seem to punish the innocent along with the guilty and the risk is that this leads to resentment from those who are currently 'on side'. Maybe you should turn this on its head and operate a system where there is a class reward for keeping the noise below a certain level for a set period of time. I've seen people use a simple noise meter based on a cardboard circle divided into red, amber and green segments. Green represents

(Continued)

(Continued)

the desired noise level, amber is a warning that it is becoming too noisy and the level needs to be adjusted, and red means it is too noisy. You would move the pointer to the appropriate section. A class reward could be linked to staying out of the red zone. This encourages a similar sort of peer group pressure to a whole-class sanction but directs it in a more positive manner. It also enables you to direct praise to those who have noticed the position of the pointer and adjusted their behaviour.

Analysis

The mentor is right to express concern. Previous government guidance has clearly stated that schools should 'avoid whole group sanctions that punish the innocent as well as the guilty' (DCSF, 2009, p 31). As the Elton Report (DES, 1989) pointed out, such approaches are always likely to be seen as unfair by children and the resulting sense of grievance is likely to be damaging to the school atmosphere. From a behaviour for learning perspective, it is an approach that raises some additional concerns. We would see self-efficacy as an important component of an individual's relationship with self. Self-efficacy can be thought of as a person's estimate that a given behaviour will lead to certain outcomes coupled with their belief in their ability to successfully execute this behaviour (Bandura, 1977). The strategy used by the teacher potentially undermines the individual's sense of self-efficacy. Even if an individual chose to take personal responsibility (a positive learning behaviour) in order to get on with the task quietly and attempted to filter out distractions from others (a positive learning behaviour), this is neither rewarded nor recognised and still leads to the same negative outcome (i.e. staying in), unless sufficient others make similar positive choices. Such a strategy risks sending the unhelpful message that, as an individual, the child is able to exert little influence over what happens to them; it is the behaviour of others that determines whether the individual receives the sanction. We might also speculate on the potential damage to children's relationships with others. The inherent unfairness may be damaging to the children's relationship with the teacher but we can look further than this and consider what it might do to peer relationships. Though the assumption underpinning this strategy is often that it

(Continued)

makes use of peer group pressure, it is essentially underpinned by a 'divide and conquer principle' (Kohn, 1999, p. 5). If the peer group pressure moved beyond the 'shushing' in class to take the form of the perceived culprits subsequently being socially isolated by their classmates, or even experiencing physical coercion, it would be a concern.

The tutor's suggestion represents a more positive alternative, though the form taken by any peer group pressure on those perceived to be preventing the class receiving the reward would still need careful monitoring. The noise meter (Rogers, 2011) encourages the class to take more responsibility for monitoring their own behaviour. It is a positive strategy that can be used throughout the lesson – though the teacher's original strategy could also be used in this way rather than reactively, it sets a very negative tone based on threat of punishment. This overt focus on the sanction conveys low expectations – the implication is that the class are bound to lose minutes. In contrast, the noise meter can be presented as part of a wider consideration of appropriate noise levels for different types of activity when learning in a group setting. Some teachers, for example, will distinguish between 'partner voices', 'table voices', 'classroom voice' and 'playground voice'.

The noise meter was a positive, potentially useful strategy to suggest. It does fit with the principle of protecting the three behaviour for learning relationships and, in the way it is presented to the class and subsequently referred to, could contribute to the development of learning behaviour. However, prior to simply replacing one questionable behaviour management technique with a better one, there was a need to look at possible reasons why noise levels were too high and whether there were other routes to addressing this concern. For example, do the problems result from children getting stuck and not knowing what to do? Unable to continue, they may become restless and find other ways of occupying their time. In this situation the priority might be to teach problem solving strategies. These could be supported by a poster displaying the steps to take when stuck that the teacher can then remind the children of. The noise levels might also prompt a need to look at the level of challenge. Are children getting stuck so frequently because the task is too difficult? Conversely the level of challenge may be too low, meaning either that children can complete it and talk at the same time or it is experienced as boring, so to relieve this they find other distractions. If the level of challenge is the issue then differentiation strategies rather than behaviour management strategies may be the priority.

Summary

This chapter has looked at some generic behaviour management systems and techniques through a behaviour for learning lens, considering their compatibility with the general principles reflected in the behaviour for learning conceptual framework. Behaviour for learning represents a different way of thinking that encourages schools and teachers to harness the cognitive, social and emotional components of classroom relationships to support the development of learning behaviour. There is explicit recognition that the route to securing these learning behaviours will often lie in a different direction from a quest to identify more behaviour management strategies in the hope that these will enable the teacher to cope with anticipated classroom disruption (Powell and Tod, 2004).

For many children, it will suffice simply to focus on the general learning behaviours necessary to develop in learners at their age and stage of development, while keeping a watchful eye on the effect of any practice on the three relationships. However, the flexible nature of the behaviour for learning approach means that, when this is not sufficient, it can be applied in a more systematic way as an assessment and planning tool for groups and specific individuals whose behaviour causes particular concern. The conceptual framework (Figure 9.1) provides a means of understanding the cognitive, social and emotional factors influencing their current behaviour and supports the planning of appropriate strategies and approaches. Where the teacher feels positive change will be achieved by developing one or two target learning behaviours this would involve identifying strategies and approaches that have the potential to contribute to the development of these. The strategies and approaches are likely to be recognisable as cognitive, social and/or emotional in their focus (see Figure 9.2). This knowledge can help the teacher recognise if, for example, one of these three areas is being underused currently as a source of strategies and approaches. Monitoring and evaluation would be based on the emergence of the identified target learning behaviours.

For a more complex case, a teacher may consider that the current problematic behaviour results from a significant weakness in one or more of the three relationships. Learning behaviours remain important but the focus would shift to the development of a specific relationship area. Self-esteem might be an example. We would associate low self-esteem with the child's relationship with self. The teacher would identify a cluster of learning behaviours (or specific significant learning behaviour) that they feel they need to promote in order to have a pervasive, positive effect on the target relationship. Adaptations to standard practice and any additional or different strategies and approaches would be identified in order to promote this cluster of learning behaviours (or specific significant learning behaviour). Monitoring and evaluation would be based on the emergence of the cluster of learning behaviours (or specific significant learning behaviour) previously identified that indicate that the target relationship area has been strengthened.

Questions for discussion

- What observable differences in practice might you see if a teacher was adopting a behaviour for learning approach as opposed to focusing on behaviour management?
- What aspects of your current practice might you change to more closely align it with the behaviour for learning approach described in this chapter?
- Identify an activity you regularly require children to take part in. What learning behaviours do they need within their repertoires to tackle the different parts of this activity?
- Reflect on common strategies and approaches used to manage behaviour in your setting. Are they compatible with the principle that any practice ideally enhances but, at the very least, does not carry a predictable risk of impacting negatively on the three behaviour for learning relationships?
- To what extent do you agree with the suggestion of McNally et al. (2005, p. 183) that attaching too much priority to the management of behaviour potentially distracts from 'a superior focus on learning, trivialises the life problems of pupils and demeans the place of teacher–pupil interactions in relation to these problems'?

Further reading

Ellis, S. and Tod, J. (2015) *Promoting Behaviour for Learning in the Classroom: Effective Strategies, Personal Style and Professionalism*. Abingdon: Routledge.
This book provides more detailed coverage of the behaviour for learning approach introduced within this chapter.

Hart, R. (2010) 'Classroom behaviour management: Educational psychologists' views on effective practice', *Emotional and Behavioural Difficulties*, 15 (4): 353–71.
This article focuses on a small-scale research project collecting educational psychologists' views on effective classroom behaviour management strategies.

Lever, C. (2011) *Understanding Challenging Behaviour in Inclusive Classrooms.* Harlow: Pearson.
This book is concerned with understanding why certain behaviours occur and how to deal with them. It offers strategies for how to deal with challenging behaviour on an individual level, by looking at the needs of the individual.

McNally, J., I'anson, J., Whewall. C. and Wilson, G. (2005) '"They think swearing is OK": First lessons in behaviour management', *Journal of Education for Teaching*, 31 (3): 169–85.
Drawing on the experiences of beginning teachers, this article argues that an overemphasis on behaviour management is problematic as it can lead to insufficient recognition of links between behaviour and learning, the experiences pupils bring with them and the powerful influence of teacher–pupil relationships.

Rogers, B. (2015) *Classroom Behaviour*, fourth edn. London: Sage.
This is one of many books Bill Rogers has written on behaviour management over the years. In presenting a range of practical strategies and approaches he retains a strong focus on maintaining positive relationships with pupils. Within his work, Rogers places particular emphasis on teacher language when managing behaviour.

References

Bandura, A. (1977) *Social Learning Theory.* Englewood Cliffs, NJ: Prentice Hall.
Brophy, J. (1981) 'Teacher praise: A functional analysis', *Review of Educational Research*, 51 (1): 5–32.
Department for Children, Schools and Families (DCSF) (2009) *School Discipline and Pupil-Behaviour Policies – Guidance for Schools.* Nottingham: DCSF.
Department for Education and Science (DfES) (1989) *Discipline in Schools* (the 'Elton Report'). London: HMSO.
Department for Education and Science (DfES) (2005) *Learning Behaviour: The Report of the Practitioners' Group on School Behaviour and Discipline* (the 'Steer Report'). Nottingham: DfES.
DfE (2013) *Teachers' Standards.* London: DfE.
DfE (2014) *Behaviour and Discipline in Schools: Advice for Headteachers and School Staff.* Available at: www.gov.uk/government/uploads/system/uploads/attachment_data/file/277662/Behaviour_and_Discipline_in_Schools_-_A_guide_for_headteachers_and_school_staff.pdf (accessed 6 February 2014).
DfE (2016) *Behaviour and Discipline in Schools: Advice for Headteachers and School Staff.* Available at: https://www.gov.uk/government/uploads/system/uploads/attachment_data/file/488034/Behaviour_and_Discipline_in_Schools_-_A_guide_for_headteachers_and_School_Staff.pdf (accessed 8 February 2017).
Ellis, S. and Tod, J. (2009) *Behaviour for Learning: Proactive Approaches to Behaviour Management.* Abingdon: Routledge.
Ellis, S. and Tod, J. (2015) *Promoting Behaviour for Learning in the Classroom: Effective Strategies, Personal Style and Professionalism.* Abingdon: Routledge.

Faupel, A., Herrick, E. and Sharp, P. (1998) *Anger Management: A Practical Guide*. London: David Fulton.

Jude, R. (2014) 'Is using running as punishment the right message?' Available at: www.sports gazette.co.uk/section.php?aid=1121&sid=36 (accessed 31 January 2017).

Kohn, A. (1999) *Punished By Rewards*. New York: Houghton Mifflin.

McLean, A. (2009) *Motivating Every Learner*. London: Sage.

McNally, J., I'anson, J., Whewall, C. and Wilson, G. (2005) '"They think swearing is OK": First lessons in behaviour management', *Journal of Education for Teaching*, 31 (3): 169–85.

Office for Standards in Education (Ofsted) (2014) *Below the Radar: Low-level Disruption in the Country's Classrooms*. Available at: https://www.gov.uk/government/uploads/system/ uploads/attachment_data/file/379249/Below_20the_20radar_20-_20low-level_20disruption _20in_20the_20country_E2_80_99s_20classrooms.pdf (accessed 8 February 2017).

Powell, S. and Tod, J. (2004) *A Systematic Review of how Theories Explain Learning Behaviour in School Contexts*. London: EPPI-Centre, Social Science Research Unit, Institute of Education, University of London.

Rogers, B. (1990) *You Know the Fair Rule*, first edn. London: Pitman Publishing.

Rogers, B. (1997) *The Language of Discipline*, second edn. Plymouth: Northcote House.

Rogers, B. (2011) *Classroom Behaviour*, third edn. London: Sage.

Teaching Agency (TA) (2012) *Improving Teacher Training for Behaviour*. Available at: http:// dera.ioe.ac.uk/14683/7/improving%20teacher%20training%20for%20behaviour%20with out%20case%20studies.pdf (accessed 8 February 2017).

10

Personal, Social, Health and Economic Education (PSHE)

Richard Palmer

By the end of this chapter you should:

- understand the relevance of personal, social, health and economic education (PSHE) to children's learning and well-being (Teacher Standard 5.3)
- know the underpinning principles of an effective whole-school PSHE programme and how that relates to effective PSHE in class (Teacher Standards 3.1, 3.2)
- demonstrate greater confidence in teaching effective and 'safe' PSHE lessons that meet children's needs (Teacher Standards 1.1, 1.2, 2.2, 4.1, 4.5, 5.4, 8.5)
- identify aspects of PSHE as a focus for professional development within and beyond your initial teacher training (ITT) (Teacher Standards 3.2, 4.4).

Introduction

Children today are growing up in a fast-paced world that offers them many new and exciting possibilities, but with this comes a host of risks, pressures and anxieties that they will need help to navigate at school, and in preparation for their adult lives. Personal, social, health and economic education (PSHEE), more commonly shortened to PSHE, is the subject in the curriculum that allows children and young people to explore the knowledge, skills and attitudes needed to help them stay safe, healthy (mentally and emotionally as well as physically), and develop positive relationships with others. Within this learning children can also gain a better understanding of their self-worth and develop resilience to assist them in reaching their full potential.

It is difficult, then, to understand why in a report published by the Office for Standards in Education (Ofsted) in 2013, entitled *Not Yet Good Enough*, the findings suggest that PSHE is poorly taught in many schools (Ofsted, 2013). There are a number of reasons for this including the subject's non-statutory status, a lack of subject-specific training for teachers, and an overcrowded National Curriculum with an emphasis on academic results. This can sometimes mean that PSHE is not prioritised, and is why the government have proposed that relationships and sex education (RSE) will be made compulsory for all schools in England, with the changes coming into effect by 2019. There will also be a consultation about PSHE with a view to making this a statutory curriculum subject (House of Commons, 2017). This has been campaigned for by a range of education, social and health organisations headed by the National PSHE Subject Association (2016).

While this chapter can only be a starting point for your development as a teacher of PSHE, it will aim to provide you with a better understanding of the subject and help you consider some practicalities of how to teach it in your early stages as a primary teacher. These ideas will be based upon the PSHE Subject Association's Ten Principles of Effective PSHE Education (PSHE Subject Association, 2014).

Reflective task

As a starting point for this chapter begin by reflecting individually or with others on the following questions:

- Consider how life has changed for children and young people in the past 15 years? What do they need now compared to then?

Table 10.1 Summary of the PSHE Subject Association Principles of effective PSHE practice

1. Don't assume a pupil's prior knowledge. Find out what they know before you teach.
2. Plan a 'spiral' PSHE programme that builds upon prior knowledge and skills.
3. Take a positive approach that does not attempt to induce shock or guilt.
4. Use a range of participatory and interactive learning strategies.
5. Provide information which is realistic and relevant and which reinforces positive social norms.
6. Encourage young people to reflect on their PSHE learning and apply it to their lives.
7. Recognise that PSHE is part of a whole-school SMSC provision (spiritual, moral, social, cultural).
8. Underpin PSHE with work on positive relationships.
9. Help pupils reflect on healthy and safe choices.
10. Provide a safe and supportive learning environment.

The status of PSHE within the National Curriculum

At the time of writing, PSHE remains a non-statutory subject in the National Curriculum for state schools and academies. However, this does not mean that it is optional, something that can be misunderstood by student teachers. The non-statutory status means unlike other curriculum areas there is no formally recognised programme of study for schools to follow; instead each school is free to devise their own PSHE programme. Section 2.5 of the National Curriculum (DfE, 2015, p. 5) states,

> All state schools 'should make provision for personal, social, health and economic education (PSHE), drawing on good practice'.

The National Curriculum also requires that maintained schools' curricula are made available online, and this includes their provision for PSHE, within:

'A broad and balanced curriculum' which:

- promotes the spiritual, moral, cultural, mental and physical development of pupils at the school and of society, and
- prepares pupils at the school for the opportunities, responsibilities and experiences of later life. (DfE, 2015, p. 5)

Much of the new safeguarding guidance for schools (DfE, 2015) also suggests that it would be difficult for a school to meet their duties unless they were teaching PSHE effectively (see Chapter 11). As discussed in the latest House of Commons Education Committee Report on PSHE (House of Commons, 2015), changing the subject's status may not mean that high-quality teaching and learning are achieved. However, the report does recognise that removing the 'non-statutory' label would help improve PSHE's profile in schools and give a mandate to improve teacher training in this curriculum area. However, it is still unclear whether the government's proposals will provide a definitive programme of work for PSHE.

PSHE and initial teacher training

Many student teachers find it challenging to identify when PSHE is being taught within their teaching practice schools (Mead, 2004, p. 22). PSHE can often be embedded within other lessons rather than being taught as a discrete subject. It is also a subject that is more likely to be removed from the weekly timetable to make room for other activities (Formby, 2011), therefore limiting student teachers' experience of the subject further. Some of the comments from trainees and more experienced primary teachers in Boddington and colleagues' *Understanding Personal, Social, Health and Economic Education in Primary Schools* (Boddington et al., 2014, p. 3) suggest that PSHE in initial teacher training (ITT) is still a 'hit and miss' affair. If this resonates with your experiences so far, while not a substitution for effective training, this chapter will give you some of the essentials so that you can begin to plan and teach effective PSHE lessons.

Reflective task

Look at Table 10.2. Identify where each PSHE theme supports the different levels in Maslow's Hierarchy of Needs.

Table 10.2   Possible themes that could be explored within a whole-school PSHE programme

- Diversity and difference – gender diversity, differences between families, cultural and racial and ethnic diversity (see also Chapter 14 in this book), personal differences including likes and dislikes and personal choice, physical differences (important starting point for work on puberty and body image work), LGBTQ issues
- Rights and responsibilities – individual, within school, families and wider society. Universal rights of the child, global citizenship, behaviour for learning (see Chapter 9)
- Fundamental British values, Prevent, anti-radicalisation education – although this is covered in a separate chapter (Chapter 15) within this book, much of a school's work on British values will come within PSHE
- Health education – healthy eating, importance of physical activity, personal hygiene
- Drug education including medicine safety, smoking, alcohol and other legal drugs, illegal drugs, emergency aid
- Relationship and sex education (RSE) – names of body parts, physical and emotional changes at puberty, life cycles, conception and childbirth, different types of families, friendship, safe and unsafe touch (safeguarding), e-safety, bereavement
- Social and emotional development – social skills, managing feelings, mindfulness, getting on and falling out, conflict resolution, empathy, positive mental health, hopes and dreams
- Resilience – peer pressure, being a resilient learner, facing challenges, overcoming obstacles, positive self-esteem, motivation, coping with change, stress management
- Safety education – personal safety, e-safety, fire safety, water safety, railway and road safety, sun safety, safety in the home, accessing help
- Critical thinking – skills of investigation, debating and weighing arguments, making choices, understanding fact and opinion, role of the media
- Body image
- Safeguarding (links to personal safety, child online exploitation, female genital mutilation, forced marriage), see also Chapter 15
- Bullying, including online and through social media
- Citizenship, careers and financial education

Planning your programme of work

Table 10.2 is a 'suggested' list of topics that could be taught within a primary PSHE programme. This is not an exhaustive list and, as suggested by the PSHE Association's Principle 1, any PSHE programme should be based on *children's needs*, and this may vary from class to class and school to school.

When looking at this list it is important to understand that some of these topics are not mutually exclusive and at first glance some can seem wholly inappropriate to teach in primary school. This is where the *spiral* nature of a school's PSHE programme and *age-appropriateness* are important factors (PSHE Subject Association Principle 2).

However, we must be careful when generalising the term 'age-appropriate'. What we mean is educationally appropriate – are the children intellectually and emotionally ready for these lessons? Social constructivists, sociologists and public health experts agree that a 'person-centred' approach is effective in promoting positive healthy behaviours (Boddington et al., 2014). However, thinking about this practically, it simply makes sense to understand what your children know or don't know so that you can plan your lesson and ensure there is an appropriate progression of skills and concepts.

There are numerous teaching techniques that can be used to pre-assess children's understanding in PSHE (see Mosely and Murray, 1996; Boddington et al., 2014). If you are fortunate enough to be teaching in a school that uses a comprehensive scheme of learning for PSHE such as Jigsaw PSHE (www.jigsawpshe.com) there will be further examples at your disposal.

If using a published lesson plan, it is imperative that you reflect on the planned content and adjust it if necessary, with *the needs of your children in mind*. Not all published PSHE resources do this, so you may need to employ some of your own pre-assessment so you can be confident that the resources are appropriate *for your children*.

Work in school

Student 1:   On my last placement, I had to teach a lesson about bullying with Year 3. The school used circle time to teach all its PSHE. It didn't go well because all the children started 'naming and shaming' other children in the class. It has really made me nervous about teaching PSHE again.

(Continued)

Student 2:   I agree, I had to teach a lesson about alcohol in Year 6 and was asked by the children if I had ever been drunk! I didn't know how to respond. It has put me off PSHE.

Mentor: Circle time can be a useful method in PSHE, but without the appropriate safeguards it has the potential to be exactly like you describe. Bullying and alcohol are examples of the many 'sensitive' subjects in PSHE and need to be handled carefully. You could have used distancing techniques. Sometimes circle time is not always the most appropriate teaching method. Don't be afraid to change something if you feel that it is not appropriate. Did the school have any special circle time or PSHE ground rules to use with the children? Don't let these negative experiences put you off PSHE. It can be an enjoyable subject to teach and there are simple but effective methods you can use to overcome problems like you described.

Analysis

There are several issues to be considered here and these will be addressed in the 'Creating a safe "space" for PSHE' section of this chapter below.

Creating a safe 'space' for PSHE

It is clear that both trainees were not made aware of suitable teaching strategies to use in planning. PSHE is personal because we are helping children explore and make sense of what it means to be human. Children and adults will bring their own understanding, experiences, values, beliefs, and skills to every PSHE lesson, and some of this will be deeply personal.

Therefore, an *essential* consideration for good PSHE education is the establishment of a 'safe' classroom climate (PSHE Subject Association Principles 8 and 10). We need to ask ourselves certain questions from the children's perspective to get this climate right:

- Am I comfortable learning about this subject?
- Am I able to say what I think about this subject even if I'm the only one who thinks like this?
- Do I feel valued and that what I say is valued?
- How do I talk about negative experiences, things that worry me or mistakes I have made?
- Is it okay to be honest?

A commonly seen starting point is the PSHE Learning Charter or 'PSHE Ground Rules' (King and Wetton, 2003). When working with a new class, the first PSHE lesson(s) should focus on the creation of a set of PSHE principles that the children and adults agree to abide by. This can be simply enacted by asking the children to work in groups and come up with a list of characteristics they would like to see in a good friend. The children will come up with things like 'Being a good listener' and 'Being kind'. The skill of the teacher is to guide them towards (not impose) a PSHE Learning Charter that includes the following ideas and agree with them that these would be good 'rules' for PSHE lessons where we sometimes talk about 'tricky subjects':

- We listen to each other.
- We have the right to 'pass'.
- We use kind and positive words.
- We only use people's names if we are being positive or giving compliments.
- We take turns to speak.
- We respect each other's privacy (confidentiality).

(Taken from Jigsaw PSHE, www.jigsawpshe.com)

It is worth noting the right to pass and confidentiality principles. As we have seen in the Work in School example some subjects may be difficult for children to talk about. The 'right to pass' gives children a get out clause if something is just too awkward or difficult to share. The rule is equally applicable to the teacher and can be used to get out of the 'awkward question' situation.

Realistically it is unlikely that complete confidentiality will be also be observed but it is important that the children are taught to respect the privacy of others and do their best to keep what is said in PSHE confidential. This 'rule' also allows the teacher to explain their limits of confidentiality and that they cannot promise to keep something 'secret' if there are safeguarding concerns. On occasion a child may divulge something that will need to be reported in line with the school's safeguarding policy (see Chapter 11).

If the trainee teachers in the Work in School example had used a PSHE Learning Charter their lessons may have had more positive outcomes. Their tutor also mentioned 'distancing techniques'. As the name suggests distancing is a way of discussing a subject through a 'third party'. In PSHE we can use:

- characters and situations in stories and scenarios
- picture books
- images and photographs depicting a specific scene or scenario
- puppets

- drama (be wary using this in lessons about bullying because we can inadvertently 'rehearse' bullying situations, which is not the intent)
- TV, internet, video and audio sources
- an anonymous 'question box' (particularly helpful when discussing bullying issues and RSE)
- visitors.

When choosing resources for distancing make sure they are age-appropriate and inclusive, taking into account the wide range of religious, cultural and physical diversity that reflects twenty-first-century society. Visitors can be an excellent source of information for the children but always ensure that you have discussed with them in good time what they are going to say and the classroom activities they want to use. This should identify in advance if there are any possible concerns with their input before they get in front of the children!

Managing awkward questions

Reflective task

With a friend discuss how you might answer the following questions from children. Would any of the techniques discussed previously support you with your answer?

- Miss/Sir, do you have sex?
- Why does God let people suffer?
- My dad says all immigrants should be sent home. What does he mean?
- Why do people watch porn?
- Jonny said my trainers were gay? What's gay?

Despite having a Learning Charter and using distancing, considering in advance what questions might arise and how you will answer them is helpful, but even then, you may not have thought about an answer for everything!

Never feel 'under pressure' to answer immediately. You can always respond by saying 'That's a good question, I'm going to need some time to think about that. Is that okay?' If you are unsure about what you are permitted to say, share the question with another member of staff and look at relevant school policies if you feel the question strays into 'controversial' territory. Sometimes we may not always have an answer, so we are also permitted to model this.

Some questions can be depersonalised by the answer you give. Staying positive, factual and normalising healthy choices is also helpful (PSHE Subject Association Principles 3 and 5). Equally the answer, 'I think it's important for you to make up your own mind so I'm not going to influence what you think' is a good way of deflecting a question back to the child and reinforces the importance of making their own choices.

The age-appropriateness of a child's question should also be considered carefully. The question about porn is a case in point, where this may indicate a pupil welfare issue. Refer to Chapter 11 for more on safeguarding.

Some questions worry teachers because they may conflict with parental views. Being sure about what it says in your school policy documents is essential. It is perfectly acceptable to answer the question in the Reflective Task about 'being gay'. Again, staying factual is helpful, 'It's when two men or two ladies love each other'. Primary schools have a legislative duty to address all forms of bullying including homophobia, such as the inappropriate use of the pejorative gay (Education Act 2006; Equality Act 2010; DfE *Preventing and Tackling Bullying*, 2014; Ofsted, 2016). The teacher could then add, 'Jonny was wrong to call your trainers gay, that word shouldn't be used in an unkind way'.

Where parental views appear to conflict with the values upheld by the school, a teacher would be correct in reinforcing the school policy, while depersonalising at the same time, as in the question about immigrants, 'Some people do think immigrants should be sent home, but in our school, we believe they have a right to be in our country. What do you think?'

Children look to their teachers as role models and we need to consider whether it is always appropriate or necessary to put our own personal values 'out there'. Exploring our own values and seeing where these might come into conflict with PSHE is important so that we know how to respond in class (Blake and Katrak, 2002). It is not 'wrong' to share our beliefs with the children, we are trying to model being human, but what we need to avoid is for them to *always* see us giving the 'right' answer (sometimes there will be). In PSHE, children need to learn to gather and evaluate a range of evidence so they can formulate their own ideas. Therefore, where there may be a conflict with a teacher's personal values, the techniques previously discussed to depersonalise, stay factual and within the school's values and policy frameworks are helpful. A range of participatory, active learning strategies such as those listed in Table 10.3 also allows children to explore a topic within PSHE and develop skills of enquiry without necessarily focusing on the teacher as a 'giver of information'.

Table 10.3   Some active teaching learning strategies for use within PSHE

Triads – groups of three, two children voicing different sides of a debate, the third in an observing/recording role.

Matching activities – two sets of cards for each group to match, e.g. rights/responsibilities or risk/consequence.

Continuum – an imaginary or physical line (on paper, in the classroom). Children are told one end represents one extreme viewpoint and the other end of the line is the opposite viewpoint. Children position and discuss where they are 'on the line'.

Carousel – two rows of chairs facing each other in a circle. Give the children a topic to discuss. After an agreed amount of time move the children in the inner circle one chair to the right/left so they have a new partner and begin the discussion again.

Storyboards – children create a storyboard of a situation or scenario. Can also do this as a 'road-map' to represent the children's personal 'journeys' within a PSHE theme. For example, how to be an effective learner, overcoming obstacles, friendship roadmaps (with bumps in the road sometimes).

Graffiti wall – children write or draw their responses to a question/discussion/scenario, etc. on a large display in the classroom. Can be used as a question wall, which collates the children's questions about a topic that they research in the next session(s).

Snowballing – children discuss in pairs, then those pairs join to make groups of four, then groups of eight.

Diamond nine – nine cards are given to each group with statements on each card. Children rank and lay out the cards as a large diamond in 1, 2, 3, 2, 1 formation. The most significant statement being at the top of the diamond and so on.

Envoying – children are assigned different tasks/topics in a group. After an agreed period of time children feed back what they have done/learnt to other groups in turn.

PSHE and bullying

Work in school

Mrs J is a PSHE subject lead. Her school does have a PSHE framework, but this does not specify detail beyond the topics to be taught in each year group. PSHE is a timetabled lesson in each class on a Friday afternoon. Mrs J is aware PSHE is often cut from the timetable due to time constraints. She has received numerous complaints from teachers and parents about bullying and has been asked what the school is doing about it. The school programme includes bullying in Year 2, and in Year 4 the pupils have a visitor to talk about cyber-bullying. One child in Year 6 has received 'nasty text' messages from her classmates. In Year 1, two children have fallen out but despite parental complaints Mrs J can't see any evidence of bullying. In the short term, Mrs J has planned for every class to focus on bullying during a specific week. In the long term, she has asked the school to

(Continued)

(Continued)

invest in a published scheme of work (Jigsaw PSHE) and to move the timetabled PSHE slot from a Friday to a Monday morning.

Consider:

1) Is the school doing enough anti-bullying work?
2) Is there a shared understanding within the whole school community about what is and isn't bullying?
3) If there is bullying happening (perhaps the strongest evidence is in Year 6) what measures are being put in place to stop it?

Analysis

It is important to stress that even with a whole-school approach to anti-bullying, it will sometimes occur. Consequently, it is vital that the school's bullying policy reflects all the preventative work it is doing, as well the procedures in place for supporting any children involved in bullying, as perpetrators, targets or bystanders. One of the most important aspects of any school bullying policy is the definition of bullying, which must be understood and owned by the whole school community. Because of different perceptions, a school's policy should clearly state its position and many schools use the definition contained within the Department for Education (DfE) Preventing and Tackling Bullying guidance (DfE, 2014).

Regardless of whether the action is repeated or otherwise, picking on somebody else so that it damages them physically or emotionally is unacceptable, and this is the fundamental message that needs to be taught to children repeatedly in PSHE and should pervade the school's ethos. In our example, there may not be a consistent understanding of what bullying 'looks like' in the school. The children in Year 1 may have just fallen out – this isn't necessarily bullying. PSHE is placed to support children to understand a range of conflicts within personal relationships and helps them to discriminate whether they are being bullied or not. It also teaches them to value and respect each other.

Clearly in Mrs J's school she is trying to 'plug the gap' with her short-term plan because PSHE has not been taught consistently. However, in the longer term she wants the school to invest in a detailed resource that focuses on PSHE skills as well as knowledge, and by moving the timetabled slot to earlier in the week, it is less likely to 'fall off' the weekly timetable. Moving PSHE to Monday mornings may also support the children to settle into a new week at school.

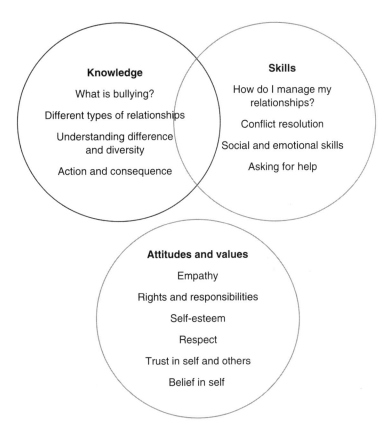

Figure 10.1 The interdependence of knowledge, skills, attitudes and values in anti-bullying work

Much of what we teach in PSHE supports anti-bullying, and that is why the short-term measures Mrs J is putting in place may only work for a few weeks at best, and why she wants to develop a much more coherent and consistent PSHE programme. Figure 10.1 identifies some of the PSHE that contributes to anti-bullying work.

In the light of this diagram it is easy to see why Mrs J's short-term measures are not likely to succeed. The skills and knowledge children need to recognise and deal with bullying situations can't be taught in a 'one off' bullying lesson.

We also cannot ignore the impact of the internet in bullying situations. The arrival of social media means that bullying perpetrators can now reach their intended targets virtually, potentially all day, every day. Many schools do teach about cyber-bullying as part of their information and communication technology (ICT) curriculum, but like bullying per se, this needs to be underpinned by effective PSHE if it is going to result in sustained learning. For further information on cyber- and other types of bullying, organisations such as the Anti-bullying Alliance (www.antibullyingalliance.org.uk) and the Child Exploitation and Online Protection Centre (CEOP, www.ceop.police. uk) offer a range of guidance and support for pupils, teachers and schools.

How do I support children that are involved in a bullying situation?

The focus of this chapter has been about PSHE education rather than pastoral care, although the two are not mutually exclusive. One of the most effective strategies for managing bullying incidents in school is 'The Support Group Approach' developed by Maines and Robinson (1991) (formerly called The No Blame Approach). For further information on this refer to *Bullying: A Complete Guide to the Support Group Method* (Robinson and Maines, 2008).

Relationships and sex education (RSE)

Reflective task

Discuss with a friend or group of friends about whether teaching relationships and sex education in Key Stages 1 and 2 destroys children's innocence.

RSE is perhaps the most contentious and misinterpreted aspect of PSHE education. When one hears the phrase 'sex and relationships education' our focus is drawn towards the word sex rather than relationships, which in turn leads us think about the narrow biological aspects of 'sex education': sexual intercourse and reproduction. The government's decision to make RSE statutory by 2019 puts more emphasis on 'relationships'. This has been done for good reason.

Children will have many relationships in their lives, acquaintances, friends, relatives, colleagues and classmates, and one day someone with whom they might share a loving and sexual relationship. Their relationships will change and shift over time, and in some cases, they will have to learn to move on, whether this is through a natural process such as death and bereavement, or by choice, where they or the other party has chosen to change the status of the relationship.

They may have a wide variety of physical and social contact within these relationships, from handshakes to more intimate gestures such as hugging, holding hands or kissing. Children need to start learning from an early age what is appropriate for the different relationships they have, what feels comfortable to them and what doesn't.

They also need to develop a relationship with themselves and their bodies. Part of this is an understanding of the physical, emotional and social changes that happen when we 'grow up'. Preparing children in advance for this is fair and just, and isn't spoiling their innocence, an argument that is often raised by some schools that do not want to teach RSE. Ignorance is different from innocence as we will go on to explore. RSE is also much more nuanced than 'sex education' and is not just about biology!

Adult and child perspectives

Children will also be exposed to a wide range of sexual imagery and language on a daily basis, more so because of the immediacy of the media and the internet. Some might say that a lot of this 'goes over the children's heads'. This is not true; in fact from a constructivist viewpoint they will be gathering information and trying to make sense of it. Where this works well, the new information makes the right connections and the child develops a true understanding. Where it's not so effective is where the child connects things wrongly, which means the whole concept needs unpicking and must be relearnt. Apply this to RSE and it is easy to see that children could create a whole host of their own explanations and become easily confused. Consider this example. Children are often told that to make a baby there needs to be a 'special cuddle'. I have taught primary aged children that were genuinely worried about this terminology, some so frightened they feared any type of physical contact for fear of making a baby!

The other issue to reflect upon is what we as adults bring to the subject before we even start teaching it. Many schools do not feel comfortable teaching the correct terminology for the sex organs in Key Stage 1. As adults, we bring an 'adult level' knowledge to these words. To a 4- or 5-year-old they are just words, and children will happily use them to describe parts of their bodies without the 'baggage' that adults bring. From a safeguarding perspective alone this is important so that children have the correct vocabulary rather than a whole array of colloquial language that could potentially be misinterpreted should they need to describe abusive behaviour.

Are we therefore empowering the children or destroying their innocence? There is an evidence base that suggests that a comprehensive RSE programme does not sexualise children, and teenagers that have been given quality age- and stage-appropriate RSE within a PSHE programme from a young age are less likely to engage in risky sexual behaviours and have effective skills to keep themselves safe within relationships (Brook, 2014). This resonates with what young people say about their sex education (Brook, 2014, p. 3) where many describe the RSE they have had as 'too little, too late and focused on biology'.

Legislation for RSE

The same requirements that relate to PSHE discussed earlier in this chapter also apply to RSE. However, there is also some more specific guidance to be aware of:

- DfE guidance on PSHE states that 'Sex and Relationships Education is an important aspect of PSHE' (DfE, 2013).
- There is a parental right to withdraw their children from all or part of RSE lessons (except aspects relating to human life cycles and biology, which are a statutory part of the science curriculum) (DfEE, 2000; Brook, 2014).
- All state schools must have an up-to-date sex and relationships education policy (DfEE, 2000), which must be made available to parents and carers (academies and free schools are advised but not compelled to do the same) (Brook, 2014).

So how do you teach RSE?

RSE should be a component part of PSHE, so *everything we have discussed in this chapter also applies to RSE specifically*. It is sometimes the 'content' of RSE that can make it 'feel' different for teachers, but good quality PSHE is good quality RSE: they are one and the same! Use the same approaches we have discussed previously.

For an example of a spiral programme of learning, see Chapter 9 in Boddington et al. (2014), or if your school is using the Jigsaw PSHE programme, the Relationships and Changing Me units (Jigsaw PSHE, 2013).

Partnership with parents and carers is also vital. Your school will almost certainly have a sex and relationships education policy, either as a discrete policy statement or included within another policy. Families should be made aware of this and the parts of the programme of study where children are likely to ask questions (e.g. puberty, conception and childbirth). This allows parents and carers to be involved and adequately prepared to support their children at home. We live in a culturally diverse community and some families will inevitably choose to withdraw their children from RSE, however the majority don't (Brook, 2014). A useful text that discusses RSE, faith and values by Blake and Katrak (2002) is a helpful source of further reading.

Mental health

Professor Katherine Weare (2015), a leading voice on children's and young people's social, emotional, and mental health, offers guidance to schools in both the promotion of positive mental health and tackling the mental health problems of those pupils who are already in difficulty. Her document sets out the importance of implementing well-designed programmes that support children's emotional and social development that can:

- improve children's capacity to learn through motivation and commitment
- help children feel happier at school and outside of school
- promote the development of social and emotional skills that are fundamental to positive mental health in life
- reduce mental health problems such anxiety, stress and depression
- improve pupil behaviour including reductions in low-level disruption, fights, bullying, exclusions and absence
- support children to manage risk such as impulsiveness, uncontrolled anger, violence, bullying, crime, drug use and unhealthy relationships.

It is quite deliberate that this chapter will close with a short section about mental health. As you can see from the list above, PSHE has a fundamental role to play in this, and the social and emotional skills Katherine Weare refers to underpin everything we teach in PSHE. The importance of addressing emotional health cannot be overestimated when reviewing the following statistics:

- 20 per cent of adolescents may experience a mental health problem in any given year.
- 50 per cent of mental health problems are established by age 14 and 75 per cent by age 24.
- 10 per cent of children and young people (aged 5–16 years) have a clinically diagnosable mental problem, yet 70 per cent of children and adolescents who experience mental health problems have not had appropriate interventions at a sufficiently early age. (Mental Health Foundation, 2010)

Many schools still use the social, emotional, aspects of learning (SEAL) resources (DfE, 2005), which is a planned programme focusing on five emotional literacy domains or Philosophy for Children (www.p4c.com). However, while these resources do teach children some skills of emotional and social literacy, they are not a substitute for a comprehensive PSHE programme.

If we teach PSHE well, we will help children recognise their own and others' emotions, which is crucial in maintaining healthy relationships and to make healthy and safe choices. Therefore a programme such as SEAL, that albeit unintentionally artificially separates emotional intelligence from PSHE rather than seeing them as whole, isn't particularly helpful. However, lessons such as those found in Jigsaw PSHE successfully include social and emotional development, embedding these skills as the foundation for quality PSHE, which is a far better approach (Wostenholme et al., 2016).

Summary

This chapter has only scratched the surface relating to the importance of effective PSHE education, but hopefully this has initiated reflection about how you will approach it within your teaching practice, as a newly qualified teacher and beyond. Indeed, if the DfE proposals come to fruition in 2019, there may be additional legislation and guidance to support you in your endeavours. While some of the subject matter can make PSHE seem daunting, we have discussed ways that you can explore a range of issues with children within a safe learning climate that values everyone. We have considered some specific aspects of PSHE, such as anti-bullying, emotional and social skills and RSE, and that an integrated PSHE programme is potentially more effective than a parade of unrelated 'topics', a series of visitors to the classroom/school or 'one off' lessons.

We have not covered assessment within PSHE or other curriculum areas, such as medicine, drug and alcohol education, personal finance education (including careers advice and skills at primary level) and safety education. However, more about these can be found by referring to the Further Reading list below.

Questions for discussion

Consider how this chapter has changed your perceptions of PSHE as a subject. What was your starting point and where are you now?

What further development in your PSHE teaching would you like to build into your continuing professional development plan?

Consider where this chapter challenged your awareness of your own personal values and how these might potentially influence the teaching of PSHE.

What are the complexities of bringing in a prescriptive national framework for PSHE as part of the DfE proposals?

Further reading

Boddington, N., King, A. and McWhirter, J. (2014) *Understanding Personal, Social, Health and Economic Education in Primary Schools*. London: Sage.
This text is a comprehensive guide to teaching PSHE. It offers further pedagogical insights, theory, practical advice and teaching strategies to ensure that PSHE lessons are relevant and meet the needs of children.

Formby, E (2011) '"It's better to learn about your health and things that are going to happen to you than learning things that you just do at school": Findings from a mapping study of PSHE education in primary schools in England', *Pastoral Care in Education*, 29 (3): 161–73.

Wostenholme, C., Willis, B. and Culliney, M. (2016) 'Does Jigsaw the mindful approach to PSHE work?', Sheffield Hallam University. Available at: www.jigsawpshe.com/does-jigsaw-work/ (accessed 18 March 2017).
A research study about schools who have been using the Jigsaw PSHE programme, which is a progressive spiral whole-school PSHE programme from Foundation to Year 6, underpinned by mindfulness practice.

Websites

PSHE Subject Association, www.pshe-association.org.uk.

A comprehensive source of support for school leaders, PSHE coordinators and class teachers. It contains guidance materials, further training and updates. Student teachers and newly qualified teachers have discounted membership fees (£15 annual fee for the first year, then £35 annual fee – prices at March 2017). It is free to join the Association mailing list.

Sex Education Forum, www.ncb.org.uk/about-us/our-specialist-networks/sex-education-forum.

References

Blake, S. and Katrak, Z. (2002) *Faith, Values and Sex and Relationships Education: Addressing the Issues*. London: National Children's Bureau.
Boddington, N., King, A. and McWhirter, J. (2014) *Understanding Personal, Social, Health and Economic Education in Primary Schools*. London: Sage.
Brook (2014) 'Sex and relationships education (SRE) for the 21st century: Supplementary advice to the Sex and Relationships Education Guidance DfEE (0116/2000)', London, Sex Education Forum, hosted by the National Children's Bureau. Available at: https://www.brook.org.uk/data/SRE-supplementary-advice.pdf (accessed 18 March 2017).

Department for Education (DfE) (2005) *Social, Emotional, Aspects of Learning (SEAL)*. Nottingham: DfE. Available at: http://webarchive.nationalarchives.gov.uk/content/20081117141643/http://standards.dfes.gov.uk/primary/publications/banda/seal/ (accessed 18 March 2017).

Department for Education (DfE) (2013) *Guidance for Personal, Social, Health, Economic education*. Available at: https://www.gov.uk/government/publications/personal-social-health-and-economic-education-pshe (accessed 17 March 2017).

Department for Education (DfE) (2014) *Preventing and Tackling Bullying*. Available at: https://www.gov.uk/government/uploads/system/uploads/attachment_data/file/444862/Preventing_and_tackling_bullying_advice.pdf (accessed 12 March 2017).

Department for Education (DfE) (2015) *National Curriculum: Primary Curriculum*. Available at: www.gov.uk/government/publications/national-curriculum-in-england-primary-curriculum (accessed 14 December 2016).

Department for Education (DfE) (2015) *Working Together to Safeguard Children*. Available at: www.gov.uk/government/publications/working-together-to-safeguard-children--2 (accessed 14 December 2016).

Department for Education (DfE) (2016) *Multiagency Statutory Guidance on Female Genital Mutilation*. Available at: www.gov.uk/government/publications/multi-agency-statutory-guidance-on-female-genital-mutilation (accessed 14 December 2016).

Department for Education and Employment (DfEE) (2000) *Sex and Relationships Education Guidance DfEE(0116/2000)*. Available at: https://www.gov.uk/government/publications/sex-and-relationship-education (accessed 1 March 2017).

Formby, E. (2011) '"It's better to learn about your health and things that are going to happen to you than learning things that you just do at school": Findings from a Mapping Study of PSHE Education in Primary Schools in England', *Pastoral Care in Education*, 29 (3): 161–73.

House of Commons (2015) *Life Lessons: PSHE and SRE in Schools: Fifth Report of Session 2014–2015*. Available at: www.publications.parliament.uk/pa/cm201415/cmselect/cmeduc/145/145.pdf (accessed 14 December 2016).

House of Commons (2017) *Sex and Relationships Education: Written statement – HCWS509*. Available at: www.parliament.uk/business/publications/written-questions-answers-statements/written-statement/Commons/2017-03-01/HCWS509/ (accessed 5 March 2017).

Jigsaw PSHE (2013) 'Jigsaw and the PSHE Association's Programme of Study: Making connections'. Available at: www.jigsawpshe.com/jigsaw-and-the-pshe-association-programme-of-study-2013-making-connections/ (accessed 28 February 2017).

Jigsaw PSHE (2017) *Scheme of Work*. Available at www.jigsawpshe.com (accessed 12 March 2017).

King, A. and Wetton, N. (2003) *Real Health for Real Lives*. Cheltenham: Nelson Thornes.

Maines, B. and Robinson, O. (1991) 'Don't beat the bullies', *Educational Psychology in Practice*, 7: 168–72.

Mead, N. (2004) 'The provision for personal, social, health education (PSHE) and citizenship in school-based elements of primary initial teacher education', *Pastoral Care*, June: 19–26.

Mental Health Foundation (2010) 'Mental health statistics children and young people'. Available at: https://www.mentalhealth.org.uk/statistics/mental-health-statistics-children-and-young-people (accessed 18 March 2017).

Mosely, J. and Murray, P. (1996) *Quality Circle Time in the Primary Classroom*. Positive Press. Available to buy at: www.circle-time.co.uk (accessed 4 September 2017).

Office for Standards in Education (Ofsted) (2013) *Not Yet Good Enough: Personal, Social, Health and Economic Education in Schools*. Available at: www.ofsted.gov.uk/resources/not-yet-good-enough-personal-social-health-and-economic-education-schools (accessed 12 December 2016).

Office for Standards in Education (Ofsted) (2016) *School Inspection Handbook*. Available at: https://www.gov.uk/government/publications/school-inspection-handbook-from-september-2015 (accessed 1 March 2017).

PSHE Subject Association (2014) *10 Principles of PSHE Education*. Available at: www.pshe-association.org.uk/curriculum-and-resources/resources/ten-principles-effective-pshe-education (accessed 12 December 2016).

PSHE Subject Association (2016) *A Curriculum for Life: The Case for Statutory PSHE Education*. Available at: www.pshe-association.org.uk/curriculum-and-resources/resources/curriculum-life-case-statutory-pshe-education (accessed 12 December 2016).

Robinson, G. and Maines, B. (2008) *Bullying: The Complete Guide to the Support Group Method*. London: Sage.

Weare, K. (2015) *What Works in Promoting Social and Emotional Wellbeing and Responding to Mental Health Problems in School?* London: National Children's Bureau. Available at: www.youngminds.org.uk/assets/0002/2178/NCB__2015__What_works_sociall_emotional_wellbeing_and_mental_health_in_schools.pdf (accessed 13 February 2017).

Wostenhome, C., Willis, B. and Culliney, M. (2016) 'Does Jigsaw the mindful approach to PSHE work?' Sheffield: Sheffield Hallam University. Available at: www.jigsawpshe.com/does-jigsaw-work/ (accessed 18 March 2017).

11

Safeguarding

Nicky Batty and Jayne Metcalfe

By the end of this chapter, you should:

- have an informed understanding of safeguarding related to yourself and children in school
- have considered fundamental documents and questions concerning safeguarding
- recognise the breadth of areas that come under the safeguarding 'umbrella'
- understand your statutory responsibilities regarding safeguarding.

Introduction

This chapter will focus on safeguarding, recognising the breadth and scale of what it encompasses for you as a professional. It will consider why safeguarding is important, the development of safeguarding national policies and practice, including statutory requirements, and how these have influenced school policy and procedures. It will explore safeguarding online and offline, how you can empower children to take responsibility for their own safety and how you can be aware of your own personal safeguarding.

As a teacher you need to be aware of and meet the Teachers' Standards (DfE, 2013a) as part of your professional role. Safeguarding requirements are made explicit in Part Two of the Standards:

> A teacher is expected to demonstrate consistently high standards of personal and professional conduct. The following statements define the behaviour and attitudes, which set the required standard for conduct throughout a teacher's career.
>
> Teachers uphold public trust in the profession and maintain high standards of ethics and behaviour, within and outside school, by:
>
> * treating pupils with dignity, building relationships rooted in mutual respect, and at all times observing proper boundaries appropriate to a teacher's professional position
> * having regard for the need to safeguard pupils' well-being, in accordance with statutory provisions.

(DfE, 2013a, p. 14)

What is safeguarding?

Safeguarding is often a term that student teachers, newly qualified teachers (NQTs) and even experienced teachers are cautious of, worried about and want to feel knowledgeable and confident about. They want to be aware of what to do in any situation related to safeguarding. Safeguarding, child protection, grooming, abuse and historical crimes against children seem to be in the news constantly and it is therefore understandable why people working with children feel concerned about the enormity of their responsibility to safeguard the children in their care. Perhaps the emphasis needs to change: people working with children should feel proud and honoured, first to be working with them, and second, to the best of their ability, to be part of a rigorous safeguarding process and team of people who professionally care about the whole child and not just the academic child (see Chapter 10 where Palmer discusses personal, social and health education).

Statutory guidance from the Department for Education (DfE), courses from your Local Safeguarding Children Board (LSCB), school policy documents, university-based training and chapters like this one help towards supporting and developing your knowledge, understanding, awareness and practice. However, it is also worth noting that, whilst every case may have similarities to others, it will also be different and unique to the child in focus. This is why it is vital for you to engage with reputable reading, statutory documents, policies and continued professional training to be able to support the children with whom you work.

Safeguarding is defined as,

> protecting children from maltreatment; preventing impairment of children's health or development; ensuring that children grow up in circumstances consistent with the provision of safe and effective care; and taking action to enable all children to have the best outcomes. (DfE, 2016a, p. 5)

It can be seen as an umbrella term to incorporate a number of terms, such as: children's health and safety, providing first aid, educational visits, addressing bullying, intimate care, internet or online safety, the use of reasonable force, drugs, female genital mutilation (FGM), faith abuse, mental health, radicalisation, private fostering, sexting, child trafficking and meeting the needs of children with medical conditions and forced marriage – this list is not comprehensive and more examples can be found in Part 1 of *Keeping Children Safe in Education* (DfE, 2016a). Whatever term is attached, it is imperative that safeguarding is taken seriously, correct procedures are followed and you engage with the expert and professional organisations in that particular field, as they are the most reliable, up-to-date sources of support. (See paragraph 43 of *Keeping Children Safe in Education* (DfE, 2016a), websites and courses at the end of the chapter to develop and support your understanding.)

Safeguarding children in our care has to be at the centre of what we do as teachers. Maslow (1943, 1968) highlighted the importance of meeting the needs of children in his 'Hierarchy of Needs model'. Children cannot function if these needs are not met or are ignored or abused. Children need to feel safe, settled and cared for before they can develop personally and socially, and can engage in learning, and with the expectations of the academic curriculum and statutory academic tests.

Possible indicators of abuse or neglect

What to Do If You're Worried a Child is Being Abused: Advice for Practitioners (DfE, 2015a) draws attention to some key indicators teachers, and those working with children, need to note.

> Some of the following signs might be indicators of abuse or neglect:
>
> • Children whose behaviour changes – they may become aggressive, challenging, disruptive, withdrawn or clingy, or they might have difficulty sleeping or start wetting the bed;

- Children with clothes which are ill-fitting and/or dirty;
- Children with consistently poor hygiene;
- Children who make strong efforts to avoid specific family members or friends, without an obvious reason;
- Children who don't want to change clothes in front of others or participate in physical activities;
- Children who are having problems at school, for example, a sudden lack of concentration and learning or they appear to be tired and hungry;
- Children who talk about being left home alone, with inappropriate carers or with strangers;
- Children who reach developmental milestones, such as learning to speak or walk, late, with no medical reason;
- Children who are regularly missing from school or education;
- Children who are reluctant to go home after school;
- Children with poor school attendance and punctuality, or who are consistently late being picked up;
- Parents who are dismissive and non-responsive to practitioners' concerns;
- Parents who collect their children from school when drunk, or under the influence of drugs;
- Children who drink alcohol regularly from an early age;
- Children who are concerned for younger siblings without explaining why;
- Children who talk about running away;
- and Children who shy away from being touched or flinch at sudden movements.

(DfE, 2015a, p. 6)

What you should do

You cannot take any of the above in isolation and think a child is being abused. You must not investigate disclosures, hunches or hearsay on your own. If you have any worries about a child you *need to*:

- *recognise* the signs
- *respond* appropriately
- *report* them to the Designated Safeguarding Lead (DSL)
- *record* you have done this
- *re-refer* and challenge if the situation does not seem to be improving or does not seem to have been dealt with.

You must not:

- investigate any concerns yourself
- ignore the situation, thinking someone else will deal with it
- get into deep conversations with the child, asking leading questions
- dismiss them or the situation as fabricated

- take evidence in the form of interviews or photographs
- keep it to yourself
- tell the child you will keep it confidential and not tell anyone else.

Reflective task

Developing your own knowledge and understanding is vital as you read through this chapter so that you are not just being 'fed' information but are also reflecting on it, extending it and applying it to your own experiences. Read the Summary and Part 1 of *Keeping Children Safe in Education* (DfE, 2016a). On a page with a wide margin make notes and highlight key points.

In the margin note:

- whether you have been shown the three school policies in paragraph 12 or discussed safeguarding with your mentor
- any questions which arose as you read the document
- whether, reflecting on your own schooldays, you may have encountered a child who may have suffered any form of abuse.

In a group, share and discuss your notes.

Policy

Relevant historical documents, cases and inquiries

It is a regrettable fact that certain people in society, for whatever reason, harm children and in some cases are responsible for their deaths. Some victims' names, remembered due to the shocking cases and related news reports are: James Bulger, Stephen Lawrence, Holly Wells and Jessica Chapman, Victoria Climbié, Baby P, Shannon Matthews and Daniel Pelka. There are also the high profile celebrity cases detailing prosecutions including Jimmy Saville, Rolf Harris and the recent football coaching abuse allegations. If you remember the reports, you will still hold feelings of shock and disbelief. If you do not remember the names, then a search on the internet will provide endless links due to the enormity of the cases. Such events have had an impact on policy and practice as will become evident.

Four main types of abuse

- *Physical abuse*: a form of abuse which may involve hitting, shaking, throwing, poisoning, burning or scalding, drowning, suffocating or otherwise causing physical harm to a child
- *Emotional abuse*: the persistent emotional maltreatment of a child such as to cause severe and adverse effects on the child's emotional development
- *Sexual abuse*: involves forcing or enticing a child or young person to take part in sexual activities, not necessarily involving a high level of violence, whether or not the child is aware of what is happening
- *Neglect*: the persistent failure to meet a child's basic physical and/or psychological needs, likely to result in the serious impairment of the child's health or development.

(DfE, 2016a, p. 11)

The Victoria Climbié Inquiry

The extract below is taken from the *The Victoria Climbié Inquiry* (Laming, 2003), which can be accessed in full on the internet. Even though it was some years ago its impact in shaping and developing safeguarding provision is still as important today, and Victoria should not be forgotten. With the four main types of abuse in your knowledge base, try to identify the types of abuse Victoria suffered and how they could possibly have been prevented.

1 Introduction

'Victoria had the most beautiful smile that lit up the room.' Patrick Cameron

1.1 This Report begins and ends with Victoria Climbié. It is right that it should do so. The purpose of this Inquiry has been to find out why this once happy, smiling, enthusiastic little girl – brought to this country by a relative for 'a better life' – ended her days the victim of almost unimaginable cruelty. The horror of what happened to her during her last months was captured by Counsel to the Inquiry, Neil Garnham QC, who told the Inquiry:

'The food would be cold and would be given to her on a piece of plastic while she was tied up in the bath. She would eat it like a dog, pushing her face to the plate. Except, of course that a dog is not usually tied up in a plastic bag full of its excrement. To say that Kouao and Manning treated Victoria like a dog would be wholly unfair; she was treated worse than a dog.'

1.2 On 12 January 2001, Victoria's great-aunt, Marie-Therese Kouao, and Carl John Manning were convicted of her murder.

Abuse and neglect

1.3 At his trial, Manning said that Kouao would strike Victoria on a daily basis with a shoe, a coat hanger and a wooden cooking spoon and would strike her on her toes with a hammer. Victoria's blood was found on Manning's football boots. Manning admitted that at times he would hit Victoria with a bicycle chain. Chillingly, he said, 'You could beat her and she wouldn't cry … she could take the beatings and the pain like anything.'

1.4 Victoria spent much of her last days, in the winter of 1999–2000, living and sleeping in a bath in an unheated bathroom, bound hand and foot inside a bin bag, lying in her own urine and faeces. It is not surprising then that towards the end of her short life, Victoria was stooped like an old lady and could walk only with great difficulty.

1.5 When Victoria was admitted to the North Middlesex Hospital on the evening of 24 February 2000, she was desperately ill. She was bruised, deformed and malnourished. Her temperature was so low it could not be recorded on the hospital's standard thermometer. Dr Lesley Alsford, the consultant responsible for Victoria's care on that occasion, said, 'I had never seen a case like it before. It is the worst case of child abuse and neglect that I have ever seen.'

1.6 Despite the valiant efforts of Dr Alsford and her team, Victoria's condition continued to deteriorate. In a desperate attempt to save her life, Victoria was transferred to the paediatric intensive care unit at St Mary's Hospital Paddington. It was there that, tragically, she died a few hours later, on the afternoon of 25 February 2000.

(Laming, 2003, p. 1)

The Children Act

The Children Act 1989 (National Archives, 1989) was a parliamentary act to ensure the safeguarding of children. It places responsibility on Local Authorities as well as parents/ guardians to protect and consider the welfare of a child. In 2004 the act was revised in response to Lord Laming's report, *The Victoria Climbié Inquiry* (Laming, 2003), following the death of Victoria Climbié: 'Not one of the agencies empowered by parliament to protect children in positions similar to Victoria's – funded from the public purse – emerge from this Inquiry with much credit' (Laming, 2003, p. 3). The safeguarding measures in place to safeguard children did not protect Victoria. The recommendations from this report increased the expectation and requirement that agencies worked together to safeguard children. The *Every Child Matters* policy was introduced (see https://www.gov.uk/government/publications/every-child-matters).

The Bichard Inquiry Report

The Bichard Inquiry Report (2004) further informed the safeguarding legislation and statutory expectations placed on people who want to work with children. The inquiry was actioned in response to the Soham murders, where two schoolgirls, Jessica Chapman and Holly Wells, were murdered by the school caretaker, Ian Huntley, who, 'it became clear … had been known to the authorities over a period of years' (Bichard, 2004, p. 1). The inquiry led to Criminal Records Bureau (CRB) checks becoming statutory, which is the predecessor to the Disclosure and Barring Service (DBS) – a process student teachers, teachers and others who want to work with children are required to adhere to, and gain certification for, to tackle the safer recruiting agenda.

The Munro Review and The Wood Report

Munro (DfE, 2011) reviewed the child protection system and believed her final report would, 'help to reform the child protection system from being over-bureaucratised, and concerned with compliance, to one that keeps a focus on children, checking whether they are being effectively helped, and adapting when problems are identified' (DfE, 2011, p. 5). More recently, *The Wood Report* asks that the government 'reform our framework for multi-agency arrangements and improve learning from serious events affecting children' (DfE, 2016b, p. 4). The message from these historical reports is that safeguarding policy and practice is ongoing; it needs to be continually challenged, evaluated and developed. Children and young adults rely on us to protect and keep them as safe as possible.

Practice

Keeping children safe and keeping yourself safe

Laming (2009) was commissioned to carry out a further report into safeguarding after the Baby P case. He begins the report with these words, 'Please keep me safe. This simple, but profoundly important hope is the very minimum upon which every child and young person should be able to depend' (p. 2).

Reflective task

Return to your notes and engagement with *Keeping Children Safe in Education* (DfE, 2016a). Now engage with *What to Do If You're Worried a Child is Being Abused – Advice for Practitioners* (DfE, 2015a) and make more detailed notes on types of abuse and neglect. Reflect on why it is important to be aware of such abuse in your role as a student teacher or teacher.

There is a situation below for you to consider in the light of your reading (Work in School section). Reflect how your deeper knowledge, understanding and awareness may support you in safeguarding children.

The readings, policies and national cases you have engaged with so far should help to give you an understanding and awareness of the breadth of safeguarding. By reflecting on the above you will start to develop your own personal confidence, alertness and understanding of how to support children in keeping them safe. The following 'Work in School' focus is designed to make you think about your practice in schools and what you would do if faced with a possible situation. Would you panic? Would you ignore it, as you have a class of 30 with other minor issues to deal with? Would you take a minute to remember what you have read here and react in a professional, caring and informed manner? It is normal for all three to go through your mind, yet the final one will, with continued reading and awareness in safeguarding, be your default position.

When faced with any sensitive issue or disclosure it is vitally important that you do not show shock, anger, disgust, and so on to the children. You are their role model, their safe and protecting adult. You need to keep calm, neutral and in control, professionally. A diagram in *Keeping Children Safe in Education* (DfE, 2016a, p. 10) shows actions that a school needs to take when there are concerns about a child.

It does not encourage you to act on your own, make decisions or decide what has happened. When asking for help you will need to have made some notes on behaviours that are concerning you, and the DSL may ask you some more questions. The matter may then be referred. Remember, there are systems in place in schools that need to be followed to safeguard the children in a planned and protected approach.

Sometimes, as part of your busy day as a teacher, you will come upon situations you are not expecting. It is easy to react without thinking things through. You need to try, in such situations, to take a few minutes to reflect and seek advice if needed, before reacting in the wrong way and alarming the children or making them feel scared and fearful of what has happened. Consider the following scene and what you would do.

Work in school

Student: A lunchtime supervisor says that she overheard a boy in my class saying how his dad is always drunk and how he often has to put himself to bed as his dad is out or is asleep downstairs. He is from a single parent family as his mum died last year. He is often late for school in dirty clothes, tired and extremely hungry. I'm not sure what I should do.

Should I act on something overheard in the playground?

Mentor: You do not act on hearsay, but you do need to act appropriately on your discussion with the lunchtime supervisor. He or she will have been trained in safeguarding so it is important to discuss the sensitive nature of the case and that at the moment it remains with those who need to know.

Student: Should I ask to see the boy and interrogate him to get the facts – or should I ask to see his dad straight after school?

Mentor: No, you must not ask to see the father independently, without seeking advice, nor should you ask to see the boy about what he has been saying. You take the information given to you and pass it on to the DSL.

It may be that the DSL arranges a meeting with the father to check how things are since his wife has died and if the school can provide any support.

By being alert, noting the situation and referring it to the DSL you have acted appropriately.

Children's books to use

Children's books can be a means of supporting a child in a non-threatening way. Of course, as with any book dealing with sensitive issues, it would have to be introduced in a well-planned way, appropriate to the situation and child. Discussions with the DSL would be recommended. Children relate to stories from authors such as: Jacqueline Wilson, Michael Morpurgo, Anthony Browne, Malorie Blackman and Babette Cole because of the accessible way they address issues that are very real to some children, but do not exclude those for whom they are not real.

Reflective task

Former Children's Laureate, Michael Morpurgo, says that any subject is appropriate for a children's book so long as it is handled properly. Do you agree?

What could he mean by 'handled properly'?

Some of the books are not directly linked to safeguarding, but could be a way into thinking about it.

Which of the books listed below would you be prepared to have, and to justify having, in your (Key Stage 2) classroom? Which would you not have? Why?

- racial abuse (*Noughts and Crosses*, Malorie Blackman)
- sex (*Mummy Laid an Egg*, Babette Cole)
- homosexuality (*ABC: A Family Alphabet Book*, Bobbi Combs; *And Tango Makes Three*, Justin Richardson)
- disability (*Wonder*, R.J. Palacio)
- parental manic depression (*The Illustrated Mum*, Jacqueline Wilson)
- bullying (*Cloud Busting*, Malorie Blackman; *Stop Picking on Me*, Pat Thomas)
- drug use (*The House that Crack Built*, Clark Taylor)
- divorce (*Goggle-Eyes*, Anne Fine, *Mum and Dad Glue*, Kes Gray)
- asylum seekers/refugees (*The Silence Seeker*, Ben Morley; *The Journey*, Francesca Sanna; *The Arrival*, Shaun Tann)
- sexual interest (*I Said No! A Kid-to-Kid Guide to Keeping Your Private Parts Private*, Kimberly King; *Talking PANTS*, NSPCC)
- secrets (*Some Secrets Should Never Be Kept*, Jayneen Sanders)
- worries (*The Huge Bag of Worries*, Virginia Ironside; *The Colour Monster*, Anna Lienas).

If you do not know the books, they are worth reading up about. Books are such a good catalyst for discussing certain situations or issues. They are also supportive to children after events, knowing they are not alone. See also Chapter 14 where Warner and Elton-Chalcraft provide examples for using resources to learn about anti-racism, and Chapter 10 where Palmer discusses strategies for dealing with bullying.

Online safety

Rapid advances in digital technology have brought new ways of communicating and interacting online; they inspire children to be creative as well as foster new approaches to teaching and learning. However, these new opportunities bring increased levels of risk. Byron (2008), in the first independent review of the dangers children face online, believed that through empowering children to understand and manage risk and develop their resilience to material online, they are more able to take responsibility for their behaviour online and reap the educational and social benefits the internet and technology afford. Education, rather than prohibition, is seen as the way forward, and the role of schools in keeping children safe online is highlighted. In your role as a teacher you are seen as a fundamental player in this process.

Professional responsibilities

As already highlighted, Part Two of the Teachers' Standards makes reference to your responsibilities in terms of safeguarding (DfE, 2013a). There are a number of key areas that you need to understand in order to fulfil your professional responsibilities and in turn protect yourself and the children in your care when using online technologies. These will be explored in the remainder of the chapter and include:

- children's use of technologies; the risks and benefits
- school policy and practice relating to the safe use of technology
- protecting your professional reputation.

Children's use of technology

It is important that you develop an awareness of children's use of technology in order to better understand the benefits and risks children and adults face online, and in turn appreciate the importance of online safety education. Children's online behaviour is now regularly monitored by organisations such as Ofcom, Childwise and EU Kids Online, who carry out and publish research, usually on an annual basis.

Data extracted from the *Children and Parents: Media Use and Attitudes* report (Ofcom, 2016) highlight the following key trends:

- Television is still the most important media activity for children aged 5–11.
- Children as young as 3 and 4 years old go online using a wide range of media devices, including mobile phones and tablet computers.
- The amount of time children spend online is rising; children aged 3–4 now spend 8 hours and 18 minutes a week online.
- YouTube is an important destination for children of all ages, with over one-third of 3–4-year-olds, half of 5–7-year-olds and nearly three-quarters of 8–11-year-olds using the YouTube website or app to view content.
- Social media are central to the lives of many older children; nearly a quarter of 8–11-year-olds have a profile; this figure nearly doubles between the ages of 10 and 11 (21 per cent to 43 per cent).

- Facebook still remains the profile of choice, although there has been a decline in its popularity as the use of sites with group chat facilities such as WhatsApp, SnapChat, Facebook Messenger and Instagram increases; this is despite a minimum user age of 13, which indicates children are bypassing the age restrictions in order to join.
- Gaming devices continue to be popular, although 10 per cent of 8–11-year-olds admit to playing games online with people they have never met, as well as using the chat facility with people they do not know.

Risks and benefits

Whilst it is evident that the internet brings real opportunities in terms of interaction and communication, there is concern that not all children have the digital skills to manage privacy and personal disclosure, which is worrying, considering the potential worldwide audience for information shared online. There is also the risk of children being exposed to negative behaviours, such as bullying and grooming. Exposure to adverts and pop-ups, for example on social media sites and YouTube, is also a worry, especially as children say they feel pressured to make in-app purchases. Similarly, the internet provides access to a wealth of information, but content may be inappropriate or unreliable. Children's trust of online content continues to be a challenge with over a quarter of 8–11-year-olds believing that if Google lists a website it means that it can be trusted. It is evident that children need to develop a more critical understanding of the digital environment, which includes where information comes from and advertising.

Current trends in children's use of technologies and some of the benefits and risks of children playing online games, using social media and watching YouTube have been highlighted, but the surface has only really been scratched here. So what are the key risks children face through their use of digital technologies and associated apps?

The 3Cs conceptual framework for e-safety in Table 11.1 developed by the EU Kids Online Project (Hasebrink et al., 2008) is seen as a practical way of thinking about online risk. It has been adopted by many national bodies including Ofsted (2014) and the DfE (2016a). It categorises risk into three main areas: content, contact and conduct.

It can be seen that the risks are often determined by the user's behaviour rather than by the technology itself, and that whilst children can be victims of abuse they can also be the perpetrators, for example cyber-bullying. Both emphasise the need for children to be taught the importance of being responsible and respectful users. Two of the many risks that you need to be aware of are sexting and cyber-bullying.

Sexting

Childnet (2016a) defines sexting as the use of technology to send sexually explicit content, which usually refers to still or video images, although parents, and some

Table 11.1   3Cs conceptual framework

Content: where the child is exposed to illegal, inappropriate or harmful material.	This includes pornographic or unwelcome sexual content, biased, racist, inaccurate or misleading information, violent or hateful content as well as exploitation of children through commercial content such as adverts and, junk email and use of personal information
Contact: where the child is subjected to harmful online interaction with other users	Such as being bullied and groomed online. Children can also be subjected to unwelcome persuasions online such as self-harm and pro anorexic sites.
Conduct: where the child's own personal online behaviour increases the likelihood of, or causes, harm.	This can include children involved in illegal downloading, gambling, terrorism, cyberbullying or harassing others, creating and uploading inappropriate material and sexting, plus consequences for children's health and well-being, through for example addictive behaviours and excessive time spent online. It is important therefore that children fully understand the implications of their online behaviour.

children and young people, also include sexually explicit messages in their definition. For clarification, the police refer to sexting images as 'youth produced sexual imagery' (UKCCIS, 2016, p. 5). You need to be aware that creating, possessing or sharing 'indecent' imagery of anyone under the age of 18 is illegal under the Sexual Offences Act 2003 (England and Wales) and therefore any incidences of sexting must be managed and escalated appropriately in line with policy. There is new guidance to help schools deal with incidents, *Sexting in Schools and Colleges: Responding to Incidents and Safeguarding Young People* (UKCCIS, 2016). It adopts a structured, but child-centred approach, which aims to avoid criminalising children. The South West Grid for Learning (SWGfL), in conjunction with UKCCIS, offers the following succinct advice if any sexting incident comes to your attention:

- If a device is involved – confiscate it and set it to flight mode or, if not possible, switch it off. Do not email the images to anyone as this constitutes sharing and would be illegal.
- Seek advice – report to your DSL via your normal child protection procedures.

Work in school

Student: I have seen Reception children of both sexes in the toilets showing each other their 'private parts' and giggling.

What should I have done immediately? I wasn't sure...

(Continued)

(Continued)

Should I involve their parents?

Or should I get the whole class together and tell them that this behaviour is not acceptable?

Mentor: You need to talk to the DSL about this.

It is difficult, and not helpful, to give a concrete solution. But this is a possible solution for this particular situation where no other signs or practices have been noted. Children have always explored their bodies at a young age and compared notes! We will all remember playing kiss chase and mummies and daddies in the home corner.

On the surface this looks like an innocent scenario where the children are making sense of their world and themselves. It is not a case for overreacting and setting off alarm bells, although it does need to be noted and acted upon. Check with the DSL what you should do in this situation. It may be that they suggest you need to talk with the children involved, quietly, and say that even though it is normal to look at how boys and girls are different it is not really appropriate to do it in the toilets. Explain that as a class you can talk about and look at books to show the differences between boys and girls and then they can ask questions and you will answer them.

This is a controlled reaction and the children will get answers to their inquisitiveness without it becoming sexualised or being something to discuss in the toilets.

At the end of the school day it would be sensible to talk with the parents of the children to explain what has happened. Stress that you are not worried and it is a part of growing up, as they will understand. If they could emphasise the messages you gave at school with their children at home that would be helpful.

You have informed the parents and made them aware. This prevents worry and questions if the children were to go home and say they had been looking at each others' bodies in the toilets.

Student: Thank you. That's really helpful.

But now I come to think about it, these were Reception children. I have heard of older children taking photographs and sharing them electronically. What on earth should I do if that happened?

(Continued)

Mentor:	Think carefully about what you think you should do in each of these circumstances, and why. Then we can discuss it further.
	Much of what I have already said is relevant. Remember you must always confiscate any devices when an indecent image is shared and report to the DSL. You must not share the images further as this is illegal.
	This is a very useful video clip to use with slightly older children:
	NSPCC 'I saw your willy', https://www.youtube.com/watch?v=sch_WMjd6go

Cyber-bullying

Childnet International (2016b) defines cyber-bullying as 'the use of technologies by an individual or by a group of people to deliberately and repeatedly upset someone else' (p. 5). Cyber-bullying can take many forms. You may have experienced some of these. They can include: intimidation and threats; harassment and stalking (e.g. repeatedly sending unwanted texts or instant messages); defamation of character; exclusion or peer rejection; impersonation; and unauthorised publication of personal information and/or images.

Whilst all bullying is harmful, lack of face-to-face contact means it can be easier to behave in more inappropriate ways online than offline. It could also be argued that cyber-bullying can have more impact than face-to-face bullying due to a number of factors. For example, cyber-bullying:

- can take place anytime, anywhere, which means perpetrators have access to previous safe places like home and can attack 24/7
- can be anonymous and content can be quickly shared again and again with potentially large audiences
- is difficult for the victim as they may not know the bully and are unsure of who has viewed the abusive content
- content is difficult to remove.

Cyber-bullying does, however, leave an evidence trail, and whilst a victim may be tempted to delete any abusive content, they should be encouraged to keep this to help with any investigations, as well as urged not to reply or retaliate. You can access the new cyber-bullying guidance for schools, which focuses on preventing and responding to cyber-bullying to fill any gaps in your knowledge and understanding at: www.childnet.com/resources/cyberbullying-guidance-for-schools.

There is significant unease from schools and parents on these issues, given how easily images and content can be shared, plus the potential for further exploitation, such as unwanted attention and even blackmail. Such events can have a negative impact on children's social and emotional well-being and, in some cases, result in self-harm and even suicide.

School policy and practice

As well as having an awareness of key online safeguarding issues such as cyber-bullying and sexting, you need to have a clear understanding of school policies and procedures and their role in keeping children safe online. Schools will have a range of policies such as child protection, anti-bullying and behaviour policies, which are likely to make reference to online safety. Schools will also have a dedicated online safety policy, often referred to as an acceptable use policy (AUP), which details acceptable and unacceptable behaviours and sanctions for misuse. Staff, parents, children and visitors are often asked to sign an AUP to show that that they are in agreement and will operate within these guidelines. Whenever you are in school ensure that you familiarise yourself with the AUP and sign as appropriate.

Whilst there is an expectation from Ofsted (2016) that 'appropriate filters and monitoring systems' (p. 12) will be in place to regulate children's use of technology, a planned, broad and balanced, age-related curriculum is also seen as key (DfE, 2016a; Ofsted, 2016). In your role as a teacher you will be responsible for teaching children about online risks and empowering them to manage their behaviour online in order to keep themselves safe. This includes the dangers of radicalisation and extremism as part of the Prevent Duty. You can find out more about this from the website section at the end of the chapter. (See also Chapter 15, where Elton-Chalcraft, Revell and Lander discuss this issue in detail.)

Teaching online safety

The introduction of the new Computing National Curriculum (NC) in September 2014 (DfE, 2013b) positively supports ongoing online safety work in schools. There are precise statements in the aims and programmes of study (POS) about using technology 'safely' and 'respectfully' (DfE, 2013b, p. 2).

Table 11.2   National Curriculum guidance on using technology safely

At Key Stage 1 children should be taught to:	At Key Stage 2 children should be taught to:
Use technology safely and respectfully, keeping personal information private; identify where to go for help and support when they have concerns about content or contact on the internet or other online technologies	Use technology safely, respectfully and responsibly; recognise acceptable/unacceptable behaviour; identify a range of ways to report concerns about content and contact Be discerning in evaluating digital content

At *Key Stage 1* children should be aware of the main risks associated with the internet, and recognise that they should not share certain types of personal information online and the reasons why. Children should also develop their sensitivity to others online, and learn about the importance of positive online communication and showing respect for others' privacy.

Key Stage 2 builds on skills learnt in Key Stage 1. As well as teaching children how to keep themselves safe and to treat others with respect, the programme of study introduces an emphasis on responsible use of technology. Children need to consider how their online actions impact other people. They need to be aware of their legal and ethical responsibilities, such as showing respect for intellectual property rights (e.g. musical, literary and artistic works), keeping passwords and personal data secure, and observing the terms and conditions for the web services they use (such as the 13+ age restriction on most US websites, including Facebook). Children should also develop some awareness of their digital footprint and how those data are or could be used.

At both Key Stages children should have an age-appropriate understanding of their responsibilities under the school's AUP and abide by these. They should also have a clear understanding of what to do if they have concerns about inappropriate online behaviour or inadvertently access inappropriate content. Telling a teacher or parent should normally be the first response, but children should also know that they can report their concern to the Child Exploitation and Online Protection Centre (CEOP) (https://www.ceop.police.uk/Ceop-Report/) or get support from Childline (https://childline.org.uk/get-support/) about such matters. Some schools also have their own reporting systems, so ask about these.

Assemblies and pastoral activities can also be used to reinforce key online safety messages, as well as personal health and social education (PHSE) and other subject areas (see Chapter 10, Palmer). The importance of teaching digital citizenship is highlighted in the recent *Growing Up Digital* report (Children's Commissioner, 2017), which states that despite positive developments in education around online safety since the Byron Report (2008), children are not sufficiently prepared to deal with the internet. The report calls for a digital citizenship programme for children aged 4–14, where they learn not only about how to be a responsible citizen online, but also about their rights online. It is envisaged the latter will be linked to the iRights initiative (2015), where children and young people have:

- **The Right to REMOVE** content they have created.
- **The Right to KNOW** who has access to their data, why and how it is being used.
- **The Right to SAFETY AND SUPPORT** when they encounter distressing situations online.

- **The Right to INFORMED AND CONSCIOUS CHOICES** about whether to engage with the internet, but also knowing it can be switched off/when to disengage.
- **The Right to DIGITAL LITERACY** so that they have the critical understanding and skills to use digital technologies creatively but safely.

Online safety education is high on the political agenda, so look out for further developments in this area.

Teaching resources

There is currently a plethora of materials specially designed for primary teachers, children and their families to teach online safety. The challenge for you is selecting appropriate resources from this rich bank.

A useful starting point is:

The UK Safer Internet Centre (UKSIC) website (www.saferinternet.org.uk/advice-centre/teachers-and-professionals/teaching-resources), which provides links to a range of free teaching resources for use with children and parents, such as: animated and real life story videos, interactive activities and stories, as well as a wealth of lesson plans and supporting resources for teachers.

It includes links to:

Childnet resources (www.childnet.com/resources)

South West Grid for Learning (SWGfL) digital literacy and citizenship curriculum (www.digital-literacy.org.uk/)

Childnet's guide to online safety in the computing curriculum (www.childnet.com/resources/esafety-and-computing)

Child Exploitation and Online Protection Centre (CEOP) (https://www.thinkuknow.co.uk/Teachers/)

London Grid for Learning (https://www.lgfl.net/online-safety/resource-centre).

You should also look out for Safer Internet Day (SID; www.saferinternet.org.uk/safer-internet-day), which takes place annually in February. Education packs, designed to help deliver sessions and raise awareness of online safety issues on a selected theme, can be downloaded from the website so try and find ways to get involved.

The following sites also offer useful advice and resources for you as a professional:

www.saferinternet.org.uk/professionals-online-safety-helpline

www.saferinternet.org.uk/advice-centre/teachers-and-professionals

www.childnet.com/teachers-and-professionals

Reflective task

Working with others if possible, list the ways in which you feel confident to teach children about online safety.

List the areas in which you feel less confident to do this.

Discuss ways in which you can become more confident in these areas and when you will address them. Include these notes in your notes on safeguarding.

Professional conduct and reputation online

It is highly likely that you will have some form of online presence or professional reputation created through use of, for example, search engines, blogs, wikis, music sharing and social media sites either by yourself or from references and posts by others. It is critical for you as a teacher to have a positive online presence or reputation and to maintain this, because how you are perceived online can have a significant impact on your personal and professional life. Parents and children will probably seek you out online in an effort to find out more about you. Research (Microsoft, 2010) also shows employers are accessing online profiles and making judgements about the suitability of candidates on the basis of this, so it is crucial that you consider your digital footprint at all times.

Reflective task

- What would someone find if they searched for you online?
- What does this information say about you?
- What kind of measures have you taken to protect your online reputation?
- Access the following link to additional resources on this topic (www.saferinter net.org.uk/advice-centre/teachers-and-professionals/professional-reputation).

After engaging with the Reflective Task above, consider the key strategies below to help you manage your online reputation:

- *Discover what is on the internet about you* – search for yourself regularly online.
- *Evaluate your online reputation* – how are you presented online? What does this say about you? What do you want it to say about you? Make content private, remove previous online content, deactivate and delete unwanted accounts and profiles.
- *Protect your online reputation* – think before you share, regularly review and adjust your privacy settings, create secure strong passwords and protect them, remember to log out of accounts, make clear expectations with friends about digital content you do and do not want shared, respect the privacy and reputation of others.
- *Know how to report a problem.*

Summary

This chapter has introduced you to the breadth of safeguarding areas and issues you need to be aware of for your own and children's protection. This has included: engagement with key statutory policy and practice, reflection on your thinking and professional responsibilities, practical strategies and resources for developing and supporting safeguarding in school, and further suggestions for keeping up to date with the ongoing changing nature of such a fundamental area.

Questions for discussion

- Consider the implications of this chapter for your own learning and practice. What will your next steps be in terms of continuing your safeguarding understanding?
- How will you empower children to take responsibility for their own safety?
- What safeguarding issues relating to children have been highlighted recently? What are the implications for you as a teacher?
- Reflect on a safeguarding issue you are aware of or have been involved with. How would you now respond after reading this chapter? Would you respond in the same way?

Further reading

The following chapters and journal articles provide useful supplementary reading about safeguarding in schools and your role as a teacher.

Appleton, J. (2013) 'Safeguarding in education', *Child Abuse Review*, 22 (2): 75–9.
Cremin, A. and Arthur, J. (eds) (2014) *Learning to Teach in the Primary School*, third edn. Section 8: Partnership in Practice. Abingdon: Routledge.
Lindon, J. and Webb, J. (2016) *Safeguarding and Child Protection*, fifth edn. London: Hodder Education.
Macpherson, P. (2015) 'Safeguarding children', in A. Hanson (ed.), *Primary Professional Studies*, third edn (pp.187–203). London: Sage.
Metcalfe, J. and Simpson, D. (2013) 'Lost in cyberspace? Children and social media', in J. Metcalfe, D. Simpson, I. Todd and M. Toyn (eds), *Thinking Through New Literacies for Primary and Early Years* (pp.117–140). London: Sage.
Tarr, J., Whittle, M., Wilson, J. and Hall, L. (2013) 'Safeguarding children and child protection education for UK trainee teachers in higher education', *Child Abuse Review*, 22 (2): 108.

Websites

Childline: www.childline.org.uk

DfE: https://www.gov.uk/topic/schools-colleges-childrens-services/safeguarding-children/latest

Educate against hate: http://educateagainsthate.com/

Internet matters: https://www.internetmatters.org/

NSPCC: https://www.nspcc.org.uk/preventing-abuse/

TES: https://www.tes.com/articles/safeguarding-teaching-resources

To develop your awareness of preventing radicalisation and FGM engage with the following two online courses and website:

Channel general awareness course: http://course.ncalt.com/Channel_General_Awareness/01/index.html

FGM: recognising and preventing FGM: www.safeguardingchildrenea.co.uk/resources/female-genital-mutilation-recognising-preventing-fgm-free-online-training/

References

Bichard, M. (2004) *The Bichard Inquiry Report*. Available at: http://dera.ioe.ac.uk/6394/1/report.pdf (accessed 16 November 2016).
Blackman, M. (2002) *Noughts and Crosses*. Croydon: Corgi.

Blackman, M. (2005) *Cloud Busting*. London: Corgi Yearling.

Byron, T. (2008) *Safer Children in a Digital World: The Report of the Byron Review*. Nottingham: DCSF publications.

Childnet International (2016a) *Sexting*. Available at: www.childnet.com/parents-and-carers/hot-topics/sexting (accessed 18 January 2017).

Childnet International (2016b) *Cyberbullying: Understand, and Respond Guidance for Schools*. Available at: www.childnet.com/resources/cyberbullying-guidance-for-schools (accessed 18 January 2017).

Children's Commissioner (2017) *Growing Up Digital: A Report of the Growing Up Digital Taskforce*. Available at: www.childrenscommissioner.gov.uk/sites/default/files/publications/Growing%20Up%20Digital%20Taskforce%20Report%20January%202017_0.pdf (accessed 14 February 2017).

Cole, B. (1993) *Mummy Laid an Egg*. London: Red Fox.

Combs, B. (2012) *ABC: A Family Alphabet Book*. Ridley Park, PA: Two Lives Publishing.

Department for Education (DfE) (2011) *The Munro Review of Child Protection: Final Report. A Child-Centred System*. Available at: https://www.gov.uk/government/uploads/system/uploads/attachment_data/file/175391/Munro-Review.pdf (accessed 13 February 2017).

Department for Education (DfE) (2013a) *Teachers' Standards*. Available at: https://www.gov.uk/government/uploads/system/uploads/attachment_data/file/301107/Teachers__Standards.pdf (accessed 14 February 2017).

Department for Education (DfE) (2013b) *National Curriculum: Computing Programmes of Study: Key Stages 1 and 2*. Available at: https://www.gov.uk/government/publications/national-curriculum-in-england-computing-programmes-of-study (accessed 14 February 2017).

Department for Education (DfE) (2015a) *What to Do If You're Worried a Child is Being Abused – Advice for Practitioners*. London: DfE.

Department for Education (DfE) (2015b) *Working Together to Safeguard Children*. London: DfE.

Department for Education (DfE) (2016a) *Keeping Children Safe in Education: Statutory Guidance for Schools and Colleges*. London: DfE. Available at: https://www.gov.uk/government/uploads/system/uploads/attachment_data/file/550511/Keeping_children_safe_in_ education.pdf (accessed 14 February 2017).

Department for Education (DfE) (2016b) *Wood Report: Review of the Role and Functions of Local Safeguarding Children Boards*. Available at: https://www.gov.uk/government/uploads/system/uploads/attachment_data/file/526329/Alan_Wood_review.pdf (accessed 14 February 2017).

Gray, K. (2010) *Mum and Dad Glue*. London: Hodder Children's Books.

Hasebrink, U., Livingstone, S. and Haddon, L. (2008) *Comparing Children's Online Opportunities and Risks Across Europe: Cross-national Comparisons for EU Kids Online*. London: EU Kids Online. Available at: http://eprints.lse.ac.uk/24372/ (accessed 14 February 2017).

Ironside, V. (2011) *The Huge Bag of Worries*. London: Hodder Children's Books.

King, K. (2008) *I Said No! A Kid-To-Kid Guide to Keeping Your Private Parts Private*. Weaverville, CA: Boulden Publishing.

Laming, H. (2003) *The Victoria Climbié Inquiry*. London: TSO.

Laming, H. (2009) *The Protection of Children in England: A Progress Report*. London: TSO.

Lienas, A. (2015) *The Colour Monster*. London: Templar.

Maslow, A.H. (1943) 'A theory of human motivation', *Psychological Review*, 50 (4): 370–96.

Maslow, A.H. (1968) *Toward a Psychology of Being*. New York: D. Van Nostrand Company.

Microsoft (2010) 'Data Privacy Day: Your online reputation is on the line'. Available at: https://news.microsoft.com/2010/01/26/data-privacy-day-your-online-reputation-is-on-the-line/#bdmcCgT8vvIedpVV.99 (accessed 14 February 2017).

Morley, B. (2009) *The Silence Seeker*. London: Tamarind Books.

National Archives (1989) *Children Act 1989*. Available at: www.legislation.gov.uk/ukpga/1989/41/enacted (accessed 16 November 2016).

National Society for the Prevention of Cruelty to Children (NSPCC) (2016) 'Talking PANTS'. Available at: https://www.nspcc.org.uk/preventing-abuse/keeping-children-safe/underwear-rule/ (accessed 13 February 2017).

Office of Communications (Ofcom) (2016) *Children and Parents: Media Use and Attitudes Report*. Available at: https://www.ofcom.org.uk/__data/assets/pdf_file/0034/93976/Children-Parents-Media-Use-Attitudes-Report-2016.pdf (accessed 3 January 2017).

Office for Standards in Education (Ofsted) (2016) *Inspecting Safeguarding in Early Years, Education and Skills Settings*. Manchester: Ofsted.

Palacio, R.J. (2013) *Wonder*. Croydon: Corgi.

Richardson, J. (2005) *And Tango Makes Three*. London: Simon and Schuster.

Sanders, J. (2011) *Some Secrets Should Never Be Kept*. Macclesfield, Victoria: Upload Publishing PTY Ltd.

Sanna, F. (2016) *The Journey*. London: Flying Eye Books.

South West Grid for Learning (SWGfL) (n.d.) 'Advice for schools: Responding to and managing sexting incidents'. Available at: http://swgfl.org.uk/magazine/Managing-Sexting-Incidents/Sexting-Advice.aspx (accessed 3 April 2017).

Starishevsky, J. (2014) *My Body Belongs to Me*. Minneapolis, MN: Free Spirit.

Tann, S. (2007) *The Arrival*. London: Hodder Children's Books.

Taylor, C. (1992) *The House that Crack Built*. San Francisco, CA: Chronicle Books.

The IRights Report (2015) *Enabling Children and Young People to Access the Digital World*. Available at: http://5rightsframework.com/static/The-iRights-Report-2015.pdf (accessed 18 March 2017).

Thomas, P. (2010) *Stop Picking on Me*. London: Wayland.

UK Council for Child Internet Safety (UKCCIS) (2016) *Sexting in Schools and Colleges: Responding to Incidents and Safeguarding Young People*. Available at: www.gov.uk/government/uploads/system/uploads/attachment_data/file/551575/6.2439_KG_NCA_Sexting_in_Schools_WEB__1_.PDF (accessed 18 March 2017).

Wilson, J. (2007) *The Illustrated Mum*. London: Yearling.

12

Language and Learning in a Multilingual World

Jean Conteh

By the end of this chapter you should be able to:

- understand what it means to live in a multilingual world, with particular reference to the United Kingdom
- have awareness of current research into multilingualism in education and the implications for teaching and learning
- understand the importance of language in learning across the whole school curriculum
- have awareness of the key elements of pedagogy to promote learning for English as an additional language (EAL) pupils and what constitutes good practice for all.

These objectives are linked to the four sections of this chapter. These are:

- multilingual Britain
- learning multilingually
- language in learning across the whole curriculum
- EAL in the curriculum – good practice for all.

Multilingual Britain

We all live in a multilingual world. In our daily lives, we may speak, read or write different languages or use different accents, dialects and varieties of the

English language. On the other hand, we may only use English, and never really encounter different varieties of English or different languages. But there are no countries in the world, even in Western Europe, where only one language is used in everyday communication, in official, commercial and educational discourses, or in the media. All the pupils you teach, not just those who may be categorised as EAL, have knowledge and experiences of different languages and of varieties of English outside school that are different from those that they use and learn in school. English is still one of the most important languages in the world, but in our increasingly multilingual world, more people speak English as a second or foreign language than as their native one (Centre for Applied Linguistics, 1999). People all around the world are learning English, not because they want to become monolingual, but rather to become more multilingual.

The rapid growth of social media over recent years has sped up the spread of multilingualism globally and in individual lives. All of this means that all the pupils you teach – even those who may only speak English and so may be thought of as 'monolingual' – experience multilingualism in their lives; they are all members of multilingual societies. England is a multilingual country. We are all continually exposed to different languages and different forms and varieties of the English language in our everyday lives. We may hear and speak different dialects of English, which have grammar and vocabulary that vary from standard English, or we may speak English with our families and friends using accents that are different from the ones most commonly used in school. It is perfectly fine to use these varieties of English at different times and for different purposes, but they may not be considered appropriate in schools and workplaces. This does not mean that they are 'wrong'. We all have our own repertoires, or personal resources, of language, which we learn to use as we go through life (Blommaert and Backus, 2011). In our interactions with others, we are free to choose different ways of speaking and writing, depending on whom we are interacting with, what we are trying to do and how we are trying to accomplish it. But in order to succeed in society, we all need to be able to use the forms of English taught in school and usually associated with power and privilege.

Blommaert and Backus (2011) call language repertoires our 'indexical biographies', suggesting that they are linked closely to the social and cultural experiences we have had in our lives. Our repertoires change as we go through our lives, dependent on where we live, whom we meet and what we do. In the light of the discussion in this section, think about your own language repertoire, and how it has changed throughout your life. Try to write a brief 'language autobiography' describing your own language repertoire.

Superdiversity and EAL

The superdiversity of British society is clearly reflected in our schools. In England, up until quite recently, no data were systematically collected in relation to pupils who did not speak English as their first language, but schools are now required to collect increasingly detailed data about the languages their pupils speak at home and in their communities. Current data reveal that there are over a million pupils, about one in six in mainstream schools in England, who speak languages other than English at home (NALDIC, 2017). Indeed, we need to remember that some pupils will already speak more than one language and may be learning English as their third or fourth language. English is, of course, number one on the list – still by far the most commonly recorded home language among pupils in our schools, with over 5.5 million who speak it as their first language. After this, the list for the 12 most commonly recorded languages continues as follows:

Table 12.1　Languages spoken by pupils in mainstream schools in England who do not speak English as their main language (2012 statistics)

2.	Punjabi	1136,350	1.7%
3.	Urdu	109,730	1.6%
4.	Bengali	87,945	1.3%
5.	Polish	53,915	0.8%
6.	Somali	42,215	0.6%
7.	Gujerati	40,490	0.6%
8.	Arabic	39,135	0.6%
9.	Portuguese	24,305	0.4%
10.	Tamil	24,605	0.4%
11.	French	22,415	0.3%
12.	Turkish	20,490	0.3%

This list is very interesting as it illustrates the diversity of pupils that can come under the category of EAL. Sometimes the term 'EAL' is applied only to pupils who have recently arrived in the country, and are categorised as 'new to English'. It could be argued that this points only to what is lacking in the pupil's knowledge and so carries the implication of deficit. In reality, 'new to English' is only a very small part of the picture. 'EAL' is an umbrella term, used for pupils who, between them, have a wide array of characteristics, and who bring a vast range of experience and knowledge of languages, cultures, schooling and literacies to their classrooms in mainstream schools. A brief analysis of the languages list in Table 12.1 will show this. The languages can be divided into three groups. The first group includes the first three languages on the list, along with the seventh (Gujerati). These languages are largely spoken by pupils who are British nationals. The vast majority were born in the

UK as descendants of people who came from the Indian subcontinent or from East Africa in the 1950s and 1960s, usually to work in factories where their labour was vital to the economy. Eventually, they formed settled communities, mostly in larger industrial cities. For many of these pupils, English is not really an additional language, but the main one they speak in their daily lives. Other languages are used for different purposes. The second group includes Polish, Portuguese and French, and represents the languages spoken by pupils whose families came – usually fairly recently – from European countries as part of the expansion of the EU. The final group, Somali, Arabic, Tamil and Turkish, is largely representative of pupils whose families may have suffered war or political turmoil and so have had to leave their countries of origin and seek asylum in safe countries. Of course, this is not the only reason: many Turkish-speaking pupils, for example, come from families who migrated to the UK from Cyprus for different reasons. This shows how we cannot think of pupils who are learning English as an additional language as one uniform group. Here is a list of different terms that have been used over the years in policy documents to describe EAL learners:

- Learners who are second and third generation members of settled ethnic minority communities (*advanced bilingual learners*).
- Learners who are recent arrivals and new to English, some of whom have little or no experience of schooling, and others who are already literate in their first languages (*children new to English*).
- Learners whose education has been disrupted because of war and other traumatic experiences (*asylum seekers and refugees*).
- Learners who are in school settings with little prior experience of bilingual children (*isolated learners*).
- Learners whose parents are working and studying and are in England for short periods of time (*sojourners*).

Reflective task

Language diversity in school

On one of your school placements, find out about the language diversity in the school. Try to find out information such as the following:

- How many different languages are spoken by pupils in the school?
- How many pupils in school are categorised as 'EAL learners'?

(Continued)

(Continued)

- How does the school find out about the pupils' home languages?
- How does the school decide which pupils are 'EAL'?
- Is there a school policy for EAL?
- Who is in charge of EAL in the school?

Think about how easy or difficult it was to collect this information. If possible, discuss what you found out with other members of your course to discover the different ways that schools manage their EAL pupils.

Learning multilingually

Debates about multilingualism

One of the burning questions in multilingual education is about the role that learners' first languages play in learning a new language and in learning across the curriculum. The longstanding debates about whether learners should be allowed to use their home languages in the classroom or not show no signs of abating. Before beginning your training as a mainstream teacher, you may have gained qualifications and had experience in teaching English, or other languages, in different settings to different learners. For example, you may have done a course in Teaching English as a Foreign Language (TEFL) or a Certificate of English Language Teaching to Adults (CELTA). There are some parallels between English as a foreign language (EFL) and EAL pedagogies, and some ideas can work very well across the fields, but there are also crucial differences. Key ideas in EFL teaching may seem like common sense, but they turn out to be not so helpful when you are working with young learners and begin to understand something of the complexities of the experiences of many bi/multilingual and EAL learners in schools in England. In Conteh et al. (2014, pp. 159–60), we talk about some 'myths' about 'best practice' in languages teaching and learning. We argue that they can seem to be 'intuitively attractive', but they are 'not supported by research, and they need to be challenged'. Here are our 'myths' about best practice:

- Languages should be kept separate in the classroom, or learners will become confused. Instruction should be carried out exclusively in the target language without recourse to students' first language (L1).
- Translation between L1 and L2 has no place in the teaching of language or literacy.
- The ideal language teacher is a native speaker.
- The more the 'target language' is used in the classroom, the better the results.
- Language diversity is a 'problem', and it is better in multilingual classrooms if children speak English or the target language all the time.

In the remainder of this section, I present some of the research into multilingualism and multilingual learning which challenges the assumptions about language and learning that underpin these 'myths'. After this, I introduce some new theoretical ideas that could help to promote a new way of thinking about 'multilingual pedagogy' in our classrooms.

Challenging the myths

As Hakuta and Diaz (1985) point out, the early psychological research into bi/multilingualism often concluded that bilingual children suffered some linguistic disadvantage. Some researchers even suggested that bilingualism led to 'linguistic confusion that deeply affected children's intellectual development and academic performance' (p. 321). It was not until Peal and Lambert published their monograph entitled 'The relation of bilingualism to intelligence' (1962) that attitudes began to change. Since then, evidence has accumulated to show that the early fears were groundless. Indeed, more recent neuroscientific research, which shows us actual images of the brain, emphatically concludes that bilingualism brings cognitive advantages (e.g. Bialystok, 2011). This is very good news for multilingual education. But the findings from this kind of research are not influenced in any way by social, cultural or economic factors such as ethnicity, gender, family background, income and so on. And of course, as soon as we begin to think about education, these factors come to the fore.

A key figure in education research into bi/multilingualism, Jim Cummins (2001; Cummins and Early, 2011), has always been very concerned about understanding multilingual pupils' experiences in context and in developing awareness of the links between language, culture and identity. Most of his research has been carried out in Canada, initially with French/English bilingual pupils, and more recently in the kinds of schools that are increasingly common across the globe, where the languages spoken represent the complex migration histories of the communities in which they are situated.

Cummins, common underlying proficiency and linguistic interdependence

Cummins's research is based on observing and interviewing pupils as well as working with their teachers, and his ideas have been hugely influential in developing understanding of what multilingual pedagogies need to entail. A key text that brings together most of his main ideas is *Negotiating Identities* (Cummins, 2001). Perhaps the most significant contribution of his approach to second language acquisition is his argument that learners' first languages are an integral part of second language acquisition and learning processes. In other words, when we study the language development and learning of bi/multilingual pupils, we need to understand the ways in which it is different from that of so-called monolinguals, as well as the commonalities. This is why Cummins's work is more useful and relevant for teachers working with EAL learners than models taken from other theoretical frameworks of language learning, such as EFL or second language acquisition (SLA), which focus on the new language being taught, not the whole language repertoire of the learner. In understanding the ways that young bi/multilingual pupils process and use their language repertoires, two of Cummins's key ideas are particularly helpful for primary school teachers: the common underlying proficiency (CUP) and the notion of linguistic interdependence. I will discuss these here, and in the section on language across the curriculum. I will refer to another of Cummins's key ideas that has great relevance for thinking about language and learning: the notions of basic interpersonal communication 'skills' (BICS) and cognitive academic language proficiency (CALP).

As I suggested above, it used to be thought that for a bilingual person to move between their languages would be confusing and possibly dangerous. This is the fear behind the thinking that it is best to keep languages separate in the classroom. Through his observations of bi/multilingual pupils, Cummins noticed the ways that they used their languages both in oracy and literacy. He recognised that they definitely did not keep their languages separate, but that they switched between them in ways that were clearly regulated, and not just random. Many other researchers have also observed the ways that bi/multilingual people switch between and mix their languages, and would support Cummins's conclusions that, in the mind, languages are processed together as one unit, not as separate systems. His theory of the CUP is a powerful way of understanding this. It is based on the idea that we all have, in essence, the same kind of facility for processing language, whether we are monolingual or bi/multilingual. The CUP can be thought of as something like a reservoir of language understanding, knowledge and skill, which the language user can draw on to make meaning in the contexts they inhabit. This clearly links with Blommaert and Backus's notions of language repertoires (2011) that I introduced above, and means that mixing and switching between languages is not going to do any harm to anybody. Indeed, such mixing could even lead to advantages for bi/multilingual learners if they can access their full language repertoires in their learning.

Based on the concept of the CUP, Cummins and Early (2011) went on to develop the theory of linguistic interdependence, in which he argues that knowledge and understanding of one language links to knowledge and understanding of new languages, and that this is especially significant in relation to literacy.

If we relate this to practice, it directly contradicts the 'target language' model of pedagogy which demands that languages be kept separate in the classroom. In line with sociocultural models of learning more broadly, it is based on the premise that we learn new things better if they are grounded in and grow from what we already know. In terms of pedagogy, it opens up the classroom space to learners bringing their full language repertoires to their learning, with the possibilities that ensue (see Conteh and Brock, 2010). A consultation document from the Department for Education and Skills (2003: 31) provides a case study of a primary school where classroom strategies have been developed which begin to draw on pupils' bilingual skills.

It shifts the focus in the classroom from teaching to learning. Teachers' roles change from knowledge transmitters to the facilitators of learning and co-learners. They are not teachers of 'a language', but teachers of pupils who already have resources of their own, who may know things that teachers themselves do not know and who need a scaffold, not a stretcher, to help them to move on to the next stage. This approach to pedagogy is about developing relationships between teachers and learners that lead to 'empowerment', not those based on static hierarchies of power. According to Cummins (2001, p. 136), this is the only way we can realise the full potential of our EAL pupils, and achieve transformation, rather than reproduction of the status quo. In this sense, learning multilingually can become a positive pedagogy for all pupils, not just those who may be regarded as EAL.

Work in school

You overhear the following conversation in a Key Stage 2 multilingual classroom, where the class teacher is discussing with the bilingual support assistant how to work with 'her' group, many of whom are new to English, and some of whom speak Polish, the same language as she does:

Teacher: Make sure the children don't sit next to someone who speaks the same language, as they all need to practise their English as much as possible.

Assistant: Okay. What should I do if they speak to me in Polish?

Teacher: Don't tell them off, but tell them that they shouldn't speak Polish in the classroom. Tell them how to say it in English and get them to repeat this.

Assistant: Okay.

If you were the class teacher, would you have given the same instructions to the assistant? If not, what would you say?

As I have already begun to suggest, this way of thinking about pedagogy means we need to have new ways of thinking about language, learning and the roles of teachers and learners. Garcìa (2009, p. 45) argues that first we need to shift our perspectives from 'the perspective of the language itself' to those of 'the users themselves'. So, instead of seeing languages as neutral, unchanging systems, we can see them as 'sets of resources called into play by social actors' (Heller, 2007), in order to 'make possible the social reproduction of existing conventions and relations as well as the production of new ones'. To understand the ways in which people actually use their language repertoires concepts such as translanguaging can be very helpful. This is a way of thinking about what people do with language that focuses on their aims, purposes and identities, rather than just the language itself.

Translanguaging and pedagogy

In classroom terms, translanguaging is about using all the language resources you have at your disposal in order to do the things you want to do. Young bi/multi-lingual children translanguage naturally and spontaneously, both in speaking and later in writing, if they have the opportunity. For example, 9-year-old Huma, loves telling stories. Her finger puppets of Goldilocks and the Three Bears have given her and her classmates lots of fun as she retells the story in English and Punjabi. When she decided to write the story down, she chose to do it in Punjabi. Not being able to write in Punjabi script (which is similar to Arabic script) did not hold her back.

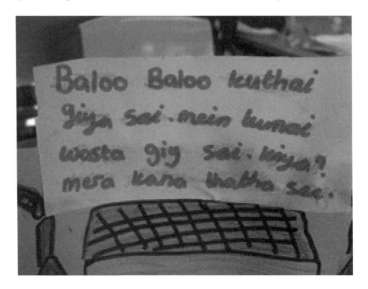

Figure 12.1   Huma's written version of the Goldilocks story

She used Roman script and Punjabi words and wrote in the style of her oral telling, in questions and answers. The translation of what she wrote is something like: 'Bear, bear, where did you go? I went for a walk. Why did you go? My food was hot.'

Once Huma had produced her translanguaged script, other pupils in the class began to follow her lead. Five-year-old Firdous produced a dual-language text about her grandma (*Dadi*). She explained that a second speech bubble was a translation of the first, though in fact it is a mix of Punjabi and English – she simply used the English word when the Punjabi did not come easily to her. For Firdous, both languages come together as one resource with which she can express her feelings about her grandmother. They allow her, in the words of Creese and Blackledge (2010, p. 109) to:

> … make meaning, transmit information, and perform identities using the linguistic signs at [her] disposal to connect with her audience in community engagement.

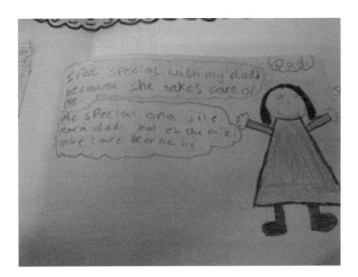

Figure 12.2   Firdous' sentences about her grandmother

These texts were produced in a complementary Saturday class (for further details, see Conteh, 2015), where multilingual pupils were given the space to use all their language resources in their learning. The outcomes reveal the benefits of what is known as a 'funds of knowledge' approach to teaching and learning. Gonzalez et al. (2005, pp. 91–2) define funds of knowledge as 'historically developed and accumulated strategies (skills, abilities ideas, practices) or bodies of knowledge', which are developed in communities in ways that provide children with 'ample opportunities to participate in activities with people they trust' in home and community contexts.

As they learn in this way, children develop a profound sense of belonging, of their own place in communities that are culturally and socially complex. Such learning entails 'maximum identity investment' (Cummins, 2001, p. 125; Cummins and Early, 2011, p. 33), a factor that has long been identified as crucial in promoting success and realising learners' full potential, particularly in literacy. The implications of all this for mainstream classrooms are very strong, and are taken up in the section on EAL in the curriculum.

Language in learning across the whole curriculum

BICS and CALP

Cummins's notions of BICS and CALP are often referred to in discussions about the needs of EAL learners, but their importance for all learners and for learning across the curriculum more generally is perhaps not so well understood. Sometimes, indeed, BICS/CALP have been written about in ways that do not reflect their full scope and their broader implications for pedagogy. They have sometimes been referred to as just 'skills' or even specific features of language to be taught and tested: sometimes BICS is characterised as spoken language and CALP as written, sometimes BICS is equated with 'playground language' and CALP with 'classroom language'. All of these ideas may capture parts of the story, but none of them really reflects the full picture. Cummins has developed the ideas over the years, and has revealed his own deepening understanding of the concepts as he has continued to work with teachers. He now emphasises the point that BICS and CALP are a continuum, not two separate, hierarchical features of language.

Essentially, BICS refers to all the social, everyday things we can do with language in face-to-face situations, such as greetings, conversations, naming and describing things, retelling stories and so on. CALP, on the other hand, refers to all the things we need to do with language in order to learn and progress academically. These are usually much more cognitively demanding, such as explaining, analysing, arguing and so on. For all of us, in language acquisition and learning, BICS relates to the kinds of language that usually develop first because we all – even small babies – want to communicate with those around us and to make sense of our surroundings. CALP usually develops from this as we begin to learn more formally in more decontextualised activities when we go to school and learn to read and write. Thus, CALP is much more strongly intertwined with literacy than BICS. It has two main dimensions: it is the kind of academic language that we find in different school subjects – in textbooks, written tests and exams, lecture notes and so on. It is also the kind of language that we need in order to do academic things, to think about complex ideas such as investigating, exploring ideas, analysing, hypothesising and solving problems. It has to be remembered, though, that we can do cognitively demanding things in simple language. It is possible for people to move back and forth across the BICS/CALP continuum according to their knowledge of the kind of language involved, and we should be aiming to develop this capacity and confidence with language in the children we teach. All pupils need opportunities in school to use a wide range of language and languages in different ways in their learning.

CALP is sometimes referred to as 'academic language', and Gibbons (2009, p. 5) has introduced the term 'disciplinary literacy', which she defines as:

> … being able to express more concisely and precisely the complex ideas and concepts that are embedded in the content of a subject and that are essential for learning in that subject.

Gibbons argues that the different academic disciplines in the curriculum demand different oracy and literacy skills, and I will show this later in this section, in relation to the National Curriculum for England. She goes on (p. 9) to show how different subjects across the curriculum hold the potential for developing pupils' academic language skills – in other words, pupils learn about language and improve their skills in English in all the subjects they do. This is an important point for all pupils, but particularly so for EAL learners, whose skills, knowledge and understanding of the English language can be enhanced through their engagement in learning in all areas of the curriculum.

In the paragraphs above, I have discussed BICS and CALP in relation to all learners and users of language. The model also has implications that are very specific to bi/multilingual learners. Cummins found that children entering school with very little English would normally develop conversational confidence (i.e. BICS) quite quickly, and could often gain fluency in their new language in about 18 months. But to gain a similar level in CALP domains could take a lot longer – Cummins concluded that this could take up to 7 years. It also became clear that the progression from BICS to CALP is not automatic, and that learners need to be supported as they move from learning through context-embedded activities to the more disembedded tasks they are expected to perform as they move up the primary school. We can link all this to the ideas about the CUP and linguistic independence I outlined above, along with another of Cummins's ideas, around the 'language threshold', where he argues that the capacity to develop competence in a new language depends on competence in the first, just as the overall strength of a building depends on the strength of the foundation. All of these ideas contribute to the argument that the more pupils have opportunities to use all their language resources in their learning of English and across the curriculum, the better their learning will be.

Language and the curriculum

The National Curriculum (DfE, 2014) embodies the 'official knowledge' that teachers are required to teach their pupils in mainstream schools in England. In terms of language, we have the subject of English as well as modern foreign languages (MFL) for 7–14-year-olds. Language is also referred to in different ways in all the other subjects of the curriculum. Thus, the English language is both the medium of instruction and a separate subject in the curriculum. The subject of English is presented in a very traditional grammar-based way, and its mastery is assessed through the formal 'SPAG' tests, done after 6 years of primary education when most pupils are 11 years old, which focus on spelling, punctuation and grammar. This is supported through a very extensive glossary of terms and definitions, which is presented as an appendix to the curriculum. Thus, the curriculum for English requires a lot of teaching of linguistic terminology in order that pupils can deal with these demands. The focus is heavily on literacy rather than oracy.

A look at the demands of other subjects reveals the importance of language for learning across the curriculum, and also shows the relevance of the ideas about BICS, CALP and academic language I have discussed above. For example, the aims of the primary maths curriculum (DfE, 2014, p. 3) resonate closely with the demands of CALP and disciplinary literacy as outlined by Cummins and Gibbons.

Aims

The National Curriculum for mathematics aims to ensure that all pupils:

- *become fluent in* the fundamentals of mathematics, including through varied and frequent practice with increasingly complex problems over time, so that pupils develop conceptual understanding and *the ability to recall and apply knowledge rapidly and accurately*
- *reason mathematically* by following a line of enquiry, conjecturing relationships and generalisations, and *developing an argument, justification or proof using mathematical language*
- *can solve problems* by applying their mathematics to a variety of routine and non-routine problems with increasing sophistication, including *breaking down problems into a series of simpler steps and persevering in seeking solutions.*

I have italicised some of the things that pupils are expected to be able to do, as part of their learning of maths, all of which are heavily dependent on language. Cognitively, they range from things that may be quite straightforward, such as 'become fluent in the fundamentals of mathematics', which, at one level, involves simple processes such as recall and naming. Other requirements clearly demand much more complex cognitive processes – and language – such as 'developing an argument' or 'breaking down problems into a series of simpler steps'. It is not unusual to find that pupils who are categorised as EAL learners can do such things with ease in their home languages, but not in English. Thus, it is often the English words and structures they need rather than the specific subject knowledge of mathematics involved, which they may already have at their fingertips.

If we look at the aims of the science curriculum for pupils at the top of primary school (10–11-year-olds) (DfE, 2014, p. 25), they can be seen to be supporting the transition from BICS to CALP in the progression of their cognitive demand from simple to more complex:

> During Years 5 and 6, pupils should be taught to use the following practical scientific methods, processes and skills through the teaching of the programme of study content:
>
> - *planning different types of scientific enquiries* to answer questions, including recognising and controlling variables where necessary
> - *taking measurements*, using a range of scientific equipment, with increasing accuracy and precision, taking repeat readings when appropriate
> - *recording data and results of increasing complexity* using scientific diagrams and labels, classification keys, tables, scatter graphs, bar and line graphs
> - *using test results to make predictions* to set up further comparative and fair tests
> - *reporting and presenting findings from enquiries*, including conclusions, causal relationships and explanations of and degree of trust in results, in oral and written forms such as displays and other presentations
> - *identifying scientific evidence* that has been used to support or refute ideas or arguments.

Again, I have italicised some of the language demands of this part of the curriculum. We see how they move from simpler to more complex language, all in terms of the specific science content and the special words with their technical meanings that are an important part of learning science. It also shows how the demands of the curriculum go beyond key vocabulary to the things that scientists need to do with their language, such as 'taking measurements' and 'reporting and presenting findings'. This suggests the language structures and text features that good scientists need to use and know. All of this opens the way to planning helpful strategies for EAL learners, as part of a model of good pedagogy for all pupils in primary classrooms.

Reflective task

Language across the curriculum

Look at another subject area of the National Curriculum, apart from English, maths and science, which have been discussed above. Identify *what* the pupils are expected to learn (i.e. the content), and *how* they are expected to learn it, using language – in other words, identify the *language demands* of the particular subject area you are considering.

Once you have done this, list all the words and phrases in the curriculum that show you the language demands; use the examples given above to help you do this.

'EAL' in the curriculum – good practice for all

The National Curriculum makes some helpful, if brief, reference to the needs of EAL learners. This is done as part of Section 4, which sets out principles for the inclusion of all pupils, under two main requirements:

- setting suitable challenges
- responding to pupils' needs and overcoming potential barriers for individuals and groups of pupils.

Though the reference to 'overcoming barriers' may take us back to the sense that EAL learners suffer from some kind of deficit (see Chapter 14, Warner and Elton-Chalcraft, and Chapter 15, Elton-Chalcraft, Revell and Lander), the actual statements that refer to what teachers need to do offer a stronger, more positive perspective on EAL learners and their families:

- 4.5 Teachers must also take account of the needs of pupils whose first language is not English. Monitoring of progress should take account of the pupil's age, length of time in this country, previous educational experience and ability in other languages.
- 4.6 The ability of pupils for whom English is an additional language to take part in the National Curriculum may be in advance of their communication skills in English. Teachers should plan teaching opportunities to help pupils develop their English and should aim to provide the support pupils need to take part in all subjects.

There is a lot packed into these 94 words, and much of what I have said above about theories of language and learning underpins the good practice that they imply. They make it very clear that schools need to find out about the home languages and prior education of their EAL learners, and take this into account in monitoring their progress. Through this, teachers can gain access to the funds of knowledge that their pupils may be bringing to the classroom, including their prior experiences of literacy. This is crucial for their engagement with literacy in a new language, with the opportunities it may afford for transfer, as well as for learning across the curriculum. Taking seriously what children bring to classrooms opens the door for teachers to take what could be termed a 'funds of knowledge' approach to their planning and teaching across the curriculum. Such an approach is not just about language. It is about finding ways to link curriculum learning objectives to pupils' cultural knowledge and experience, and providing opportunities for them to learn independently, using all their language and cultural resources. (See Chapter 14, Warner and Elton-Chalcraft, and Chapter 15, Elton-Chalcraft, Revell and Lander.) In Conteh (2015, pp. 59–60) I describe a thematic project based on family and community knowledge, where the pupils used photos of their own families to find out about their community histories. This kind of work affords opportunities for pupils to talk in ways that are not available to them in other activities, as they try to express their own meanings and achieve their own goals. Five-year-old Firdous' dual-language text about her grandmother above was a product of this project.

In terms specifically of language, research shows clearly that while a pupil's home language is stronger than English, they will learn better in that language. So, they need space to try to do this, which will also help them to keep up with their classmates in the subject. As their English language develops, they will transfer this subject knowledge to English. Some strategies that can help pupils to activate their prior knowledge are:

- When you begin a new topic, allow pupils in a talking partners activity to share their prior knowledge with each other, in any language they are able to.
- When they are doing group tasks, put pupils who share the same home language together so that they can talk to each other in any language they choose. Make sure they know that they need to report back to you in English.
- Ask pupils for key words in their own languages and bring together lists of words, invite discussion about the similarities and differences between the words related to the concepts.

Oksana Afitska (2015) demonstrates this 'translanguaging approach' in the materials and strategies she has developed for primary science at Key Stage 2. She explains the ways in which teachers were encouraged to use them with their EAL learners, giving them space to respond in their first languages:

> Firstly, where the learners had sufficient literacy skills in their first language – as measured subjectively by the learners themselves – they were invited to write their understanding of the teacher's explanations, as well as other ideas related to the topic from the lesson's content…

> Where the learners did not have sufficient literacy skills in their first language to write in sentences or phrases, they were invited to draw or sketch, and probably label, their ideas… The learners were also allowed to mix two languages – English and their first language. (pp. 10–11)

The aim of such an approach is *not* to teach pupils different languages, but to offer ways of learning using knowledge they already have and so to make bridges to their new learning. The teacher will probably not know the languages being used by their pupils, but this should not prevent them from allowing pupils to use them in the classroom at appropriate times. Of course, allowing pupils to do something which teachers feel they cannot control can be very risky – it imposes heavy demands on top of many other pressures (see Conteh, 2003, pp. 125–26). Interestingly and very helpfully, Afitska points out how the teachers she worked with were initially hesitant in adopting the strategies she suggested. But their concerns were overcome by the belief that:

> … the learners should be allowed to use whatever resources are available to them to support their learning even where teachers did not feel competent, or competent enough, to support them. (p. 11)

In this way, the teachers demonstrate the shift in role that I advocate in the section 'Learning multilingually', from transmitter of knowledge to facilitator of opportunities for learning. And the children responded positively and creatively. For example, invited to label a diagram showing three parts of flowers, a child labelled 'stem' and 'leaf' in English (though misspelled) and used her home language of Hungarian to label the root 'gyökér'. Thus, she achieves the learning objectives of the science activity. At the same time, she shows that she belongs in this classroom, that her language and identity are welcome and valued, and that it is acceptable for her to speak other languages than English, to use all the resources at her disposal in order to achieve her full learning potential.

Work in school

In a multilingual primary KS1 classroom, a student teacher decides to try out a 'translanguaging' strategy in a geography-based activity about domestic animals. He arranges the children in groups where, as far as possible, those who speak the same home language sit together. He gives each group a selection of relevant pictures and invites them to discuss them in their home languages, then write questions they wish to know about on their whiteboards, using any languages they wish. The children set off enthusiastically on their task.

In the course of the activity, the student teacher overhears the following conversation between two children in one group:

Child A: (pointing to one of the pictures) What do you call this in your language?

Child B: It's inek (cow in Turkish). What do you call it in yours?

If something like this happened in your classroom, how would you feel about it, and why?

Questions for discussion

1. In what ways do you think you could introduce a 'funds of knowledge' approach to planning and teaching in the primary classrooms that you work in? Remember that the approach is not just for EAL learners.
2. What do you think are the general issues around assessing EAL learners, and what are the implications for assessment of the theories about language and learning that are discussed? (See Chapter 4, where Harris and Lowe discuss assessment.)
3. Some people would argue that a pedagogy for EAL learners is good pedagogy for all learners. Do you agree with this? If so, what would be involved in such a pedagogy? If not, how do you think a pedagogy for EAL learners would differ from one that met the needs of all learners?
4. Do you consider yourself bilingual or multilingual? How do you think your identity influences your role as a primary teacher?
5. What gaps do you think you have in your knowledge about language diversity and EAL learners in schools in England? How do you think you can address these gaps?

Further reading

Conteh, J. (2015) *The EAL Teaching Book: Promoting Success for Multilingual Learners in Primary and Secondary Schools*. Learning Matters. London: Sage.
A comprehensive guide to working with EAL pupils across primary and secondary phases with case studies written by practising teachers; covers many of the ideas and principles outlined in this chapter.

Conteh, J. and Brock, A. (2010) '"Safe spaces"? Sites of bilingualism for young learners in home, school and community', *International Journal of Bilingual Education and Bilingualism*, 14 (3): 347–60.
This article reviews a range of classroom-based research with bi/multilingual learners from early years to age 11 and their teachers, which open out 'safe spaces' for learning that recognise and value the 'funds of knowledge' of both teachers and learners.

Cummins, J. (2001) *Negotiating Identities: Education for Empowerment in a Diverse Society*, second edn. Ontario: CABE/Trentham.
A full account of Cummins's work with bi/multilingual learners; gives a full discussion of his ideas as covered in this chapter.

Garcìa, O. (2009) *Bilingual Education in the 21st Century: A Global Perspective*. Oxford: Wiley-Blackwell.
This is a comprehensive overview of bi/multilingual education from philosophy to policy to practice. It contains a substantial section on translanguaging, which fully expands the ideas introduced in this chapter.

Gonzalez, N., Moll, L.C. and Amanti, C. (eds) (2005) *Funds of Knowledge: Theorising Practices in Households, Communities and Classrooms*. Mahwah, NJ: Lawrence Erlbaum.
This is a book about researching funds of knowledge by teachers and university-based researchers, and also the ways that the findings of such research can be brought into classroom practices.

References

Afitska, O. (2015) *Scaffolding Learning: Developing Materials to Support the Learning of Science and Language by Non-native English-speaking Students*. Innovation in Language Learning and Teaching. Abingdon: Taylor and Francis.
Bialystok. E. (2011) 'Coordination of executive functions in monolingual and bilingual children' *Journal of Experimental Child Psychology*, 110 (3): 461–8.
Blackledge, A. and Creese, A. (2010) *Multilingualism: A Critical Perspective*. London: Continuum.
Blommaert, J. and Backus, A. (2011) 'Repertoires revisited: "Knowing language" in superdiversity', *Working Papers in Urban Language and Literacies*, 67, King's College, London.

Centre for Applied Linguistics (1999) *A Global Perspective on Bilingualism and Bilingual Education.* Available at: www.cal.org/resources/Digest/digestglobal.html (accessed 15 March 2017).

Conteh, J. (2015) '"Funds of knowledge" for achievement and success: Multilingual pedagogies for mainstream primary classrooms in England', in P. Seedhouse and C. Jenks (eds), *International Perspectives on ELT Classroom Interaction.* Basingstoke: Palgrave Macmillan. pp. 49–63.

Conteh, J. and Brock, A. (2010) 'Safe spaces'? Sites of bilingualism for young learners in home, school and community', *International Journal of Bilingual Education and Bilingualism*, 14 (3): 347–60.

Conteh, J., Copland, F. and Creese, A. (2014) 'Multilingual teachers' resources in three different contexts' in J. Conteh and G. Meier (eds), *The Multilingual Turn: Opportunities and Challenges.* Bristol: Multilingual Matters. pp. 158–78.

Creese, A. and Blackledge, A. (2010) 'Translanguaging in the bilingual classroom: A pedagogy for learning and teaching', *Modern Language Journal*, 94: 103–115.

Cummins, J. (2001) *Negotiating Identities: Education for Empowerment in a Diverse Society,* second edn. Ontario: CABE/Trentham.

Cummins, J. and Early, M. (2011) (eds) *Identity Texts: The Collaborative Creation of Power in Multilingual Schools.* Stoke-on-Trent: Trentham Books.

Department for Education (DfE) (2014) *National Curriculum in England: Framework for Key Stages 1 to 4.* Available at: https://www.gov.uk/government/publications/national-curriculum-in-england-framework-for-key-stages-1-to-4/the-national-curriculum-in-england-framework-for-key-stages-1-to-4 (accessed 27 March 2017).

Department for Education and Skills (DfES) (2003) *Aiming High: Raising the Achievement of Minority Ethnic Pupils, DFES/0183/2003.* Available at: www.education.gov.uk/consultations/downloadableDocs/213_1.pdf (accessed 4 September 2017).

Garcìa, O. (2009) *Bilingual Education in the 21st Century: A Global Perspective.* Oxford: Wiley-Blackwell.

Gibbons, P. (2009) *English Learners, Academic Literacy and Thinking: Learning in the Challenge Zone.* Portsmouth, NH: Heinemann.

Gonzalez, N., Moll, L.C. and Amanti, C. (eds) (2005) *Funds of Knowledge: Theorising Practices in Households, Communities and Classrooms.* Mahwah, NJ: Lawrence Erlbaum.

Hakuta, K. and Diaz, R.M. (1985) 'The relationship between degree of bilingualism and cognitive ability: A critical discussion and some new longitudinal data', in K.E. Nelson (ed.), *Children's Language,* vol 5. Mahwah, NJ: Lawrence Erlbaum. pp. 319–342.

Heller, M. (ed.) (2007) *Bilingualism: A Social Approach.* Basingstoke: Palgrave Macmillan.

National Association for Language Development in the Curriculum (NALDIC) (2017) *Languages in Schools: More about the Languages of Bilingual Pupils.* Available at: https://www.naldic.org.uk/research-and-information/eal-statistics/lang/ (accessed 27 March 2017).

Peal, E. and Lambert, M. (1962) 'The relation of bilingualism to intelligence', *Psychological Monographs*, 76 (546): 1–23.

Vertovec, S. (2010) 'Towards post-multiculturalism? Changing communities, conditions and contexts of diversity', *International Social Science Journal*, 61: 83–95. doi:10.1111/j.1468-2451.2010.01749.x.

13

Dialogical, Enquiry and Participatory Approaches to Learning

Donna Hurford and Chris Rowley

By the end of this chapter, you should be able to:

- make connections between dialogue, enquiry and participatory approaches to learning
- discuss, in an informed way, how dialogue and participatory approaches can contribute to learning
- plan for a variety of enquiry and participatory approaches in the primary classroom.

Introduction

Dialogical enquiry and participatory approaches

This chapter is concerned with approaches to leading children into active participation and enquiry, through involvement in their own learning, both at Key Stages 1 and 2. The terms 'enquiry', 'learning' and 'active participation' are closely related. We link these approaches to dialogue and discussion because these aspects of learning are often dealt with separately in the literature and yet clearly they are a form of enquiry and participatory learning. We draw upon a range of literature and research in order to justify these approaches and we offer some examples of how they might be put into practice in the primary curriculum. Dialogical enquiry and participatory approaches apply across educational stages and have much in common with the concept of 'sustained, shared thinking' identified in the Researching Effective Pedagogy in the Early Years (REPEY) project (Siraj-Blatchford et al., 2002). This project found that the most effective strategies and techniques for promoting learning in the early years involved adult–child interactions in which the adult responds to the child's understanding of a subject or activity, the child responds to what is to be learnt, what is in the adult's mind, and both contribute to and are involved in the learning process, although the project also found that such exchanges do not occur frequently and that freely chosen play activities often provided the best opportunities for adults to extend children's thinking (Cooper, 2004, pp. 1–2). Sustained shared thinking is discussed in Chapter 7.

A rationale for dialogical, enquiry and participatory approaches

Theories

In many ways, it seems strange to need to articulate a rationale for using enquiry and participatory approaches in a primary classroom. Why would we not want children to enquire, participate, be involved with learning and to work with each other? There is research evidence that asserts the importance of oracy and dialogue in the classroom and their vital contribution to learning (Alexander, 2012; Higgins et al., 2014). To affirm the place of participatory approaches to learning, we can draw on a variety of literature. Dewey (1902) provides a rationale for child-centred education. Pollard (2008) gives a summary of Constructivist and Social Constructivist models of learning in school classrooms. Freire (1970) argues for transformative and emancipatory education for communities that are otherwise unheard of and oppressed. Emergent theories of creative approaches (Craft, 2000, 2005) and global education (Hicks and Holden, 2007; Oxfam, 2015; Think Global, n.d.) emphasise the importance of talk and interaction. Alexander argues for dialogic teaching where 'exchanges … chain together into coherent and deepening lines of enquiry' (Alexander, n.d.).

Policies

Although current education policies in England are inexplicit in their advocacy of dialogical, enquiry and participatory approaches, there are encouraging signs. The statutory requirements in the National Curriculum at all stages (DfE, 2013, p. 17) place emphasis on listening and responding to adults and peers, asking questions to extend understanding, articulating arguments and opinions, participating actively in collaborative conversations, hypothesising, imagining and exploring ideas, participating in discussions, evaluating viewpoints and building on the contributions of others. Currently, the National Curriculum (DfE, 2013) forms only part of each school's individual school curriculum, facilitating variation in content and approaches to teaching and learning as illustrated by schools that integrate Philosophy for Children (P4C) (SAPERE, n.d.) in all children's education. In addition, the current commitment to inclusive education (DfE, 2013), as explained in Chapter 10 on personal and social development, affirms children's rights to an accessible, high-quality education. This entitlement, together with assessment for learning's (ARG, 2002) principled learner-centred approach to teaching and learning, endorses the need for pedagogic approaches that stimulate curiosity and engage learners and teachers.

In these challenging, global times there is recognition of the need for children to engage with sensitive and controversial issues and to be equipped with the necessary skills and knowledge (DfE, 2015). The Prevent Duty (DfE, 2015) looks to personal, social and health education (PSHE) to facilitate this engagement and skill development (see Chapter 10, by Palmer, on PSHE, and also Chapter 15, by Elton-Chalcraft, Revell and Lander, on fundamental British values). But besides PSHE and RE's rich knowledge base for dialogic enquiries (Prescott, 2015, 2017), cross-curricular approaches to teaching and learning provide a wealth of opportunities to stimulate curiosity, motivate learner engagement and develop contextualised skills (Barnes, 2007; Rowley and Cooper, 2009). And if we extend cross-curricular learning to inter-curricular learning we will find participatory approaches that stem from community learning and action (Chambers, 2002; Oxfam, 2015).

Theory and policy in practice

Research also provides us with approaches to teaching and learning and, by critically reviewing these from practitioner perspectives, we can explore ways to enhance learning. You may wish to consider how the statements in Table 13.1 reflect your own practice. In many ways, these are challenging lists, setting high expectations for teachers and facilitators to keep learners engaged, motivated and challenged. Elements of the lists suggest that the teacher or facilitator needs to be a risk-taker and innovator. It could be argued that the very notion of learner participation requires an element in which the teacher 'lets go' of some element of control to the learners. This requires, however, a strong grasp of both the subject matter and the pedagogy on the part of the teacher, who must adopt practices that are well illustrated by the FACTS (feedback, application, challenge, thinking, self-esteem) model from Nottingham (2010), summarised in Table 13.1. In order to evidence the widely recognised significance of the FACTS model, Table 13.1 maps five relevant resources onto its key headings: feedback, application, challenge, thinking and self-esteem. Table 13.1 is designed to provide a helpful overview of the congruence between relevant theoretical and practical resources with regard to dialogical, enquiry and participatory methods.

Table 13.1   Shared characteristics of enquiry learning, dialogic teaching and participation

Nottingham (2010) 'FACTS'	Alexander (2017) 'Dialogic teaching' http://robinalexander.org.uk/dialogic-teaching/	Oxfam (2015, p. 8) *Education for Global Citizenship – a Guide for Schools*	Barnes (2007, p. 134) *Cross-curricular Learning 3–14*, 'How teachers can help children learn creatively'	Chambers (2002, pp. 8–9) *Participatory Approaches*, 'Do's for facilitating participatory approaches'
Feedback				
Provide information related to the task, which helps move pupils towards their learning objectives	Informs and leads thinking forward as well as encourages	Build on what learners already know (see Table 13.2) Promote assessment for learning (ARG, 2002)	Show respect for the child's background Identify the areas of strength in each child	Empower and support, be confident ('they can do it'); watch, listen, learn
Application				
Apply activity to a learning goal related to value and expectation	Professional engagement with subject matter that liberates classroom discourse from the safe and conventional	Belief that people can bring about change; commitment to social justice, equity, participation and inclusion	Give plentiful opportunities for holistic, contextualised and meaningful learning (see Table 13.2)	Innovate and invent – try new things, be bold, take risks; be optimally unprepared and flexible
Challenge				
Make a situation more demanding or stimulating to encourage learning	Discussion and argumentation that probe and challenge rather than unquestionably accept	Ability to manage complexity and uncertainty; self-awareness and reflection	Learn the arts of pedagogy. Give attention to subject knowledge	Embrace error, learn from mistakes
Thinking				
Develop the skills to reason and to reflect upon the ideas and concepts that you meet (see Activity, Table 13.3)	Interactions that encourage students to think, and to think in different ways	Critical and creative thinking		Be self-aware and self-critical; improvise; have fun, joke, enjoy
Self-esteem	Classroom organisation, climate and relationships that make all of this possible	Sense of identity and self-esteem	Work at engaging each child	Establish rapport; respect and be nice to people; unlearn/abandon preconceptions

Defining enquiry: curiosity-led or target-driven curriculum

The starting point for enquiry is curiosity, so perhaps we should really be considering first how we stimulate curiosity in the classroom. What do we understand by curiosity? To what extent can we rely on children's innate sense of curiosity and what role does the teacher have in ensuring that this can flourish? Is the curriculum that we have planned one which encourages curiosity? Is such a curriculum compatible with a target-driven curriculum, and if so how? These fundamental questions have to drive our approach to enquiry for, while enquiring might be a fundamental aspect of human development, it is easily forgotten in a crowded curriculum.

The basis of curiosity is often experience, and in the primary school this can take many forms. Experience can be a visit, a visitor, an activity, a story, an image or indeed anything which has an impact and which raises possibilities for questioning. An experience is generally shared and teacher-mediated. In other words, the experience alone is not the only component of a process of developing enquiry. It must be rich, yes, but children must often be helped by the teacher, in shifting the peripheral to the meaningful. One of the great early exponents of the fundamental importance of experience in learning was Dewey, and though some of his critics saw his proposed curriculum as one that left learning to the child with little teacher guidance or reference to well-established subject methodologies, careful reading of Dewey suggests otherwise. *The Child and the Curriculum* (Dewey, 1902) shows that Dewey conceived a curriculum in which the child's experience works alongside the subject curriculum:

> Nothing can be developed from nothing, nothing but the crude can be developed out of the crude and that is surely what happens when we throw the child back upon his achieved self as finality, and invite him to spin new truths of nature or of conduct out of that. (Dewey, 1956, p. 18)

In other words, Dewey recognised that the child's experiences needed mediating through the subject knowledge and expertise offered by the teacher.

Enquiry, values and dialogue

Dewey goes on to identify the importance of selecting appropriate stimuli for gaining new experience. After that, he saw what he called the 'logical' (relating to subject matter) and the 'psychological' (relating to experience *and values*) as being mutually dependent, like the dependency between 'notes an explorer makes and the finished map that is constructed' (Dewey, 1956, p. 19).

Based on our understanding of this interdependence of subject matter and values, we designed the activities below that give equal importance to the values children bring to their learning and subject knowledge. Alexander (2006, p. 32) discusses the complex relationship between 'talking' and 'knowing' as a way of testing evidence, analysing ideas and exploring values. He outlines the views of cynics to these approaches but concludes that dialogue still remains a key way by which teachers can move children's understanding forward.

Dewey did not just see education as a balance between the subject and experience. He recognised that in a world of massive and rapid change the child's social skills were equally important. (In Dewey's time, this was the continued growth of industrial society. Today it is the shift to an information society and probably in the future there will be even more radical shifts to an ecologically sustainable society.) Dewey saw the development of values as essentially part of a process that is integral to the psychological and cognitive development of the child:

> When the school introduces and trains each child into membership of society within such a little community, saturating him with the instruments of service, and providing him with the instruments of self-direction, we shall have the deepest and best guarantee of a larger society which is worthy, lovely and harmonious. (Dewey, 1956, p. 29)

Dewey, then, saw the way in which we select the material that we teach as well as how we teach as intimately connected and influential, not only on how we manage an enquiry but also on the values that are embedded in it. He saw an ability to enquire as one of the essential tasks that a school should be developing. Dewey's vision of the curriculum is different from, but not necessarily incompatible with, many aspects of the curriculum that we have today, in terms of both values and enquiry learning.

Enquiry, rigour and subjects

Participation and enquiry, then, cannot be separated from values education. What is more, these methods can all be related to subject knowledge. Alexander (2006) refers to 'constructive dialogue' as more than just conversing, and this is very much the basis of the Philosophy for Children programme developed in the 1980s by Lipman (1993) and others since (Gregory et al., 2017). Alexander (2010, p. 283) refers to the Society to Advance Philosophical Enquiry and Reflection in Education's (SAPERE) contribution to the primary review, 'teachers should be given more encouragement and preparation in stimulating and managing classroom dialogue', along with 'more opportunity in the curriculum for "open enquiry"'(for an example of this approach, see Table 13.3).

Work in school

Key Stage 2

Student: I agree with the lecture where we learnt that dialogical, enquiry and participatory approaches are really useful but I'd like to find a way of making sure that they are built into my planning and practice. What do you think?

Mentor: So what is your argument for including them? How would you convince a sceptic? Let's start by making a list of what you think are characteristics of participatory learning, then you can see where you are using them, and perhaps where you might build in more.

Student (later):   Here are my characteristics of participatory learning:

1. Involving the children in developing the learning objectives (LO); giving them ownership and responding to their curiosity.
2. Including LOs for knowledge and understanding, skills and values.
3. Introducing challenges into learning activities, asking 'What if...' questions.
4. Integrating short enquiries to encourage reflection.
5. Prioritising dialogical feedback, both peer and teacher feedback.
6. Ensuring every child is engaged and has success and also learns from mistakes: be bold, take risks.
7. Ensuring everyone participates in learning and enjoys the challenges.

Mentor: You've listed a range of characteristics which contribute to participatory learning and which illustrate the facts shown in Table 13.1. I noticed you have used several already – I'll give you some feedback in my written notes. But it's important that you check on the list when you're doing your planning – and also that in your evaluations you consider what worked well – or otherwise – and why. And don't forget to plan for and analyse your questions and children's discussion.

Analysis

Here the student teacher provides a list of characteristics of participatory learning, some of which are evident in the student's practice. There's significant congruence between the student teacher's list and the compilation in Table 13.1,

(Continued)

but what do these characteristics look like in practice? The mentor advises the student teacher to check her list but if they also had to jot down an example of what each characteristic will actually look like in class, this would convert the checklist into an authentic plan, see below:

1. Involving the children in developing the LO; giving them ownership and responding to their curiosity – *We can investigate how changes in the price of bananas in our local supermarket affect a Fair Trade banana grower and a non-Fair Trade banana grower.*
2. Including LOs for knowledge and understanding, skills and values – *We can learn about cooperatives by practising cooperative learning.*
3. Introducing challenges into learning activities, asking 'What if...' questions – *What if more farmers start growing bananas? What will happen to the price of Fair Trade bananas and non-Fair Trade bananas? What does this tell us about Fair Trade?*
4. Integrating short enquiries to encourage reflection – *Use the word 'fair' as a stimulus for an enquiry.*
5. Prioritising dialogical feedback, both peer and teacher feedback – *In pairs, the children discuss how well they are working cooperatively and the teacher provides feedback on how their approach to cooperative learning compares with a cooperative.*
6. Ensuring every child is engaged and has success and also learns from mistakes: be bold, take risks – *Look at the challenges cooperative learning presents – ask the children to identify challenges they experience and to discuss and trial possible solutions.*
7. Ensuring everyone participates in learning and enjoys the challenges – *Set learning expectations so all group members have specific tasks; the task cannot be completed unless all these tasks are fulfilled.*

This visioning process would also give the student teacher confidence; by 'walking through' her lesson, she would embody what participatory learning could look like in class.

Key Stage 1

Student teacher: I have read about participatory and dialogic approaches enquiry and I try to take them on board, but in my Reception class I also think play is very important. Is there a tension here?

(Continued)

(Continued)

Mentor:	Of course, play is important! But think about the overlaps between the two approaches...
Student teacher:	I do feel that I know quite a lot about why play is important. It is a form of solving problems together, I suppose – how to use things in the environment as objects, creating imaginary situations and stories and acting them out together. I've noticed children often have different ideas – and discuss them and argue whose is best – or right... And I've watched them engage other adults in the play sometimes, and sometimes adults may ask the children questions – or vice versa, or even help them find out more, related to the play.
Mentor:	Exactly, so why don't you observe children playing when you have a chance, and jot down the ways in which participatory learning is going on?

Analysis

In the second dialogue the student teacher raises a concern about a tension between play and participatory and dialogic approaches. Why might the student teacher have suspected a tension between these two pedagogic approaches? It is not uncommon to classify different pedagogic approaches as discrete, but this can be problematic and may lead to misconceptions about learning. If we try to be aware of how we are compartmentalising and instead look for commonality between approaches rather than differences, this would help us make connections between pedagogic approaches.

Examples of planning a curriculum through participation, enquiry and values education

We shall now consider how we might manage this type of participation and enquiry in the classroom in ways that are both practical and yet rigorous in the contexts of today. Tables 13.2, 13.3 and 13.4 attempt to illustrate some of the theoretical ideas above, and in particular:

- They encourage participation where children have opportunities to make choices under guidance from the teacher.
- They encourage enquiry methods.

- They embed subject knowledge in a variety of ways, ranging from specific skills to exploring concepts.
- They make use of dialogue in the classroom and encourage the development of values.

The context for the examples in Table 13.2 and 13.3 is a short topic on 'Where did my breakfast come from and how did it get here?' The context for the example in Table 13.4 is a short topic on our water supply. The plan in Table 13.2 focuses on learning learning-specific map skills through physical participation and questioning.

Reflecting on the activity

How does the approach to identifying and developing map skills, in the activities in Tables 13.2 and 13.3, differ from more traditional map work? Possibly the most striking difference is the children's physical involvement in the creation of the map.

Table 13.2   Where did my breakfast come from and how did it get here? A people map

Resources	Open space indoors or outdoors; locality map or world map; signs of local places
Learning outcome	To develop map skills through an experiential people map
Success criteria	To show awareness of relative positions of localities or countries
Assessment	Peer review questions and group feedback. What have we learnt from this activity? What did we have to think hard about? How would we do this next time?
Organising the activity	Depending on the children's awareness of the world map, choose either to focus on the immediate locality with the school as the central point or a world map with the country where the school is located as the central point. If the children know or are ready to learn compass points, ask them to make labels for the four main compass points and to identify where they need to go. Once the compass references are in the right places, bring all children to the map's central point, all facing in the same direction (one of the four compass points). If you are standing in a large open or outdoor space, you may need to set parameters for the 'people map' so that everyone is clear about how far they can go and begin to understand relative distances
	If you are making a school locality map, you may want to provide the children with signs or symbols representing features in the local area with which they are familiar. Working either in pairs or groups, the children have to take a sign and discuss where they think the place is in relation to the school. Wait until all groups have discussed and decided where they will go and decide how they will move: all together or a group at a time. Groups will probably have to review their location once others move into their places
	As children's travel experiences will vary, you may want to explore this first in class and extend it to where family members have travelled, have lived or live and then use these experiences for the map. Consider if all children need to have personal or vicarious travel experiences to be included in this activity. Alternatively, you could either give out signs for a selection of countries or ask the children to choose a country. Arrange pair or group work as explained above

As Pollard reminds us, 'we now know that the most effective deep, long-term learning is meaningful and conceptual' (2008, p. 201). Tanner, like Pollard, recognises the value of participatory approaches and notes how they can 'motivate pupils, engage their interest and provide memorable experiences which encourage deeper learning' (2007, p. 154). It is this pursuit of deeper learning that seems so well aligned with participatory approaches. However, it is not sufficient to dot the curriculum with more participatory experiential learning experiences. While Barnes (2007) recommends that 'experiences' are interpreted through the relevant skills and subject knowledge, curricular integration would also apply to participatory approaches. Making learning deep, meaningful and conceptual requires an open-minded and flexible approach to how we enable children to engage with the curriculum.

As a group or individually, using the format in Table 13.2 as a model, plan an activity for another subject (or based on a combination of two subjects), colour-coding opportunities where pupils can: participate by making choices under the guidance of the teacher; use enquiry methods; see where skills and concepts central to the subject are embedded in the activity; and encourage discussion involving values.

Table 13.3   A journey map

Resources	A class of pupils; open space indoors or outdoors; locality map or world map; signs of local places
Learning outcome	I will be able to work well with my group
	I will find out what I already know about our breakfast food's journey, including the transport and the jobs that were needed to bring it to my table
Success criteria	I will listen carefully to others, share my own ideas and help the group members work together on the activity. I will be able to talk about what I knew about my breakfast food's journey and I will be able to say what I want to find out next
Assessment	Self/peer/teacher review of posters' fitness for purpose; teacher observation; teacher questioning; self/peer/teacher review of presentations and what has been learnt during the topic
Organising the activity	The whole class will discuss and agree on what would make effective group work and agree to adopt the agreed criteria. The group needs to decide how to share out the group tasks. Each group has a different breakfast food (each food will need to have a country of origin indicated on the label), a sheet of flip-chart paper and marker pens. The teacher will explain that the purpose of the activity is to find out what we already know about the breakfast food's journey, and what we will need to find out or check. The groups need to know that the outcome of the activity is to have a poster from each group. The poster must be a map of their food's journey, with pictures or symbols showing the means of transport and jobs that were needed to bring the food from its source to the classroom. Reassure the children that it is okay not to know everything about the food's journey, encourage them to think about what they know about other foods and to share their ideas. Allow 15 to 20 minutes for the posters to be completed
	Each group now reviews other groups' posters by walking around the room to view them. Alternatively, groups could present their posters to the rest of the class. This could be an opportunity to consider and develop presentation skills. Through the poster review, the pupils can begin to identify what they know and need to know about their food; how well they worked as a group; and what they want from their posters

The plan in Table 13.3 focuses on learning about the international transport of food, in ways that involve interactive group work and discussion of values.

Consider which areas of learning you think this activity would cover. Once you have captured your own thoughts, consider the findings in Table 13.4 that show student teachers' evaluation of the mapping activity. The headings used to evaluate the activity are taken from Oxfam's (2015, p. 8) model for Global Citizenship. Oxfam (2015) notes how participatory approaches to teaching and learning can help learners develop their critical and creative thinking skills. Enquiry and critical thinking are endorsed by the government-funded Global Learning Programme (http://glp.global dimension.org.uk) as appropriate pedagogic approaches to complex global challenges. As teachers, we are required to plan and assess learning in terms of understanding, knowledge and skills development. We may well consider the impact of learning on values and attitudes less frequently and assign these aspects of learning to religious

Table 13.4 Evaluating potential and actual learning from the participatory activity: 'mapping the journey of a breakfast food'

Knowledge and understanding	Skills	Values and attitudes
Geography: map skills; relative distances; climate; landscapes; means of transport	Creating a meaningful map; demonstrating awareness of relative distances; transferring information from a globe or world map to own group map	Developing respectful awareness of similarities and differences between home and other places
Science: properties of materials (food and packaging); preserving foods; processing foods	Interpreting factual information	Valuing food
Maths: understanding estimation and how to improve accuracy; knowing measures of distance and how they relate (metres/kilometres); knowing how to calculate	Estimating and calculating distances	Developing awareness of globalisation and how it affects us all
Literacy: understanding text has meaning; understanding how symbols can convey meaning	Reading labels for information; designing and using symbols; speaking and listening	Having an inclusive approach to sharing information through visual literacy
Group work: understanding how to contribute effectively to a group	Turn-taking; listening; critical thinking; negotiating; presenting own views; sharing ideas	Empathy; respect; cooperation
Personal, social and health education (PSHE)/assessment for learning (AfL): developing self-awareness of what I already know and don't know	Identifying what I need to find out; listening to feedback	Self-awareness; being self-critical and receptive to critically constructive feedback
PSHE/Global Citizenship: understanding the contribution others make to my well-being; developing understanding of the work needed so I have food		Respect; empathy; self-awareness

education (RE), and Prescott (2015) successfully demonstrates how P4C activities can enhance RE. However, what if we deeply embed engagement with values and attitudes into our teaching and learning practices? What difference do we think this would make? Barnes talks about how schools seek to accommodate the 'all-encompassing sphere of shared values' (2007, p. 146) and notes the importance of values arising from 'genuine and sustained conversations'. Arguably, classroom practice provides regular and meaningful opportunities for these conversations, which can in turn be facilitated through participatory activities.

The plan shown in Table 13.5 focuses on deepening understanding of a complex concept through dialogue. This plan uses as its stimulus a story by Raymond Briggs (*The Man*, 1992). The approach for Key Stage 1 would be essentially similar though the stimulus choice would need to be more suitable. (See the final reflective task in this chapter, which links to web pages supporting the choice of stimulus.)

In this case study, the children chose the question 'Who owns water?' It would be easy for a teacher to look at this question and see it as one that has an answer. It is, however, a rich question with lots of potential for dialogical enquiry.

Table 13.5   A Year 3 group studying where their water comes from

Learning outcome	The ability to reflect more deeply on the meaning of a key concept, in this case that of ownership
Success criteria	I will be able to ask thoughtful questions and, in talking about one of those, I will begin to see how we might challenge each other's ideas
Assessment	Self-assessment of my contribution to the discussion. Teacher assessment of responses to exercises carried out after the discussion
Organising the activity	A visit to the local water treatment works provided an excellent stimulus, but since the intention was to develop more philosophical questions we moved the children into the role of a group of 'little people' living on a fictional island. To do this, a story – *The Man* by Raymond Briggs – was used (1992). This story is particularly appropriate because it has embedded in it many questions. It involves a small man (he could stand on your hand) who arrives in a boy's bedroom. As the book progresses, various dilemmas become evident. Should the boy treat him in the same way that he would treat any man? Is it fair to treat him differently because of his size? After reading this book, the children were led into the fictional island where these small people depended upon the mainland for their water supply. The role of the book at this point had been both to introduce a fictional element that would distance the children a little from their own place and also to encourage a deeper level of questioning from them, modelled by the issues raised in the book. Gradually, these discussions were developed into a series of questions. At this stage, it is essential that the teacher understands the nature of a 'philosophical question', one that we could talk about together based upon our own experiences of similar yet different aspects of life. Such questions invariably encompass a range of concepts and it is these concepts (big ideas with rather fuzzy boundaries) that we want to develop different understandings of. Help in identifying and supporting children in creating this type of question can be found in numerous books on Philosophy for Children. Increasingly, I use the 'questions quadrant' developed in *20 Thinking Tools: Collaborative Enquiry in the Classroom* (Cam, 2008). Once the question is chosen, the teacher manages a whole-class enquiry, exploring the meanings using Philosophy for Children techniques

The key concept chosen by the children was ownership, emerging presumably from the notion that water is owned by the utilities company from which we buy it. In practice, however, this dilemma offers an excellent way into a dialogue that raises many sub-questions. Is it really the water that the company owns or is it the cost of collecting, purifying and transporting it that we are paying for? Do I own the water that falls upon my roof? If so, do I have responsibility for either storing it or paying someone else (another utilities company) to take ownership of it in removing it?

Children will often show remarkable creativity if encouraged to discuss in this way, providing the teacher understands the nature of the discussion. To do this, training in the nature of philosophical enquiry with children is needed and this can be found via SAPERE's website.

There are many ways of further developing children's thinking on the concept of ownership. Our aim is not to write exercises that lead to an answer so much as exercises that promote deeper thinking around the nature of the concept.

In this example, there were certain moments in the dialogue that could be seen as 'critical events' in that they had a significant impact on the dialogue. (For more information on critical events, see Woods (1993) and further examples in Rowley and Cooper (2009, pp. 132–3).) Amy, for example, suggested that water 'belongs to the Earth'. This was later challenged by Stuart, who said that 'The Earth can't own something if I can't pick it up'. Stephanie then challenged Stuart with an example: 'But a tree can own water because it takes it up from the ground'. This shows how one statement (in this case by Amy) is often critical in dialogue and whether that is picked up and developed by other children can depend a lot on the teacher's handling of it.

These examples suggest that both participatory approaches and dialogue can, if handled well, develop deeper learning through actively engaging the learner in a real enquiry.

Reflective task

We learn a great deal by trying out the activities we plan with children first: the advantages and pitfalls. In a group, at your own level, list key philosophical questions related to ownership. Decide on the question to be explored. One person records the ensuing discussion as a concept map. Following the discussion, consider what the concept map shows: ideas that led to further ideas; ideas that were contested; how through discussion the group has arrived at a deeper understanding of the concept of ownership than any individual had previously. Write individual self-assessments based on the learning objectives and success criteria of the lesson plan.

Summary

In this chapter, we have attempted to justify participation and enquiry methods as key elements of primary learning. We have argued that enquiry methods are often closely related to participation and that the method we adopt has important implications for both the knowledge and value aspects of learning. We have further investigated dialogue as an essential aspect of enquiry and participation in primary classrooms, both potentially leading to deeper learning.

Questions for discussion

- How could you integrate participatory approaches to learning into a cross-curricular theme you would like to explore with your class?
- How would you define participatory approaches to learning? What would you say are its fundamental features?
- Do methods of enquiry differ in different subjects or in 'domains of knowledge' (as defined by Alexander, 2008)?
- How important is dialogue as a method of whole-class enquiry?
- To what extent are primary children able to ask philosophical questions?
- What is the significance of the stimulus that you use to motivate children's enquiry? (See additional web materials for this chapter at https://study.sagepub.com/cooper3 to help develop both this question and the reflective task on p. 313.)

Further reading

Alexander, R. (2012) 'Improving oracy and classroom talk in English schools: Achievements and challenges'. Extended and referenced version of a presentation given at the DfE seminar on oracy, the National Curriculum and educational standards, 20 February 2012. Available at: www.robinalexander.org.uk/wp-content/uploads/2012/06/DfE-oracy-120220-Alexander-FINAL.pdf (accessed 1 August 2017).

Alexander argues for effective oracy as a necessary cognitive skill; he critiques the tendency for teachers to focus on oracy as a social rather than a cognitive skill. He provides a thorough appraisal of the history of oracy in the school curriculum and pedagogy and concludes with clear recommendations for the National Curriculum Review.

Berthelson, D., Brownlee, J. and Johansson, E. (2009) *Participatory Learning in the Early Years: Recent Research and Pedagogy*. London: Routledge.

This informative and thought-provoking book explores different ways in which the experiences and participation in learning of young children are explored and understood in theory and practice. It will encourage you to continue the discussion about infants' and toddlers' participatory learning in group settings.

Education Endowment Foundation (July 2015) *Philosophy for Children Evaluation Report and Executive Summary*. Available at: https://v1.educationendowmentfoundation.org.uk/uploads/pdf/Philosophy_for_Children.pdf (accessed 1 August 2017).
The report documents the impact of a 4-year study that evaluated the impact of P4C on pupils in 50 schools in the UK. One finding was that P4C had a positive impact on Key Stage 2 attainment in English and maths.

Fisher, R. (2012) *Teaching Thinking: Philosophical Enquiry in the Classroom*. London: Continuum.
This book shows how to encourage children to think critically and creatively through dialogue. It is concerned with the kinds of talk we already have with children but 'doing it better', to develop their reasoning, moral thinking and social education. It shows how introducing children to a 'community of enquiry' through philosophical discussion can enrich thinking in any subject area. It is illustrated by examples of the author's work with teachers and children.

Roche, M. (2011) 'Creating a dialogical and critical classroom: Reflection and action to improve practice', *Educational Action Research*, 19 (3): 327–43.
An inspirational self-study action research enquiry by a primary school teacher who wanted to create a more critical and dialogical form of pedagogy.

Further resources

Chambers, R. (2002) *Participatory Workshops*. London: Earthscan.
This guide is written for facilitators of participatory workshops. It provides thorough and clear explanations of ways to engage participants in learning. Many of the activities are directly transferable to a classroom setting and others have the potential to be easily adapted for classroom and school use.

Oxfam Education (available at: www.oxfam.org.uk/education/) provides a wide range of online and downloadable participatory activities and resources designed for global citizenship, which are easily transferable to other learning contexts.

Think Global (available at: https://think-global.org.uk/) represents a network of development education centres that provide support for the formal and informal education sectors on issues relating to global citizenship. There is currently government funding for professional development support for teachers in 'global learning', which can include enquiry and participatory approaches.

References

Alexander, R. (n.d.) 'Dialogic teaching'. Available at: www.robinalexander.org.uk/dialogic-teaching/ (accessed 1 August 2017).

Alexander, R. (2006) *Education as Dialogue: Moral and Pedagogical Choices for a Runaway World*. Hong Kong: Hong Kong Institute of Education and Dialogos.

Alexander, R. (2008) *Towards Dialogic Teaching: Rethinking Classroom Talk*, fourth edn. York: Dialogos.

Alexander, R. (ed.) (2010) *Children, Their World, Their Education: Final Report and Recommendations of the Cambridge Primary Review*. London: Routledge.

Alexander, R. (2012) 'Improving oracy and classroom talk in English schools: Achievements and challenges'. Extended and referenced version of a presentation given at the DfE seminar on oracy, the National Curriculum and educational standards, 20 February 2012. Available at: www.robinalexander.org.uk/wp-content/uploads/2012/06/DfE-oracy-120220-Alexander-FINAL.pdf (accessed 1 August 2017).

Alexander, R. (2017) *Towards Dialogic Teaching: Rethinking Classroom Talk*, fifth edn. York: Dialogos.

Assessment Reform Group (ARG) (2002) *Assessment for Learning: 10 Principles*. London: Assessment Reform Group.

Barnes, J. (2007) *Cross-Curricular Learning 3–14*. London: Sage.

Briggs, R. (1992) *The Man*. London: Random House.

Cam, P. (2008) *20 Thinking Tools: Collaborative Enquiry in the Classroom*. Camberwell: ACER.

Chambers, R. (2002) *Participatory Workshops*. London: Earthscan.

Cooper, H. (ed.) (2004) *Exploring Time and Place through Play*. London: Fulton.

Craft, A. (2000) *Creativity across the Primary Curriculum: Framing and Developing Practice*. London: Routledge.

Craft, A. (2005) *Creativity in Schools: Tensions and Dilemmas*. London: Routledge Falmer.

Department for Education (DfE) (2013) *The National Curriculum in England. Key Stages 1 and 2 Framework Document*. Available at: www.gov.uk/government/publications.

Department for Education (DfE) (2015) *The Prevent Duty: Departmental Advice for Schools and Childcare* Providers. DFE-00174-2015. London: DfE.

Dewey, J. (1902) *The Child and the Curriculum*. Chicago, IL: University of Chicago Press.

Dewey, J. (1956) *The Child and the Curriculum*. Chicago, IL: University of Chicago Press.

Freire, P. (1970) *Pedagogy of the Oppressed*. Harmondsworth: Penguin.

Gregory, M.R., Haynes, J. and Murris, K. (2017) (eds) *The Routledge International Handbook of Philosophy for Children*. New York: Routledge.

Hicks, D. and Holden, C. (eds) (2007) *Teaching the Global Dimension*. London: Routledge.

Higgins, S., Katsipataki, M., Kokotsaki, D., Coleman, R., Major, L.E. and Coe, R. (2014) *The Sutton Trust-Education Endowment Foundation Teaching and Learning Toolkit*. London: Education Endowment Foundation.

Lipman, M. (1993) *Thinking Children and Education*. Dubuque, IA: Kendall/Hunt.

Nottingham, J. (2010) *Challenging Learning*. Berwick upon Tweed: JN Publishing.

Oxfam (2015) *Education for Global Citizenship: A Guide for Schools*. Available at: www.oxfam.org.uk/education/global-citizenship/global-citizenship-guides (accessed 1 August 2017).

Pollard, A. (2008) *Reflective Teaching*, third edn. London: Continuum.

Prescott, G. (2015) 'Creative thinking and dialogue: P4C and the community of enquiry', in S. Elton-Chalcraft (ed.), *Teaching Religious Education Creatively* (pp.35–50). Abingdon: Routledge.

Prescott, G. (2017) 'Challenging assumptions and making progress', in B. Anderson (ed.), *Philosophy for Children: Theory and Praxis in Teacher Education* (pp.122–130). Abingdon: Routledge.

Rowley, C. and Cooper, H. (2009) *Cross-curricular Approaches to Teaching and Learning*. London: Sage.

Siraj-Blatchford, I., Sylva, K., Muttock, S., Gilden, R. and Bell, D. (2002) *Researching Effective Pedagogy in the Early Years* (Research Report 256). Annersley: Department for Education and Skills.

Society for Advancing Philosophical Enquiry and Reflection in Education (SAPERE) (n.d.) 'Philosophy for Children – P4C'. Available at: www.sapere.org.uk/ (accessed 1 August 2017).

Tanner, J. (2007) 'Global citizenship', in D. Hicks and C. Holden (eds), *Teaching the Global Dimension*. London: Routledge. pp. 150–60.

Think Global (n.d.) 'Who we are'. Available at: https://think-global.org.uk/ (accessed 1 August 2017).

Woods, P. (1993) *Critical Events in Teaching and Learning*. London: Falmer.

14

Race, Culture and Ethnicity Teaching in Post-European Times

Diane Warner and Sally Elton-Chalcraft

By the end of this chapter, you should be able to:

- comply with the legal requirements that promote diversity and social cohesion in a post-European context
- understand the impact of your own ethnicity and attitudes towards diversity on your role as a teacher
- reflect on research that investigates cultural awareness among teachers and primary children
- develop teaching and learning approaches that challenge intolerance and promote understanding and equality.

Introduction

We live in post-European times, where even though the UK is still part of the continent of Europe, we no longer share the community and economic basis of the European Union. This has racial and cultural implications for school populations and the consequent effect on ways of teaching and learning. In addition the identification, and language of, and the response to race and ethnicity in schools are now much less visible in the curriculum and government policy (Gillborn, 2005, 2013; Warner, unpublished thesis, 2017). This chapter links with Conteh's Chapter 12, 'Language and Learning in a Multilingual World', and Elton-Chalcraft, Revell and Lander's Chapter 15 on British values.

The national picture in UK classrooms

There are currently 4.3 million children in maintained English primary schools, of which 28 per cent of pupils are classified as being of a minority ethnic origin (DfE, 2013a). Ethnic diversity of pupils is not new because the UK has seen large-scale immigration since the 1950s, but the types of new peoples, the effect on schools and resulting government policies are constantly changing (Alexander et al., 2015).

The UK has been an ethnically diverse group of countries for centuries but the picture of children in UK schools is changing, reflecting the newer European and worldwide migration demographic. Two recent movements have been happening simultaneously in the early twenty-first century that affect schools. The first occurred when the UK, as part of the European Union, welcomed people from other countries in Europe. Children and their families came, particularly from the Eastern European countries, looking for work and a better life. This brought new languages and cultural customs into the classroom. It also brought a new idea that, although these migrant families were white not black, they often had similar needs to support their inclusion. The second movement occurred later, as war and violence in the Middle East, particularly in Syria and Yemen, caused a large-scale movement of people to leave their home countries and seek refuge in other countries, including the UK. Their status as refugees or asylum seekers brings fresh challenges and sits alongside children from black and minority ethnic (BME) groups who have been settled for decades. These include those from Caribbean, Asian and African backgrounds.

BME populations are concentrated in urban areas, mainly London, the East and West Midlands, the north and north-west regions. This results in extremes of variation, with some schools teaching 100 per cent minority ethnic children, while others, in rural or suburban areas, only have a handful of BME children or none at all. Most schools lie on the spectrum somewhere in-between.

The main characteristics of ethnic and racial diversity in the UK are shown by cultural customs. These include: religion and forms of worship, language and dialect, food, music and dress. These differences embody the values, morals and outlook of groups, and engender a strong sense of community and beliefs. However, it is important not to see groups as comprising individuals who all think, speak and live in exactly the same way. The 2011 Census alerts us to the fact that minority ethnic groups are varied within themselves:

different groups share some characteristics but there are often greater differences between the individual ethnic groups than between the minority ethnic population as a whole and the White British people. (ONS Census, 2011)

These differences reflect people's histories as well as current social phenomena. Pakistani Muslims in Lancashire, for example, may share many values and practices with Somali Muslims in west London, but there will be cultural and religious differences too, based on their past and how and where they live now. This will affect surface issues such as dress, food and daily customs, but more importantly members of these groups will have different views and opinions about deeper issues in life, based on the way they follow their religion and the way they are viewed and treated in British society. Alternatively, those whose heritage combines two or more racial backgrounds, such as a Caribbean-English or Irish-Chinese child, will embody both of these cultures, which they gained from their parents, but will also forge their own, new culture, which will develop as they express themselves in our rapidly changing society.

We are all racial and cultural beings, whether we belong to the majority or minority cultures, and this affects the way we think, act and interact with one another. However, teachers can worry about teaching religious education (RE), for example, and in making explicit and positive responses to children who come from BME backgrounds. There is a fear of offending through a lack of knowledge or being patronising in one's approach (Elton-Chalcraft, 2015). Culturally responsive teaching understands difference, recognising that different racial and ethnic groups are vibrant and are to be valued and cherished. This occurs in teaching, assemblies and extra-curricular activities, and involves equal representation of all types of children in school life. This approach recognises that all racial and ethnic groups, including white British, are diverse within themselves, rather than being homogeneous units. Therefore, recognising children as both individuals and inheritors of a particular cultural dynamic will promote positive self-esteem, racial equity and social justice.

Reflective task

Use the interactive map on the Guardian Education website to find out the ethnicity of primary school children in the area where you grew up and where you now study or work (https://www.theguardian.com/news/datablog/interactive/2011/jun/22/english-school-system-interactive-map).

(Continued)

1. What are your response and attitudes to the minority ethnic communities in these areas? Why do you think this?
2. How aware are you of your own ethnicity and how it impacts on your thinking and teaching?
3. What could you do now to develop your understanding of the ethnicity and cultures of children with whom you work?

Schools, guidance and the law

- The National Curriculum (DfE, 2014) does not specifically comment on ethnic or cultural diversity needs, only the need for children with English as an additional language (EAL) to be suitably supported. Further reading about EAL needs can be found in this book (Chapter 12 by Conteh). The general inclusion statement in the National Curriculum, based on the Equality Act 2010, specifies:

> Lessons should be planned to ensure that there are no barriers to every pupil achieving… Teachers should take account of their duties under equal opportunities legislation that covers race, disability, sex, religion or belief, sexual orientation, pregnancy and maternity, and gender reassignment. (DfE, 2013b, p. 8)

From the Teachers' Standards (DfE, 2012) there are areas that particularly reflect racial and cultural issues in Part Two: Personal and Professional Conduct. Teachers and schools therefore need to create an inclusive ethos and curriculum that also identify and respond to the promotion of British values, such as recognising and respecting difference (see Chapter 15 by Elton-Chalcraft, Revell and Lander). This involves children understanding that their own and others' religious and cultural beliefs and customs should mutually support, not work against, one another. This should be taught in a context that the UK is multicultural, built on a rich history of different racial and cultural peoples. In one London school, where 28 languages are spoken, 'British values' are promoted in many ways, including a Diversity Week, where the whole school takes part in activities that value everyone's difference, including gender, disability and so forth. Through the use of a 'core' book such as *Elmer* by David McKee, the children learn that difference is normal and leads to a vibrant society. They learn ways of living and working together in school and in their community. The school also promotes national events such as Black History and Gypsy, Roma and Traveller Months (Ofsted, 2014).

However, research has found teaching British values is not straightforward. Many teachers feel uncomfortable and unsure about such an overtly political idea, which has arisen as a 'result of the Home Office Prevent strategy for counter-terrorism' (see Chapter 15, Elton-Chalcraft, Revell and Lander; Elton-Chalcraft et al., 2017; Tomlinson, 2015). This is a similar finding to Revell (2012), who investigated how some governmental initiatives such as *Prevent* and *Community Cohesion* have imposed new levels of intervention that are questionable and, as she suggests, a possible misrepresentation and manipulation of Islam. How to address the directive to promote fundamental British values is discussed more fully in Chapter 15.

Community Cohesion

For the past 10 years schools have been under a duty to promote community cohesion in three main areas:

- *Teaching, learning and curriculum* – to teach pupils to understand others, to promote common values and to value diversity; to promote awareness of human rights and of the responsibility to uphold and defend them; and to develop the skills of participation and responsible action.
- *Equity and excellence* – to ensure equal opportunities for all to succeed at the highest level possible, removing barriers to access and participation in learning and wider activities and eliminating variations in outcomes for different groups.
- *Engagement and ethos* – to provide a means for children, young people and their families to interact with people from different backgrounds and build positive relations, including links with different schools and communities locally, across the country and internationally. (DCSF, 2007; DfE, 2011)

Equality Act 2010

The Equality Act 2010 (https://www.gov.uk/guidance/equality-act-2010-guidance) states that schools are not allowed to discriminate against children and young people because of their: disability, gender, race, religion or belief, or sexual orientation. In addition the United Nations (UN) Convention on the Rights of the Child states that all children have the right to:

- believe what they want and to practise their religion
- receive education and its benefits, as any other child, while seeking refuge
- learn and use the language, customs and religion of their family, whether or not these are shared by the majority of the people in the country where they live (OHCRH, 1990).

The Equality Act 2010 makes it unlawful for direct or indirect discrimination, harassment or victimisation of any one of three groups: those who *belong* to one of the nine protected characteristics, those who are *associated with* someone from one of the nine protected characteristics or those who are *perceived to be a member*. Thus, everyone is, in fact, covered by this all-encompassing Act.

The Equality Act 2010 legalises tolerance and acceptance for all, including children. It runs in parallel to the requirements for teachers *to not undermine fundamental British values, including democracy, the Rule of Law, individual liberty* as stated in the Teachers' Standards (DfE, 2012). Therefore, in response to this statutory and non-statutory guidance, schools have to provide support and guidance for children from minority ethnic groups, to ensure they are properly equipped to engage fully and well in their communities and in society. Teachers have a duty to respond positively to the rich diversity in their classrooms and provide knowledge and insight about other UK cultures. It may not be straightforward and there are never easy answers to changes and new opportunities; however, an open and inclusive mindset is necessary for inclusion and learning to take place.

The role of the teacher is never straightforward and you may have already realised that some of these characteristics may be in conflict with each other – for example, some members of some Christian denominations and some Muslims, Hindus and other faiths may disagree, in principle, with the practice of homosexuality, but the Equality Act 2010 demands that homosexuals should not be victimised or discriminated against. Similarly, some women feel that some religious groups discriminate against women in their hierarchy. There are no easy answers to these dilemmas – but perhaps a healthy and open debate following the spirit of the law can assist children to see why the Equality Act 2010 was introduced, and the list below offers examples of how you can ensure you adhere to the law.

The implication of the Equality Act for schools, with particular reference to race and ethnicity, includes making sure you:

- draw on resources that are from a variety of cultures – for example, authors outside the 'traditional canon' (not always using white, male and British authors)
- use images that reflect other perspectives – for example, displays that show a variety of families from a range of different cultures, using maps with Australia at the top (whilst avoiding 'tokenism'– see 'Types of multiculturalism')
- seek opportunities for other voices to be heard – for example, not always white, male, Christian, but rather a variety of views/opinions and not just the dominant standpoint in the catchment area of your school

- adopt a critical multiculturalist stance whilst avoiding tokenism (see Table 14.1), for example, discuss why different dating systems exist, such as BCE (Before Common Era) and CE (Common Era), the Christian BC (Before Christ) and AD (*Anno Domini*), Muslim and Jewish calendars, etc.
- project appropriate 'institutional body language' (Dadzie, 2000) – for example, displays, ethos which celebrate a variety of cultures and viewpoints.

Reflective task

- Look at your school's policies on inclusion that include aspects of anti-racism, community cohesion and cultural diversity.

1. How is the policy demonstrated in practice at a whole-school level?
2. Do you see the policy demonstrated in other classrooms? If yes, how? If not, what do you think are the reasons?
3. How is the policy demonstrated within your own classroom? What changes would you need to introduce and sustain activities that develop understanding and equity through challenging children's thinking?

Developing a mindset

The law promoting equality is an important framework, and the Teachers' Standards have to be complied with, but it is up to schools and teachers to create and practise in an environment that is educationally positive and affirming for its pupils. It is therefore important to develop a mindset that is broad and supportive (see also the section below headed 'Teachers seeing and understanding race and culture in the classroom'). Research by Warner (unpublished PhD thesis, 2017) reveals that about 8 per cent of primary teachers are from BME backgrounds. This means that the majority are white. If we belong to the majority culture and a comfortable social class, it is easy to expect certain privileges in life and not see how difficult and distressing it can be for those from minority groups who either have been settled here for two or three generations or are fairly new settlers. They will suffer indignities and hostilities, which can be violent but are more often subtle and 'hidden'. This means their daily lives are spent negotiating what happens to them, based on their colour, culture and religion. To help teachers recognise their position as powerful as well as responsible, the three concepts of critical race theory (CRT), critical multiculturalism and cultural capital will briefly be considered.

The concept of CRT seeks to show up inadequacies in curriculum content and a colour-blind pedagogy that often presents children from BME backgrounds as under-achieving and difficult (Solórzano and Yosso, 2002; Ladson-Billings, 2005). It aims to increase and widen awareness of the ethnic and cultural needs of pupils and turn negative attitudes into positive ones. CRT also addresses casual, unintended, daily racisms, which are often considered not worthy of comment and are then 'hidden' from our collective social consciousness (Warmington, 2008).

Critical multiculturalism (May, 2005; May and Sleeter, 2010; Gillborn et al., 2016), like CRT, recognises the negative effect of powerful structures such as schools on children from BME backgrounds. It recognises that diversity and differences in identities in the curriculum and practices within the classroom are complex and multilayered, and advises that teachers should draw on children's knowledge and experiences. In this way teachers, can understand better how their powerful-majority position can be negated to see and include difference and give pupils more voice and power.

Cultural capital is an idea that can influence the way in which teachers can understand and become more compassionate in their outlook and practice in the classroom. Cultural capital was developed by sociologist Pierre Bourdieu in the 1980s and 1990s, who studied how people in a society have differing amounts of privilege and its consequent effect on their lifestyle, expectations and performances. (For access to Bourdieu's ideas, try Grenfell, 2012.) How much 'capital' or privileges people possess depends on the type of employment, material wealth, family and education they encounter. Bourdieu called these areas 'fields' and understood them to influence personal life chances and social position; determining higher or lower status. So, for example, a child in an area where there is a high percentage of professional families will be in an educative environment that prizes and extends academic, innovative and ambitious activities. The cultural capital in this type of school is high, leading to high-status outcomes such as university and professional employment for a higher proportion of the pupils. This is in contrast to a child from a minority ethnic group who may live in social housing and have parents in low-level employment or unemployment. This child's ability to engage well in school life is more negatively influenced. For teachers, trying to understand what a child 'brings' to school, will allow them to work more effectively with individual needs and a whole-school policy aimed at promoting well-being and life chances.

Teachers seeing and understanding race and culture in the classroom

In developing your awareness of culturally responsive education, this section (outlining our own research on teachers' and children's attitudes) aims to deepen your understanding.

Research among 40 student teachers showed a dichotomy between a desire to meet all children's needs alongside a lack of racial and cultural awareness (Warner, 2010). This lack of awareness, in their thinking and attitudes, caused them to make automatic responses and assumptions that were based on their own cultural heritage. Reasons for this cannot be easily pinned down and neither would it be right to simplify what is a complex area, but the research identified factors that could be seen as useful starting points for everyone, whatever your cultural background. These were family, schooling and community, and the social context of one's upbringing. Such factors can be seen as highly influential aspects of our identity formation and affect, in some way, how we see others.

All of the students in the study were white British. One had a part Ukrainian heritage. All had been educated and lived in white communities in the UK, and were currently studying at a mainly white university (Warner, 2010). It is pertinent to consider what values and assumptions they might have already formed about cultures, resulting from this monocultural focus of their backgrounds, and to think about how much this applies to all of us. Lander (2011) describes a lack of willingness, by student teachers and new teachers, to see children from minority backgrounds as different because of a fear not understanding their culture, while Ambe (2006) speaks of 'deep-rooted patterns' that are part of our unconscious being.

The students acknowledged their monocultural backgrounds, with one stating, 'you simply draw on what you know'; while another, who lived in the countryside as a child, explained:

> I'd never seen anybody of a different colour; you just knew people in the village. You didn't even think there was an outside world.

Commenting on the use of multicultural children's literature in the classroom, one stated:

> I understand why we have multicultural books because we have a multicultural society, so obviously we need to but I do feel sometimes that by making a book specifically for reading that is on an Asian subject matter, I think that can also make it more of an issue than it actually is.

Other students were worried about appearing ignorant of other cultures and religions, particularly while on placements in racially diverse schools. One commented:

> In 100 per cent Asian school I might see it as more of a challenge because you are not as aware of the culture and beliefs; you're more of an outsider in some ways. Because you're not fully aware of their culture or beliefs I think I'd be more worried that I'd do something that'd offend them or be seen as wrong.

King (2004) suggests that a wariness of approaching cultural differences can result in following known attitudes and approaches, which only affirm the high status of the prevailing cultural majority, and the lower status of minority cultures.

The student teachers (all names are pseudonyms) in the research displayed and discussed areas of their lives that resisted a white privilege mindset and displayed a deep desire to teach with equity and understanding. Recognising his own cultural position and the desire to teach with equity, Will, part Ukrainian and part English, articulated his difference:

> My granddad was dark skinned and my mother was a single teenage mum, so although I did not know it at the time, I grew up understanding what it meant to be different.

His later employment, before coming to university, was in a firm which employed many black and Asian peoples. This also affected his outlook:

> You want school to reflect what's life. The reality is that you might grow up in a white area ... but that's not how the world is... As educators we have the opportunity to make sure that children experience as many opportunities as they can.

Lou, who lives in the white part of a racially segregated northern town, has been able to hold on to her existing positive beliefs about racial diversity. While on placement at a white school, an incident involving the negative reaction of some parents about a new Asian child jarred against Lou's sensibilities and understanding about teaching children equitably:

> We need to reduce ignorance and provide models to help children know they are important and reduce feelings of isolation. Some say 'teaching's teaching', but I think it's [racially aware teaching] important... It brings a different experience and that's important.

Becoming a culturally responsive teacher

Participants in the research discussed above had begun to recognise that they did not exist in a cultural vacuum, but that they were coming from the cultural majority and white privileged position. As both of these factors influence the way we teach, educators should aim for the 'critical-multiculturist' position (Table 14.1), by questioning the underlying cultural assumptions of the curriculum and developing anti-discriminatory, inclusive pedagogies.

Initial teacher training and ongoing continuing professional development (CPD) are important catalysts in replacing entrenched ideologies and self-satisfied thinking and actions with challenging and transforming practices that reflect the complex and shifting nature of our multicultural society.

Children's awareness of race

Research in both predominantly white and also diverse schools found that the majority of 10-year-old children displayed anti-racist attitudes, but nevertheless had internalised the prevailing Western white privilege mindset, whatever their own ethnicity (Elton-Chalcraft, 2009). While recognising that the sample was comparatively small (about 80 children from four schools), it became apparent that most children in the multi-ethnic schools who were reasonably knowledgeable about their own culture and other cultures displayed anti-racist behaviour and attitudes (Figure 14.1, Quadrant A). Many children from all four schools were anti-racist even though they displayed limited knowledge (Quadrant B). A handful of children, mainly white boys from a low socio-economic background and in the low sets for maths and literacy, expressed racist comments. In this example, Bart, a white boy, and Kurt, a boy whose mother is white and whose father is of Jamaican heritage, discuss people of different cultures:

Kurt: They're ugly. [giggles]

Sally: They're ugly – so you think people who aren't the same culture as you are ugly?

Kurt: Yeah.

Sally: Why do you say that?

Kurt: Because they've got funny eyes and different to ours – ours are like that, theirs are bozeyed. [making facial gestures]

Bart: Yeah but Heidi [Kurt's girlfriend] is a different culture to you and everyone else in, and some people in, this thing, in this school, has [a] different culture to you but you like 'em – you're friends with 'em. So I don't know what you're pointing that for – ugly… And so if Heidi's got a different culture to you are you gonna dump her?

Kurt: [embarrassed giggle] Nnooo.

(Elton-Chalcraft, 2009, p. 114)

This interchange is interesting because Bart, who had himself expressed racist sentiments, was criticising Kurt's remarks. Thus, Bart and Kurt display racist attitudes towards a particular group but anti-racist attitudes towards a particular individual whom they dissociate from that group (Troyna and Hatcher, 1992; Elton-Chalcraft,

2009, p. 114). As a beginning teacher, are you aware of the stances towards different cultures held by the children in your placement schools? Is there an ethos of mutual respect or white Western privilege, particularly post Brexit?

A small number of children in the research were deemed to be knowledgeable about their own and other cultures but still displayed racist viewpoints (Figure 14.1, Quadrant C). These children were either expressing disgust at an unfamiliar culture, while in the main expressing anti-racist sentiments towards numerous cultures, or they exhibited racist behaviour that they almost instantly regretted. Rachel, a girl of Caribbean heritage, also made a gesture with her eyes but instantly said, 'I shouldn't have done that', possibly because I asked her why she was making a gesture with the corner of her eyes (Elton-Chalcraft, 2009, pp. 110–11).

Schools may attempt to be inclusive, refrain from stereotyping and promote community cohesion and anti-racism. Yet there may still exist within schools a white Western privileged outlook which assumes that the dominant culture of white Western mindset is superior (Gaine, 2005; Elton-Chalcraft, 2009; Revell, 2012). It has been acknowledged that since Brexit hate crimes have increased, suggesting a resurgence of negative attitudes towards diversity (Katwala et al., 2016, p. 18)

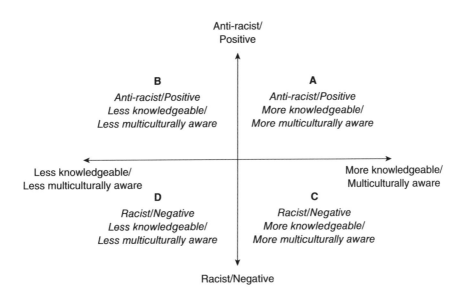

Figure 14.1 The range of children's attitudes and knowledge (Quadrants A, B, C and D) (from Elton-Chalcraft, 2009)

Multicultural stances in schools

The previous section invited you to consider the teachers' and children's awareness of race but there is a need to understand the school's 'institutional body language' too (Dadzie, 2000). Table 14.1 offers a rudimentary tool to consider how well a school, or class or teacher, approaches issues of diversity, ranging from tokenistic to critically multicultural.

Where would you place yourself, schools you have visited or individual teachers?

Table 14.1   Types of multiculturalism (Elton-Chalcraft, 2009, p. 82, adapted from Kincheloe and Steinberg, 1997)

1	Conservative multiculturalists (monoculturalism)	are 'tokenist'. They attempt to address multicultural issues but, deep down, they believe in the superiority of Western (white) patriarchal (male dominated) culture. *This is a starting place for many teachers, but this stance is superficial – there needs to be a genuine celebration of diversity*
2	Liberal multiculturalists	are dedicated towards working to 'one race'. They attempt to gloss over differences in an attempt to make everyone equal and the 'same' ('they' are the 'same' as 'us' – they just happen to be a different colour). *Some teachers think this is 'equality in action' but actually they are adopting a 'colour-blind' stance, denying that diversity exists*
3	Pluralist multiculturalists	believe pluralism is a virtue, where diversity is pursued and exoticised. There is cultural 'tourism' where 'they' (as opposed to 'us') live in an exotic parallel world. For example, Hanukkah is the Jewish Christmas. *These teachers attempt to celebrate diversity but they use their 'own' cultural language to describe the 'other' (inferior) culture. There is not genuine equality*
4	Left essentialist multiculturalists	are extreme in promoting the minority culture, to the extent that the dominant culture is seen as 'bad' and the marginalised as 'good'. *This stance is the opposite of pluralist – here the teacher elevates the 'other' culture and demotes the dominant culture. Again there is not genuine equality*
5	Critical multiculturalists	believe in the promotion of an individual's consciousness as a social being. They promote an awareness (self-reflection) of how and why his/her opinions and roles are shaped by dominant perspectives. *This teacher appreciates that there are differences within, as well as between, cultures and there is open discussion of the dominance of one culture over another, while celebrating diversity and equality*

Reflective task

Consider a critical incident you have encountered in school that presents a challenge with reference to issues of diversity, for example, low-level racist name-calling in the playground of a recently new child, who wears a prominent religious dress (turban, headscarf), at which the other children quietly join in.

1. What would be your initial response?
2. Would this reflect the school's policy?
3. How would you, as their class teacher, attempt to educate and develop the understanding of the whole class in subsequent weeks?

Teaching and learning for cultural and ethnic diversity

Being aware of ourselves as racial and cultural beings is an important position and enables an authentic and viable teacher–pupil relationship. This is a valuable attitude to foster in all schools to avoid a 'colour-blind' approach, an approach that comes from a failure to acknowledge race and ethnicity, or an uncertainty about how to notice it and then avoidance of the issue (Gaine, 2005; Pearce, 2005). This type of stance can lead to the formation of negative racist attitudes in children because, according to Pearce, 'unthinking racist insults and unintentional stereotypical racial references' are not linked to racism and therefore not challenged (2005, p. 35).

The following two examples of classroom practice will provide ideas and stimulate thinking for further teaching and learning in the area of valuing and raising awareness of racial and ethnic diversity.

Work in school 1: a Key Stage 1 approach – Persona Dolls

Brown (2001, 2008) gives practical advice on how to use Persona Dolls in the early years to combat discrimination. Her ideas can be extended for Key Stage 1 and Key Stage 2 children, particularly within RE lessons. Used alongside other approaches, Persona Dolls can provide a rich resource for learning 'about' and learning 'from' a particular religion/culture/way of life within the safety of the classroom (Elton-Chalcraft, 2015).

Introducing Jeetinder

Jeetinder sits on the class teacher's knee answering questions. Through the teacher as 'mouthpiece' Jeetinder provides information about his life and religion; children can see similarities and differences between their life and his and also understand how to deal with racism.

Izaak:	What's your name?
Jeetinder:	My name is Jeetinder Singh. I am a Sikh which means I follow Guru Nanak... What's your name?
Izaak:	Izaak but people spell it wrong; I'm named after a famous fisherman.
Judith:	What language do you speak?
Jeetinder:	I speak Punjabi and English. Do you speak other languages?

(Continued)

(Continued)

Judith:	I only speak English but Maria speaks Italian because her mum's from there.
Ryan:	Do you have brothers and sisters?
Jeetinder:	My brother Tejpreet is 11 and my sister's 14 and called Manjit. She is doing a GCSE in Punjabi; she visited my grandma and grandpa in the Punjab last year, it's in north-west India and south-east Pakistan. What are your brothers and sisters like?
Ryan:	I have three older brothers who tease me because I'm the smallest.
Jeetinder:	I get teased sometimes.
Hydar:	What's your favourite food?
Jeetinder:	Fish and chips from the chip shop round the corner. My mum cooks yummy vegetable curry too. What is your favourite food?
Hydar:	Chicken nuggets.
Lucy:	Why do you wear that cloth thingy on your head?
Jeetinder:	It's a jura – top knot. My mum used to help me tie it but I can do it myself now. Some Sikhs have long hair and we have to tie it up; my dad wears a turban. I have a best friend Jagdeep who doesn't wear a jura and he has cut hair – he's a different kind of Sikh. I sometimes get teased for wearing my top knot. I really don't like being teased. Ryan, what do you do when you get teased by your big brothers?
Ryan:	I hit them back but they chase me!
Jeetinder:	My dad told me I mustn't hit back but I have to stand up for myself and defend why I wear my jura, but it's really hard.
Colin:	I get called four eyes sometimes, I ignore it or I tell a teacher and she tells the class why I wear them.
Jeetinder:	Maybe I should tell a teacher about the bullies. I could explain why I wear the jura and many Sikhs have kesh (uncut hair) and wear a kangha (comb) and why we have to stand up for our faith, that's part of the 5 Ks.

(Continued)

Colin: We could tell the teacher and also tell the bullies and other children in assembly about your 5 Ks, whatever they are, and maybe they won't tease you anymore.

While this is obviously a scripted scenario, it provides an example of how you can 'direct' the conversation, through the persona doll, to help children learn about different cultures, the variety within a particular culture/religion and also engage in anti-discriminatory problem solving, which is at the heart of the Persona Doll approach (Brown, 2001, 2008; Elton-Chalcraft, 2015).

Work in school 2: a Key Stage 2 approach

The Island by Armin Greder (2007)

This picture book is an excellent and challenging resource to help children understand migration, immigrations and being a refugee. The story follows a lost and desperate man, washed up on an island where he is confronted by forbidding walls and hostile islanders. He is allowed to stay but because he is different he is treated as an outcast. He is finally set adrift in his burning raft and the islanders return to their heavily fortified, narrow existence. It includes themes of:

- racial and cultural difference
- racism
- effects of immigration, including refugees and asylum seekers
- human responses and the role of community.

The suggested teaching plan (full details can be found on the adjoining Sage website, https://study.sagepub.com/cooper3e) covers five sessions, although it could easily be extended to cover a 2-week period. This length of time allows for a development of understanding of diversity through the effect and appreciation of the narrative and linked activities designed to draw learners towards greater awareness and knowledge of how we should live together. It uses a cross-curricular approach, which includes literacy and PSHE.

(Continued)

(Continued)

1 Preparatory activity

Ask children to think of between two and four aspects of their lives at home, school and in their communities that they really like and wouldn't want to be changed by anyone new coming in. Provide them with 'bricks' made from brown sugar paper to write their ideas on. Stick the bricks on a large display board, or hang them from a line suspended across the room, to symbolise a wall. This 'wall' will later be dismantled as the children discuss and discover positive ways of embracing change and difference.

2 Introducing the book

The book contains powerful black and white images that will elicit thoughtful discussion, so a good way of sharing it is to scan each page into a computer program to project onto a whiteboard. Look at the front cover; ask for predictions and responses. Read the first part of the story and talk about the children's initial feelings. Make links to their earlier feelings about wanting to keep things the same in their community. In pairs, children should now discuss the man and his feelings. Write these on one side of the wall. Discuss how there seems to be a contradiction between their feelings of things staying the same in their community and the predicament of new people coming in and new things happening. Leave it as an open dilemma at this point.

3 Beginning to explore the story and its messages

Use drama activities to explore this open dilemma by focusing on the actions and motives of the villagers. These could include:

- *Freeze frames* – the children adopt the pose and view of a villager. You go round tapping different shoulders to allow them to appropriately voice their feelings. Do not allow the children to use inappropriate language however and have clear signs for going into and out of 'role', for example, snapping your fingers.
- *Hot-seating* – the teacher adopts the role of the man, taking questions from the 'villagers'. Place children in groups of two or three to think of questions that reflect how their village might feel. Encourage thoughtful questions and ensure there are no racially negative or inappropriate questions through giving some examples and by appointing a group leader to guide and monitor the others.

(Continued)

- *Conscience alley* – this is a good point at which to show the children that not everyone would be hostile towards the man. Divide the class into two lines and choose a child to walk slowly down the middle, twice. On the first walk, one side should call out reasons why they do not like having him in their community. On the second walk, the other side should call out reasons why he could stay, what he has to offer, and to indicate how their minds have been changed since he came to their island.

4 Reflecting so far

Link the children's responses back to the wall, emphasising that although these early comments are natural responses, they may not be helpful and supportive. Discuss and take predictions about the ending of the story, including how a negative or a positive ending would affect the villagers and the man.

Summary

In this chapter, we have enabled you to begin to appreciate and understand what it means to be a culturally responsive and anti-discriminatory teacher. This includes the suggested ways in which you can adhere to, but also go beyond, the legal requirements for promoting equality by tackling racism and discrimination, and valuing and celebrating children's cultural and racial heritages. You have been challenged to consider the impact of your own ethnicity and attitudes towards cultural diversity on your role as a teacher and have been offered the opportunity to engage with current research, which discusses white privilege, colour-blindness and a limited teacher mindset.

Teachers are always on a journey of discovery where constant re-evaluation of attitudes and ways of seeing the world becomes a key characteristic of their learning.

Even if the pupils in your school appear to be of a similar cultural position, for example, they are mainly Indian and Pakistani Muslims or are all white, it is important for teachers to dismantle notions of perceived social norms of race and class, which may characterise children as 'cultural others', who don't quite 'fit in'. Teaching instead should centre on a more accurate picture of the existing pluralistic society of the UK and enable what Townsend (2002) calls 'culturally responsive pedagogy'. Culturally responsive pedagogy alters personal and professional behaviours, paradigms and judgements by trying to understand and see into the world of pupils from cultures different from your own. Teachers therefore need to draw on culturally plural modes of teaching that recognise, celebrate and raise the status of minority cultures; and on anti-racist modes that challenge the power imbalance experienced by ethnic minority pupils. This involves engaging in teaching that develops identity and gives pupils a sense of playing an equal part in building and sustaining their school and community. These attitudes and practices, alongside a critical multicultural approach, should be adopted by teachers in both multi-racial and white schools, so that our pedagogies are transformed.

Further reading

Alexander, C. and Weekes-Bernard, D. (2017) 'History lessons, inequality, diversity and the national curriculum', *Race, Ethnicity and Education*, February. Available at: www.tandfonline.com/doi/abs/10.1080/13613324.2017.1294571 (accessed 24 March 2017).
The authors argue that it is not only the content of what children and young people are taught in schools that is at issue, but how teachers are supported to teach diverse curricula effectively and confidently.

Arshad, R., Wrigley, T. and Pratt, L. (eds) (2012) *Social Justice Re-Examined: Dilemmas and Solutions for the Classroom Teacher.* Stoke-on-Trent: Trentham Books.
This text is helpful for both new and student teachers because it covers issues of race and culture as well as other social justice issues that teachers face in their schools, including gender, poverty, class and religion. Insights into the subtle ways in which inequality often works are presented alongside classroom situations and strategies that can support teachers as they engage in constructive ways of working.

Gillborn, D., Rollock, N., Warmington, P. and Demack, S. (2016) *Race, Racism and Education: Inequality, Resilience and Reform in Policy and Practice.* Report to the Society for Educational Studies. Available at: http://soc-for-ed-studies.org.uk/documents/GillbornD-et-al_Race-Racism-and-Education.pdf (accessed 24 March 2017).
This report, based on a 2-year funded project, suggests that little has changed for the better for black young people in Britain in the past 20 years since the death of Stephen Lawrence, and race issues are of even less significance for policy makers today.

Warner, D. (2010) 'Moving into the unknown', *Race Equality Teaching*, 28 (3): 39–43.
This article presents research findings about white student teachers' understandings of racial and cultural diversity, through children's books.

References

Alexander, C., Weekes-Bernard, D. and Arday, J. (2015) 'Race and education – contemporary contexts and challenges', *Race, Education and Inequality in Contemporary Britain*. London: Runnymede Trust. Available at: www.runnymedetrust.org/uploads/The%20School%20Report.pdf (accessed 24 March 2017).
Ambe, B. (2006) 'Fostering multicultural appreciation in pre-service teachers through multicultural curricular transformation', *Teaching and Teacher Education*, 22 (6): 690–9.

Brown, B. (2001) *Unlearning Discrimination: Persona Dolls in Action*. Stoke-on-Trent: Trentham Books.

Brown, B. (2008) *Equality in Action: A Way Forward with Persona Dolls*. Stoke-on-Trent: Trentham Books.

Dadzie, S. (2000) *Toolkit for Tackling Racism*. Stoke-on-Trent: Trentham Books.

Department for Children, Schools and Families (DCSF) (2007) *Guidance on the Duty to Promote Community Cohesion*. Nottingham: DCSF. Available at: http://webarchive.nationalarchives.gov.uk/20130401151715/https://www.education.gov.uk/publications/eOrderingDownload/DCSF-00598-2007.pdf (accessed 2 August 2017).

Department for Education (DfE) (2011) *Community Cohesion and Prevent: How Have Schools Responded?* Available at: https://www.gov.uk/government/publications/community-cohesion-and-prevent-how-have-schools-responded (accessed 2 August 2017).

Department for Education (DfE) (2012) *Teachers' Standards*. Available at: www.gov.uk/government/publications/teachers-standards (accessed 4 September 2017).

Department for Education (DfE) (2013a) *Statistical First Release*. Available at: https://www.gov.uk/government/uploads/system/uploads/attachment_data/file/207670/Main_text-_SFR21_2013.pdf (accessed 2 July 2013).

Department for Education (DfE) (2013b) *The National Curriculum in England. Key Stages 1 and 2 Framework Document*. Available at: https://www.gov.uk/government/uploads/system/uploads/attachment_data/file/425601/PRIMARY_national_curriculum.pdf (accessed 2 August 2017).

Department for Education (DfE) (2014) *National Curriculum for England*. Available at: www.gov.uk/government/publications/national-curriculum-in-england-framework-for-key-stages-1-to-4 (accessed 4 September 2017).

Elton-Chalcraft, S. (2009) *It's Not Just About Black and White Miss: Children's Awareness of Race*. Stoke-on-Trent: Trentham Books.

Elton-Chalcraft, S. (ed.) (2015) *Teaching RE Creatively*. London: Routledge.

Elton-Chalcraft, S., Lander V., Revell, L., Warner, D. and Whitworth, L. (2017) 'To promote, or not to promote fundamental British values? Teachers' standards, diversity and teacher education', *British Educational Research Journal*, 43 (1). Available at: http://onlinelibrary.wiley.com/doi/10.1111/berj.2017.43.issue-1/issuetoc (accessed 2 August 2017).

Gaine, C. (2005) *We're All White, Thanks: The Persisting Myth about White Schools*. Stoke-on-Trent: Trentham Books.

Gillborn, D. (2005) 'Educational policy as an act of white supremacy: Whiteness, critical race theory and educational reform', *Journal of Education Policy*, 20: 485–505.

Gillborn, D. (2013) 'The policy of inequity: Using CRT to unmask white supremacy in education policy', in M. Lynn and A. Dixson (eds), *Handbook of Critical Race Theory in Education* (pp.129–139). Abingdon: Routledge.

Gillborn, D., Rollock, N., Warmington, P. and Demack, S. (2016) *Race, Racism and Education: Inequality, Resilience and Reform in Policy and Practice*. Report to the Society for Educational Studies. Available at http://soc-for-ed-studies.org.uk/documents/GillbornD-et-al_Race-Racism-and-Education.pdf (accessed 24 March 2017).

Greder, A. (2007) *The Island*. Crows Nest, NSW: Allen & Unwin. (This publisher's webpage will provide further details on *The Island* and more teaching ideas: www.allenandunwin.com/default.aspx?page=94&book=9781741752663.)

Grenfell, M. (ed.) (2012) *Pierre Bourdieu: Key Concepts*, second edn. Durham: Acumen Publishing.

Katwala, S., Rutter, J. and Balinger, S. (2016) 'What next after Brexit? Immigration and integration in post referendum Britain'. Available at: http://socialwelfare.bl.uk/subject-areas/services-client-groups/minoritygroups/britishfuture/178816What-next-after-Brexit.pdf (accessed 17 February 2017).

King, J.E. (2004) 'Dysconscious racism: Ideology, identity and the miseducation of teachers', in G. Ladson-Billings and D. Gillborn (eds), *The RoutledgeFalmer Reader in Multicultural Education*. Abingdon: RoutledgeFalmer. pp. 71–83.

Ladson-Billings, G. (2005) 'The evolving role of critical race theory in educational scholarship', *Race Ethnicity and Education*, 8 (1): 115–19.

Lander, V. (2011) 'Race, culture and all that: An exploration of the perspectives of White secondary student teachers about race equality issues in their initial teacher education', *Race, Ethnicity and Education*, 14 (3): 351–64.

May, S. (ed.) (1998) *Critical Multiculturalism*. Abingdon: Routledge Falmer.

May, S. and Sleeter, C. (eds) (2010) *Critical Multiculturalism: Theory and Praxis*. London: Routledge.

McKee, D. (2007) *Elmer*. London: Andersen.

Office for National Statistics (ONS) Census (2011) *Census*. Available at: www.ons.gov.uk/ons/datasets-and-tables/index.html?pageSize=50&sortBy=none&sortDirection=none&newquery=ethnicity+data&content-type=Reference+table&content-type=Dataset (accessed 1 July 2013).

Office for Standards in Education (Ofsted) (2014) *Creating a School Community that Celebrates Diversity*. Available at: https://www.gov.uk/government/publications/good-practice-resource-creating-a-school-community-that-celebrates-diversity (accessed 1 August 2017).

Office of the United Nations High Commissioner for Human Rights (OHCHR) (1990) *Convention for the Rights of the Child*. Available at: www.ohchr.org/EN/ProfessionalInterest/Pages/CRC.aspx (accessed 2 August 2017).

Pearce, S. (2005) *You Wouldn't Understand: White Teachers in the Multi-ethnic Classroom*. Stoke-on-Trent: Trentham Books.

Revell, L. (2012) *Islam and Education: The Manipulation and Misrepresentation of Religion*. Stoke-on-Trent: Trentham Books.

Solórzano, D. and Yosso, T. (2016) 'Critical race methodology: Counter storytelling as an analytical framework for educational research', in E. Taylor, D. Gillborn and G. Ladson-Billings (eds), *Foundations of Critical Race Theory in Education*. London: Routledge.

Tomlinson, S. (2015) *Race, Education and Inequality in Contemporary Britain*. London: Runnymede Trust.

Townsend, B. (2002) 'Leave no teacher behind', *Qualitative Studies in Education*, 15 (6): 727–38.

Warmington, P. (2008) 'The 'R' Word: Voicing race as a critical problem and not just a problem of practice', in J. Satterthwaite, M. Watts and H. Piper (eds), *Talking Truth, Confronting Power*. Stoke-on-Trent: Trentham Books. pp. 143–57.

Warner, D. (2010) 'Moving into the unknown', *Race Equality Teaching*, 28 (3): 39–43.

15

Fundamental British Values: Your Responsibility, to Promote or Not to Promote?

Sally Elton-Chalcraft, Lynn Revell and Vini Lander

By the end of this chapter you should:

- have a clearer understanding of the legal and political background to the governmental requirements to promote and not undermine fundamental British values (FBV)
- appreciate that the requirement to promote FBV could be viewed as problematic and could be viewed as 'veiled racism' rather than achieving its purpose of preventing radicalisation and of forging a common and uniting notion of Britishness
- know how to approach this requirement in your professional role – ensuring you provide safe spaces for critical debate and exploration of similarities and differences.

Introduction – what the chapter aims to achieve

There is a phrase in the Teachers' Standards that requires you to uphold public trust in the profession by 'not undermining fundamental British values' (DfE, 2012), and a policy document for schools that requires you to actively 'promote fundamental British values' (DfE, 2014). Fundamental British values are defined as 'democracy, the Rule of Law, individual liberty and mutual respect, and tolerance of those with different faiths and beliefs' (DfE, 2012, p. 10).

In this chapter we encourage you to think about these requirements in a critical way, considering why you have been asked to promote FBV, and how you could, or indeed whether in fact you should, do this. The authors of this chapter undertook some research to uncover what teachers and student teachers thought about the introduction of promoting FBV and our findings are critical of this requirement (Elton-Chalcraft et al., 2017). In each of our universities, drawing on our findings, we have discussed issues such as ethnicity, inclusion and meeting the needs of black and minority ethnic (BME) children with our groups of student teachers. In this chapter we aim to engage you in a challenging debate to interrogate the implications of the requirements to promote FBV in schools and why this might be problematic or possibly even detrimental to learners, if not approached in a critical fashion. We conclude with suggestions, drawn from evidence-based practice, for a more appropriate way to promote a sense of unity and shared values in our communities, and address radicalisation issues, through work in schools that does not vilify groups or inculcate fear but rather encourages an exploration of difference and similarities within a critical but respectful context (Bryan and Revell, 2016; Revell and Elton-Chalcraft, 2016).

What are FBV and why are we required to promote them?

Background

To understand why the requirement for teachers not to undermine FBV could be understood as controversial we need to understand how the 2012 Teachers' Standards differ from previous professional guidelines and the unique circumstances in which they are being implemented (Gearon, 2015). A period of international instability that has prompted new counter-terrorism strategies (Home Office, 2011), in which fear of Islam plays a significant role, is in part shaping a transformation of teacher professionalism (Bryan and Revell, 2016). Teachers have always been expected to act in ways that are considered professional, but what is considered to be professional for teachers has changed over time. Some aspects of professionalism for teachers would be deemed unacceptable today. For instance up until 1944 a marriage bar meant that women teachers had to resign or were sacked when they married; up until 1986 teachers in state-run schools may have been expected to deliver corporal punishment to their pupils. Until recently it would have been unthinkable that government ministers would have directly written policy that dictated what values teachers should promote in their classroom. When the National Curriculum was introduced in 1988, although the content of the curriculum was described, no specific values were mentioned. And even as late as 2007 the Teachers' Standards only mentioned that teachers should hold 'positive values'. So why do the most recent Teachers' Standards not only dictate the values teachers should promote in school but also require them to uphold those values inside and outside the school?

The current Teachers' Standards should be understood in the context of a succession of counter-terrorist initiatives that identify education as a tool in a struggle to stop the spread of extremism (O'Donnell, 2015). The salience of the focus on a promotion of British values lies in the way government has identified ideas as the major source of radicalisation and extremism. Original counter-terrorist strategy CONTEST, developed in the wake of 9/11, placed no particular significance on education or on non-violent extremism; its focus was extremist actions not extremist ideas (Farrell, 2016).

CONTEST, the counter-terrorism strategy of the UK government, comprises four strands, one of which is Prevent, a collection of approaches designed to prevent radicalisation from happening. It was not until the July London bombings of 2012 that the essentially dormant Prevent of 2007 was revived, and each successive Prevent initiative has more tightly prescribed what teachers and pupils may say in the classroom. Teachers must now promote FBV inside and outside of the school; they must monitor pupil conversations and online discussions where they take place in school; and are are expected to be able to identify signs of radicalisation and report this to the Home Office. There are voices of dissent around the Prevent strategy and FBV (Thomas and Beauchamp, 2011; Shain, 2013; O'Donnell, 2015; Miah, 2017). Some commentators have noted that the values themselves are not exclusively British and that to claim them as such creates a distinction between 'us' and 'them' that is not only divisive but also inaccurate (Sian, 2013). For example the identification of democracy as an FBV suggests that it is a uniquely British value as well implying that all those who are not British are not democratic. Others have observed that promoting FBV legitimises hostility against all groups that dare to be different (Arthur, 2015). The question for teachers though is more basic. Does the promotion of FBV undermine and compromise their status as independent professionals?

Reflective task

Schools have been asked to promote FBV because the government holds schools and teachers accountable for 'home grown terrorists'; for example, Jihadi John and the fleeing Syrian girls. But what about another interpretation – perhaps Jihadi John and the Syrian girls turned 'away' from British values because they didn't feel included?

(Continued)

(Continued)

Read the quotation below and discuss with your peers your attitude towards Prevent and counter-terrorism strategies?

We have overlooked these vulnerable British girls for too long, writing them off while we focus on their ostensibly more violent brothers. It's time to burst this dangerous bubble and it's up to us – as friends, teachers, lawmakers, community leaders and fellow British citizens – to somehow make these educated but ignored girls feel valued in our society. (Barnett, 2015)

Is promoting FBV problematic?

The section above explains why, as an intending teacher, legislation (rightly or wrongly) requires you to promote and not undermine FBV. In this chapter we challenge you to consider the implications of promoting FBV. We ask you to think about how this directive fits within your conception of what teaching and learning should involve. So we begin by asking you some fundamental questions – what are your aims as a primary school teacher? What are you trying to achieve?

What are your aims as a teacher?

Several chapters in this book aim to stimulate and support questions about the purpose of primary schooling; for example, Cooper (Chapter 2) invites you to philosophise about what primary education is for. Issues of inclusion and social justice are discussed in numerous chapters, for example in Soan, Chapter 8. Conteh addresses teaching pupils with English as an additional language in Chapter 12. Warner and Elton-Chalcraft discuss issues of race and ethnicity in Chapter 14, and promoting children's personal and social development is addressed by Palmer in Chapter 10. In this chapter we challenge you to think about the directives discussed in the section above and we ask you to consider whether you agree that your role should include promoting FBV. As a primary classroom teacher should you be asked to impart a set of values to your children and be responsible for ousting radicalisation, or should you be encouraging children to critically evaluate rules and values in order to grow into politically aware citizens able to take their role in society as active members of a democratic community?

We purposely avoid the term teacher training with its emphasis on teaching skills and types of behaviour, preferring the term teacher education, with an emphasis on educating intending teachers to prepare themselves for their professional lives, with our support.

What values should underpin teaching?

Our story begins with a group of teacher educators, including the authors of this chapter, who met at a conference in 2012 to discuss the introduction of 'not undermining fundamental British values' in the Teaching Standards 2012. Five of these teacher educators (working in the fields of inclusion, religious education (RE), diversity, race and ethnicity) questioned whether teachers and student teachers should be required to promote FBV and so we designed a research project to collect the views of students and teachers in four geographical areas (Elton-Chalcraft et al., 2017).

We asked teachers and student teachers what values they thought should underpin teaching, and answers included notions of equality and inclusion, respect, honesty, Christian values and conceptions of teacher as facilitator, Socratic dialogue and other educational approaches (Elton-Chalcraft et al., 2017, p. 35). The range of views suggested that many student teachers did not share common values and some student teachers confessed they had not considered this. A further question in our research asked about attitudes towards values that could be described as specifically British. We ask you to pause a moment before seeing what our respondents said and think about your own responses.

Reflective task

What values underpin your teaching?

What do you understand by the term British values?

What teachers and student teachers said about FBV

We asked our participants from the four geographic areas whether they thought there were values that could be described as British: 53 per cent thought there were specific values that were British and 47 per cent said there were not, or they did not know. Responses are recorded below.

Yes, there are specifically British values and these are:

Being polite, queuing, caring for animals, being patriotic, support for the monarchy.

No, there are no values that are specifically British because:

Britain is too diverse and so shared values are impossible. This is a meaningless concept, FBV is a social construct. Using the term FBV challenges inclusive practice. I don't know.

Three common themes in the responses to British values as espoused by the student teachers in our research emerged, ranging from a superficial to a nuanced conception:

1. Naïve and unsophisticated understandings of FBV (e.g. some students defined British values as 'drinking tea' and 'complaining', although one respondent did not think such values were worthy of being encouraged!).
2. Britain is very diverse so shared FBV is not possible.
3. Being asked to promote FBV is 'veiled racism', creating insiders and outsiders.

One primary female teacher in our study voiced assimilationist language:

> We are English and this is the UK so everyone in the education system should be taught and know British values in order to fit in. (Elton-Chalcraft et al., 2017, p. 40)

This contrasts significantly with another primary female teacher, who said:

> Honestly I think it's a horrendous knee jerk reaction to all the propaganda currently surrounding immigration. I think it's a right-wing government pandering to the people who read *The Daily Mail* or *The Sun* without engaging in an intelligent debate about the reality of immigration. They constantly claim there is an 'erosion' of British values but as I said earlier, I believe values are largely individual and certainly constantly shifting, and they feel the need to be seen to address this 'erosion'. I think it's ridiculous, what makes their values superior and what exactly are these elusive 'British' values?' I also think it's loaded with a veiled racism, suggesting British values are superior. (Elton-Chalcraft et al., 2017, p. 40)

In addition to this it has been argued that the government believes a stronger society is one where there is a shared set of values, hence the imposition of FBV within the education system (Kundnani, 2007; Meer and Modood, 2009). Similarly, a weaker society associates difference with dissent, fragmentation and absence of unity (Ware, 2007; Garner, 2012; Elton-Chalcraft et al., 2017).

So according to the government shared FBV means 'one voice' and 'one set of values', which the government says makes a stronger society. However, such homogeneity does not allow for difference or other voices to be heard (Bhopal and Rhamie, 2014). Thus, those people with a different voice are silenced and marginalised. It has been argued that the Teachers' Standards (DfE, 2012) imply that difference within society is to be feared and brings about a weaker society (Bryan and Revell, 2016). So diversity is being marginalised. But if this is the case, then which voices are being privileged? Which shared values are being promoted and which values are being ignored? Thus, any values that are not seen as fundamentally British are marginalising and to be feared. The assimilationist language with its emphasis on 'tolerance' suggests a 'putting up with' or tolerating rather than celebrating diversity. So we would argue that these 2012 Teachers' Standards suggest a homogeneity of values, practice and behaviour. Evidence shows us that teacher education doesn't prepare students to engage with difference, or counter racism or inequality in the classroom (Goodwin, 2001; Bryan, 2012; Smith, 2012; Maylor, 2016). Where do you stand – look at the reflective task box and consider your own views?

Reflective task

Read our article – Elton-Chalcraft, S., Lander, V., Revell, L., Warner, D. and Whitworth (2017) 'To promote or not to promote fundamental British values? Teachers' standards, diversity and teacher education', *British Educational Research Journal*, 43 (1): 29–48.

Which of the three responses on p. 344 would you have subscribed to before reading the chapters in this book and our article?

Have your views changed as a result of thinking through these issues?

Do you think the chapter authors are unduly sensitive towards promoting FBV and adherence to this directive is not problematic? What is your evidence?

Do you think 'promoting FBV' is problematic? What is your evidence?

Adopting a critical stance on FBV

Our argument thus far suggests that:

1. Teachers have been required by the government to promote and not under-mine FBV with the intention to promote a shared set of values that will thereby reduce radicalisation.
2. Authors of this chapter and many other scholars would question whether it is possible to have a shared understanding of FBV given the diverse nature of Britain (Shain, 2013; Panjwani, 2016). In reality different teachers interpret FBV differently (Farrell, 2016; Maylor, 2016).
3. Some teachers have a limited understanding of what is meant by the term FBV and meet the requirements superficially. Some teachers draw on FBV to reinforce an 'us' and 'them' standpoint that could be described as 'veiled racism' and this actually reinforces white, patriarchal hegemony. Other teachers appreciate the complexities of trying to promote a set of values that can be interpreted either negatively or superficially, and these teachers endeavour to challenge their learners to look at discriminatory practices, while also ensuring no group is marginalised and thus prey to radicalisation (see Elton-Chalcraft et al., 2017).
4. So FBV are problematic because teachers might not even be aware of dif-ferent interpretations.
5. We appreciate that busy teachers need guidance and support to under-stand the complexities and interpretations and to find an appropriate standpoint that will facilitate appropriate courses of action, celebrating diversity, encouraging community cohesion and investigating accusations of radicalisation.
6. We would encourage teacher educators, intending and in-service teachers to critically challenge the directive to promote FBV and consider issues raised by implementing the policy in an uncritical way.
7. In this chapter we have tried to scaffold your understanding so you can critically engage with the directive to promote FBV.
8. In the next section we present suggestions for classroom practice that will ensure the law is not broken but creatively interpreted and addressed (ideas can be found elsewhere in this book too – e.g. see Chapter 14, Warner and Elton-Chalcraft).

Reflective task

1. What values do you hold?
2. Are these values inclusive?
3. To promote or not to promote FBV – what will you do?

Work in schools, policy to practice – RE and citizenship

Schools are approaching the statutory obligation to promote FBV in different ways. In some schools there is an emphasis on visual signs; that is, there are numerous posters and displays that showcase the school's values, and pupils' work is displayed around them. Other schools have introduced specific lessons on particular British values in citizenship education, RE and personal, social, health and economic education (PSHE). Assemblies and school focus days/weeks, where pupils can be introduced to related themes, provide alternative opportunities for teaching about FBV (see Revell and Elton-Chalcraft, 2016).

A growing range of resources is now available from educational publishers on FBV, far more for the early and primary years than for any other age phase. These tend to fall into two groups: those resources that celebrate Britishness (bunting, posters of icons and artefacts associated with Britishness and stories of great British heroes) and textbooks that can be used to facilitate learning about individual British values and guides to support teachers fulfilling their obligations to the Prevent Duty.

This section of the chapter aims to provide you with ideas for engaging with the requirement to promote and not to undermine FBV in ways that are critical and challenging. This means you will be expected to reflect on the way you understand and define your professional responsibilities in relation to statutory requirements as well as your integrity as a teacher. Some have raised concerns that the Prevent Duty and the requirement to promote FBV will inhibit discussions in the classroom (Ramsay, 2017), and one aim of this chapter is to support teachers to encourage debate with pupils. It will begin by encouraging you to reflect on the term Britishness and what this implies for issues of identity and inclusiveness. It will then examine in turn each of the values identified in the 2012 Teachers' Standards as fundamentally British.

Britishness

A great deal of research has been carried out on what children understand by the term Britishness (Jerome and Clemitshaw, 2012; Keddie, 2014). One of the things that the research tells us is that children of all ages find it confusing and they are generally unable to talk about Britishness in ways that are not full of clichés and stereotypes (Clay and Barrett, 2011). Some writers argue that this is because the notion of Britishness is inherently problematic as it is based on ideas of colonialism and Empire that are intrinsically racist (Modood, 1992; Joppke, 1999; Andrews and Mycock, 2006; Sears et al., 2011; Smith, 2016).

Pupils could be asked to consider how the notion of Britishness has changed through discussing images associated with Britishness over time. For example:

- pictures of children celebrating Empire day at the beginning of the century, often 'blacked up' and seen showing the subservience of the colonial people to Queen Britannia
- images of Liverpool Town Hall decorated with carvings of slaves
- the arrival of the *SS Empire Windrush* (the ship that brought people from the Caribbean who came to work in Britain to fill the labour shortage after World War II)
- photographs of Team GB celebrating after the Olympics.

Pupils can be asked to consider what emotions and values they would associate with each image of Britishness. They could discuss which values they think still exist today and why they might have changed. Teachers could encourage pupils to consider alternative approaches to national identity and values in relation to education. For example, pupils could be asked to enact the scenario below.

In America the Stars and Stripes hangs in every school, often on a flagpole in the school grounds, in the halls and common areas, in the main school offices and in some schools in every classroom. In elementary schools in America the day will usually begin with the pledge. This will involve the teacher and all pupils turning to face the flag, placing their hands on their hearts and saying 'I pledge allegiance to the Flag of the United States of America and to the Republic for which it stands, one Nation under God, indivisible, with liberty and justice for all'.

Pupils could talk about:

- How would the ceremony make them feel?
- Would everyone in the class want to join in?
- What positive things might come out of everyone having the same values?
- If they thought up school or class values should everyone have to believe in them?

Rule of Law and democracy

The Rule of Law is probably the most misinterpreted value in the British values canon. Resources and schemes of work produced by schools suggest that many teachers interpret the Rule of Law as obedience to the law and the idea that citizens should not break laws. Resources produced for primary schools often promote activities that encourage pupils to make up their own laws for games or fictional events and then discuss how they could be enforced, penalties for breaking the laws and possible consequences for the group if laws are broken. This approach to the Rule of Law neglects the salient point: that the Rule of Law means that all governments and states are also obliged to be just and lawful; that is, no government must ever pass laws or act in ways that are unjust because literally no one is above the law. Historically and politically this aspect of democracy is truly empowering, as it presents the law and democracy as dynamic and responsive to the will of the people. Laws may be challenged and redrawn if they are unjust and historically this process is part of a dynamic and thriving democracy.

There are numerous instances of laws in British history that could be used as illustrations of this value with pupils: slavery, limited franchise, capital punishment, for example (Wolton, 2017). However, there are also contemporary examples of laws and acts by government that are controversial and could be explored: the Sus laws, Clause 28, the right of employers to ask people to remove religious symbols and the Blasphemy law. These laws could be used to discuss the following questions:

- Where different groups disagree over whether a law is just, what are the most important factors to consider?
- Would it ever be acceptable to use force to oppose an unjust law (see the box on the suffragettes)?
- How do we decide if a law is unjust?

Work in school

Democracy and the Rule of Law

Student: In a history lesson on International Women's Day I decided to focus on voting and the suffragettes. I introduced the children to the lives of Emily Pankhurst and Emily Davison and to some of the events that resulted in women gaining the vote. I explained that partial women's suffrage was introduced in 1918 and that women achieved full parity with men only in 1928. I showed them photographs and a video clip of women's mass protests, chaining themselves to railings, violent

(Continued)

(Continued)

demonstrations, throwing bombs, attacking policemen and resisting arrest. One of the children knew about the incident where Emily Davison threw herself under King Edward VII's horse and about the force-feeding of women prisoners who went on hunger strike.

Then some children started talking about terrorists today and asked if the suffragettes were terrorists because they were violent and threw bombs. To be honest I felt out of my depth and it all got a bit out of hand. Then one little girl said that her mum never votes and nor do any of the ladies in her family and they are quite happy: 'My mum and aunties would never throw bombs'. What should I have said?

Mentor: It is very tricky to navigate political issues in the classroom with young children. While, on the one hand, you are required to follow government policy, on the other hand you are involved in 'educating', which is itself a political act. Wolton (2017) talks about the 'democratic deficit' and how many people in Britian have grown to distrust politicians and hence do not use their right to vote. She also discusses dilemmas faced when teaching about suffragettes. Controversial issues can be explored with children – you can ask children to think about reasons why some groups in the past were not allowed to vote, why some people nowadays choose not to vote and, after reading Wolton (2017) and Chapter 15 by Elton-Chalcraft, Revell and Lander, you can support the children's developing understanding of external influences. You can also encourage children to consider what it means to be 'radical' – Jesus was thought of as radical in his time and many other famous figures both religious and political have challenged governments and laws. So long as you encourage children to consider issues carefully, from all viewpoints, and within a safe, respectful and informed context, you can have a lively and interesting debate, which is one of the characteristics of free speech and individual liberty, which are at the heart of democracies.

Individual liberty and mutual respect

Individual liberty is a key value in all liberal democracies but it is also a very abstract concept. One of the ironies of the fact that the Teachers' Standards identifies it as a British value is that it can serve to limit individual liberty through the way it restricts free speech in schools. Pupil understanding of the importance and significance of individual liberty and mutual respect can be developed through activities and discussions that challenge the limits of individual liberty and reasons for why it is curtailed in some contexts.

Discussions and activities can be focused on experiences and situations that might take place in a school. For example:

- Uniforms – Does a uniform policy restrict the individual liberty of pupils to choose what they would like to wear to school every day? Do the reasons the school gives for making the wearing of a uniform compulsory outweigh the individual liberty of pupils? Should pupils from certain religious groups be exempt from the uniform rule?
- The United Nations Convention on the Rights of the Child, Clause 1 (Respect for the views of the child), says that all children, at the age at which they are able to explain themselves rationally, have the right to make significant decisions in their lives. This could mean that they refuse to go to the school of their parents' choice. In cases where the liberties of two groups collide (in this case parents and children), how do we decide whose liberty is the most important?

Work in school

Tolerance of those with different faiths and beliefs

Tolerance can be an uncomfortable word here because it implies an unequal relationship between the tolerated and the tolerator. Others object to tolerance because it implies a tepid acceptance of difference. Rather than an approach to those who are different from us that is infused by warmth or an attitude to those who are different from us that is celebratory, tolerance also implies a disapproval of others. Teachers could discuss alternatives to tolerance as a value as well asking pupils to explore their own feelings about being tolerated:

- Pupils can be invited to explore both the merits and weaknesses of toleration in relation to the range of beliefs and faiths in their own school and community. How do the rules and customs in their school show that they tolerate one another? What are the behaviours and beliefs that are not tolerated in their school?
- They could discuss and plan how they would respond to a group of pupils visiting their school from another country. What would they do if they wanted to show the visitors that they:

respected them

tolerated them

thought of them as neighbours?

Tolerance and diversity

In an RE lesson the teacher has planned for a discussion on marriage customs as part of an introduction to a unit on special occasions and rites of passage. The pupils have been shown a clip of a wedding ceremony in a Muslim family in Pakistan. The clip shows how the couple are introduced through members of the family and that the marriage can be understood as 'an arranged marriage'. In the clip the narrator stresses that respect for parents and grandparents is very important for this community and in the following discussion a pupil asks what would have happened if either the bride or the groom had refused the marriage. Some pupils said they thought the practice was unfair and that even if the couple were not forced to marry it was not something that could be tolerated.
How would you respond?

Conclusion

Throughout this chapter we have endeavoured to challenge you to think deeply about your professional role in promoting and not undermining FBV. We have cited a range of research, including our own, which highlights the problematic nature of adherence to the governmental directives. The aim of this chapter has been to prompt and provoke new ways of understanding policy and the role of the teacher. When this happens many teachers are able to see the ordinary with fresh eyes and ask unexpected questions (Goodwin, 2001). We acknowledge the need to reduce terrorism but would question whether a directive to promote FBV in schools to prevent radicalisation is the most appropriate way of limiting a terrorist threat. However, we have offered some suggestions for practice, which we hope you will find useful.

Questions for discussion

Is it legitimate to understand the requirement to promote FBV as an unjust law and therefore, according to the Rule of Law, illegitimate?

Do you think challenging government directives is acceptable?

Do you agree with the chapter authors that the phrase 'promote FBV' is problematic?

Are you aware how to avoid exclusionary and racist behaviour?

Further reading

Bryan, H. and Revell, L. (2016) 'Calibrating fundamental British values: How head teachers are approaching appraisal in the light of the Teachers' Standards 2012, Prevent and the Counter-Terrorism and Security Act, 2015', *Journal of Education for Teaching*, 42 (3): special issue: Fundamental British Values.
School practices in relation to the promotion of British values are now subject to Office for Standards in Education (Ofsted) inspection. This article considers the policy and purpose of appraisal in such new times, and engages with 48 school leaders from across the education sector to reveal issues in emerging appraisal practices. Zygmunt Bauman's concept of Liquid Modernity is used to fully understand the issues and dilemmas that are emerging in new times and argue that fear and 'impermanence' are key characteristics of the way school leaders engage with FBV.

Farrell, F. (2016) '"Why all of a sudden do we need to teach fundamental British values?": A critical investigation of religious education student teacher positioning within a policy discourse of discipline and control', *Journal of Education for teaching*, 42 (3): special issue: Fundamental British Values.
This paper presents a critical investigation of a group of 11 RE student teachers' views of the promotion of FBV undertaken in 2015. Drawing from the perspectives of Foucauldian methodology and critical theory, it examines the extent to which student teachers were able to align the FBV discourse with their own personal and professional positioning. The paper argues that it is through the development of teacher subjectivity in the alternative discourses of critical RE and research that practitioners will be able to make adjustments that can accommodate and re-appropriate the demands of policy.

Maylor, U. (2016) '"I'd worry about how to teach it": British values in English classrooms', *Journal of Education for Teaching*, 42 (3): special issue: Fundamental British Values.
What is meant by fundamental British values? How are they constructed and can they be taught in schools? This article considers the extent to which schools delivered a diverse curriculum (reflecting the composition of Britain as an ethnically diverse society). It aims to challenge conceptions of British values being shared by teachers. The teacher discourses highlighted present challenges for teacher education in developing teacher understanding and practice, especially where student teachers bring uninformed views about particular ethnic groups to the classroom.

Panjwani, F. (2016) 'Towards an overlapping consensus: Muslim teachers' views on fundamental British values', *Journal of Education for Teaching*, 42 (3): special issue: Fundamental British Values.
This paper presents the findings of a small-scale research project carried out to understand Muslim teachers' perspectives on the Standards, and FBVs in particular. Though the teachers made several criticisms of FBVs, they did not see any incompatibility between FBVs and their conception of Islamic values. The paper proposes that the teachers' responses reflect Rawlsian 'overlapping consensus', and situates the roots of this consensus in contemporary Muslim intellectual history and the modernist reforms. A case is made that the teachers' responses

problematise the essentialised understanding of terms such as 'Islam' and 'the West' and indicate the interpretive and open-ended nature of cultures.

Smith, H. (2016) 'Britishness as racist nativism: A case of the unnamed "other"', *Journal of Education for Teaching*, 42 (3): special issue: Fundamental British Values.
The construct of Britishness continues to be used by politicians and the media as a powerful exclusionary force. This paper employs the concept of racist nativism, developed to explain the dialectic relationship between nativism and racism in America, to analyse both political constructions of Britishness with media portrayals of this and student teachers' comprehension of FBV as an aspect of the Teachers' Standards in England. It explores distinct differences between the manifestations of racist nativism in the sociopolitical context, compared to student teachers' perceptions in a professional context, and highlights perturbing issues for critical teacher educators.

References

Andrews, R. and Mycock, A. (2006) 'Dilemmas of devolution: The "politics of Britishness" and citizenship education', *British Politics*, 3: 139–55.

Arthur, J. (2015) 'Extremism and neo-liberal education policy: A contextual critique of the Trojan Horse Affair in Birmingham schools', *British Journal of Educational Studies*, 63 (3): 311–28.

Barnett, E. (2015) 'British girls join Islamic state and we dismiss them as Jihadi brides', *The Telegraph*, 22 January. Available at: www.telegraph.co.uk/women/womens-life/11360581/Islamic-State-British-girls-join.-We-dismiss-them-as-jihadi-brides.html (accessed 2 August 2017).

Bhopal, K. and Rhamie, J. (2014) 'Initial teacher training: understanding "race", diversity and inclusion', *Race Ethnicity and Education*, 17 (3): 304–25.

Bryan, H. (2012) 'Reconstructing the teacher as a post secular pedagogue: A consideration of the new Teachers' Standards', *Journal of Beliefs and Values*, 33 (2): 217–28.

Bryan, H. and Revell, L. (2016) 'Calibrating fundamental British values: How head teachers are approaching appraisal in the light of the Teachers' Standards 2012, Prevent and the Counter-Terrorism and Security Act, 2015', *Journal of Education for Teaching*, 42 (3): special issue: Fundamental British Values.

Clay, D. and Barrett, M. (2011) 'National identifications and attitudes towards a "traditional enemy" nation among English children', *European Journal of Developmental Psychology*, 8 (1): 25–42.

Department for Education (DfE) (2012) *Teachers' Standards*. Available at: https://www.gov.uk/government/uploads/system/uploads/attachment_data/file/301107/Teachers__Standards.pdf (accessed 24 March 2015).

Department for Education (DfE) (2014) *Promoting Fundamental British Values as part of SMSC: Department Advice for Maintained Schools*. Available at: https://www.gov.uk/

government/uploads/system/uploads/attachment_data/file/380595/SMSC_Guidance_
Maintained_Schools.pdf (accessed on 26 February 2015).

Elton-Chalcraft, S., Lander, V., Revell, L., Warner, D. and Whitworth, L. (2017) 'To promote or not to promote fundamental British values? Teachers' standards, diversity and teacher education', *British Educational Research Journal*, 43 (1): 29–48. Available at http://onlinelibrary.wiley.com/doi/10.1111/berj.2017.43.issue-1/issuetoc.

Farrell, F. (2016) '"Why all of a sudden do we need to teach fundamental British values?" A critical investigation of religious education student teacher positioning within a policy discourse of discipline and control', *Journal of Education for Teaching*, 42 (3): special issue: Fundamental British Values.

Garner, S. (2012) 'A moral economy of whiteness: Behaviours, belonging and Britishness', *Ethnicities*, 12 (4): 445–64.

Gearon, L. (2015) 'Education, security and intelligence studies', *British Journal of Education Studies*, special issue, 63 (3): 263–79.

Goodwin, A. (2001) 'Seeing with different eyes: Reexamining teachers' expectations through racial lenses', in S. King and L. Castenell (eds), *Racism and Racial Inequality: Implications for Teacher Education* (pp.69–76). New York: American Association of Colleges for Teacher Education.

Home Office (2011) *Prevent Strategy*. Available at: https://www.gov.uk/government/publications/prevent-strategy-2011 (accessed 28 April 2016).

Jerome, L. and Clemitshaw, G. (2012) 'Teaching (about) Britishness? An investigation into trainee teachers' understanding of Britishness in relation to citizenship and the discourse of civic nationalism', *The Curriculum Journal*, 23 (1): 19–41.

Joppke, C. (1999) *Immigration and the Nation State*. Oxford: Oxford University Press.

Keddie, A. (2014) 'The politics of Britishness: Multiculturalism, schooling and social cohesion', *British Educational Research Journal*, 40 (3): 539–54.

Kundnani, A. (2007) *The End of Tolerance*. London: Pluto Press.

Maylor, U. (2010) 'Notions of diversity, British identities and citizenship belonging', *Race Ethnicity and Education*, 13 (2): 233–52.

Maylor, U. (2016) '"I'd worry about how to teach it": British values in English classrooms', *Journal of Education for Teaching*, 42 (3): special issue: Fundamental British Values.

Meer, N. and Modood, T. (2009) 'The multicultural state we're in: Muslims, "multiculture" and the "civic rebalancing" of British multiculturalism', *Political Studies*, 57 (3): 473–97.

Miah, S. (2017) *Muslims, Schooling and Security: Trojan Horse, Prevent and Racial Politics*. London: Palgrave Macmillan.

Modood, T. (1992) *Not Easy Being British: Colour, Culture and Citizenship*. London: Runnymede Trust and Trentham Books.

O'Donnell, A. (2015) 'Securitisation, counterterrorism and the silencing of dissent: The educational implications of Prevent', *British Journal of Educational Studies*, 64 (1): 53–76.

Panjwani, F. (2016) 'Towards an overlapping consensus: Muslim teachers' views on fundamental British values', *Journal of Education for Teaching*, 42 (3): special issue: Fundamental British Values.

Ramsay, P. (2017) 'Is Prevent a safe space?' *Education, Citizenship and Social Justice*. Available at: https://doi.org/10.1177/1746197917693022.

Revell, L. and Elton-Chalcraft, S. (2016) 'Religious education, racism and citizenship: Developing children's religious, political and media literacy', *Teaching Citizenship: Faith and Citizenship*, 44. Available at: https://www.teachingcitizenship.org.uk/journals.

Sears, A., Davies, I. and Reid, A. (2011) 'From Britishness to nothingness and back again', in A. Mycock and C. McGlynn (eds), *Britishness, Identity and Citizenship: The View from Abroad*. Bern: Peter Lang. pp. 291–312.

Shain, F. (2013) 'Race, nation and education an overview of British attempts to "manage diversity" since the 1950s', *Education Inquiry*, 4 (1): 63–85.

Sian, K.P. (2013) 'Spies, surveillance and stakeouts: Monitoring Muslim moves in British state schools', *Race, Ethnicity and Education*, 18 (2): 183–201.

Smith, H. (2012) 'A critique of the Teaching Standards in England (1984–2012): Discourses of equality and maintaining the status quo', *Journal of Education Policy*, 1–22: iFirst Article.

Smith, H. (2016) 'Britishness as racist nativism: A case of the unnamed "other"', *Journal of Education for Teaching*, 42 (3): special issue: Fundamental British Values.

Thomas, L. and Beauchamp, C. (2011) 'Understanding new teachers' professional identities through metaphor', *Teaching and Teacher Education*, 27 (4): 762–9.

Ware, V. (2007) *Who Cares About Britishness? – A Global View of the National Identity Debate*. London: Arcadia Books.

Wolton, S. (2017) 'The contradiction in the Prevent Duty: Democracy vs "British values"'. Education, Citizenship and Social Justice. Available at: http://journals.sagepub.com/doi/10.1177/1746197917693021.

Part 3

FROM TRAINEE TO TEACHER

In reading Parts 1 and 2 of this book, you will have realised that complex, professional judgements are required in all aspects of teaching. You should have become increasingly aware of the kinds of questions to ask and evidence to consider in making them. There is rarely a single correct answer because there are so many variables to consider. By now, you should have developed, discussed and examined your personal educational philosophy, which informs these judgements. In Part 3, Chapters 16 to 20 aim to show you, in practical contexts, how to take your professional thinking further, in reflecting on and thinking critically about educational issues and the statutory professional responsibilities you need to take into account in doing so. Chapter 16 shows you how to be responsible for developing your own practice in school; Chapter 17 shows how you can do this through in-depth reflection on your practice in order to develop it; Chapter 18 explains your statutory professional responsibilities; and Chapter 19 considers how your increasing responsibility for your own professional development will move you on to take a Master's degree. The final chapter gives an overview of the wide range of Teachers' Standards that have been addressed at increasingly advanced levels throughout the book, and suggests the ways in which you should be supported, as a qualified teacher, by networks of like-minded colleagues and the specific competences you will require for a Master's and later a doctoral degree.

'Learning Teaching' in School

Pete Boyd

By the end of this chapter, you should understand:

- that your continued professional learning is essential to maximise pupil learning
- that you need to be proactive in managing your work and workplace learning
- that you should work on the development of your professional identity as a teacher
- that you should question public (published) knowledge and the practical wisdom of teachers
- that metaphors for learning are useful tools.

Learning to teach

Many teachers and trainees will insist that 'you mostly learn to teach by teaching'. But inspirational teaching is an extremely complex activity that, to the untrained eye of those who have never had to do the job, looks easy (Labaree, 2000). This chapter presents seven workplace learning tools so that you do not end up, having established yourself as a professional teacher, claiming for example to have '10 years of classroom experience' when in fact you merely have '1 year of classroom experience, ten times'. The seven workplace learning tools provided here will help you to develop throughout your career by becoming an enquiry-based teacher who continually gains professional learning from classroom and school experiences. These tools are developed from workplace learning theory, but as Kurt Lewin, the inventor of action research, famously claimed (1951), 'there is nothing so practical as a good theory'. Ironically, if you are to add these tools to your professional toolkit, then you will need to try them out for real, not just read about them. So take your time in reading this chapter, or read it more than once. You need to take ownership of the tools by using them in practical ways to shape your professional learning from classroom and school experiences.

Seven workplace learning tools

Great teaching is a complex, challenging and relational activity that requires a professional commitment to lifelong professional learning. In the short term the busy classroom teacher may claim to be prioritising the needs of their learners, but in the medium term those learners will benefit from the continued professional learning of their teacher. It is important to find time and space for your own professional development because your learning will enhance the learning of the children you teach. As proposed by John Hattie (2012) you need to continually ask the question 'what is my impact?', meaning what effect are you having on pupil learning? It is possible to aim beyond merely raising attainment by asking the question 'what is my impact on learning and on learners?' (Boyd et al., 2015). Asking this daily question is a first step to becoming an enquiry-based teacher, a powerful professional who is able to contribute fully to curriculum development and school leadership.

The seven teacher workplace learning tools proposed here for your practical use are:

1. conceptions of an 'outstanding teacher'
2. teacher enquiry
3. pedagogical content knowledge
4. teacher identities
5. learning communities
6. expansive workplace learning environments
7. a situated metaphor for teacher learning.

Workplace learning tool 1: personal conceptions of an 'outstanding teacher'

One of the initial problems with becoming a teacher is that all of us, including even newly appointed ministers for education, have experienced a mix of school, college and university as learners. That adds up to thousands of hours of observing teachers at work. Many of us will have at least one lasting memory of a really outstanding and inspirational teacher. Of course, all this experience is of value if we seek to become great teachers ourselves, but we are likely to have built up conceptions of an 'outstanding teacher' based on fragile assumptions and with ourselves positioned as 'the learner'. These personalised conceptions of teaching and learning are 'folk pedagogies' and need to be questioned (Bruner, 1996). Learning to teach also means that we need to shift attention away from our 'performance' as a teacher onto the experience of our learners. As a beginning teacher you will have opportunities to observe teaching and learning in classrooms. It is important that you focus on the learning outcomes for the learners and how the lesson might influence their dispositions or 'habits of mind' (Costa and Kallick, 2014). You must question the underlying assumptions you have about what makes a good teacher. This kind of 'unfreezing' of existing ideas is very challenging and may lead to a period of uncertainty for you, but it is essential if you are to develop as a teacher. Chapter 2 began this process by asking you what you thought primary education is for and to define your philosophy of education. It may be that you have already started to develop or modify these ideas.

Even when you have gained experience as a teacher in one or more schools, your own practice history will be both a support and a potential limitation when you attempt to improve practice or when you move to a new school workplace. Awareness of your history, your developing identity as a teacher and your current repertoire of teaching and learning strategies will help you to be a critically aware practitioner who is able to keep on learning and able to adapt to different educational workplace contexts.

To become a great teacher it is not sufficient to merely mimic the approach of other teachers. You need to gain some insight into what they are doing and why. This is because classrooms are varied, complex and dynamic workplaces involving relationships, and you will need to respond to your own classroom and develop your own personal approach to working with learners and other adults (Bauml, 2009). The effective teachers that you observe may find it difficult to explain what they are doing: much of their practical wisdom is held as tacit, instinctive and hard to explain to others. Teachers' professional learning may be understood as a social 'interplay' that involves identity, relationships and emotions, as well as knowledge of subject content and pedagogy. It is a personal and career-long, rewarding and challenging journey, through which you will be continually *becoming* a teacher. That teaching is complex creates a challenge for sure, but it also makes becoming a teacher enjoyable and continually satisfying.

Being prepared to continue your professional learning requires resilience and this is all about your emotional experience of everyday teaching. Teacher 'resilience' means the ability to bounce back and may be defined as the ability to 'recover strengths of spirit quickly in the face of adversity' (Gu and Day, 2007, p. 1302). Based on their large study of over 300 teachers, Gu and Day argue that resilience is closely connected to your sense of vocation as a teacher and to your self-efficacy. In relation to vocation they mean your sense of commitment to improving children's learning and lives, and by self-efficacy they mean your belief that you can continue to improve as a teacher and make a positive contribution. Resilience is not simply a personal trait of 'bouncebackability'; rather it is relational and can be nurtured in both teachers and pupils through developing supportive learning environments (Gu and Day, 2007). Early in your career you will need to respond to both positive and negative experiences within your school workplace learning environment. Based on your own educational experiences you may have an idealised view of what kind of teacher you wish to be and you may need to make compromises in the face of the reality of your school workplace and the wider educational policy framework. A first step is always to find a friend, collaborate with a colleague!

Reflective task

Start to create a written mission statement about the kind of teacher you want to be. Reflect on how your conceptions of good teaching have been shaped by your own educational experiences as a learner. What kind of teacher do your current learners need? What kind of teaching maximises their learning? How do your personal ambitions as a developing teacher fit into your current school workplace and the wider educational policy framework? Whom might you work with to help build trust and resilience and support for your continued professional learning?

Workplace learning tool 2: teacher enquiry

Teacher enquiry is a broad term covering critical questioning of practice at different levels, from everyday evaluation of lessons through to a full practitioner research project. Enquiry-based teacher learning will involve some level of data collection and analysis, including observation, gathering and analysing pupils' voices or pupils' work, and analysing basic statistical data on pupil progress. It may also involve engagement with different perspectives such as sharing practice with other teachers and critical engagement with published professional guidance and educational research.

Through your initial teacher education programme and continuing professional development, you will come across a range of different enquiry-based activities, including some of the following:

- *Evaluation of teaching*: based on assessment of children's work and/or test scores.
- *Observation of teaching*: followed by professional conversation.
- *Student voice*: gathering and analysing the views of children.
- *Action learning*: a group of teachers sharing issues and supporting each other.
- *Lesson study*: collaboratively plan, teach, evaluate and re-teach a specific lesson.
- *Achievement data analysis*: using grades or other measures of student progress.
- *Practitioner research*: systematic collaborative research projects.

The most ambitious activity proposed, a systematic collaborative practitioner research project, is a powerful way to lead change in practice and drive school improvement (Lankshear and Knobel, 2004; Baumfield et al., 2014). Most initial teacher education programmes will include an introduction to practitioner research. In order to become a confident and skilful practitioner researcher, for example, capable of leading a challenging whole-school project, many teachers will initially take part in a collaborative research project or will complete a Master's level practitioner research focused course. Many qualified teachers choose to study towards a Master's award after gaining some experience in the classroom. A suitable programme will help you to develop research and leadership skills in addition to building an in-depth understanding of educational issues in your chosen area of specialism.

For teacher enquiry to reach the highest level of 'practitioner research', a key requirement is that the investigation is 'systematic' (Lankshear and Knobel, 2004, p. 20). Characteristics of teacher 'research' identified by Lankshear and Knobel are:

- a carefully framed research question or issue that is manageable
- a research design that matches your research question
- an analytical framework … a concept or theory used as a lens to study the problem
- a feasible and ethical approach to gathering or generating data
- systematic analysis and interpretation of the data
- a research report or presentation that draws conclusions, identifies implications for practice and is subject to peer review.

The level of teacher enquiry you are able to pursue will depend on your work situation, the support available and your access to public (published) knowledge including theory and research evidence. You need to develop some degree of research literacy so that you are able to adopt a critical stance towards different forms of research evidence and understand both its value and its limitations. For example, the online research meta-review Teaching and Learning Toolkit from the Educational Endowment Fund (EEF, 2015) is a powerful and accessible source of research evidence but is limited by the narrow scope of selected research on which it is based (randomised control trial intervention studies), and by the contested approach to measuring and summarising the impact of classroom interventions on learning. It is important that you adopt a critical questioning stance to research evidence in all its forms. Increasingly research is becoming open access but it is important to be able to identify and give priority to more reliable peer reviewed research journal papers.

Reflective task

Identify a key issue that you are currently dealing with in your development of classroom practice. Are you able to refine a clear enquiry question? What theory, research evidence and professional guidance materials seem relevant to your question and how are you engaging with these forms of public knowledge? To what extent are you experimenting by making (small) changes in practice within your classroom and then evaluating them? How are you gathering and analysing data (evidence of learning) and sharing your findings with other teachers?

Workplace learning tool 3: developing pedagogical content knowledge

There are conflicting views about what is meant by the professional 'knowledge' of a teacher and it is a contested area of theory. However, one well-established idea is that the teacher brings at least two kinds of knowledge together. These are 'content knowledge' and 'pedagogical knowledge'. The 'content knowledge' means the curriculum subject being taught, for example, geography or mathematics, and the 'pedagogical knowledge' means how to teach. The overlap of these two areas of teacher knowledge is sometimes referred to as pedagogical content knowledge (PCK). PCK means the teacher's grasp of key concepts in the subject and how to teach them effectively, including knowing the most powerful explanations, metaphors, demonstrations and practical examples to make the subject comprehensible to learners (Shulman, 1986; Banks et al., 2005). This relationship is shown in Figure 16.1.

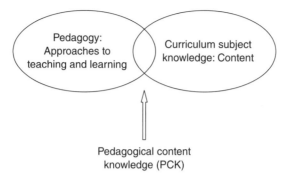

Figure 16.1   Illustrating the concept of pedagogical content knowledge

Primary teachers in the UK generally teach across the curriculum and so have the considerable challenge of developing curriculum subject knowledge in a wide range of subject disciplines. It may be feasible for you to learn new curriculum content knowledge from colleagues, a suitable text, online resources or a taught course, but the development of PCK requires work-based learning through enquiry-based experimentation in your own classroom.

Planning, both short-term for lessons and medium-term for topics or units of work, is often focused on the identification of tightly defined learning outcomes. Although they are useful planning tools, it is important to be aware that learning outcomes might be viewed as forming the cutting edge of high accountability educational systems such as in England. School inspectors in such a system may be seeking evidence of measurable progress and this may distort the purpose of learning outcomes. The purposes of education are about more than raising attainment in standardised tests (see Chapter 2). Lessons and units of work should include some degree of open enquiry so that children might learn to take their place as global citizens and have space to develop as unique individuals (Biesta, 2010). A useful way to focus on PCK is to step back from the planning or evaluation of a lesson and ask 'what is the big idea or key concept, within the subject discipline, that underpins the purpose of this lesson?' This approach may also have a social justice element because *all* children should develop knowledge and enthusiasm for learning by tasting rich cultural knowledge at school and it is not sufficient or equitable for some to be served with the thin gruel of 'teaching to the test' (see Chapter 3).

Reflective task

Evaluating a lesson or sequence of lessons consider the following prompt questions and discuss your reflections with a trusted colleague. What were the intended learning outcomes and did they include some space for children to respond creatively and individually to the lesson(s)? What teaching and learning activities did I use and to what extent do they extend my repertoire of pedagogical strategies? What key concepts within the subject discipline were pupils engaging with? How did the lesson(s) help children to build rich cultural knowledge and develop as citizens and as individuals, as well as preparing them for their next test?

Workplace learning tool 4: professional identity

It is necessary to 'become a teacher' through gaining teaching experience and critically reflective learning on that experience. It is not effective to simply 'tell' someone how to teach. Teaching is emotional and relational work, it involves you in building relations with children and with colleagues. Therefore, becoming a teacher means building a professional identity, a developing story that you tell about yourself, concerning the kind of teacher you are. As an individual you will have multiple identities, interweaving professional identity with other aspects of your life, and these develop over time to form trajectories of identity, as illustrated in Figure 16.2.

Your identity as a teacher may have different strands within it, for example, from your first degree you may have an identity associated with a subject discipline, such as 'historian' or 'physicist'. You may be an enthusiast in a hobby or leisure activity that

Figure 16.2   Showing trajectories of identity: multiple interwoven stories about self developing over time

helps to define you and influences your practice as a teacher, such as 'movie critic' or 'mountaineer'. You will also have distinctive cultural characteristics that shape your identity. Within your workplace you should try to identify one or two identity role models – these will be teachers whom you might model yourself on. It may just be a particular characteristic of a teacher that you admire and seek to develop. It is also worth considering what teacher identities are highly valued within your workplace and how closely they align to the kind of teacher you want to be. Your professional identities will develop in negotiation with your practice, meaning that the story you tell about yourself as a teacher is related to your approach to classroom teaching (Wenger, 1998). This means that it is helpful to add 'practice and identity' to the teacher knowledge diagram, as in Figure 16.3.

This more complex diagram suggests that your practice and identity are overlaid with content and pedagogical knowledge to make your professional knowledge more personal and more grounded. The area surrounding the three overlapping circles represents the wider context of your teacher knowledge, including the school in its community and wider society, within an often rapidly changing educational policy framework. This diagram emphasises the interrelationship between the cognitive, emotional and social aspects of being a teacher. The central overlapping area represents great lessons when everything comes together to promote effective learning. It is important for teachers to do 'identity work' as part of ongoing professional learning. This means reflecting explicitly on your development of identity as a teacher, using one or more collaborative activities with other new teachers, such as writing and sharing narratives. But it is important to realise that your identity as a teacher is likely to be developing whenever you reflect on your work, particularly where you are collaborating with peers, for example, in analysing classroom video or the work your children have produced.

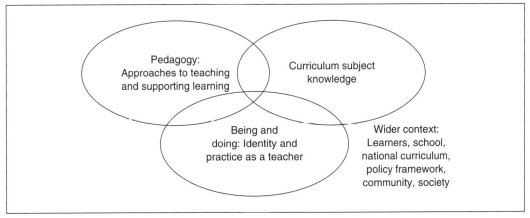

Figure 16.3   Illustrating how your teacher knowledge, identity and practice are related

Reflective task

Do some thinking around your developing identity as a teacher and develop it within a written mission statement. What are the strands that I bring together to form my identity as a teacher? What kind of teacher am I and what kind do I want to be? What teachers or combination of teacher characteristics have I seen that provide an identity role model for my development as a teacher? How effectively do my lessons, and my relationships with children and colleagues, reflect the teacher identity that I wish to develop? What are my medium- and long-term goals in terms of making a strong professional contribution as a teacher?

Workplace learning tool 5: professional knowing in learning communities

From a situated learning perspective, teachers working within a school may develop a shared sense of trust and purpose and so form a 'community of practice', by developing a collaborative repertoire, for example, of teaching strategies and ways of working. Membership of such a collaboration is voluntary, although sometimes formal groupings, such as a teaching team, may develop into a community of practice. A student or beginning teacher interested to join such a group will hopefully be welcomed as a newcomer and through negotiation will gradually build a sense of belonging and eventually become a full member of the group (Lave and Wenger, 1991; Wenger, 1998). The formation of professional learning communities of teachers has been widely introduced as part of school improvement efforts (Bolam et al., 2005) but these formal groupings may not always manage to develop open dialogue; for example, they may be too dominated by managers and thus fail to support enquiry that challenges established ways of working (Fenwick, 2001; Watson, 2014).

Teacher expertise from the sociocultural perspective of communities of practice becomes more about professional *knowing* than knowledge (Blackler, 1995). This teacher 'knowing' is dynamic, situated, social, contested and shaped by the tools, rules (including unwritten rules), values and key ideas within the school as a workplace. As a newcomer teacher it is important to understand the history of the group of teachers you are joining, to acknowledge the unwritten rules in force, to recognise that you are able to bring new knowledge and can aim to participate and also contribute. You will need to appreciate the power involved in any community of practice, with some teachers in the group claiming status, for example, by long membership or by holding a promoted post. The newcomer will need to be resilient and determined to learn from setbacks as well as successes, and to handle disappointing learner behaviour, challenging feedback and even occasional knock-backs from more established teachers in the school. This is close to the kind of resilience we would hope to develop in our learners.

The concept of 'communities of practice' has been developed through the study of apprentices (Wenger, 1998). Arguably the teachers' workplace is more complex and the practice of teaching is more contested than many apprentice crafts (Fuller et al., 2005). More recent thinking on communities of practice (Wenger, 1998) takes account of modern, complex professional workplaces by considering a workplace as a 'constellation' of overlapping communities of practice. The overlapping communities or networks that you might experience or seek to develop include: a formal teaching team in your school; a less formal group of colleagues in school that you find you can relate to and tend to share and collaborate with; a group of teachers in partnership schools with a shared interest; a subject specialist national network of teachers, for example, the Geography Association or the Association for Science Education (see Chapter 20). The group may be one or two colleagues that you trained with and keep in touch with, an informal mentor teacher you use occasionally for informal support, a group of teachers that are completing a part-time Master's programme with you, and so on. These examples range from networks both within and external to your school and from more formal professional arrangements to more informal social contacts. Some networks will be face-to-face and others will be blended or fully online. You will need to be personally proactive in developing such networks as they will support your professional learning and career development. If you fail to get promotion or a particular post in the future, it is no good reflecting back and blaming the head teacher or the school for not providing sufficient opportunities or training. Much professional learning is informal and can be pursued whatever your work situation; even formal professional development programmes requiring fees will mainly provide a framework to provoke or support your workplace learning.

Reflective task

Identify relevant professional learning communities and action plan to strengthen your membership and contribution. Is there a community of practice, a group of teachers with a shared purpose and repertoire, that I might join within my school workplace? What are the unwritten rules and who holds different kinds of power

(Continued)

(Continued)

within the community? In what ways am I gaining membership of the community and how might I contribute? Who are my current mentors and am I proactive in managing those relationships and making the most of their support? If there does not seem to be a community of practice within my current workplace, then is it possible to start one collaborating with a colleague? What wider teacher networks might I join to support my professional learning?

Workplace learning tool 6: expansive workplace learning environments

The concept of an expansive workplace learning environment, originally developed in a wide range of workplaces, was applied in a study of secondary school teachers and the researchers developed a continuum of expansive to restrictive workplace environments, shown in Table 16.1. You should evaluate your current workplace against the continuum in Table 16.1 and consider how expansive or restrictive your workplace seems to be.

Table 16.1 Illustrating the workplace learning environment expansive–restrictive continuum for teachers (Hodkinson and Hodkinson, 2005)

<<<Expansive	Restrictive>>>
Close collaborative working	Isolated, individualist working
Colleagues mutually supportive in enhancing teacher learning	Colleagues obstruct or do not support each other's learning
An explicit focus on teacher learning, as a dimension of normal working practices	No explicit focus on teacher learning, except to meet crises or imposed initiatives
Supported opportunities for personal development that go beyond school or government priorities	Teacher learning mainly strategic compliance with government or school agendas
Out-of-school educational opportunities, including time to stand back, reflect and think differently	Few out-of-school educational opportunities, only narrow, short training programmes
Opportunities to integrate off-the-job learning into everyday practice	No opportunity to integrate off-the-job learning
Opportunities to participate in more than one working group	Work restricted to teaching teams within one school
Opportunity to extend professional identity through boundary crossing into other departments, school activities, schools and beyond	Opportunities for boundary crossing only come with a job change
Support for local variation in ways of working and learning for teachers and work groups	Standardised approaches to teacher learning are prescribed and imposed
Teachers use a wide range of learning opportunities	Teachers use a narrow range of learning approaches

Even if you are fortunate to work in a school with a more expansive workplace learning environment, you will require resilience – an ability to sustain your commitment and manage tensions between your personal and professional identities (Gu and Day, 2007). In considering your workplace learning environment it is important to bear in mind that we all have agency: we are able to shape our workplaces as well as experience them. By acting with integrity, being willing to openly share our practice with trusted colleagues and by maintaining an ethical code, we can help to influence our workplace learning environment. Even in a restrictive workplace environment, it will be possible to form a community of practice with like-minded colleagues in or beyond the school. This is a key point of this chapter: although school managers have a responsibility to develop an expansive workplace learning environment, you also have a responsibility to be proactive in pursuing your professional learning and career development. Some teachers claim that they are too busy to pursue their own learning and that they prefer to focus on the needs of their learners. But you need to prioritise your professional learning for the benefit of your pupils because you will soon be of little use to pupils if you do not continue to learn.

A particular issue in schools is that teachers and other school leaders are often operating within very high levels of accountability, including measurement of school performance by test or exam results, high-stakes school inspection systems and school league tables. At least three of the 'restrictive' characteristics in the continuum in Table 16.1 seem relevant to those schools where responding to school inspector expectations, post-inspection action plans and inspection system criteria seem to dominate professional development activity. It is an important element of professional integrity that the learners' needs, in their broadest sense, are the number one priority for all teachers and schools. This is a dilemma that you will come across and need to handle carefully, understanding the pragmatic priorities of school managers in response to inspectors but also working to go beyond those requirements to achieve excellence in terms of wider educational outcomes for learners.

The continuum in Table 16.1 helps to show how professional learning is situated and social, and the issue around review bodies and school inspection highlights the contested nature of teachers' professional knowing.

Reflective task

Develop an action plan for your professional learning so that you are making the most of the learning environment in your current workplace. How does your current school workplace learning environment seem to fit into the

(Continued)

(Continued)

expansive-restrictive continuum? How are you contributing to your workplace learning environment? How are you proactively seeking learning opportunities within your workplace? To what extent does your workplace environment encourage teachers to move beyond school inspector requirements and strive for excellence in responding to learner needs?

Workplace learning tool 7: a metaphor for professional learning

In our everyday talk as teachers we use metaphors, linguistic representations, as a powerful method of capturing the experience of learning (Lakoff and Johnson, 1980). For example, two important metaphors for student learning in higher education have been proposed as 'acquisition' and 'participation', reflecting in turn transmissive (learning as being told) and Social Constructionist (learning through dialogue) theories of learning (Sfard, 1998) (Social Constructivist Theory is explained in Chapter 1). As an example, language used by a teacher such as 'I delivered the topic' may reveal the underlying use of the acquisition metaphor for learning.

Despite their apparent usefulness, some popular metaphors may be misleading. An example of this is the flawed metaphor of a 'gap between theory and practice'. The theory–practice gap metaphor is very widely used in teacher education and development. It is often used subconsciously and underpins statements such as 'we need to apply theory to practice' or 'all that theory is irrelevant because we know in practice what works in our school'. The theory–practice gap presents professional knowledge or knowing as either one or the other, either abstract theory or what works here, whereas these kinds of knowledge are interwoven within the complexity of the successful classroom teacher's approach.

An alternative metaphor is that teachers' professional learning is an 'interplay' between the vertical public (published) knowledge domain and the horizontal practical wisdom of teachers' knowledge domain (Boyd and Bloxham, 2014; Boyd et al., 2015) as illustrated by Figure 16.4.

In this metaphorical framework, public knowledge is seen as foregrounding published work, including theory texts, research papers, professional guidance books or other resources and also policy documents. This public knowledge is seen as a vertical knowledge domain because of the way it is hierarchically structured and the way that it holds power because of its published and peer reviewed status. The horizontal domain of practical wisdom of teachers foregrounds 'ways of working' in particular

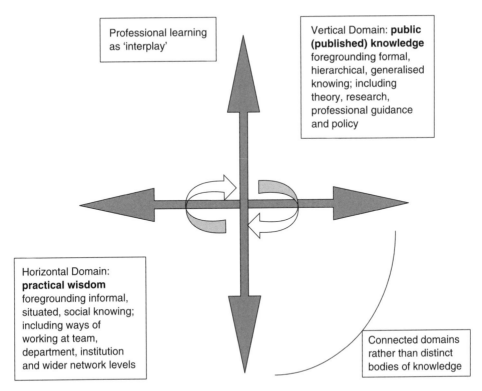

Figure 16.4 A situative metaphor for teacher learning (Boyd et al., 2015).

classrooms and educational workplaces. This knowledge is situated and socially held by teaching teams and foregrounds tacit knowledge and unwritten rules, although it is also likely to include elements whose origins could be traced back to forms of public knowledge. This horizontal knowledge domain holds power because of its practical credibility, because the teachers are the ones doing the actual job and they know 'what works here'.

Professional learning may be considered as an 'interplay' between these two domains. The metaphorical term 'interplay' helps to capture the complexity, dynamism and element of power involved in this learning. It is important for teachers to critically consider the metaphors they hold and use, for their own professional learning and for the learning of their students (Martinez et al., 2001).

The metaphors we hold for our own professional learning and for children's learning are important because they shape our practice. In this case we propose that you consider your professional learning as a teacher to be interplay between the vertical public knowledge domain and the horizontal practical wisdom domain.

When considering critical incidents or your general progress as a teacher, this metaphor recognises the high value of local, socially held ways of working but challenges you to also critically question and engage with relevant public knowledge, policy, professional guidance and learning theory. Teachers are busy professionals and are usually embedded in their particular school. Clearly they will place high value on the practical wisdom held by the teachers and other staff in their workplace. However, this may make it too easy for teachers to limit their repertoire of teaching strategies and adopt locally held assumptions and expectations about the children in their school. Engaging critically with public knowledge adds an element of externality to your professional learning and helps to avoid circular thinking and conservatism in your school improvement efforts. The metaphor of interplay helps to capture the power play and complexity involved in developing research-informed practice as a teacher. Classrooms are complex and education as a field is multi-paradigm, meaning there are different theoretical perspectives available by which to understand a single practical problem. This complexity makes education interesting and challenging, it is all part of the fun and satisfaction of being an educator.

Reflective task

Adopt the teacher professional learning as 'interplay' metaphor. Use this metaphor to check that your approach to evaluation includes critical consideration both of accepted ways of working within your school and of relevant external public knowledge. Consider how you are maintaining critical engagement with public (published) knowledge as part of your ongoing professional learning. Be aware that some theory is seductive, it seems like common sense and appears to be clear cut, and so it is important to adopt a questioning stance of critical engagement that asks 'how reliable is this information and what does it mean for my teaching and my children's learning?'.

Using the seven workplace learning tools

As an alternative to considering one tool at a time to review a critical incident or issue that you are handling in your work, you might prefer to reflect on the incident or issue using all of the tools. Table 16.2 provides a framework for this approach (also see Chapter 19).

Table 16.2 Showing how the seven workplace learning tools may be applied to a particular critical incident in your work

Workplace learning tool	Key idea	Key question
1 Conceptions of an 'outstanding teacher'	We all hold conceptions of a good teacher and good teaching based on our personal experiences	What beliefs have I brought to this incident or issue from my personal history?
2 Teacher enquiry	Teacher enquiry is a necessary process in order to interpret and use policy, guidance, research evidence and theory in our classrooms	What data have I collected and analysed, and how do my findings relate to policy, guidance, research evidence and theory?
3 Pedagogical content knowledge	Curriculum subject knowledge must be combined with knowledge of teaching, learning and assessment	In this topic what are the key curriculum subject concepts and what teaching strategy am I using to engage students with them?
4 Teacher identities	Teachers develop multiple trajectories of identity– beliefs about themselves as a teacher that are in negotiation with their classroom practice	What kind of teacher do I want to be and what are the implications for my response to this incident or issue?
5 Learning communities	Collaboration with other teachers, staff, parents and wider networks is an essential element of a teacher's workplace	How is collaboration with colleagues helping me to resolve this incident or issue?
6 Expansive workplace learning environments	Expansive workplace learning environments encourage teacher learning, collaboration, experimentation and boundary crossing	How does my workplace environment support or restrict my response to this incident or issue?
7 A metaphor for teacher learning	My learning as a teacher is an interplay between the vertical public knowledge domain and the horizontal practical wisdom of teachers in my workplace	How am I engaging with relevant knowledge from vertical and horizontal domains to inform my response to this incident or issue?

The following scenario illustrates how the seven workplace learning tools might apply to one scenario involving a student teacher, Phil, following a visit from his university tutor.

Work in school

A student teacher, Phil, is considering feedback from his mentor, who is a class teacher in the school. He discusses this with his visiting university tutor:

Phil: I was really pleased with the way my teaching placement was going. I have good control of my Year 5 class and I have taken care to implement

(Continued)

(Continued)

the class teacher's schemes and routines. She's so pleased with me that she has given me a considerable level of independence. So I was surprised and disappointed when my school-based mentor observed my literacy lesson and was very critical of a lack of challenge and assessment.

Tutor: Perhaps her feedback has challenged your conceptions about what good teaching looks like (Tool 1). You need to gather evidence of children's learning through formative assessment strategies and analyse the level of challenge in your lessons (Tool 2). Identify the key concepts that the lesson is focused on and consider how they are best taught and assessed (Tool 3). Perhaps you should reflect on the value you place on achieving a quietly busy classroom through good behaviour management? You seem to admire the 'strict' teachers in the school but need to decide if you want to be the kind of teacher who manages behaviour or nurtures learning (Tool 4).

Phil: I do agree that in this school there is a big emphasis on behaviour management. However, the other Year 5 teacher seems very interested in experimenting with innovative learning activities so maybe I should ask to observe some of her teaching (Tool 5)? I am not sure if that is what student teachers in this school normally do, but I guess it will not hurt to ask (Tool 6).

Tutor: I also think that you might go back to read again about some of the principles of assessment for learning with its emphasis on creating opportunities for formative assessment and the development of a positive classroom learning climate where it is okay to make mistakes and to struggle with challenging tasks (Clarke, 2008). You might experiment with some challenging learning activities and consider how your children respond (Tool 7).

Phil: I agree that seems to be a good next step but I must admit it might be a bit awkward if I start to change some of the classroom routines that the class teacher has in place. I guess I need to go one step at a time, negotiate with the class teacher, and see if I can involve her in my enquiry by observing or helping to assess the children's work.

(Continued)

This final modest action plan by Phil reflects the influence of several of the tools introduced in this section but above all it shows that he is willing to be proactive in terms of his professional learning and in terms of influencing his workplace. Making a contribution to the development of children's learning, appropriate to his current situation, is part of being a professional teacher and of becoming a member of a learning community. It is also important to recognise that each of us is able to shape our workplace and help to make it more expansive.

Reflective task

Select a critical incident or issue that you are currently dealing with in your classroom teaching and use one or more of the workplace learning tools to help to critically reflect on what happened and what action you will take in response.

Managing workload and priorities

Teachers work hard – in the UK primary teachers work on average around 50 hours per week during term time (OME, 2008). To remain effective and healthy it is important that you manage your workload and maintain a sense of control and of confidence in your impact as a teacher. You may feel that this chapter is giving you yet another task to fit into your busy week as a teacher. And you would be right about that! But by adopting 'enquiry as stance' (Cochran-Smith and Lytle, 2009), equipped with the seven workplace learning tools, you will be more resilient and more effective.

Teachers have experienced intensification of their work over the past 20 years; they are handling increasing pressures from the external policy framework, from parents and from school leaders. A useful study of Belgian primary teachers found that when they experience 'calls for change', they are motivated by their commitment to children's learning to filter these demands and use professional judgement in implementing new top-down initiatives (Ballet and Kelchtermans, 2009). The study showed that the mediating effect of school leaders, the quality of the collaborative workplace environment and the strength of individual teachers' professional identity were all important factors in controlling intensification. A study in Canada highlighted the importance to new teachers of social support from colleagues to create a feeling of all 'being in this together' (Pomaki et al., 2010). This study suggests that it is important for new teachers to find ways to interact with colleagues and build informal alliances, as well as using the more formal support offered such as a formal mentor and your programme teaching team.

Much of the general guidance on time management for busy professionals focuses on prioritising tasks and making lists. However, it is important to clarify your personal mission before time management is likely to become effective (Covey, 2004). You need to be clear on what kind of teacher you want to be and what your career ambitions are. Once these are identified, they form a basis for planning work effort. It is all too easy to become distracted by seemingly urgent but actually unimportant tasks and to ignore important non-urgent longer-term goals. Long- or medium-term planning, building long-term relationships with colleagues and making steps towards being the kind of teacher you want to be are the kind of mission-critical activities that you need to prioritise (Covey, 2004). By planning your work on a weekly basis, including personal, family and social priorities, you should be able to plan some time to devote to your strategic priorities, including your continued professional learning.

Children are entitled to support from teachers who maintain their continuing professional development, who experience a reasonable work–life balance and who have collaborative support from their colleagues. Despite the undoubted constraints in some schools, teachers have some autonomy and ability to influence workplace culture and to prioritise their own work effort.

Formal professional development opportunities

This chapter has emphasised how you should make the most of informal workplace professional learning, but this is not intended to diminish the possibilities of powerful learning from more formal professional development programmes and projects. Gaining a Master's level award will establish you as a practitioner researcher and prepare you to lead curriculum development through enquiry. Joining a collaborative research project should support your development of researcher knowledge and skills. A research review entitled *Developing Great Teaching* is available online and provides a useful checklist of the characteristics of effective professional development for teachers (Higgins et al., 2015). Some of the characteristics of effective professional learning for teachers identified in the report have been summarised here:

- The provision provides time but also has a rhythm that enables teachers to engage with new ideas and follow up the activity, for example, through classroom experimentation and further consideration.
- The content is able to capture the attention of teachers because of its relevance for pupil learning and their day-to-day work in the classroom.

- The provision builds a shared sense of purpose among the teachers and being voluntary or compulsory is less important than this.
- The 'activities for teachers' has some alignment with the principles of student learning being promoted.
- The provision focuses on pedagogy but is embedded in a particular curriculum subject.
- There is a focus on translating the content of the professional development into the classroom, for example, by experimentation and evaluation, including analysis of evidence of learning.
- An external facilitator may be associated with the provision, acting as a coach or mentor and often in tandem with school-based colleagues, introducing new knowledge and building the leadership capacity of participating teachers.
- There is a good level of trust and collaboration.
- The professional development activity is supported by proactive school leadership so that it is part of a strategic vision and development plan.

You might use this list of characteristics as a checklist, when deciding on which formal professional development opportunities you wish to engage in.

Managing your mentors

Some kind of formal mentoring is likely to be part of the support provided for you as a new teacher. If the formal arrangements are not in place then you should do your best to find an informal mentor yourself. Identify a colleague that you respect and trust – usually they will be within your school but that may not always be possible, particularly in a small primary school. Having a mentor is potentially a very positive and useful resource but in itself it does not represent an enquiry-based strategy. You should aim to use the workplace learning tools proposed in this chapter in collaboration with your mentor so that you have a useful framework and data to consider. It is very important that you are proactive in managing your relationship with your mentor in order to make the best use of the opportunity. If you are wary of your formally appointed mentor, then work to build trust but also draw your own boundaries concerning what you are willing to share with them and seek another informal mentor with whom you feel able to share practice honestly. This issue of being proactive in managing your own professional learning is an important message on which we can close this chapter. School workplaces vary enormously as learning environments. Rather than relying on the school or blaming colleagues, it is for you to take charge. Decide what kind of teacher you wish to become and then start the work of achieving that goal. Many experienced teachers will claim that being a great teacher is a natural gift. Some of them are in senior positions and really should know better. There are many very effective teachers with a wide range of styles and you will need to work hard and with a proactive approach to your own learning to develop your own style and become the teacher you want to be.

Summary

This chapter emphasises the importance of teachers planning proactively for their professional learning while teaching in schools, in order to develop their teacher identity and their capacity to make decisions about their practice, rather than being clones of a particular policy or context. The seven 'workplace learning tools' are presented for your practical use in answering the everyday question of an enquiry-based teacher: what is my impact on learning and on learners? Above all this chapter argues that the seventh workplace learning tool, the metaphor for professional learning as the interplay between public published knowledge and the practical wisdom of teachers, is the key to your continued professional learning.

Questions for discussion

- To what extent do working conditions, resources and the culture of schools support teacher enquiry with critical questioning of both the practical wisdom of teachers and public knowledge?
- How proactive are you being in planning for your professional development? What are your next steps in prioritising your workplace learning?

Further reading

Baumfield, V., Hall, E. and Wall, K. (2013) *Action Research in Education*. London: Sage. Teacher practitioner research is a powerful approach to enhancement of your practice and your children's learning. This text provides a thorough overview of research design, ethics, data collection and analysis. It will help you to complete formal research assignments as part of your initial teacher education and Master's programmes, and to use a collaborative practitioner research project as a driver for change in your school.

Boyd, P., Hymer, B. and Lockney, K. (2015) *Learning Teaching: Becoming an Inspirational Teacher*. St Albans: Critical Publishing.

This compact book focuses on learning power and is designed around five of the most critical dilemmas that teachers face in their everyday work: belief vs. ability; autonomy vs. compliance; abstract vs. concrete; feedback vs. praise; and collaboration vs. competition.

Eaude, T. (2012) *How Do Expert Primary Class Teachers Really Work? A Critical Guide for Teachers, Headteachers and Teacher Educators.* St Albans: Critical Publishing.
If you want to learn more about workplace learning theory, then this concise and accessible guide will be of interest. It introduces key ideas around the nature of expertise and then discusses how some primary teachers use their expertise to maximise children's learning.

References

Ballet, K. and Kelchtermans, G. (2009) 'Struggling with workload: Primary teachers' experience of intensification', *Teaching and Teacher Education*, 25 (8): 1150–7.
Banks, F., Leach, J. and Moon, B. (2005) 'Extract from new understandings of teachers' pedagogic knowledge', *The Curriculum Journal*, 16 (3): 331–40.
Baumfield, V., Hall, E. and Wall, K. (2013) *Action Research in Education.* London: Sage.
Bauml, M. (2009) 'Examining the unexpected sophistication of preservice teachers' beliefs about the relational dimensions of teaching', *Teaching and Teacher Education*, 25 (6): 902–8.
Biesta, G.J.J. (2010) *Good Education in an Age of Measurement.* Boulder, CO: Paradigm.
Blackler, F. (1995) 'Knowledge, knowledge work and organizations: An overview and interpretation', *Organization Studies*, 16 (6): 1021–46.
Bolam, R., McMahon, A., Stoll, L., Thomas, S. and Wallace, M. (2005) *Creating and Sustaining Professional Learning Communities.* Department for Education and Skills Research Report 637. Available at: http://dera.ioe.ac.uk/5622/1/RR637.pdf.
Boyd, P. and Bloxham, S. (2014) 'A situative metaphor for teacher learning: The case of university teachers grading student coursework', *British Educational Research Journal*, 40 (2): 337–52.
Boyd, P., Hymer, B. and Lockney, K. (2015) *Learning Teaching: Becoming an Inspirational Teacher.* St Albans: Critical Publishing.
Bruner, J. (1996) *The Culture of Education.* London: Harvard University Press.
Clarke, S. (2008) *Active Learning Through Formative Assessment.* London: Hodder Education.
Cochran-Smith, M. and Lytle, S.L. (2009) *Inquiry as Stance: Practitioner Research for the Next Generation.* New York: Teachers College Press.
Costa, A.L. and Kallick, B. (2014) *Dispositions: Reframing Teaching and Learning.* London: Sage.
Covey, S.R. (2004) *The 7 Habits of Highly Effective People: Powerful Lessons in Personal Change.* London: Simon and Schuster.
Day, C.W., Stobart, G., Sammons, P., Kington, A., Gu, Q., Smees, R. et al. (2006) *Variations in Teachers' Work, Lives and Effectiveness.* Final report for the VITAE Project. London: DfES.

Education Endowment Fund (EEF) (2015) 'Teaching and learning toolkit'. Available at: https://educationendowmentfoundation.org.uk/resources/teaching-learning-toolkit (accessed 3 August 2017).

Fenwick, T. (2001) 'Questioning the concept of the learning organisation', in C. Paechter, M. Preedy, D. Scott and J. Soler (eds), *Knowledge, Power and Learning* (pp.74–88). London: Paul Chapman.

Fuller, A., Hodkinson, H., Hodkinson, P. and Unwin, L. (2005) 'Learning as peripheral participation in communities of practice: A reassessment of key concepts in workplace learning', *British Educational Research Journal*, 31 (1): 49–68.

Gu, Q. and Day, C. (2007) 'Teachers' resilience: A necessary condition for effectiveness', *Teaching and Teacher Education*, 23 (8): 1302–16.

Hattie, J. (2012) *Visible Learning for Teachers: Maximising Pupil Learning*. New York: Routledge.

Higgins, S., Cordingly, P., Greany, T. and Coe, R. (2015) *Developing Great Teaching: Lessons from the International Reviews into Effective Professional Development*. Teacher Development Trust. Available at: http://tdtrust.org/wp-content/uploads/2015/10/DGT-Summary.pdf.

Hodkinson, H. and Hodkinson, P. (2005) 'Improving schoolteachers' workplace learning', *Research Papers in Education*, 20 (2): 109–31.

Labaree, D. (2000) 'On the nature of teaching and teacher education: Difficult practices that look easy', *Journal of Teacher Education*, 51 (3): 228–33.

Lakoff, G. and Johnson, M. (1980) *Metaphors We Live By*. Chicago, IL: Chicago University Press.

Lankshear, C. and Knobel, M. (2004) *A Handbook for Teacher Research: From Design to Implementation*. Maidenhead: Open University Press.

Lave, J. and Wenger, E. (1991) *Situated Learning: Legitimate Peripheral Participation*. Cambridge: Cambridge University Press.

Lewin, K. (1951) *Field Theory in Social Science: Selected Theoretical Papers* (D. Cartwright (ed.)). New York: Harper & Row.

Martinez, M.A., Sauleda, N. and Huber, G.L. (2001) 'Metaphors as blueprints of thinking about teaching and learning', *Teaching and Teacher Education*, 17 (8): 965–77.

Office of Manpower Economics (OME) (2008) *Teachers' Workloads Diary Survey: March 2008*. London: Office of Manpower Economics. Available at: www.ome.uk.com.

Pomaki, G., DeLongis, A., Frey, D., Short, K. and Woehrle, T. (2010) 'When the going gets tough: Direct, buffering and indirect effects of social support on turnover intention', *Teaching and Teacher Education*, 26 (6): 1340–6.

Sfard, A. (1998) 'On two metaphors for learning and the dangers of choosing just one', *Educational Researcher*, 27 (2): 4–13.

Shulman, L.S. (1986) 'Those who understand: Knowledge growth in teaching', *Educational Researcher*, 15 (2): 4–14.

Thomas, L. and Beauchamp, C. (2011) 'Understanding new teachers' professional identities through metaphor', *Teaching and Teacher Education*, 27 (4): 726–69.

Watson, C. (2014) 'Effective professional learning communities? The possibilities for teachers as agents of change in schools', *British Educational Research Journal*, 40 (1): 18–29.

Wenger, E. (1998) *Communities of Practice: Learning, Meaning, and Identity*. Cambridge: Cambridge University Press.

17

Reflective Practice

Andrew Read

By the end of this chapter, you should be able to:

- reflect on descriptive accounts of your own practice
- plan for and provide evidence of your own reflective practice
- begin to establish an overview of your own developing reflective practice.

Introduction

Chapters and books on reflection and reflective practice tend to open with a section describing various theories and frameworks. But theory can distance us from the process of reflection itself: *being* reflective and *applying* this to your own practice is what makes the difference. Sometimes it is also important to be able to *articulate* this process of reflection, especially when you are required to write an essay about it. So this chapter begins with an example of a trainee's descriptive lesson evaluation and identifies some potential starting points for reflection, including dealing with *unforeseen situations* and recognising *theories in use*, and puts this into a theoretical context. Questions to ask when looking back at lesson evaluations and observations are suggested: these may support those who are less familiar with what reflection is about.

An example of a discussion between a trainee and a mentor serves as a basis for thinking about reflecting on values. Opportunities to consider the *cognitive dissonance* between *theories in use* and *espoused theory* are identified, leading to *critical reflection on practice*.

Drawing on an individual trainee's experience, an example of what the *reflective process* might look like is provided. Ways of organising evidence in order to demonstrate meeting the Teachers' Standards, and a model for viewing this reflective process from a *meta-reflective* perspective, are suggested.

Starting points for reflection

Put simply, reflection involves thinking about something. But we think about things in different ways: we recall (e.g. what we were told about behaviour management in a lecture), we consider (e.g. what the lecturer meant by the phrase 'assertive discipline'), we interpret (e.g. we settle, perhaps temporarily, on what 'assertive discipline' means). The characteristic of reflection, the element that makes it different from other ways of thinking, is that it is thinking that leads to a 'useful outcome' (Moon, 1999, p. 4). In the context of the classroom, this is thinking that leads to 'a steady increase in the quality of the education provided for children' (Pollard, 2014, p. 68). The case study below shows how Anna thought about her lesson early in her first placement.

Case study

Anna, Placement A, Day 7. Year 2 class, 28 pupils. Written lesson evaluation

Today I read the text we will be using this week to the class. I made sure all the children were listening before I started by reminding them of my rules. I gave J and R a sticker each because they had their arms and legs crossed first and I wanted to see good listening. I asked G to sit on the carpet by my feet so I could keep an eye on him. I read the story with a clear voice and all the children were engaged because they were looking at me. I had to stop once because B started talking to his neighbour. I asked him to share what he had to say with the rest of the class. I wrote B's name on the board and drew a sad face next to it. B said he couldn't see the pictures. I told him to put his hand up next time he had something to say. B remained quiet for the rest of the story. When I had finished reading the story I asked the children to put their thumbs up if they had enjoyed the story. All the children put their thumbs up so this was a successful lesson.

This is the beginning in two senses for Anna: it is the beginning of her experience in school within the context of her course; this is also, potentially, the beginning of a process of reflection. Her evaluation is descriptive: the term *descriptive* sometimes implies a need for further analysis – when tutors write 'too descriptive' on essays they are usually referring to a lack of analysis. However, description can be a positive starting point, providing context and a basis for exploration (Ghaye and Ghaye, 2011). In addition, Anna's lesson evaluation is the result of an experience: Kolb argues that 'immediate personal experience is the focal point of learning' (1984, p. 21). But something is missing from this lesson evaluation, at least on the surface, preventing it from leading into a reflective process: it is a recollection, an account of something that happened. What sets reflection apart is that it leads to a *useful outcome*. In a sense, Anna's evaluation is complete in itself.

Having said this, there are several aspects within this piece of descriptive writing that suggest opportunities for reflection. For a start, it is packed with theory. Brookfield argues that 'most workers … are theorists': 'they are constantly testing out hunches, intuitions, and guesses about what will work against their own reality' (1987, p. 152). When one of these approaches is effective in one particular context, it is put aside to be reused when a similar situation arises. Brookfield argues that these effective approaches are similar to Schön's *theories in use* (1987): an effective approach is identified, some explanation is provided for why the approach is effective and the theorist demonstrates an openness to change in the light of shifting circumstances (Schön, 1987). Such *theories in use* may also evolve from what we observe or from what we understand to be the accepted model in the particular situation. *Theories in use* may stem from our own prior experience as pupils: we think back to our favourite teachers, or perhaps to those with the strategies we feel in retrospect were the most effective – these strategies may form the basis of our theories. These theories form what we know, and what we think we know, about 'good practice'. Instead of using the phrase 'good practice' we might talk about 'what works well with these pupils'.

Reflective task

Look at Anna's lesson evaluation

What theories does Anna bring to her lesson? What effective approaches does she identify? What does she see as 'good practice'?

What explanations for these approaches does Anna provide?

What evidence for the effectiveness of these approaches is there in Anna's evaluation?

Anna's lesson evaluation also indicates that she had not anticipated some of the pupils' responses. Schön talks about the element of surprise, where 'something fails to meet our expectations' (1987, p. 26). Brookfield suggests that these 'unforeseen situations' trigger the need for us to 'question our habitual ways of working' (1987, p. 151). Tripp states that, when introducing the idea of critical incidents, 'we have to ask both what happened and what allowed or caused it to happen' (2012, p. 9). Schön uses the notion of *surprise* as the basis for a discussion of 'reflection in action' (1987). Schön argues that reflection in action occurs when we are in the middle of doing something (e.g. in the middle of reading a story) and 'our thinking serves to reshape what we are doing while we are doing it' (1987, p. 26). Anna's evaluation suggests that surprise, reflection in action and some reshaping took place: 'I had to stop once because B started talking to his neighbour. I asked him to share what he had to say with the rest of the class.' This is complicated, however, because Anna's lesson evaluation is written *after* the event and in part is a recount of her reflection in action. She may, indeed, be unaware of her reflection in action. A next step could be for Anna to explore the ways in which she responded to the unexpected within the lesson, or, as Schön puts it, to 'reflect *on* her reflection-in-action' (Schön, 1987, p. 31).

Reflecting on reflection in action

One of the challenges of this is that it may be difficult to see where and when something unexpected has happened. When we write a lesson evaluation after the event, we are already filtering and editing the experience, summarising what happened and quite possibly missing important details. Descriptive writing in this context can be very useful: a detailed description of what happened during the course of the

Table 17.1   Anna, Placement A, Day 7. Year 2 class, 28 pupils. Lesson observation by mentor

---

3.15 – Anna has all pupils on carpet – some quiet talking from pupils; Anna waits for 10 seconds, folds her arms; gives stickers to J and R – says, 'Well done, good sitting'. Anna continues to wait – looks at G, raises her eyebrows, puts finger to her lips – G continues to talk to his neighbour. Anna says, 'G, come and sit next to me – I want to be sure you're listening'. G moves. Anna raises her eyebrow at other pupils, says, 'I can't see anyone else who deserves a sticker' – the talking stops. Anna shows the front cover of a picture book – *Not Now Bernard*.

3.18 – Anna asks, 'Does anyone know this story?' Most of the pupils raise their hands. B says, 'I like the bit when …'. Anna says, 'B – you must remember to put up your hand'.

3.20 – Anna reads the story – holding the book to her right, the pages are open towards the pupils, Anna looking around the book to see the text. Most pupils are engaged – M and N are playing with something on the carpet; B is whispering to his neighbour – M, N and B are sitting to Anna's left.

3.22 – Anna notices B, stops reading, says 'B, would you like to share what you've got to say with the class?' B doesn't reply. Anna writes 'B' on board and draws a sad face. B says, 'But I can't see the pictures'. Anna says, 'I've already told you – you must put up your hand'.

---

lesson, without any interpretation or analysis, can support the writer in identifying key moments. A lesson observation by a peer or mentor can provide this descriptive detail; an audio recording might provide a useful and more manageable alternative. Table 17.1 shows a lesson observation by Anna's mentor.

Even where the lesson is recounted in detail, it can still be hard to spot where reflection in action has taken place. It can be harder still to know what to do with the reflection in action once you have spotted it. However, spotting it can be the start of a reflective process. There are lots of models of reflective processes. When reflecting, people 'recapture their experience, think about it, mull it over and evaluate it' (Boud et al., 1985, p. 19). The *recapturing* might be a descriptive account recorded in a journal or part of a lesson evaluation or a lesson observation; the *thinking/mulling* is where the process becomes potentially reflective. *Evaluating* involves making some kind of judgement. When we judge something, we compare it, often subconsciously, with a set or sets of criteria. These criteria are external (e.g. the Teachers' Standards) or internal (e.g. our own set of values and beliefs or our own personal philosophy). It could be argued that Boud et al. (1985) miss the crucial next step in their simplified

Table 17.2 Shows how Anna might move from describing her practice to reflecting on it

Descriptive		Reflective (reflecting on reflection in action)	
Recapturing experience		Thinking about it/mulling it over	Evaluation
Unforeseen situations	My response/ reflection in action	Questioning my response	Identifying an aspect to develop – leading to an outcome
B is whispering to his neighbour	I write 'B' on board and draw a sad face	Why did I draw a sad face on the board? Where does this approach come from? What was my aim? How did B's whispering make me feel? What was my aim in writing B's name and drawing the sad face? To what extent was my response a reflection of my needs? What impact did drawing the sad face on the board have on B's behaviour?	How does my response fit with my values? To what extent did I achieve what I wanted to (short term/long term)? To what extent did I understand and address the needs of the pupil/s? How else could I have handled this unforeseen situation?
B says, 'But I can't see the pictures'	I say, 'I've already told you – you must put up your hand'	Why did I repeat the rule? Where does this approach come from? What was my aim? How did B's objection make me feel? To what extent was my response a reflection of my needs? What impact did the repetition of the rule have on B?	

definition: when reflecting, people evaluate then *respond* in some way that moves the process towards a *useful outcome* (Moon, 1999). Table 17.2 shows an example of how Anna might move from the descriptive to the reflective.

The questions in *questioning my response* could be generalised and applied to any descriptive account of practice in order to step into a reflective process: Why did I act in this way? What led me to this approach? What did I aim to achieve by acting in this way? How was I feeling when I did this? How did this approach relate to the needs of the pupil/s? What impact did my action have?

The *evaluation* column specifically addresses the trainee's own values. Closer thinking about how our practice in the classroom relates to our values provides a further opportunity to enter a reflective process.

Reflecting on values

Table 17.3 shows an excerpt from a dialogue between a trainee, Khadija, and her mentor.

Khadija has a rationale for how she has organised the groups. This is one of her *theories in use*. The discussion with the mentor begins to challenge this. Khadija cautiously suggests an alternative arrangement but comes up against a barrier: 'we put the pupils in literacy groups for history'. This is in line with Ghaye and Ghaye's notion of *critical reflection on practice* (2011, p. 41) in which the status quo, in this case the

Table 17.3   Khadija, Placement A, Day 9. Year 4 class, 27 pupils. Lesson focus: history. Discussion with mentor

---

Mentor: Tell me about how you organised the pupils today.

Khadija: They were in their ability groups with the less able group at the table at the back where the teaching assistant can work with them – they were labelling the pictures – they needed something simple to keep them on task. The most able group were with me – I wanted to challenge them, get them to think about how they could use the artefacts to build up a picture of what life was like during the war. The middle-ability groups had the worksheets – I wanted them to work in silence so that the noise level in the classroom was kept down.

Mentor: What information was the ability grouping based on?

Khadija: I had the pupils in their literacy groups. The most able group are all developing mastery in reading and writing.

Mentor: How did their reading and writing skills support them during the discussion work with the artefacts?

Khadija: Well, one of them needed to scribe down the ideas they came up with on the paper. But ... I suppose it was really more about the discussion ... asking questions ... suggesting what the objects could have been used for.

Mentor: How might you have organised the groups differently?

Khadija: I guess more of the pupils could have been involved in this kind of activity. The teaching assistant could have supported the less able group – she was doing that anyway. The middle groups would struggle though: they're not very good at collaborating or getting their ideas down on paper and I couldn't scribe for them all. I could have put them into mixed-ability groups but that would be tricky to manage because we put the pupils in literacy groups for history.

'accepted routine' of children working in literacy groups for history, is challenged. By bringing it closer to the surface Khadija has an opportunity to clarify her understanding and to question 'assumptions made about effective teaching'. It is important to recognise that 'critical' here, as Ghaye and Ghaye make clear, is *not* a synonym for cynical, destructive or negative: *critical reflection on practice* is not an invitation to Khadija to denounce school practice, it 'has the intention of being creative and constructive' (Ghaye and Ghaye, 2011, p. 63).

However, the challenge to accepted routine is only implicit in the mentor's questions. The mentor could suggest to Khadija that she puts the pupils in mixed-ability groups for the next history lesson. But, as Dewey (1926) argues, the student 'can't see just by being "told", although the right kind of telling may guide his seeing' (in Boydston, 1984, p. 57). Reflection is significantly about ownership, and it is important that Khadija works through this and understands for herself that a *shift* in her idea of 'good practice' could be beneficial for the pupils.

Within this discussion, Khadija's *theories in use* clearly imply a set of values that underpins her practice. But these values are not necessarily the values she shares publicly. We may all do this at various points: we tell our friends or colleagues that we live by one set of values but in practice we may be less consistent. For example, we may tell our friends that we are committed to reducing our use of non-recyclable plastic packaging but then find ourselves buying the same products in their non-recyclable packaging because nothing else tastes as good or works as well. This is linked closely to the idea of *theory in use* (what we do in practice) and *espoused theory*, which Brookfield describes as 'the theories that people claim to follow, even when their own actions contradict this claim' (1987, pp. 152–3). Before starting this placement, Khadija shared her theories with her peers; these *espoused theories*, shown in Table 17.4, imply a set of underlying values.

Brookfield describes the friction 'between what we say we believe and what we privately suspect to be true' as *cognitive dissonance* (1987, p. 153). While it can be uncomfortable to recognise that our thinking may be inconsistent and that *cognitive dissonance* is present in our own dealings with theory and practice, this recognition can provide a springboard for reflection. Dissonance demands resolution, and this resolution represents the *useful outcome* that is central to reflection. However, it would be misleading to suggest that the reflective practice model, *in practice*, is a simple one.

Table 17.4 Khadija's espoused theories

Pupils need to discuss their ideas in order to construct new knowledge and understanding
All pupils need to be challenged in order to achieve to the best of their ability
It is important to support pupils in their development of independence and autonomy

Reflective task

Look at the discussion between Khadija and her mentor and the list of Khadija's *espoused theories*.

What values underpin Khadija's *espoused theories*?

What *theories in use* are evident in Khadija's comments? What values do these suggest?

What *cognitive dissonance* might there be between Khadija's theories in use and her espoused theories?

Work in school

Student: After reflecting on the lesson I think it would be useful to group the children in a different way, but it was made very clear to me that school policy is to group the children as I am currently doing. How can I act on the conclusions I have reached?

Mentor: We think that the way we organise children here has had a very positive impact on outcomes over the past two years. How certain are you that changing the way you group children will have a positive impact? What evidence do you have?

Student: I noticed that the children in the two least able groups found it difficult to come up with ideas. When it came to the writing task they hadn't anything to start them off, so I ended up giving them things to write.

Mentor: How could you stimulate the children's thinking within the familiar grouping context? What might help them to come up with ideas?

Analysis

The trainee has identified a challenge and feels that the solution lies in adopting an approach that is different to established school practice. The trainee can provide some broad evidence about the issue, and it is possible that school policy in this respect is a barrier. The trainee's thinking may be prompted by concerns about the children's attainment, or by her own sense of feeling restricted by school practice. However, the mentor is keen to encourage the trainee to think of solutions within the existing framework. The mentor's thinking may be prompted by an unerring commitment to school policy or by a wish to challenge the trainee to explore more creative solutions.

The reflective process in action

Table 17.5 shows how Khadija's practice in history lessons developed over several weeks.

Khadija adapts her practice, emerging with an alternative *theory in use*. She tries out a number of strategies: the 'discussion time', the mixed-ability grouping and the distribution of roles. The strategies she experiments with are not new to the

Table 17.5   Shows how Khadija's practice in history lessons developed over several weeks

Khadija's practice (i.e. what she does in class)	Khadija's rationale	Khadija's evaluation (sometimes after mentor observation and discussion)	The reflective process
Day 9: All pupils work in 'ability groups' Some pupils work in silence	'We put the pupils in literacy groups for history' Manages noise level	'The lesson worked well because the pupils who find collaboration difficult did the worksheets and the noise level was kept down'	*Descriptive reflection on practice* (Ghaye and Ghaye, 2011) in Khadija's account of lesson to mentor Opportunity for *critical reflection on practice* (Ghaye and Ghaye, 2011) with possible challenge to routine identified *Cognitive dissonance* between Khadija's *espoused values* and *theories in use* recognised (Brookfield, 1987; Schön, 1987)
Day 14: Introduces a 5-minute 'discussion time' at the start of group work	'... to help pupils clarify with each other what they have to do'	'The most able group seemed to use "discussion time" most effectively'	*Collecting, analysing and evaluating evidence from her own classroom* (Pollard, 2014) *Perceptive reflection on practice* (Ghaye and Ghaye, 2011), drawing links between descriptions and Khadija's feelings
Day 19: Introduces mixed-ability grouping in the history lesson	'I thought the more able pupils could model discussion'	'Some of the less able pupils were just sitting there – not taking part at all – it was frustrating' (*reflecting on reflection in action*, Schön, 1987)	A new *theory in use* emerging. Khadija hypothesising and 'deducing new implications for action' (Kolb, 1984, p. 21)
Day 19: Stops the lesson – gives each group six roles (manager, scribe, time-keeper, etc.) to distribute	'I needed to do something to get them all joining in' (*reflecting on reflection in action*, Schön, 1987)	'It worked quite well. There was more participation although the more able pupils tended to dominate – they often took the manager role'	
Day 24: Introduces group activity where the outcome is collaborative – includes a focus in the lesson introduction on different roles	'They knew they had to talk about what their own role was'	'It was all about talking – some of the less able pupils had quite a lot to say – they were quite articulate in front of the class. We still need to do some work on collaboration, though'	*Cognitive dissonance* resolved to some extent – discussion of ideas integrated into practice *Useful outcome* (Moon, 1999) achieved *Quality of education increased?* (Pollard, 2014)

world of teaching and learning, but this is not a problem. It could be argued that there is nothing new in education: it has all been tried before. However, the strategies Khadija introduces during her placement are *innovatory* because they are *new to Khadija's practice* and may also be *new to the pupils* or *new to the learning context* (i.e. that classroom, that subject or that time of day). Khadija is reflecting 'systematically on the effectiveness of lessons and approaches to teaching' (Teachers' Standard 4), and introducing, in response to her reflections, 'approaches which enable pupils to be taught effectively' (Teachers' Standard 5). She is taking 'responsibility for improving teaching' and drawing effectively on interaction with her mentor (Teachers' Standard 8).

When we try something new in the class, it may often initially 'fail' because of our own uncertainty and the pupils' unfamiliarity with the novelty. It is important, however, to use this 'failure' to move forward. In order to improve practice, we need to refine and try again, rather than return to the safe ground of the status quo. Reflective practitioners are, essentially, learners and risk takers. The experience of trying something out and finding that it does not quite work involves risk: this parallels the experience of pupils. By participating in the reflective process, practitioners can become a role model to 'guide pupils to reflect on the progress they have made and their emerging needs' and 'encourage pupils to take a responsible … attitude to their own … study' (Teachers' Standard 2).

Work in school

Student: I want to try something new but I'm worried that if it doesn't work I could fail this placement. What should I do?

Mentor: Introduce one new element at a time, maintaining everything else that has worked previously. If I'm going to observe you, let me know what the new element is and ask for feedback on it. (This demonstrates that you know what you are doing and are taking responsibility.) Be clear about the purpose of the innovation: what do you want to achieve by introducing this new element? I could feed back specifically on how well the innovation met this objective.

Student: But I can't be sure if it'll work. How can I avoid chaos?

(Continued)

Mentor: Think about what is likely to go wrong and ensure you have addressed these potential issues in your plan – with an 'escape route' in place if the lesson seems to be falling apart. In the worst-case scenario you'll return to a tried and tested (and successful) formula in the lesson and need to rethink the introduction of this innovation. In the best case, you'll introduce the innovation without any hiccups and see a positive impact on pupils' learning. Either way, you are demonstrating the capacity to take responsibility for improving your teaching.

Analysis

The trainee is clearly anxious about change. This may be rooted in the trainee's fears about jeopardising her own progress or jeopardising the pupils' learning and, possibly, well-being. The anxiety may also stem from the expectations of the school: if there is a specific approach evident throughout the school, then innovation may seem more daunting. However, there is a shift away from trainees being judged on their 'performance' in individual lessons, towards a judgement based on the trainee's impact on pupil progress *over time*. This could reduce the potential anxiety for trainees seeking to innovate. Mentors are also more likely to support innovation where they are confident about the trainee's capacity to manage the change successfully: the mentor's encouragement in this case suggests that confidence in the trainee's capacity is already established.

Providing evidence of your own reflective practice

As part of your teacher training course, induction year or further professional development, you may be required to assemble a portfolio of evidence demonstrating

Table 17.6   Teachers' Standards (TS) relating to the process of reflection on practice

---

A teacher must

TS4 – reflect systematically on the effectiveness of lessons and approaches to teaching

TS5 – know when and how to differentiate appropriately, using approaches which enable pupils to be taught effectively

TS8 – take responsibility for improving teaching through appropriate professional development, responding to advice and feedback from colleagues

  – develop effective professional relationships with colleagues, knowing how and when to draw on advice and specialist support

---

that you have met or are in the process of meeting the Teachers' Standards. But how might you provide evidence of taking responsibility for improving teaching, of your effective relationships with colleagues (Teachers' Standard 8), and of your capacity to adapt to meet pupils' strengths and needs (Teachers' Standard 5)? Table 14.6 lists Teachers' Standards which relate explicitly or implicitly to reflective practice.

One way of demonstrating in a portfolio that you have taken on this responsibility is through *organisation*: evidence needs to be organised in a way which implies the reflective process that has taken place and suggests an impact or shift in practice or thinking. Returning to the example of Khadija's developing practice (pp. 391–2), evidence could be provided through an appropriately sequenced selection of lesson plans, lesson observations, lesson evaluations and reflective journal entries, as suggested in Table 17.7. The evidence here is for both the former, less effective practice and the new practice, because without acknowledgement of what worked less well the shift would not be evident.

Published work may also have had an impact on Khadija's thinking. She may have read articles or chapters on encouraging pupils to work collaboratively, or on enabling participation in group work. However, when constructing your portfolio, a photocopied chapter, article or excerpt on either of these only provides evidence of your ability to photocopy. The links between theory and practice, between what you have seen or read and what you do, need to be explicit.

This reflective process can be made more explicit through *annotation*. However, annotation needs to be brief. The word 'annotation' implies notes rather than an essay. If these notes become lengthy, the annotation may become too descriptive. Overly descriptive annotations may suggest that the examples you give do not provide sufficient evidence. A simple set of conclusions to draw from this is that you need to *welcome* observation and discussion, retain *all the evidence, keep it organised* in a way that is easy for you to explain, and *maintain a reflective journal*.

Table 17.7 Taking responsibility for improving teaching: Khadija's evidence

Khadija's practice (i.e. what she does in class)	Evidence indicating shift (from Day 9 to Day 14)
Day 9: All pupils work in 'ability groups'	Lesson plan: *ability groups*
Some pupils work in silence	Lesson evaluation: 'the lesson worked well'
	Reflective journal: recognition of *cognitive dissonance* following discussion with mentor
Day 14: Introduces 5-minute 'discussion time' at the start of group work	Lesson plan: *discussion time*
	Reflective journal: *rationale* ('to help pupils clarify…')
	Lesson evaluation: *discussion time* worked for *some* pupils

Maintaining a reflective journal

A reflective journal may be a requirement or a recommendation. What it can do is remind you about how you used to think and how and why this thinking has shifted. However, writing 'Reflective Journal' on the cover of an exercise book will not ensure that the contents are reflective. By interrogating *yourself* about the evidence, its source, location or embedded values, opportunities to evaluate and analyse the evidence (Pollard, 2014) emerge. This can lead you to think about *innovatory* ways of doing things, active experimentation (Kolb, 1984) and useful outcomes (Moon, 1999). Table 17.8 gives examples of questions you could use as a starting point for interrogating your own thinking.

Table 17.8   Examples of starting points for interrogating your own thinking

Location/ source	Interrogating yourself
My thinking	What experience leads me to think this?
	What other philosophies are there?
	What barriers are preventing me from thinking differently?
Plans	To what extent does this represent what actually happens/happened?
	To what extent did this lesson meet the objectives I sought? (Teachers' Standard 4)
	To what extent did *all pupils* develop understanding/skills/knowledge/values? (Teachers' Standards 5 and 6)
	How effective were the different elements of the lesson: differentiation, assessment, resources, etc.? (Teachers' Standards 4, 5 and 6)
Lesson evaluations	How effectively did I teach? How appropriate were my approaches in the context of this lesson? (Teachers' Standard 4)
	What did pupils learn? (Teachers' Standard 6) How do I feel about this?
	How could I have done this differently … in a way that reflects my developing personal philosophy? (Teachers' Standard 4)
Written lesson observations	To what extent does this reflect my own thinking about the lesson?
	How clear am I about my strengths and the areas I need to develop? (Teachers' Standard 8)
	What questions does this raise about my practice? (Teachers' Standard 8)
Annotated examples of pupils' work	What does this show about pupil learning? (Teachers' Standard 6)
	What does this show about *my understanding* of pupil learning? (Teachers' Standards 3, 5 and 6)
	To what extent does this work provide evidence that my practice echoes my developing philosophy?
Records of discussions with mentors and tutors	What was the purpose of this discussion?
	To what extent was my own learning enhanced by this discussion? (Teachers' Standard 8)
	What do I need to do now? (Teachers' Standard 8)
Reflective journal	Why is this passage particularly descriptive?
	Why did I choose to write about this particular event?
	What incident/s caused me to reflect on my reflections-in-action or on my values?

You can also interrogate your thinking about the reflective journal itself.

The process of reflecting on reflection has already been touched upon in relation to reflecting on reflection in action. However, by extending this, moving from your reflection on a single event to your approach to reflection in general, opportunities to engage in meta-reflection emerge. These can form the core of thinking and writing about reflective practice and can be supportive when working at Master's level (see Chapter 19, Darbyshire, Harrop and Duckworth).

Meta-reflection

At its simplest level, reflection is about finding a solution: you identify a concern, think about it, try something out, and, when it works, refine your practice accordingly. Khadija's reflective experience sees just such a change in practice. Once this outcome is achieved, you start again: a new reflective cycle kicks off when a new concern is identified.

However, there are problems with this model. One is that, as a trainee or as a teacher, you will encounter several concerns, simultaneously or on successive days, all of which require some kind of resolution. As a reflective practitioner, several reflective cycles will be running at the same time.

Another more complex issue is that the reflective process is not really circular, although the simplified visual models (Kolb, 1984; Pollard, 2014) may suggest this, and it is not an 'evenly progressive sequence' (Illeris, 2006, p. 151). Once a solution has been found, you will not, as a reflective practitioner, re-enter the process at the same starting point. You will have acquired a new set of reflective skills, new understanding around the role of the teacher and have refined the values that underpin your thinking; you will be drawing on a broader range of experience. Your re-entry into the reflective process will be deeper than your previous entry. So rather than a cycle, the process is a *reflective spiral*. This, in essence, is similar to Bruner's spiral curriculum model (1960): Bruner argues that 'any subject can be taught effectively in some intellectually honest form to any child at any stage of development' (1960, p. 33). If we consider reflection to be a spiral process, then the reflective practitioner might return repeatedly to the same element of practice (e.g. behaviour management) but each visit would involve a deeper response, acknowledging the practitioner's *stage of development.*

When looking at this spiral in a meta-reflective way, you need to step back. You can create your own analogy for this stepping back. *Helicoptering* is one that serves as an example: as you rise above the reflective process, the details of the reflective landscape (e.g. what you said to the class, how the pupils responded, how well you thought the lesson went) become less clear; the overall geography (e.g. the way your values shifted from the beginning to the end of a placement, the kinds of concerns that occupied your thoughts) becomes clearer. Meta-reflection is about reflecting on the whole reflective process, identifying themes and patterns, recognising changes in depth and breadth.

Take Anna, for example. Her initial concerns focused on pupils following the rules and ensuring that pupils were quiet. By the end of Placement A, she had developed a range of strategies to *manage classes effectively, using approaches which are appropriate to pupils' needs* (Teachers' Standard 7). She became much more aware that different pupils had different requirements, so by the beginning of Placement B her focus was on *adapting teaching to respond to the strengths and needs of all pupils* (Teachers' Standard 5), particularly those with English as an additional language (see Chapter 12 by Conteh). This in turn led her into developing her knowledge of approaches to assessment (Teachers' Standard 6). Her confidence in using formative assessment strategies developed but she recognised that she always prompted pupils to self- and peer-assess. By the beginning of Placement C, Anna's focus was on guiding learners to *reflect on the progress they had made and their emerging needs* (Teachers' Standard 2), characterised by the expectation that pupils would initiate self- and peer assessment (see Chapter 4 by Harris and Lowe).

Looking at this from a meta-reflective perspective, Anna might argue that her initial reflections were about getting the pupils to do what she told them. She was focused on establishing her authority, but was less aware of (or concerned about) the pupils as individuals. As her confidence in her classroom presence increased, she began to acknowledge pupils' individual needs, adapting her practice accordingly. In her final placement, her focus shifted to enabling pupils to operate independently. Anna could think about this process as a meta-reflective continuum, moving from *what I want pupils* to *learn to pupil decision-making*.

Summary

Descriptive accounts of your practice such as lesson evaluations and observations form a practical starting point for the reflective process. By questioning these accounts, concerns related to practice may emerge. Sometimes these concerns will relate to the cognitive dissonance between what you say you believe and what you do in practice. Resolution of this dissonance, in which *critical reflection on practice* (Ghaye and Ghaye, 2011) plays a part, is at the heart of the reflective process. As you gain experience and confidence, your engagement with reflection will become deeper and broader: a reflective spiral. By retaining a broad bank of evidence, and by organising and questioning this appropriately, you demonstrate reflective development. By stepping back from the evidence, a broader perspective emerges and opportunities to reflect on your own reflective development arise.

Questions for discussion

- How do you respond to unforeseen situations in the classroom? Why do you respond in this way?
- What are your *espoused theories* and what *cognitive dissonance* is there between these and your *theories in use*?
- What were your key concerns about practice at the start of your training? To what extent have these shifted as your experience has broadened?
- Where do you stand on the teacher-centred to pupil-centred continuum?
- What would a continuum which more effectively represented your own reflective development look like?
- What are the obstacles to your engagement with reflective practice? How might you overcome these?

Further reading

Boud, D. (2001) 'Using journal writing to enhance reflective practice', *New Directions for Adult and Continuing Education*, 90. Available at: https://pdfs.semanticscholar.org/64c3/dd98c303d082341aa39ffbeeb3d.
Boud discusses *occasions of reflection*, the ways that journal writing can be used, and identifies some of the barriers to journal writing.

Ewens, T. (2014) *Reflective Primary Teaching*. Northwich: Critical Publishing.
Ewens includes chapters on each of the Teachers' Standards, as well as a chapter on Part Two of the Standards. He uses an accessible framework for reflective tasks and encourages us to consider why something went well rather than focusing our thinking only on what was unsuccessful.

Hansen, A. (ed.) (2012) *Reflective Learning and Teaching in Primary Schools*. London: Learning Matters.
Hansen presents a range of approaches to improving teaching and learning, including chapters on encouraging children's reflectiveness and on using children's talk.

Illeris, K. (2006) *How We Learn: Learning and Non-learning in School and Beyond*, second edn. Abingdon: Routledge.
Illeris discusses models of learning and suggests versions that might better reflect reality.

Roche, M. (2011) 'Creating a dialogical and critical classroom: Reflection and action to improve practice', *Educational Action Research*, 19 (3): 327–43.
Roche chronicles her journey, as an experienced teacher, from a silent, passive classroom to one in which children have the confidence and capacity to participate fully. She notes that children's questions led her to 'critique practices and norms'.

References

Boud, D., Keogh, R. and Walker, D. (eds) (1985) *Reflection: Turning Experience into Learning*. Abingdon: RoutledgeFalmer.

Boydston, J. (ed.) (1984) *John Dewey: The Later Works Volume 2: 1925–1927*. Carbondale, IL: SIU Press.

Brookfield, S. (1987) *Developing Critical Thinkers: Challenging Adults to Explore Alternative Ways of Thinking and Acting*. Maidenhead: Open University Press.

Bruner, J. (1960) *The Process of Education*. Harvard, CT: Harvard University Press.

Ghaye, A. and Ghaye, K. (2011) *Teaching and Learning through Reflective Practice*, second edn. London: David Fulton.

Illeris, K. (2006) *How We Learn: Learning and Non-learning in School and Beyond*, second edn. Abingdon: Routledge.

Kolb, D. (1984) *Experiential Learning: Experience as the Source of Learning and Development*. Englewood Cliffs, NJ: Prentice Hall.

Moon, J. (1999) *Reflection in Learning and Professional Development*. Abingdon: RoutledgeFalmer.

Pollard, A. (2014) *Reflective Teaching in Schools*, fourth edn. London: Bloomsbury.

Schön, D. (1987) *Educating the Reflective Practitioner: Toward a New Design for Teaching and Learning in the Professions*. San Francisco, CA: Jossey-Bass.

Tripp, D. (2012) *Critical Incidents in Teaching: Developing Professional Judgement*. Abingdon: Routledge.

18

Statutory Professional Responsibilities

Nerina Díaz

By the end of this chapter, you should understand:

- the differences between statutory and non-statutory legislation, how they inform school policies and the implications for you as a teacher
- how statutory and non-statutory legislation is made and how it is changed
- that interpreting professional values can involve ethical dilemmas requiring discussion and reflection and examination of your personal values.

Introduction

This chapter explains what is meant by statutory responsibility. It explores the implications of statutory legislation. The examples cover employment, the curriculum, race relations, inclusion, and safeguarding children's health and well-being. The chapter explores the implications of statutory legislation through scenarios and examples of events you may encounter in school. As you will by now be aware, education is integrally connected with politics. Therefore, changes in government are frequently accompanied by changes in educational legislation, which are inevitably value-laden and controversial. As a professional educator and a citizen, it is important that you have an informed view about proposed changes and are prepared to participate in debates about them. This chapter will raise your awareness of these issues.

Legislation, statutory instruments and non-statutory guidance

Education in the United Kingdom is the responsibility of devolved national governments: the Northern Ireland government, the Scottish government and the Welsh Assembly government. Education in England is the responsibility of the UK government. Teachers' professional duties are framed by legislation, statutory instruments, and statutory and non-statutory guidance. The latest Education Act to receive Royal Assent was in 2011. It amended parts of the Education Act 2002, but statutory legislation still refers to areas of this act that remain applicable.

Legislation

Legislation, statutory instruments (which provide the necessary detail that would be considered too complex to include in the body of an Act) and statutory guidance are all legal documents that teachers should comply with. Schools and Local Authorities must follow statutory guidance unless they can show they are doing something just as good or better. The Department for Education's (DfE) *Induction for Newly Qualified Teachers 2016* (DfE, 2016a) is an example of statutory guidance. Statutory guidance is indicated within the first few pages of a government report and is available on the government websites.

Non-statutory guidance

Schools do not have a legal duty to adhere to non-statutory guidance. They may, however, find it helpful in understanding their duties and in deciding how they should implement the statutory requirements. For example, the pamphlet, *Religious Education in English Schools* (DCFS, 2010) is non-statutory. However, there is a statutory requirement for a head teacher and governing body to establish a behaviour policy for a school, and there is non-statutory guidance to help with this process (see Chapter 9, Ellis and Tod).

Legislative procedure

Legislative procedure consists of a Bill going through several stages in both the elected House of Commons and the unelected House of Lords before being enacted by royal consent and becoming an Act of Parliament. This Act is binding, even if, after a general election, the governing party does not support the policies enshrined. It requires a new Act of Parliament to supersede any existing Acts. When a general election is announced, the government needs to decide which Bills to proceed with before parliament is dissolved – this is called the 'wash-up'. Some Bills do not survive the 'wash-up', even though the Act has been anticipated and potential statutory information has been made available in the public domain. The incoming government may then withdraw the proposed legislation. This happened with the Rose Review of the National Curriculum for England and Wales, which was published in 2009. Many schools were creating strategies for implementing the new curriculum, which was withdrawn by the Conservative/Liberal Democrat Coalition government in 2010. Consequently, the National Curriculum framed in the Education Act 2002 remained statutory in England until it was replaced by new legislation. By 2017 the National Curriculum for maintained schools remained under the direction of the 2002 Education Act, but the curriculum for academies should be in accordance with the 2010 Academies Act.

Statutory frameworks within which you work

Induction and qualified teacher status

Teaching in England

Anyone wishing to work as a qualified teacher in a maintained school or non-maintained special school in England, including a maintained nursery school or a pupil referral unit, must have qualified teacher status (QTS) and have completed an induction period equivalent to three school terms. The National College for Teaching and Leadership (NCTL) is the competent authority in England for the teaching profession, being responsible for the award of QTS on behalf of the Secretary of State. At present it can also award QTS to trained teachers from the European Economic Area (EEA) and Swiss nationals, although when the UK leaves the European Union (EU) there may be implications for this arrangement. Overseas trained teachers can also apply for QTS.

The Induction Arrangements for School Teachers (England) Regulations 2012, underpinned by the Education Act 2002, are effective from September 2012 with further statutory guidance published in 2016 (DfE, 2016a). A significant element of the induction regulations is that newly qualified teachers (NQTs) may only complete induction in relevant institutions. Normally, these would be in the maintained sector. Independent schools, including academies, free schools and British schools overseas, may choose to offer statutory induction to their NQTs, but if they do so, must adhere to the regulations and statutory guidance. If you are considering applying for your first job in a setting other than a maintained school, you are advised to check whether you are able to complete your induction year there. If you are considering taking a post in a nursery setting, you are also advised to find out whether the post is suitable for induction. If you never intend to work in the maintained sector, there is no requirement to complete an induction period.

Note though that, whilst NQTs are encouraged to start their induction as soon as possible after gaining QTS, there is no requirement to complete induction within a certain time frame. There is a time limit on doing supply teaching, which is now 5 years from the date of QTS. During this period you can do as much supply as you want – odd days or years. After this your supply must count towards your induction period and must be for at least a term. But you do not have to do the whole induction period in one school, or even consecutively.

Schools requiring special measures are not able to offer induction, except in cases where the Office for Standards in Education (Ofsted) have judged a school, or part of a school, to be suitable to host induction. However, if you have already started your NQT year before the school entered special measures you may continue with the induction.

Head teachers and principals have the responsibility to ensure that an NQT has an appropriate induction programme, provided by a nominated induction tutor, and make a recommendation to the appropriate body on whether the NQT has met the Teachers' Standards. Overseas trained teachers can choose to be assessed against the Teachers' Standards at the same time as QTS standards. If they choose not to, or do not meet these standards, they will be required to undertake induction like any other NQT.

An NQT has only one chance to complete statutory induction. An NQT who has completed induction, and is judged to have failed to meet the relevant standards at the end of their induction period, is not permitted to repeat induction (although they may appeal against the decision). This does not, however, result in a loss of QTS, but they cannot be employed in a maintained school and their name is included on the list of persons, held by the Teaching Agency, who have failed to satisfactorily complete an induction period.

There is no legal requirement to satisfactorily complete an induction period if an NQT intends to work solely in the independent sector, including an academy, a free school, an independent nursery school or further education institution.

An NQT cannot start their induction until their appropriate body has been agreed (see Table 18.1).

If you obtain a post in a teaching school it is important to note that a teaching school that is an accredited initial teacher education (ITT) provider cannot be the appropriate body for an NQT for whom it recommended that the award of QTS

Table 18.1   Types of institution in which an NQT may be employed, and the body responsible for managing the induction process, in each type of institution

Type of institution	Appropriate body
Community, foundation or voluntary schools	A Local Authority with which the school reaches agreement
Community or foundation special schools	A teaching school (subject to the conditions)
Maintained and non-maintained nursery schools or children's centres	The National Induction Panel for Teachers (NIPT)
Non-maintained special schools	The Local Authority in which the school is situated, if agreement cannot be reached with one of the above
Pupil referral units (PRUs)	
Academies, free schools or city technology colleges	A Local Authority with which the school reaches agreement
	A teaching school (subject to the conditions)
Other independent schools including independent nursery schools	The NIPT
British Schools Overseas	The Independent Schools Teacher Induction Panel (ISTIP) (for their members and associates or additional members only)

should be made, nor can a teaching school be the appropriate body for an NQT whom it employs, or who has served any part of their induction at that school.

Once an NQT has been appointed, the head teacher must notify the appropriate body in advance of the NQT taking up the post, otherwise the start of the induction period may be delayed. At registration the appropriate body should provide the NQT with a named contact with whom they may raise any concerns about their induction programme that they are unable to resolve. This person should not be directly involved in monitoring or supporting the NQT nor in making decisions about satisfactory completion of induction

The duties assigned to the NQT and the conditions under which they work should be such as to facilitate a fair and effective assessment of the NQT's conduct and efficiency as a teacher against the relevant standards.

The head teacher/principal of the institution and the appropriate body are jointly responsible for ensuring that the supervision and training of the NQT meets their development needs. As an NQT you must be provided with the necessary employment tasks, experience and support to enable you to demonstrate satisfactory performance against the relevant standards throughout and by the end of the induction period:

- You should have an induction tutor with QTS.
- You should have a reduced timetable to enable you to undertake activities in the induction programme. This should consist of no more than 90 per cent of the timetable of other mainscale teachers in the school. This is in addition to the timetable reduction in respect of planning, preparation and assessment time (PPA) that

all teachers receive. NQTs in independent schools, including academies and free schools, independent nursery schools and further education colleges must also have a reduced timetable on a comparable basis, but it is important to note that independent schools are not obliged to provide PPA time.

- You should not be subject to unreasonable demands; including not normally being required to teach outside the age range and/or subject(s) for which you have been employed to teach.
- You should not be expected to deal, on a day-to-day basis, with discipline problems that are unreasonably demanding for the setting.
- You should be regularly teaching the same class(es).
- You should be involved in similar planning, teaching and assessment processes to those of other teachers working in similar posts.
- You should not be expected to be involved in additional non-teaching responsibilities without the provision of appropriate preparation and support.
- You should receive a suitable monitoring and support programme, personalised to meet your professional development needs (see Chapter 16, Boyd, and Chapter 19, Darbyshire, Harrop and Duckworth). This must include:

  o Support and guidance from a designated induction tutor who holds QTS and has the time and experience to carry out the role effectively.
  o Observation of your teaching and follow up discussion. Observations may be undertaken by your induction tutor or another suitable person who holds QTS from inside or outside the institution.

- You should meet with the observer to review any teaching that has been observed. Feedback should be prompt and constructive. Arrangements for review meetings should be made in advance and a brief written record made on each occasion. It should indicate where any development needs have been identified.
- You should receive regular professional reviews of progress, which are informed by evidence from your teaching. Objectives should be reviewed and revised in relation to the relevant standards and your needs and strengths. You should record evidence of progress towards objectives and agreed steps to support you in meeting your objectives. Evidence should come from practice. You will have three formal assessments during the year, and formal assessment forms completed for the first two assessments. The final assessment is at the end of the induction period and will form part of the induction report. Interim assessment is required if you leave a post during the induction year.
- You should have the opportunity for observation of experienced teachers either in your own institution or in another institution where effective practice has been identified.

The length of time required to complete NQT is normally one school year, with the minimum time contributing to the NQT, one school term, either full-time or part-time pro-rata. Extensions to the induction year may be agreed with the appropriate body for absence during the year or other reasons.

Cohort 1 teachers, those who completed QTS between 1 May 2000 and 30 April 2001, are required to have passed the numeracy skills test before they can satisfactorily complete induction.

The NCTL keeps records of teachers who have completed or part-completed induction, and these are available to employers. The NCTL also keeps records of all appeals. It is recommended that assessment reports are retained by both the institution and the appropriate body for a minimum of 6 years. You are advised to retain the original copies of your assessment reports.

Please be aware that legislation relating to induction, teaching, pay and conditions of service, and the curriculum in Wales, Scotland and Northern Ireland, is given in the references at the end of this chapter.

Teaching in Wales

Anyone wishing to teach in Wales is required to have QTS and to be registered as a qualified teacher with the Education Workforce Council (EWC). The requirements are set out in the School Teachers' Qualifications (Wales) Regulations 2012. The position on who may carry out teaching work in maintained schools or non-maintained special schools in Wales is also set out in the Education Workforce Council (Main Functions) (Wales) Regulations 2015.

NQTs are required to complete an induction period of three school terms or the period of time equivalent to 380 school sessions (one session is equivalent to a morning or afternoon of teaching), and NQTs without regular employment can accrue school sessions until 380 sessions have been completed.

From 1 September 2016, NQTs are required to complete the induction profile via the Professional Learning Passport on the EWC website. Support for NQTs includes a school-based mentor and an external mentor, as well as the head teacher. The appropriate body makes the final decision as to whether the NQT has completed induction satisfactorily.

The roles and responsibilities of the different parties involved in induction of NQT are stated in the *Learning Wales, Raising Standards Together* document (2016) as follows.

Trainee and newly qualified teachers

- Build on their Career Entry Profile (CEP).
- Complete their Professional Learning Passport (recommended but not currently mandatory).

- Actively engage with mentoring support provided.
- Participate in training and development activities.
- Take responsibility for their ongoing professional learning and use self-review to identify priorities for further development.
- Identify and agree opportunities for lesson observations.
- Identify and maintain a record of evidence of meeting the Practising Teacher Standards (PTS).
- Ensure EWC is kept fully informed of status and is notified of each period of employment.

School-based mentor (SBM)

- Provide day-to-day coaching and mentoring support to the NQT throughout the induction period.
  - Liaise with the external mentor (EM).
  - Agree NQT's professional learning priorities for the year based on CEP and PTS.
  - Observe the NQT teaching.
  - Support the NQT in identifying evidence of meeting the PTS.
  - Provide evidence to the EM of NQT's progress.
  - Liaise with appropriate body as required.

Head teacher

- Assign an SBM to provide day-to-day support as part of the school's overall mentoring arrangements.
- Ensure the NQT receives a 10 per cent reduced timetable in addition to the 10 per cent reduction for PPA.
- Ensure School Development Plans take account of the professional learning needs of NQTs.
- Ensure observation arrangements form part of the school's overall arrangements for sharing best practice.
- Ensure NQTs have access to the range of experiences necessary to meet the PTS.
- Work in collaboration with the SBM and EM to provide evidence that will contribute to the final assessment.
- Provide EWC with required notifications.

External mentor

- Meet the NQT at least twice in the year.
- Quality assure induction arrangements by working with other EMs, the SBM and head teacher.

- Provide additional mentoring support to the NQT.
- Support NQTs undertaking the Master's in Educational Practice (MEP).
- Monitor NQTs' progress in meeting priorities.
- Observe the NQT teaching.
- Gather assessment evidence from the head teacher and SBM.
- Assess induction profile against PTS.
- Make a recommendation on assessment to the appropriate body.
- Provide evidence to the appropriate body.
- The MEP for NQTs commencing their induction period has been withdrawn for new students. However this does not mean Master's level work is irrelevant: on the contrary, Boyd (Chapter 16), and Darbyshire, Harrop and Duckworth (Chapter 19) discuss strategies for high calibre continuing professional development.

Teaching in Scotland

It is a legal requirement for any teacher teaching in a Scottish school, state or independent, to be registered with GTC Scotland (GTCS). Teachers who qualified outside of Scotland are not automatically allowed to teach. If you qualified outside Scotland you must apply for registration and be assessed against 'Registration and Standard Rules and the Statement of Principles and Practice'. You may also be asked to undertake an initial period of probation. If you gained QTS without a Postgraduate Certificate in Education (PGCE), you will need to complete a PGCE top-up award, currently available through the University of Northampton.

On successful completion of a PGCE, graduates attain the Standard for Provisional Registration (SPR). To meet the Standard for Full Registration (SFR), graduates undertake a period of probationary teaching. The Scottish government guarantees a 1-year (190 teaching days) probationary placement on the Teacher Induction Scheme (TIS) for all eligible graduates in public sector schools. To be eligible for the TIS scheme, graduates need to have obtained a teaching qualification from a Scottish university and be a citizen of the EU.

Probationers in independent schools complete the Flexible Route. The Flexible Route also allows those not eligible, who do not wish to join the TIS, would prefer part-time work, or want to achieve full registration in a second subject, another way to gain the SFR. If you're undertaking the Flexible Route in public sector (state) schools, it will be through supply work and fixed-term contracts. This means that the length of probation service will vary and be partly dependent on employment opportunities. For those on fixed-term contracts or long-term supply, the probation year should follow a fairly structured process. Those on short-term supply may find that the process is much less structured. It is the NQT's responsibility to ensure that the interim and final reports are completed satisfactorily. Probation teachers following this route have 5 years to achieve SFR.

Probationers may be given a place in one of five preferred authorities they choose, or they can choose to go on the Preference Waiver Scheme, which offers an £8000 incentive payment to secondary teachers and £6000 payment to primary teachers to undertake their probationary year in any authority the GTCS chooses. All graduating initial teacher education (ITE) students are guaranteed a 1-year training contract with a reduced maximum class commitment time, the remaining time being available for professional development. Probation will be limited to 1 year and permanent employment restricted to fully registered teachers.

Teaching service elsewhere in the UK may be acceptable towards reaching the SFR, as long as it is relevant to your teaching qualification, and interim and final reports are submitted to the GTCS.

In independent schools, probationers have access to a similar experience to those completing the TIS. However, due to the different alignment of the school year, probation can take up to 270 days to complete and probationers must find their own post. The Scottish Council for Independent Schools (SCIS) offers an extensive professional learning programme to probationers.

Teaching in Northern Ireland

In Northern Ireland, you must register with the General Teaching Council Northern Ireland (GTCNI). The requirement to fully register applies to full-time, part-time and substitute teachers.

The Northern Ireland public (state) education is administered centrally by the Education Authority, created in 2015. Catholic schools fall under the jurisdiction of the Council for Catholic Maintained Schools (CCMS), but the Department of Education is responsible for promoting education and for ensuring implementation of policy.

Northern Ireland has introduced the concept of continuous professional development from the training stage. New entrants are required to complete a Career Entry Profile (CEP), which will inform development at induction level. When applying for jobs the CEP will be available to the principal and the governing body. On recommendation from the principal, a teacher will be able to pass through induction and begin the Early Professional Development programme (EPD). The period of induction lasts for 1 year, and if necessary, an extension of one term is allowed to demonstrate fulfilment of the required standards. A comprehensive description of the *Teacher Education Partnership Handbook* (2010) is available at: https://www.education-ni.gov.uk/sites/default/files/publications/de/the-teacher-education-partnership-handbook---august-2010.pdf.

Employment
Teachers' pay and conditions
England and Wales

There is a statutory document published by the government that refers to England and Wales. The *School Teachers' Pay and Conditions Document* (STPCD) (which may also be sometimes referred to as 'the blue book') outlines the standards and pay for the different grades of professional staff employed by all schools maintained by the Local Authority. It is a requirement that pay scales are reviewed annually. Schools with independent funding are not subject to the STPCD, and neither are state-funded academies or free schools, although in practice many schools follow the STPCD standards. Advice concerning pay and conditions for work in academies and free schools is available from teaching unions.

Whilst in Wales the conditions for pay are negotiated through the same body as England, other conditions of service are administered through the EWC. It undertakes, on behalf of the Welsh government, tasks in relation to the administration and confirmation of QTS, administering Induction including hearing Induction Appeals, the Master's in Educational Practice (MEP), Early Professional Development (EPD), and developing and hosting the Professional Learning Passport.

Scotland

In Scotland, negotiations about teachers' pay and conditions are dealt with by the Scottish Negotiating Committee for Teachers (SNCT), comprising representatives of teaching organisations, Local Authorities and the Scottish government. The *SNCT Handbook of Conditions of Service* (SNCT, 2007) gives full details of current agreements.

Northern Ireland

In Northern Ireland the terms of conditions on teachers' pay and conditions of service are decided by the Teachers' Salaries and Conditions of Service Committee (Schools), which is composed of the employing authorities/employer representatives, the Department of Education and the five recognised teachers' unions (Irish National Teachers' Organisation, National Association of Schoolmasters and Union of Women Teachers, Ulster Teachers' Union, Association of Teachers and Lecturers, and National Association of Headteachers).

There are several categories of school in Northern Ireland:

- controlled schools: these come under the control of the ELBs.
- maintained schools: these come under the control of the CCMS.
- voluntary grammar schools: these come under the control of the school's board of governors.

- grant maintained integrated schools: these come under the control of the school's board of governors.
- Irish-medium schools: these come under the control of the school's board of governors. These schools educate pupils through the medium of the Irish language.

Teachers in the controlled, maintained and voluntary sectors are paid by the Department of Education.

Reflective task

It is worth considering, throughout the whole of the UK, how the teachers' pay and conditions legislation is subject to changing policies.

In England, could national pay agreements be retained under the government's academy and free school ambitions? Could the unions' ability to negotiate pay and conditions be affected by government principles that any primary or secondary school judged outstanding by Ofsted can be fast-tracked to academy status, or that failing schools are mandatorily transformed into academies? How do multi-academy trusts affect pay negotiations? Is it going to be possible to retain any cohesive national England and Wales pay agreement? What would the implications of differing pay scales be for the teacher workforce and their interest for teaching in different schools?

Fitness to teach

In *England*, statutory regulations concerning fitness to teach are detailed in the Education (Health Standards) (England) Regulations 2003. The regulations indicate the prescribed activities that teachers should be fit for, and the procedure to be followed if a teacher is no longer considered fit for the job. However, employers also have a duty to have regard to the provisions of the Disability Discrimination Act 1995 and Equality Act 2010.

In *Wales*, guidance was drafted in 2013. Capability procedures (i.e. discipline and potential dismissal) for teachers can be instigated at any time. Governing bodies in Wales are required (by Regulation 7 of the Staffing of Maintained Schools (Wales) Regulations 2006/873) to establish procedures to deal with teacher capability and competence issues.

Schools must also take into account other statutory requirements such as the Employment Act 2002. The Employment Act requires that the following three steps are completed in all cases that may lead to dismissal:

- a statement in writing of what it is the employee is alleged to have done
- a meeting to discuss the situation
- the right of appeal.

In *Northern Ireland*, fitness to teach is determined by the board of governors in consultation with an occupational health physician and the Local Education Authority. There is an appeals procedure. The regulations can be found at:

https://www.education-ni.gov.uk/sites/default/files/publications/de/tnc-2013-1-termination-of-employment-ill-health-or-capability.pdf.

In *Scotland*, you will demonstrate fitness to teach against the Scottish Standards, detailed in the *Code of Professionalism and Conduct* published by GTCS in 2012. GTCS is responsible for regulating teachers' professional conduct and competence.

Work in school

Student 1:   My sister developed epilepsy in her twenties. I fear that this could happen to me. If it did, would I have to give up my career as a teacher?

Mentor: If you did develop epilepsy there should be no barrier to working as a class teacher or head teacher. Some people have faced barriers in getting the support they need but this is disability discrimination and is unlawful; however, decisions to continue to teach must be made on an individual basis. To support a person to carry out their duties safely, risk assessments, re-definition of role and reasonable adjustments might be needed. Depending on your support needs, your employer might want to talk about the job role. This will include possible 'reasonable adjustments' that can be made to the job. Reasonable adjustments can be made to help you to do the job effectively and to help keep you and the people in your care safe, should a seizure occur.

Student 2:   I understand that, as a teacher, I am responsible for the safety of the children in my care. But accidents do happen – and children should be allowed to take risks. So where do I stand if someone has an accident?

Mentor: You would need to demonstrate that all reasonable care had been taken, with regard to the age of the child, to prevent an accident in which a child is injured. For example, make sure a climbing frame is not too high for the safety of children who use it, and that there is a surface beneath it that will cushion a child's fall. If a floor is slippery, find a way to prevent children walking on it. Otherwise you could be considered legally responsible for a child being injured.

Teachers' conditions of service

The statutory requirements for teachers' conditions of service for maintained schools in England and Wales, which schools and Local Education Authorities must abide by, are set out in the *Conditions of Service for School Teachers in England and Wales*, sometimes referred to as 'the burgundy book' as it had a burgundy cover. This represents the national agreement between the six teacher associations and the Local Authorities and contains sections about:

- appointment, resignation, retirement
- sick pay scheme
- maternity scheme
- other leave
- grievance and disciplinary procedures
- miscellaneous conditions.

It also includes information concerning the following:

- premature retirement compensation
- memorandum of agreement for the release of teachers
- agreement on facilities for representatives of recognised teachers' organisations
- relations between teachers' organisations and Local Education Authorities: collective dispute procedures
- insurance and travelling allowances
- teachers and the school meals service.

If large numbers of schools become academies or free schools, negotiation of teachers' conditions of service may become unviable centrally, and unions may spend their resources on monitoring the variety of employment conditions within the education sector. Whilst all employers have to comply with employment legislation, this is related to EU employment legislation and may change once links to the EU are severed.

In Scotland, pay and conditions of service for teachers and associated professionals employed by Scottish Councils are set out in the *SNCT Handbook of Conditions of Service* (SNCT, 2007).

Contractual entitlements to leave

All teachers have the following contractual rights to leave of absence:

- for examinations
- for jury and other public service
- for accredited representation of recognised teachers' organisations.

Leave for other purposes

Although there are no national agreements for leave with or without pay for other purposes, such as participation in parliamentary elections or as a national representative in sport, an authority should make known to their teachers any provision they may have.

Leave of absence agreements and policies

It is important to distinguish between agreements that give rise to contractual entitlements and school policies that merely assist in the interpretation of the application of the contractual provision.

Leave of absence agreements established at Local Authority or diocesan levels may give rise to contractual entitlements for teachers. This occurs if an agreement is expressed in such a way as to give individual entitlements to teachers rather than giving 'advice' to governing bodies, and the teacher is employed by the Local Authority, or employed by a governing body which has accepted that such agreements are incorporated into the contracts of teachers at their school. There is no power for contractual agreements that have been established at Local Authority or diocesan level to be undermined at school level.

The following categories of absence are included in agreements and are usually taken as paid leave:

• hospital, GP, clinic and dental appointments
• compassionate leave for bereavement and illness of close relatives where there is a caring responsibility
• moving house
• accompanying children and close relatives to hospital or GP appointments
• domestic emergencies such as a gas leak or flood
• attendance at children's milestone celebrations, for example, graduations or school performances.

There may also be provision for leave for religious observance and celebration of festivals.

Discretionary leave arrangements

There is a potential for difficulty when diocesan or Local Authority policies contain certain categories of leave granted at the discretion of the head teacher and/or the governing body.

Academies (and academy trusts), free schools and independent schools will have their own contracts, which include terms and conditions. It is advisable to read the contracts carefully before committing to employment offers.

Professional conduct

England

Guidance for teachers' professional conduct was published in 2011 and is presented as Part One to the Teachers' Standards document (Part Two being the Teaching Standards). A series of seven statements defining expected behaviours and attitudes concern: relationships with pupils, safeguarding pupils' well-being, tolerance and respect for the rights of others, acceptance of British values including Rule of Law, individual liberty, respect and tolerance for those of different faith and belief, and the requirement for professional behaviour and understanding of statutory frameworks.

Regulation of the teaching profession is managed by the NCTL. The NCTL must consider any referrals it receives from any school, including academies, free schools and independent schools. If serious misconduct is proven, a teacher can be barred for life. The NCTL does not deal with minor misconduct, incompetence or underperformance. Guidance on procedure is given by the government in the document, *Teacher Misconduct: The Prohibition of Teachers* (NCTL, 2015).

Wales

Wales has a statutory self-regulating general teaching council (GTCW) whose function is to ensure teachers are properly qualified and to maintain high standards of conduct and practice. It publishes a code of professional conduct which is available at: www.gtcw.org.uk

Scotland

Scotland has an independent GTC, conferred in 2012. This is the world's first independent professional, regulatory body for teaching.

GTC publishes a 'Code of Professionalism and Conduct' (2012). Whilst the code is not statutory and thus guidance only, breaches of the code can lead to the imposition of sanctions.

Northern Ireland

The GTCNI was established in 2002 and publishes a 'Code of Values and Professional Conduct' (2004). The Council advises the Department and employing authorities on standards of conduct for teachers. It has powers to remove individual teachers from its register if it finds them guilty of misconduct or serious professional incompetence.

The cases below have come before GTCs and are examples of what is generally regarded as unacceptable professional behaviour.

Reflective task

1   Consider the case of a teacher who accesses the internet and emails excessively during lesson times. Is this acceptable?

Combined with knowledge of another action involving shoplifting, this teacher was given a reprimand (of 2 years).
  What are the implications of this case for teachers and trainee teachers?

2   Consider the case of a teacher having an evening out with friends and having a few drinks. The evening was cold and the teacher needed to use the toilet. As there were bushes nearby, he used those. The teacher was caught by police and cautioned for a public order offence.

The General Teaching Council for England (GTCE) found the teacher guilty of unacceptable professional conduct in that while a registered teacher he was cautioned for committing an act outraging public decency by behaving in an indecent manner.

Legislative framework guiding practice in maintained schools

The curriculum

Prior to 1988, there was no National Curriculum for England and Wales. Provision for the National Curriculum is found in the 1988 Education Reform Act. Originally comprising large detailed documents, by 1995 the National Curriculum was reduced and simplified and became a manageable point of reference for teachers. The National Curriculum has since been changed several times and the present version has been applicable from September 2016 (DfE, 2016b, 2016c) for Key Stages 1–4. This is statutory for all pupils of compulsory school age in all Local Authority-maintained schools.

Academies, free schools and private schools are under no obligation to follow this curriculum.

Reflective task

What do you consider the advantages and disadvantages of a National Curriculum?

What might be the consequences for the concept of a National Curriculum if the majority of school provision is outside state provision?

What should the rationale be for a design of a National Curriculum, or an individual school curriculum? Are there advantages to having individual school curricula? In England if the majority of schools start working outside Local Authority control, how soon would it be before the education system returns to pre-National Curriculum times? Would the school classroom look very different to pre-1989 if this happened?

Early years

In 2006, the Childcare Act made provision for statutory requirements for children aged 0–5 years cared for in any setting other than the home. This is known as the early years foundation stage (EYFS). It details three elements considered necessary for learning and development and six areas to be covered. Early years education takes place in a variety of settings including state nursery schools, nursery classes and Reception classes within primary schools, as well as settings outside the state sector such as voluntary preschools, privately run nurseries and childminders.

In 2006, Sir Jim Rose published his final report of *The Independent Review of the Teaching of Early Reading* (DES, 2006), which made the recommendation that the teaching of phonics incorporated into early reading should be taught using synthetic phonics. Following the acceptance of the review recommendations, the National Curriculum was amended. The National Literacy Strategy and the National Numeracy Strategy, launched in 1998, were integrated into the National Primary Strategy, named *Excellence and Enjoyment* in 2003, followed by a renewed Primary Framework in 2006. All these documents were for guidance and did not include any statutory requirements.

The *Revised Statutory Framework for the Early Years Foundation Stage* was published in March 2014 (DfE, 2014), coming into effect in all early years settings, including non-maintained and independent settings, and school-based early years provision that is inspected by Ofsted from September 2014. The EYFS Framework and supporting guidance documents can be found at www.educationengland.org.uk/documents/pdfs/2014-eyfs-statutory-framework.pdf.

In Wales, children are entitled to a free part-time early years' place the term following a child's third birthday until they enter statutory education. These places can be in a maintained school or a non-maintained setting such as a voluntary playgroup, private nursery or childminder which is approved to provide education. The Foundation Phase is a holistic developmental curriculum for 3–7-year-olds based on the needs of the individual child to meet their stage of development.

In Scotland, local authorities have a duty to secure a place for every child starting from the beginning of the school term after the child's third birthday. Pre-school education can be provided by local authority centres, or private and voluntary providers under a partnership arrangement. The early years' curriculum is contained within the Curriculum for Excellence (2010).

In Northern Ireland pre-school education is designed for children in the year immediately before they enter Primary 1. Taking into account the starting age for compulsory education in Northern Ireland, this means children are aged between three years two months and four years two months in the September in which they enter their final pre-school year. The structure for Early Years education was published in 'Learning to Learn, A Framework for Early Years Education and Learning' (2013).

Assessment and Reporting Arrangements (ARA)

Assessment and reporting procedures differ for the four countries of the UK.

England

The Assessment and Reporting Arrangements (ARA) apply to maintained schools (other than hospital schools) with pupils in Key Stage 1 and Key Stage 2, including maintained special schools.

National Curriculum tests remain as statutory end of Key Stage assessments. From 2016, children were given a 'scaled score', where 100 represents the norm within a scale of 80–120 (DfE, 2016b, 2016c). Ofsted's inspections would be informed by both pupils' scores and whatever pupil tracking data schools choose to keep. Schools use their own approaches to formative assessment to support pupil attainment and progression. The assessment framework should be built into the school curriculum, so that schools can check what pupils have learnt and whether they are on track to meet expectations at the end of the Key Stage, and so that they can report regularly to parents.

Maintained nursery schools with pupils who reach the age of 6 before the end of the school year must administer the phonics screening check.

In 2017 the government published proposals to reform reception base-line testing and Key Stage 1 assessment.

If an academy's or free school's funding agreement includes an agreement to follow guidance issued by the Secretary of State for Education in relation to assessments and teacher assessment of pupils' performance, they must comply with the ARA and take part in statutory assessments on the same basis as maintained schools. Academies and free schools must have arrangements for monitoring the phonics screening check.

Children in early years settings

When a child is aged between 2 and 3, practitioners must review their progress, and provide parents and/or carers with a short written summary of their child's development in the prime areas. This progress check must identify the child's strengths, and any areas where the child's progress is less than expected. If there are significant emerging concerns, or an identified special educational need or disability, practitioners should develop a targeted plan to support the child's future learning and development involving other professionals.

In the final term of the year in which the child reaches age 5, and no later than 30 June in that term, the EYFS Profile must be completed for each child. This remains a statutory requirement for all children in registered settings in 2017. The Profile must reflect: ongoing observation; all relevant records held by the setting; discussions with parents and carers, and any other adults whom the teacher, parent or carer judges can offer a useful contribution. Each child's level of development must be assessed against the early learning goals. Practitioners must indicate whether children are meeting expected levels of development, or if they are exceeding expected levels, or not yet reaching expected levels ('emerging').

Wales

In 2016 the Welsh Government published the Statutory Assessment Arrangements for the End of Foundation Phase, and Key Stages 2 and 3. Learners will be assessed soon after entry to school, and at the end of the Foundation Phase (age seven years) and at the end of Key Stage 2. Headteachers of all maintained settings should implement the requirements fully, whilst those of non-maintained settings should 'be aware' of the requirements.

Scotland

Statutory assessment is to be re-introduced from 2017 with pilots taking place in 2016. All children in P1, P4, and P7 will be expected to take the tests. The results will inform teachers' judgements of pupil achievement within the Curriculum of Excellence levels.

Northern Ireland

From September 2012 statutory assessment arrangements were revised to support the Northern Ireland Curriculum. These include arrangements for assessment of the cross-curricular skills of Communication, Using Mathematics and Using ICT in Key Stages 1, 2 and 3.

Reflective task

What could the consequences be for schools if they are no longer using levels to indicate children's progress?

Has a statutory testing regime had definable effects on education systems, and are there any consequences for children's achievements or progression through the education system?

A wider strategy for improving children's lives: safeguarding children

Updated statutory guidance entitled *Working Together to Safeguard Children* was published by the DfE in March 2015. Following on from the Children Act 2004, which considered that collaboration between both schools and other agencies was considered essential to achieving objectives of an *Every Child Matters* agenda, the guidance details methods of working partnerships across all public services children may come into contact with.

Statutory guidance specifically for schools, *Keeping Children Safe in Education*, was published in September 2016 (DfE, 2016d). All schools, state or privately funded, and further education institutions, have a duty to safeguard and promote the welfare of pupils. They are required to create and maintain a safe learning environment for children and young people, and identify where there are child welfare concerns and take action to address them, in partnership with other organisations where appropriate.

The Early Years Childcare Act 2006 also makes it clear that all registered providers, except childminders, must have a practitioner who is designated to take lead responsibility for safeguarding children within each early years setting and who should liaise with local statutory children's service agencies as appropriate. Early years services include children's centres, nurseries, childminders, preschools, playgroups, and holiday and out-of-school schemes.

It is deemed the responsibility of the employers to ensure their employees are confident and competent in carrying out their responsibilities, and are aware of how to recognise and respond to safeguarding concerns. They should ensure that all staff have read Part 1 of the guidance, *Keeping Children Safe in Education.*

Reflective task

What are the benefits and potential difficulties involved in multi-agency working?

Consider a situation in which a child's behaviour is causing you concern. You have, over the course of approximately 6 weeks, exhausted your repertoire of strategies to help the child, and the situation only appears to be getting worse. What are the next moves for an inexperienced teacher?

(a) Ask for the child to be moved to another class?
(b) Phone the parents?
(c) Discuss the situation with a trusted colleague, possibly the child's previous teacher?
(d) Discuss the situation with the pastoral team?

The ultimate answer should be (d). It is unwise to phone the parents without knowledge of the child's background, and without the sanction of senior staff to support you. Option (c) is an intermediate step. It is important that you do not lose confidence in your abilities as a teacher, and if you feel that you are disclosing your own inadequacies as a teacher to senior staff, it may be easier to discuss the situation with another colleague initially. Nevertheless, the child's needs are the priority. Once it is established that the child is at risk, there is a hierarchical procedure that should be followed, and the potential for a number of professionals to be involved.

Draft guidance from the National Institute for Health and Care Excellence (NICE, 2017) opined that signs of abuse are being missed because staff members were reluctant to investigate 'soft signs' of children's distress such as excessive clinginess, or persistent attention seeking. There was an implication that cultural restraints could be responsible for this lack of curiosity about children's behaviour. Do cultural sensitivities affect our understanding of child abuse, whether in the acceptance of behaviour towards a child, or in a preparedness to challenge behaviour towards a child?

Health and safety

Responsibility for health and safety derives from the 1974 Health and Safety at Work etc. Act 1974. It places overall responsibility for health and safety with the employer. For maintained schools, this is the Local Education Authority; for other schools, it is usually the governing body or the proprietor. As well as the health and safety of children, staff, visitors and volunteers to the school, education employers also have duties to the health and welfare of pupils and associated adults involved with off-site visits. The employer may delegate responsibility for health and safety to an employee, but retains ultimate responsibility (see also Chapter 11, where Batty and Metcalfe discuss safeguarding issues).

Employees also have duties. They should take reasonable care of their own and others' health and safety, informing the employer of serious risks, and cooperate with their employers by carrying out activities in accordance with training and instruction. Although the employer is responsible for health and safety, the employee can be implicated if they have failed to take notice of instructions and procedures.

In response to some schools becoming reluctant to offer children out-of-school activities, or that health and safety risk assessments were seen as very onerous paper-work, the English government published *Health and Safety: Advice on Legal Duties and Powers* (UK Government, 2014), noting that whilst some activities, especially those happening away from school, or infrequent or annual activities, continued to require assessment, schools need not carry out a risk assessment every time they undertake a regular activity that usually forms part of the school day. Routine activities should be considered when agreeing the school's general health and safety policies and procedures with a regular check to make sure the precautions remain suitable.

Reflective task

When taking children on a school trip, what situations may require you to be aware of the health and safety regulations? Consider issues that may arise when:

- taking children to public toilets
- a child or accompanying adult has an accident
- an accompanying adult behaves inappropriately.

Race relations
Human rights

The Universal Declaration of Human Rights (UDHR) set out, for the first time, fundamental human rights that are to be universally protected. There are 30 Articles in the UDHR describing fundamental human rights and Art. 26 is the right to education. After the UDHR the United Nations went on to develop specific Conventions to cover a range of issues, for example, disability, racism, women's rights. The Race Relations (Amendment) Act (2000) places three general duties on all schools and other public bodies:

- to eliminate discrimination
- to promote equality of opportunity
- to promote good race relations.

All schools are required to:

- actively promote 'race' equality
- prepare a 'race' equality policy
- monitor attainment by ethnicity, using new, electronic data systems
- monitor exclusions by ethnicity
- monitor progress and make such information publicly available.

Schools have a legal responsibility to monitor and record any racist incidents. Inexperienced teachers may feel bound by the school's practices. The school's anti-racist or 'race' equality policy should set out suggestions for a response, but you are within your rights to point out that you think the response is inappropriate.

Reflective task

Consider the consequences of advice to ignore a racist comment overheard in the playground, with the view that the children 'don't mean anything by it'.

There are many factors that might determine your response, but consider whether ignoring the comment is a dereliction of your legal duty. Overt ways of responding might include involving the senior management team to talk to the perpetrators, contacting parents/carers to discuss the school's concerns, talking to the victims of the name-calling and, ultimately, if the name-calling persists, seeking advice from the Local Authority.

Pre-empting the situation could reflect a wider school ethos. How could this be achieved through the curriculum planning? Would this planning be suitable for monocultural schools?

Residential and boarding schools also have to comply with Ofsted National Minimum Standards (NMS) intended to safeguard and promote the welfare of children who live (board) at a boarding school.

In Northern Ireland, equality and human rights are mainstream responsibilities for the DoE.

Community cohesion

As a result of the Education and Inspections Act 2006, a new section 21(5) was inserted into the Education Act 2002, introducing a duty for the governing bodies of maintained schools to promote community cohesion as from September 2007.

Non-statutory guidance was published in 2007, and Ofsted was required to report on schools' performance from September 2008.

Legislation relevant to community cohesion includes the Equality Act 2006, the Race Relations (Amendment) Act 2000 and the Children Act 2004.

> Community cohesion is defined in the guidance as: working towards a society in which there is a common vision and sense of belonging by all communities; a society in which the diversity of people's backgrounds and circumstances is appreciated and valued; a society in which similar life opportunities are available to all; and a society in which strong and positive relationships exist and continue to be developed in the workplace, in schools and in the wider community. (DCSF, 2007)

The *Guidance on the Duty to Promote Community Cohesion* (DCSF, 2007) is grouped under three headings:

- teaching, learning and curriculum
- equity and excellence
- engagement and extended services.

Reflective task

Use these headings as a guide. How could you create a learning environment that will ensure your class community is cohesive? Consider issues such as valuing diversity, the concept of citizenship, human rights, removing barriers to participation, links with other communities, and opportunities for families and the wider community to take part in activities.

Think about your physical classroom environment, yourself as a role model, your approach to the curriculum, and your contact and relationship with parents and the wider community.

The guidance acknowledges that schools cannot compensate for all societal tensions. What are the potential barriers when planning activities encouraging community cohesion and how can these be mitigated?

Understanding children's rights

The UK ratified the Convention on the Rights of the Child (UNCRC) on 16 December 1991. All children, without exception, have entitlements to over 40 specific rights. (See www.unicef.org/crc/ for more information.) The Children's Commissioner for England, responsible for promoting awareness of children's views, interests and other rights guaranteed by the Convention, must make an annual report to parliament. A horrific case of neglect leading to the death of Victoria Climbié, led to the passing of the Children Act 2004, providing a legislative spine for developing more effective and accessible services focused around the needs of children, young people and families. *Every Child Matters: Change for Children* (ECM) was published in November 2004, and is concerned with the well-being of children and young people from birth to age 19.

The government's aim was for every child, whatever their background or their circumstances, to have the support they need to:

- be healthy
- stay safe
- enjoy and achieve
- make a positive contribution
- achieve economic well-being.

This document remains a guiding force, despite subsequent governments' attempts to withdraw the advice. At present they are content with efforts to re-name the advice as 'Help Children Achieve More'.

Inclusion

The National Curriculum states that schools should provide relevant and challenging learning for all children. There are three principles set out in the statutory inclusion statement:

- setting suitable learning challenges
- responding to pupils' diverse learning needs
- overcoming potential barriers to learning and assessment for individuals and groups of pupils.

Reflective task

Take each of the five aims of the ECM agenda and consider how you can ensure that you fulfil the five aims for *all* the children in the school. This could be through whole-school activities, class-based activities, out-of-school activities or individual actions. Consider how you can incorporate these into daily activities.

Identify areas of the agenda that are susceptible to ideological influence (bearing in mind these are cross-agency aims), and consider the consequences for child welfare.

Summary

This chapter has explained the legislation upon which teachers' employment and professional duties are framed. It has outlined the differences between statutory and non-statutory guidance, and the implications of legislation for changes in government policy. Teachers' conditions of employment were explored from both the employers' and employees' perspectives. Statutory professional responsibilities for the curriculum, assessment and reporting, the *Every Child Matters* agenda, including understanding about children's rights, inclusion, safeguarding children, community cohesion, health and safety and race relations were also explained.

For current legislation and guidance, visit the relevant government websites. For commentary and explanation of legislation and guidance, visit the union websites. The largest unions for England are the National Union of Teachers (NUT) (http://teachers.org.uk) and the National Association of Schoolmasters Union of Women Teachers (NASUWT) (www.nasuwt.org.uk). Other teachers' unions are Voice (www.voicetheunion.org.uk/) and the Association of Teachers and Lecturers (ATL) (www.atl.org.uk).

Questions for discussion

These questions ask what you know about your responsibilities as an employee (guidance for answering these questions can be found in the chapter):

- Do you know how to access the school's risk assessment documents?
- Are you sure that every child in your class is treated equally, free from discrimination and any sort of bullying?
- Does every child in your class experience challenging activities suitable for their abilities?
- Do your activities involve and respect the community you serve?
- Are you aware of the school procedure if you are concerned about a child's health and well-being?
- Are you keeping records that will enable you to write a constructive and comprehensive report for the children's parents?

These questions ask what you know about your employer's responsibilities to you (guidance for answering these questions can be found in the chapter):

- Are you aware of the terms and conditions of your employment if you are not in a mainstream state school?

- Do you know the pay scales and possible progression you could make through them?
- Are you aware of what you should do if you think you require time off? Will there be tensions between family or cultural expectations and your conditions of employment? How can you resolve these?
- Are you aware of who can help you if you have a dispute with your employer?

References and further reading

England

Department for Children, Schools and Families (DCSF) (2007) *Guidance on the Duty to Promote Community Cohesion*. Nottingham: DCSF. Available at: http://webarchive.nationalarchives. gov.uk/20130401151715/https://www.education.gov.uk/publications/eOrderingDown load/DCSF-00598-2007.pdf.

Department for Children, Schools and Families (DCSF) (2009*) Independent Review of the Primary Curriculum: Final Report*. London: DCSF. Available at: www.educationengland. org.uk/documents/pdfs/2009-IRPC-final-report.pdf.

Department for Children, Schools and Families (DCSF) (2010) *Religious Education in English Schools: Non-statutory Guidance*. Available at: www.re-handbook.org.uk/media/display/ Religiouseducationguidancein-ennglish-schools2010.pdf (accessed 4 September 2017).

Department for Education (DfE) (2012) *Statutory Framework for the Early Years*. Available at www. foundationyears.org.uk/wp-content/uploads/2012/07/EYFS-Statutory-Framework-2012.pdf.

Department for Education (DfE) (2013a) *The National Curriculum in England*. London: DfE. Available at: https://www.gov.uk/government/uploads/system/uploads/attachment_data/ file/244223/PRIMARY_national_curriculum3.pdf.

Department for Education (DfE) (2013b) *Working Together to Safeguard Children (2013)*. London: DfE. Available at: www.workingtogetheronline.co.uk/documents/Working%20 TogetherFINAL.pdf.

Department for Education (DfE) (2013c) *Teachers' Standards*. Available at: https://www.gov.uk/ government/uploads/system/uploads/attachment_data/file/301107/Teachers_Standards.pdf.

Department for Education (DfE) (2014) *Statutory Framework for the Early Years Foundation Stage*. London: DfE. Available at: www.educationengland.org.uk/documents/pdfs/2014-eyfs-statutory-framework.pdf.

Department for Education (DfE) (2016a) *Induction for Newly Qualified Teachers (England) Statutory Guidance for Appropriate Bodies, Headteachers, School Staff and Governing Bodies*. Available at: www.gov.uk/government/publications.

Department for Education (DfE) (2016b) *2017 Key Stage 1 Assessment and Reporting Arrangements*. Available at: https://www.gov.uk/government/publications/2017-key-stage-1-assessment-and-reporting-arrangements-ara.

Department for Education (DfE) (2016c) *2017 Key Stage 2 Assessment and Reporting Arrangements*. Available at: https://www.gov.uk/government/publications/2017-key-stage-2-assessment-and-reporting-arrangements-ara.

Department for Education (DfE) (2016d) *Keeping Children Safe in Education*. Available at: https://www.gov.uk/government/uploads/system/uploads/attachment_data/file/550511/Keeping_children_safe_in_education.pdf.

DfE (2016e) *2017 Early Years Assessment and Reporting Arrangements*. Available at: https://www.gov.uk/government/publications/2017-early-years-foundation-stage-assessment-and-reporting-arrangements-ara.

Department of Education and Skills (DES) (2006) *Independent Review of the Teaching of Early Reading*. Available at: https://www.education.gov.uk/publications/.../0201-2006pdf-EN-01.pdf.

National College for Training and Leadership (NCTL) (2015) *Teacher Misconduct: The Prohibition of Teachers*. Available at: https://www.gov.uk/government/publications/teacher-misconduct-the-prohibition-of-teachers--3.

UK Government (2014) *Health and Safety: Advice on Legal Duties and Powers*. Available at: https://www.gov.uk/government/uploads/system/uploads/attachment_data/file/335111/DfE_Health_and_Safety_Advice_06_02_14.pdf.

Scotland

General Teaching Council for Scotland (GTSC) (2012) *The Student Teacher Code*. Available at: www.gtcs.org.uk/web/files/teacher-regulation/student-teacher-code-0412.pdf.

General Teaching Council for Scotland (GTSC) (2016) *Code of Professionalism and Conduct*. Available at: www.gtcs.org.uk/fitness-to-teach/complaints/copac.aspx.

GTC Scotland (n.d.) 'Into teaching'. Available at: www.in2teaching.org.uk/home/about.aspx.

Scottish Government (2011) *Curriculum for Excellence. Building the Curriculum 5: A Framework for Assessment*. Available at: www.educationscotland.gov.uk/Images/BTC5_tcm4-605259.pdf.

Scottish Government (2012) *Getting it Right for Children and Families: A Guide to Getting it Right for Every Child*. Available at: www.scotland.gov.uk/Resource/0042/00423979.pdf.

Scottish Government (2016) *2017 National Improvement Framework and Improvement Plan for Scottish Education*. Available at: www.gov.scot/Resource/0051/00511513.pdf.

Scottish Government (2017) *Curriculum for Excellence*. Available at: www.gov.scot/Topics/Education/Schools/curriculum.

Scottish Negotiating Committee for Teachers (2007 with updates to 2017) *SNCT Handbook of Conditions of Service*. Available at: www.snct.org.uk/.

Northern Ireland

Council for the Curriculum, Examinations and Assessment (2017) Documents are available at: www.nicurriculum.org.uk.

NI Government (2004) *Code of Values and Professional Practice: Building Dynamic and Professional Communities*. Available at www.gtcni.org.uk/uploads/docs/gtc_code.pdf.

NI Government (2013a) *A Framework for Early Years Education and Learning*. Available at: https://www.education-ni.gov.uk/publications/framework-early-years-education-and-learning-october-2013.

NI Government (2013b) *TNC Circular 2013/1 Termination of Employment of Teachers on the Grounds of Ill Health or Capability*. Available at: https://www.education-ni.gov.uk/sites/default/files/publications/de/tnc-2013-1-termination-of-employment-ill-health-or-capability.pdf.

NI Government (2014) *Health and Safety on Educational Excursions A Good Practice guide*. Available at: https://www.education-ni.gov.uk/publications/pastoral-care-schools-child-protection.

NI Government (2016) *Overview of Teachers' Pay and Conditions.* Available at: https://www. education-ni.gov.uk/articles/overview-teachers-terms-and-conditions.

Perry, C. (2012) *Programme for Government Pre-school Commitment.* Available at: www.ni assembly.gov.uk/globalassets/documents/raise/publications/2012/education/3912.pdf.

Wales

Education Workforce Council (EWC) (2016–2017) *Fitness to Practice.* Available at: www.ewc. wales/site/index.php/en/about/what-is-the-ewc-and-what-do-we-do.

General Teaching Council for Wales (DERA) (2017) *Code of Professional Conduct and Practice for Registered Teachers.* Available at: http://dera.ioe.ac.uk/13734/1/GTCW_Professional_Code.pdf.

Welsh Government (2011) *Revised Professional Standards for Educational Practitioners in Wales.* Available at: http://learning.gov.wales/docs/learningwales/publications/140630-revised-professional-standards-en.pdf.

Welsh Government (2013a) *Safeguarding Children and Education: The Role of Local Authorities and Governing Bodies under the Education Act 2002 in 2010.* Available at: http://dera.ioe. ac.uk/18167/2/270813-draft-guidance-en.pdf.

Welsh Government (2013b) *Teaching and Teaching Qualifications.* Available at: http://dera. ioe.ac.uk/18052/1/240513-teaching-and-teachers-qualifications-en.pdf.

Welsh Government (2016a) *Learning Wales. Raising Standards Together.* Available at: http:// learning.gov.wales/resources/collections/induction?lang=en.

Welsh Government (2016b) *Foundation Phase.* Available at: http://gov.wales/topics/education andskills/foundation-phase/?lang=en.

Welsh Government (2016c) *Statutory Assessment Arrangements for the Foundation Phase and End of Key Stages 2 and 3.* Available at: http://learning.gov.wales/docs/learningwales/ publications/161011-statutory-assessment-arrangements-en.pdf.

General

National Association of Head Teachers (NAHT) (2015) *Health and Safety in Schools.* Available at: www.naht.org.uk/_resources/assets/attachment/full/0/48712.pdf.

National Institute for Health and Care Excellence (NICE) (2017) *Child Abuse and Neglect.* Draft copy for consultation. Available at: https://www.nice.org.uk/guidance/indevelopment/gid-scwave0708/documents.

Outdoor Education Advisors Panel (OEAP) (2017) *National Guidance for the Management of Outdoor Learning.* Available at: http://oeapng.info/.

Research

Research briefings informing education policy are available at:
http://researchbriefings.parliament.uk/
www.gov.scot/Topics/Research/by-topic/education-and-training
https://www.education-ni.gov.uk/topics/statistics-and-research-1
http://gov.wales/topics/educationandskills/?lang=en

19

Moving on to Master's Level

Carol Darbyshire, Sue Harrop and
Vicky Duckworth

By the end of this chapter you should be able to:

- identify what it means to be a 'professional' operating at level 7 and above
- recognise the links between continuing professional development, performance in the classroom, and the progress that pupils make
- have a strong awareness of the power of educational research to inform practice
- understand the expectations for writing at level 7.

Introduction

This chapter will critically examine teaching as a level 7 Master's professional. To frame the discussion it draws on the level 7 descriptors from the *Framework for Higher Education Qualifications of UK Degree-Awarding Bodies* (QCA, 2014). The key themes explored exemplify how pertinent statements from the framework are applied in a meaningful and critical way in practice. Therefore, rather than conceptualising 'Master's level' as a qualification, the chapter aims to define what it means to be a 'professional' operating at a high level in order to improve your own learning, performance in the classroom and, ultimately, the progress for your pupils. In order to do this we turn to the key areas signposted in the learning outcomes above, to frame the chapter in four sections that address the following themes: dealing with complex and unpredictable situations; research-informed practice; teacher as researcher; and an introduction to writing at level 7.

a) *Dealing with complex and unpredictable situations*

The descriptors for Master's degree (level 7) study require you to 'have the qualities and transferrable skills necessary to tackle and solve problems autonomously, to use initiative in order to make decisions in complex and unpredictable situations'. This requires the ability to confidently think critically to inform and shape practice.

b) *The purpose of thinking critically*

A driver for critical thinking is reflection. Reflection is a generic term that captures a process of intellectual consideration and exploration of practice, which practitioners undertake to improve their knowledge and skills to develop and refine their practice. In a nutshell it centres on nurturing the relationship between the teacher and the learner and facilitating quality practices that enable all to move forward with an enhanced understanding. Reflection is not a new concept. We only need to go back to the work of John Dewey and his classic text, *How we Think* (1910), for example, to see how it has informed the influential theories of both David Boud (Boud et al., 1985) and Donald Schön (1983), which are outlined below. Practitioners' attitudes towards reflection to improve practice differ. Many practitioners use reflection on an intermittent basis in reaction to unusual or negative experiences – perhaps a critical incident or dilemma. (See Chapter 17.) This is useful when interrogating strategies to move forward in a purposeful way. When used proactively, reflection becomes very effective, constructive and successful, which in turn positively impacts on teachers' confidence, resilience and self-efficacy. Examples of a critical incident being used as the basis for reflection during teacher training can be seen in the 'Work in School' vignette below.

c) *Reflective models and strategies*

Traditional reflective theories follow the same basic principle: that of learning through experience or, more specifically, learning through reflecting on experience. This requires the teacher to:

- describe a situation
- analyse possible causes
- identify alternatives and strategies for managing the same or similar situation through 'what if' scenarios
- decide on a new approach – and embed into own practice.

These stages are most clearly reflected in Boud's approach (Boud et al., 1985), where he invites practitioners to:

1. replay an event and document – and consider what happened
2. analyse the event at both a cognitive and emotional level
3. seek understanding – identify possible and/or actual reasons
4. plan different approaches and responses to enable change.

Kolb (1984) refers to this last point as active experimentation and Dewey (1938) as the testing of a hypothesis in practice. The testing in practice is critical for developing a continuous cycle of improvement and for developing the teacher's ability to respond to a wider range of classroom situations. According to Schön, there are two distinct means of reflection within the 'reflective practicum' or learning setting:

- reflection in action
- reflection on action.

Reflection in action is where practitioners think on their feet within a situation and make a decision to change the direction of the lesson. For example, during a mathematics lesson a practitioner may become aware that the children are finding the concept of multiplication difficult and therefore stops the class and undertakes a mini-plenary, the aim being to ensure that the lesson is moving forward in an inclusive way and that all pupils are progressing.

Reflection on action takes place after the event. The practitioner will review the event, analyse and question what happened and why, leading to a deeper reflection and thought process on an aspect of practice, finally being able to suggest a new or different strategy. For example, in one particular situation, after a lesson teaching a class of primary pupils, a decision was made to probe the learning outcomes that had been set and the children's progress in relation to them. As a result of the reflection there was a decision to recap identified questions during a mental oral starter the following day in order to further structure the learning. Additionally a teaching assistant was positioned with an identified group of learners with a specific aim of supporting the scaffolding of their learning. Furthermore, an approach where, after the main input, children who feel confident start to work, whilst others, less confident, receive further input, was adopted. This strategy was very successful in differentiating learning and teaching and facilitating each pupil to reach their potential. Vitally, the outcome of the reflection on action was a clear indication of a higher level of cognition, which impacted on the transformation of a particular aspect of practice. Clearly, reflective teaching is a means of professional development, the continual journey towards quality learning and teaching, and a higher level of thinking and practice which begins in the classroom.

Reflective task

Reflection in action. Consider a time when you have reflected, on your feet, in a lesson. How has the shape of the lesson changed? What has the impact been on learning?

Reflection on action. Reflect on an occasion when you thought about a session that had not gone as planned: you thought about why, perhaps discussed it with colleagues or read more about why, then decided how to approach the problem differently in future.

The following are useful strategies to commence the reflective process in your own practice:

- begin a daily diary
- collate learner feedback
- engage in peer observation
- construct a personal journal.

These actions align meaningfully with the requirements that are expected of a novice, a trainee teacher and an experienced teacher. In producing an assessed piece of written work relating to professional practice, the purpose of thinking critically not only impacts on practice, but supports and enhances academic writing at Master's level – an idea that is explored in detail in a later section of this chapter.

Work in school

In order to explore reflection in more detail and its impact on practice, the following provide crucial think pieces for you to consider in relation to your own practice and application at level 7. Tripp (2011) identifies that 'critical incidents' are a starting point for improvements to practice through reflection. The studies below each explore a key incident that was a catalyst to facilitating higher thinking, reflection and reflexivity.

(Continued)

(Continued)

Study one

Student: It was my 7th week of an 8-week practice when I was faced with teaching phonics to a new group of children who were not part of my Year 2 class. The children were streamed for phonics. The 'incident' I found myself writing about and discussing was the moment a 6-year-old child refused to engage with activities and failed to respond to my usual effective and appropriate strategies, resulting in the deputy head teacher being called for and having to intervene, which left me feeling incapable and vulnerable.

Mentor: In listening to your description of the event I became less worried when I realised that you had initially been shocked by the incident but acknowledged the recognition that your normal strategies which were employed were not appropriate on this occasion. I was less worried when I realised that you acknowledged that you were not dealing with this in isolation but had called for a more senior member of staff – a clear illustration of reflecting *in* action (Schön, 1983). You also engaged in reflection *on* action (Schön, 1983), looking back at the incident in order to understand and initiate change for the following sessions. You worked through a range of strategies and successfully employed these in following sessions.

Study two

Student: During my final practice I was responsible for planning and delivering a science topic. The topic focus was on forces and during this particular lesson there appeared to be a critical incident for me in relation to the practical activities. I was on my own with a class of 28 children. I had set up trays and materials on each table and, following the whole-class input, I had planned for the children to go back to their tables and undertake the practical aspect of the session and to record their observations onto a recording sheet that had been prepared and left ready for the children to engage with. It was during the independent work that I suddenly realised that the expectation I had of how the children would work collaboratively was not taking place and, more

(Continued)

importantly, I was concerned that the learning outcomes of the lesson were becoming compromised. It was through the reflection-in-action that I decided to stop the activities and return all children to the carpet. Further reflection on the incident led me to re-plan the activities but to be supported by a teaching assistant. The outcome was a much richer learning experience for the children, the learning outcomes were achieved to an expected level and as a practitioner I felt that through reflecting, analysing and thinking I had now created a new way of approaching the teaching of science for myself, which will be implemented in future practices.

Analysis

The above scenarios highlight that practitioners do not only learn from experience and 'doing'. Indeed, as identified by Moon (1999), learning is positioned as more dynamic and bound to a process of reflection, either individually or alongside a more experienced mentor or tutor. The process of reflection facilitates practitioners to learn from their experiences and to utilise the knowledge gained from this to transform and further develop their practice. The impact of this includes the enhancing of personal and professional development (Nodding, 2016). If practitioners regularly use and apply reflective theory within their practice, it offers a deeper and more critical understanding of applications of practice and a rationale for pedagogical applications. Subsequently, the established insights allow practitioners to implement changes or transform their practice based on informed decisions, for example, from the empirical data generated from the reflections. This has the potential to impact upon higher quality learning experiences for children and, importantly, to develop the philosophical underpinnings that shape a practitioner's practice.

Emotional, as well as cognitive reflection

Whichever reflective model you choose (or do not choose) to draw on, self-reflection is more than simply thinking over and over about what has happened. Reflective practice is a cognitive (thinking) process that brings together several stages of considered exploration of thoughts, feelings and evaluations focused on practitioner skills and outcomes. The approach of Boud et al. (1985) also invites practitioners to analyse the event at both cognitive and emotional levels.

A focus on our emotional responses to reflection is important: trainee teachers can be critical of themselves in their self-evaluation. For example, although the mentor/class

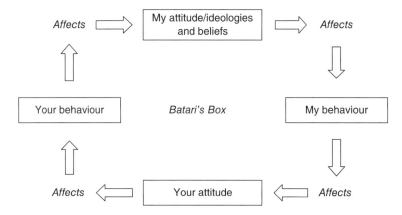

Figure 19.1   Batari's Box. (Roffey-Barentsen and Malthouse, 2013, p. 65)

teacher may feed back in a constructive professional manner, it can still be emotional when confronting the areas for development that have not gone to plan. This can be identified in the phonics lesson outlined above. Batari's box (Figure 19.1) illustrates how any interactions can affect the attitudes and behaviours of others. Indeed, how you personally think and feel can affect how you behave. This can inform the way others view us. We may be upset and this may be played out in an abruptness in behaviour. Other professionals cannot see what is being thought and felt, and the manifested behaviour may be construed as unprofessional. However, in order to ensure our behaviour is aligned to professionalism, we can move away from being reactive and instead change the way we receive information (feedback) from others and we can change our own behaviour to influence others (mentor/class teacher). This has the potential to support a more positive and developmental process. Indeed, the importance of self-reflection, and the need to reflect in order to effect change or action beyond the notion of self, cannot be underestimated as a professional teacher.

The school environment and reflection

Tarrant (2013) argues that in order to facilitate the 'reflective practitioner' schools need to have processes in place that allow this professional development to flourish; there needs to be an emphasis on:

•   strong reflective practice across the school
•   a framework for reflection
•   mentor support from colleagues

- introduction of personal portfolios to chart reflection and development
- discussions with senior members of staff, and target setting
- recordings of practice to enable practitioners to critically reflect on practice.

Daly et al. (2014) concur that if the above strategies are embraced by schools, this will result in a strong culture of reflective practice that will impact widely on the ability of practitioners to move forward professionally within a supportive environment, thus impacting on the ability of the school to move forward from within.

The specific nature of the outcome of reflection as identified above can vary: preparation for change (an action), confirmation/rejection of a theory or pedagogic approach or deeper understanding/generation of knowledge. Implicit within these outcomes is engagement with research literature. The development of a deeper understanding about an aspect of practice may inspire a practitioner to share their professional knowledge with other teachers. Similarly, the rejection of a theory may provide the motivation and curiosity for a teacher to carry out a small-scale classroom-based study. The idea of research-informed practice is explored later in this chapter.

Reflective task

Reflective teaching means looking at what you do in the classroom, thinking about why you do it and thinking about if it works – a process of self-observation and self-evaluation. Consider a scenario in your classroom to reflect on. Draw on a reflective model previously identified.

Teachers, schools and the challenges of the twenty-first century

We have reviewed the process of intellectual consideration and exploration of practice through reflection as a means of tackling and solving problems in the complex and often unpredictable situations that occur within a classroom. However, there is also a broader interpretation of 'complex and unpredictable situations'; for example, the educational challenges faced by teachers and schools in the twenty-first century. A report published in 2017 by the Teacher Education Exchange (a group of teachers, school leaders, teacher educators and researchers) envisions the kind of teachers and schools required to tackle what they describe as the demands, challenges and opportunities we face now and in the future (Teacher Education Exchange, 2017). They suggest that specific significant global challenges and their solutions are:

- *Global challenge 1*: The present reality of hyper-diverse and transient populations where society will need to ensure that respect for difference coupled with sustained attempts at inclusion are seen as *assets* for all of us. Teachers will need to listen and learn from one another.

Reflective task

How would you define 'hyper-diverse populations' in the context of twenty-first-century global challenges? How could you help your pupils to understand and respect 'difference'? How would you introduce the concept of difference in an appropriate and respectful way? Consider the language that you would use. How could your pupils listen to, and learn from, the hyper-diverse and possibly transient populations (children and families) that are associated with their school and neighbourhood? What opportunities are there in the curriculum and beyond for pupils to learn from one another? Think about the different types of primary school, for example, very small, rural versus large, inner-city, and the level of diversity that a pupil is likely to encounter (see Chapters 14 and 15).

- *Global challenge 2*: Poverty and inequality, as structural phenomena, are recognised as reducing so many people's prospects and mobility, and there is a commitment to eliminate these inequalities in order to build a more just society. Teachers can get their schools engaged in civic activities, and projects based on national charities such as 'Children in Need'.

Reflective task

Can this civic and charity-related activity be embedded into the primary curriculum? How and where? What are the opportunities for cross-curricular work? For example, how might children make use of data in order to develop their knowledge and understanding of poverty and inequality? Visit the Oxfam Education website to access a set of teaching resources that can be used to strengthen children's data handling skills. The activities would allow your class to take on an investigative role by collecting, analysing and visualising data about the lives of children in different countries. The lesson plans have clear links to the computing curriculum for upper Key Stage 2 pupils.

www.oxfam.org.uk/education/resources/data-power

- *Global challenge 3*: Environmental and sustainability challenges that are both understood and addressed by an agentic society and its schools. The hallmark of such a society would be collective agency and the ability to exercise control over the nature and quality of life (Bandura, 2001). Teachers will need to be politically literate as well as environmentally and scientifically aware.

Reflective task

How and where could this global challenge be introduced across the primary curriculum? For example, think of a project that a teacher might plan in order to support enquiry and collaborative problem solving activities in relation to a local environmental issue. Is it possible for children in the primary-age phase, as well as teachers, to be politically literate, plus environmentally and scientifically aware? How would you achieve this at an appropriate level for the children in your class?

- *Global challenge 4*: A society where technological and medical advances as well as imaginative approaches towards problem solving present new opportunities for creating a better world.

Reflective task

The computing curriculum suggests that pupils should understand that computational thinking and creativity can change the world. Lessons could therefore include opportunities to find out how the links between computing, mathematics, science, plus design and technology can be harnessed to create a better world. For example, a Google search will reveal how a simple clip-on lens for a smartphone can detect cataracts in minutes, which is helping many people in developing countries. What other examples of relatively simple yet imaginative technological solutions to world issues could you use with your pupils?

Philosophy for Children approach

Teachers might choose an approach known as Philosophy for Children (P4C) to help children to investigate global issues. This approach can facilitate ethical and philosophical conversations, promote open questions and investigations of how to be active in making a better world, and has the capacity to be open, to promote hard and critical questioning, and a built-in desire for teachers to keep learning and changing themselves (Teacher Education Exchange, 2017, p. 13).

We have presented a picture of a teacher who embraces professional reflection as a strategy to achieve successful outcomes – someone who is aware of their ability to enhance the life chances of the pupils in their classroom. Additionally, they are able to situate these outcomes in a more profound context and strive to prepare pupils to participate in a complex and unpredictable world. In this sense, there is a moral dimension to teaching, and we argue that this should be acknowledged and indeed be pivotal to the role of teachers as agents of change.

Teachers as agents of change?

Van der Heijden et al. (2015) carried out an exploratory study that provides an insight into what characterises primary teachers as change agents, and how they enact professional agency in their daily practice. These characteristics pertain to lifelong learning (being eager to learn and reflective), mastery (giving guidance, being accessible, positive, committed, trustful and self-assured), entrepreneurship (being innovative and feeling responsible) and collaboration (being collegial). Within the category entrepreneurship, 'being innovative' was mentioned most (p. 681). How the teachers use their agency and possible explanations for this behaviour are set out below.

Lifelong learning

Teachers take initiatives in order to develop themselves professionally and to improve or change their teaching practice. They ask themselves questions, and search for information to construct and reconstruct knowledge and ideas in order to be able to adapt their teaching practice or to solve problems. An explanation for this might be that teachers as change agents want to grow and develop themselves professionally from the 'inside'. They seem to strive to increase their expertise in teaching because they want to have a large impact on their students' learning and achievement. Chapter 16, 'Learning Teaching' in School, focuses on continuing professional development.

Mastery

Teachers continually strive to develop their expertise in teaching (not to be confused with mastery and assessment). A possible explanation for this would be that teachers who want to become change agents first have to develop their teaching skills to a level where they have a large impact on student learning and achievement.

Entrepreneurship

Teachers are proactive in using their agency to influence education. They are open to new insights, which they transform into opportunities for influencing or changing education at school. These change agents dare to take creative initiatives and calculated risks when experimenting with new educational approaches in their classrooms. They do not seem to be afraid of moving away from their current (possibly traditional) teaching practices. Explanations for this might be that teachers as change agents: (a) feel and take ownership of their own professional development and the quality of education at the school level in favour of their students; and (b) desire their work as a teacher to remain interesting and challenging. However, change agents also appear to be critical: they do not blindly embrace all new insights and changes at school. They use their agency in an entrepreneurial manner by taking creative initiatives accompanied by calculated risks. For many teachers in schools, the fear of taking risks might be a barrier to educational change and also, to some extent, the fear of not being appreciated by school leaders in a culture where external accountability measures are very dominant (Day et al., 2005; Le Fevre, 2014).

Collaboration

Teachers actively take initiatives in working with their colleagues. An explanation for this might be that teachers, as change agents, are aware of needing others to further develop themselves, their teaching practice and education at the school level. Collaborative expertise and being a member of a professional community are interconnected and relevant for changing education and professional development.

Reflective task

Reflect on the skills required by teachers working in the twenty-first century. Then consider your personal philosophy and your ability to enhance a child's life chances. Also consider how your position feeds into your professional identity as a teacher.

Research-informed practice

In the preceding section, we constructed a model of a teacher who is a reflective practitioner, lifelong learner and, importantly, an agent of change. The Master's level descriptor below indicates how the use of research will support this highly complex role as the teacher: searches for the information that will enable teachers to question, understand and resolve everyday occurrences in their classrooms; and gains a critical understanding of key issues related to practice, which could range from everyday behaviour management to unexpected twenty-first-century challenges, for example, the consequences of technology use (cyber-bullying). Research also offers new insights for the creative entrepreneurial risk-taker who experiments with new educational approaches in their classroom.

At Master's level you need to be able to:

use research to develop a systematic understanding of knowledge and a critical awareness of current problems and/or new insights much of which is at, or informed by, the forefront of your academic discipline, field of study, or area of professional practice. (The Quality Assurance Agency for Higher Education, 2014, p. 28)

An indication that all aspects of practice can potentially be research-informed is demonstrated in the British Education Research Association report (BERA, 2013, p. 4), which considers why educational research matters. It points to the wide scope and breadth of research, which includes studies on formal and informal schooling, special education needs, the curriculum and how we assess children's learning, innovation and the economic impacts of education, the places where learning occurs such as classrooms, playgrounds, home, and within the community (libraries). And returning to the idea of a moral dimension to teaching, it highlights how the range alone provides an indication of how education impacts on everyone and how a strong research discipline can ensure that individual lives and communities are transformed through education.

Accessing educational research

For a trainee teacher, the university library catalogue is a key location where a search for peer reviewed journal articles often begins. Other sources for research findings are outlined below. These may include BERA, which describes itself as:

a membership association and learned society committed to advancing research quality, building research capacity and fostering research engagement. It aims to inform the development of policy and practice by promoting the best quality evidence produced by educational research.

Visitors to BERA's website can see how the commitment outlined above is realised through, for example, events and conferences, 33 special interest groups, newsletters, journals, fellowships, Impact Awards, researchers' resources and projects. Student membership of this 'vibrant, forward-looking community of education experts and enthusiasts' is available at a concessionary rate.

Government publications

Research reports can be accessed from the publications area (select 'research and analysis') within the government's website (https://www.gov.uk). Filters allow you to select according to policy area, publication date, world location and key word; for example, 'primary' if you are interested in that particular age phase. An example of a report that was published in March 2017 is the evaluation of a programme to introduce breakfast clubs in high-deprivation schools.

Chartered College of Teaching

Run by teachers for teachers, the Chartered College is an autonomous member-driven organisation, established to promote the learning, improvement and recognition of the art, science and practice of teaching for the public benefit (https://www. collegeofteaching.org/). They work in partnership with associations, unions and learned societies to build on the best of teaching and emerging research evidence. They cover all phases of education and subject specialisms, and connect a diverse community of teachers to share ideas and knowledge, and provide an independent, authoritative voice for the teaching profession. The latest research, case studies, articles and good practice can be accessed from the website.

researchEd

This can be accessed from www.workingoutwhatworks.com/. It describes itself as '… a grass-roots, teacher-led organisation aimed at improving research literacy in the educational communities, dismantling myths in education, getting the best research where it is needed most'. It is more than just an online repository for research reports. Resources include video archives of what are described as key voices in education, speaking about their research. The organisation brings together as many parties affected by educational research as possible in order to pool expertise, to help educators become aware of significant obstacles such as biases in their understanding of learning and education. It aims to '… promote collaboration between research-users and research-creators so that educators become more involved in the questions posed for research to answer, the data generated in that process, and in the consideration of the meaning of that data'. This model places practitioners at the heart of research.

The Sutton Trust and the Education Endowment Foundation

The Sutton Trust is an educational charity that aims to improve social mobility and address educational disadvantage. It describes itself as 'a think-tank and a do-tank'.

It has funded over 200 programmes, commissioned over 180 research studies and influenced government education policy by pushing social mobility to the top of the political agenda. It is an independent grant-making charity. By investing in evidence-based projects relating to tackling the attainment gap, an aim is to break the link between family income and educational achievement, thereby ensuring that all children can fulfil their potential and make the most of their talents. It provides schools with access to 'the best possible evidence on which to base their professional judgments by publicly reporting an accessible summary of educational research on teaching 5–16 year olds' via its online Teaching and Learning Toolkit website. Studies are organised in strands and include information about impact, cost and evidence. For example, research into learning 'styles' is presented as being low impact for very low cost, and is based on limited evidence (see Dekker et al., 2012). Practitioners can therefore use this information to determine whether or not they would adopt this approach in their particular setting.

The Education and Endowment Fund (EEF) and the Sutton Trust are jointly designated by the government as the What Works Centre for improving education outcomes for school aged children. 'School Themes' is an area on the EEF website, which pulls together evidence from the Teaching and Learning Toolkit and published EEF projects. The focus is on ten high priority issues for schools, in response to demand from teachers and leaders for evidence around these specific challenges: character, developing independent learning, feedback and monitoring pupil progress, literacy, mathematics, parental engagement, pupils' engagement and behaviour, school organisation, science, and staff deployment and development (https://educationendowmentfoundation.org.uk/school-themes/).

Social media, connected professionals

We live in a digital society. Therefore it should be no surprise that the internet is packed with virtual spaces where those with an interest in education, from the individual teacher to large organisations, can have an online presence. However, the sources referred to here are the ones that reside on social media platforms, and not the kind of 'standard' websites cited above; for example, teacher bloggers, Twitter debates, wikis and Facebook pages. Users/visitors to these online communities will need to use the same digital literacy skills that they generally employ to evaluate what they encounter. Or, to be more direct: 'without informed scrutiny, new technologies can merely provide an echo chamber for the loudest voices offering over-simplified solutions, often driven by ideological commitments, commercial opportunism or personal ambition' (Teacher Education Exchange, 2017, p. 32).

Examples of the use of social media to connect professionals are listed below.

https://teacherhead.com/ teacher blogs

BERA has a Twitter, blog and Facebook presence

https://twitter.com/beranews?lang=en

Facebook: https://www.facebook.com/BERAUK

https://www.bera.ac.uk/blog

This blog has been established to provide research-informed content on key educational issues in an accessible manner. All content is approved for publication. However, the views of the authors are their own and the views expressed on this blog are not the official views of BERA.

National Foundation for Educational Research (NFER) (Evidence for Excellence in Education) blog https://thenferblog.org

The Chartered College of Teaching blog https://www.collegeofteaching.org/blog

UCU Further Education: Transforming lives and communities http://transforming lives.web.ucu.org.uk/.

Communities of practice (Lave and Wenger, 1991) can be real or virtual and include online forums, internal and external networks. They can be based on your work team or a cross-organisational group with a shared focus. These networks can be both refreshing and vital in sustaining the energy and commitment to teaching, keeping up to date with research, policy and initiative changes in the sector, and your professional development.

Research-rich schools and education systems

The British Educational Research Association–Royal Society of Art (2014) inquiry into the role of research in teacher education asks, 'Does research really improve the quality of the teaching professions and beyond that the quality of students' [pupils'] learning experiences?' The evidence gathered by the inquiry was 'clear about the positive impact that a research literate and research engaged profession is likely to have on learner outcomes'(p. 6).

So far in this chapter, the teacher and effective classroom practice plus pupil outcomes have been the focus of discussion. High-level knowledge, understanding and skills, plus personal characteristics have all been considered. We now move the lens from the practitioner and explore the aspects of the British Educational Research Association–Royal Society of Art (2014) report that focus on schools and the education system.

What constitutes a 'research-rich school'?

In the report it was noted that 'Teachers and students thrive in the kind of settings that we describe as research-rich, and research-rich schools and colleges are those that are likely to have the greatest capacity for self-evaluation and self-improvement' (p. 4). The findings from the inquiry led to the articulation of a vision and a set of principles for developing a research-rich self-improving educational system. At pupil and teacher level the principles are as follows.

Teaching and learning in a research-rich, self-improving education system requires:

- Every learner is entitled to teaching that is informed by the latest relevant research.
- Every teacher is entitled to work in a research-rich environment that supports the development of their research literacy, and offers access to facilities and resources (both on-site and online) that support sustained engagement with and in research.

Teachers' professional identity and practice in a research-rich, self-improving education system requires:

- Teachers share a common responsibility for the continuous development of their research literacy. This informs all aspects of their professional practice and is written into initial and continuing teacher education programmes, standards, and in registration and licensing frameworks.
- Teachers who, during the course of qualifying and throughout their careers, have multiple opportunities to engage in research and enquiry, collaborating with colleagues in other schools and colleges and with members of the wider research community, based in universities and elsewhere. (p. 7)

Reflective task

Reflect on the ways in which research can be accessed, and the range of available sources. How and why might these differ? Critically review examples of research from three of the sources outlined above. Construct a framework to support you in this review. What evaluative criteria will you use? Can you locate several different research communities of practice? How would you define each one?

Teacher as researcher

Extract from the descriptors for a Master's degree (level 7):

Teachers taking a Master's degree must have:

- the independent learning ability required for continuing professional development,
- a comprehensive understanding of techniques applicable to their own research or advanced scholarship,
- originality in the application of knowledge, together with a practical understanding of how established techniques of research and enquiry are used to create and interpret knowledge in the discipline.

The statements above indicate that a practitioner needs the procedural knowledge required to carry out a classroom-based study. Preparing a teacher/Postgraduate Certificate in Education (PGCE) trainee to plan and implement a small-scale research project is beyond the scope of this chapter. What the following section aims to do is to focus on practitioner research in the context of continuing professional development, as presented in the first bullet point above.

The previous sections in this chapter have demonstrated the need for a teacher to continually engage with professional development; to be a lifelong learner. No initial teacher training course could fully prepare a student for every aspect of the complex role of a teacher. However, what it can do is equip a newly qualified teacher with an investigative mind, and an enquiring approach to developing professional practice. The motivational power of this approach has been noted (Van Looy and Goegebeur, 2007).

Professional development

Having established the importance of professional development as an ongoing process, we turn our lens to what is meant by 'professional development'. It may be viewed as keeping up to date with the latest initiatives and guidance. However, if this were the only level of engagement, then it would be viewed as a low level of professionalism. Taber (2010, p. 27) offers a typology of teacher professionalism, portraying each of his 'levels' as follows:

- Level 0: the trained worker
- Level 1: the technician-professional
- Level 2: the scholarly professional
- Level 3: the researching professional.

At the lowest level the teacher 'feels sufficiently competent to hold down a post. The trained worker considers they are already trained for their work and will avoid engaging with any innovations (which usually require extra work and effort) if possible' (Taber, 2010, p. 28). At the highest level the teacher does not simply accept/adopt an innovation without question. Taber suggests the teacher would read around a topic and decide whether or not to trial an idea in their own teaching, and only then consider adapting and adopting the innovation in their specific context: 'The fully professional teacher therefore has to be capable and sufficiently confident in their research skills to undertake classroom-based enquiry' (Taber, 2010, p. 29).

Motivation and empowerment

Teaching is a demanding profession and, as the British Educational Research Association–Royal Society of Art report (2014) highlights, engaging with and in research need not, and must not, become a burden. They suggest that:

> this is about empowering teachers, school and college leaders, and all who work with them, to better understand how they might enhance their practice and increase their impact in the classroom and beyond. (p. 6)

Despite the view that research is time-consuming and difficult to do, it can also be more motivational to be a researching professional than a scholarly one (drawing on Taber's typology as identified above). For example, Leat et al. (2014) suggest that:

> when research is seen as a body of knowledge, teachers may or may not choose to make use of it in their practice. When research becomes a professional learning process, it can have a deep influence on how they understand research and may lead them directly towards more active engagement in undertaking enquiry themselves. (p. 18)

The idea that engaging in research in your own setting can be motivational and empowering is reflected in the feedback from the student teachers who participated in a study by Medwell and Wray (2014). They led a project that involved trainee teachers conducting classroom-based research, as an authentic way for them to increase their understanding of curriculum issues: in this case, automaticity of letter production in handwriting and the role this plays in facilitating composing processes. The authors reported that this example of evidence-based practice 'identified that it is the creation of the evidence which is important and, as this paper argues, the shared professional involvement with compelling outcomes for pupils which develops teachers as thinkers, not simply technicians' (p. 75). The study provides further exemplification of the difference between Taber's low and high levels of professionalism. Furthermore, the feedback from one of the participants suggests that the project is an example of how initial teacher training can equip newly qualified teachers with an investigative mind, and an enquiring approach to developing professional practice, so that they have every chance of becoming highly professional.

> It has led me to think about when I can do research. To solve real problems, not just as an assignment. When I have my own class or a subject in school I can see that there are some problems to be solved and now I think I could do that. (Medwell and Wray, 2014, p. 73)

Vitally, this student has recognised how empowering the research process can be.

Feedback from other students who participated in Medwell and Wray's study included reference to new ways of thinking, having an impact on children's learning, making a difference and the impact of theory. All appear to be indicators of trainee teachers who have been motivated and empowered by their experiences of classroom-based research. From the above it can be seen that the motivation to research can emanate from the satisfaction that outcomes are directly relevant to an individual teacher's classroom/pupils, and the professional pride when you better understand how to enhance your practice. Furthermore, the references to 'making a difference' and 'having an impact' remind us of the moral dimension to teaching and the motivation to research being driven by the notion of a teacher as an agent of change. This type of motivation is illustrated in research carried out by Dr Vicky Duckworth when she explored the power of adult literacy classes to transform people, their families and communities. The vignette below explores her *insider* position. Vicky (Duckworth, 2013) says that her personal position as an 'insider' with 'insider knowledge' of marginalised communities was a key motivation to becoming a basic skills tutor and becoming involved in this study. For example, my own life history, which includes being born and brought up in the same community as the learners, attending the local state school and being the first generation of my family to enter college and university and my subsequent trajectory, has greatly influenced the commitment I have for finding opportunities to enable others to take agency and aspire to reach their potential. The appeal of participatory action research (PAR) is that in claiming to 'empower' it has the potential to address the profound inequalities in power between the participants and the researcher. Indeed, as well as the knowledge gained in the form of outcomes and findings, there are additional benefits gained from the process of the research, such as the relationships formed that enrich our lives.

As part of their PGCE, students are often asked to undertake a small-scale piece of action research based on their practice while on placement. The focus of the research is chosen by the student. The research project is assessed at level 7, giving Master's-level credits, which can then be built on to complete the full Master's qualification once qualified and employed.

The first conversation we have with trainee and qualified teachers undergoing level 7 study often covers the purpose of research. This includes identifying the drive for carrying out research and how they feel it would benefit professional development and classroom practice. Often, there is a struggle to find a focus for research. Since research often demands a time commitment and is an immersive process, it makes sense to find a focus that you feel passionate about. Remember, practitioner research is exciting, enthusing, challenging and incredibly stimulating. It is also frustrating, troublesome and messy. When it goes according to plan – when all ten of your focus group members turn up on time as arranged and proceed to have a lively and interesting debate that generates lots of information for your research – it is undeniably a great feeling. Indeed practitioner research facilitates you to be a generator of knowledge, rather than a passive spectator. It is empowering and has been a driving factor of teachers' professional development.

Celebrating and sharing professional knowledge

Trainee teachers completing a PGCE course are often required to complete assessed work at level 7 (Master's level). The following are examples of possible outlets for this work.

The STeP Journal (Student Teacher Perspectives)
   http://194.81.189.19/ojs/index.php/step/issue/current
   This online journal is for student teachers. It is published by the Teacher Education Advancement Network (TEAN) and is designed to showcase excellent research and scholarly activity from student teachers everywhere. All papers are recommended by student teachers' tutors and reviewed by TEAN before publication. Most important is that all papers show student teachers as reflective practitioners, with the ability to engage with theory to enhance their practice. Examples of recent publications are:

Ashcroft, J. (2017) 'Do boys' attitudes to reading differ to those of girls? A study into the views of reading within a year three class', *The STeP Journal*, 4 (1): 2–14. Available at: http://194.81.189.19/ojs/index.php/step/issue/current/showToc (accessed 10 March 2017).
   Gibson, S. and Bradley, P. (2017) 'A study of Northern Ireland Key Stage 2 pupils' perceptions of using the bbc micro:bit in stem education', *The STeP Journal*, 4 (1): 15–41. Available at: http://194.81.189.19/ojs/index.php/step/issue/current/showToc (accessed 10 March 2017).
   Journal of Trainee Teacher Educational Research (JoTTER)
   http://jotter.educ.cam.ac.uk/

Visit the website to find out more about the type of work that can be submitted for peer review and possible publication. As a PGCE student, you will also be interested to see the range of research that has been undertaken during professional practice and to read the papers that are published on the website. The following offer some meaningful examples:

Burns, R. (2017) 'Using puppets to encourage dialogue in the primary classroom: A study of pupils' perspectives on the use of puppets in their lessons', *Journal of Trainee Teacher Educational Research*, 8: 127–52. Available at: http://jotter.educ.cam.ac.uk/ (accessed 10 March 2017).

Hammond, E.M. (2016) 'My hand is up, therefore I am a good learner: A study into Year 4 pupils' perspectives on voluntary classroom participation', *Journal of Trainee Teacher Educational Research*, 7: 107–36. Available at: http://jotter.educ.cam.ac.uk/ (accessed 10 March 2017).

An introduction to writing at Master's level (level 7)

The key questions asked by students moving to level 7 study include:

- What can be expected when writing at level 7?
- How would I recognise it?

Below are a number of key points to consider:

- It is important when approaching level 7 (as at any level) that you read the questions posed carefully and understand the learning outcomes. If they are vague and you need more clarity ask your tutor and/or discuss with your peers. It is important that you are very clear about what is being asked. This will facilitate you to develop a plan for the research that is needed to shape your writing in a critical research-informed way, producing a well argued, balanced and evidenced piece of work showing understanding of the concepts and lines of arguments.
- Discussion of issues – referenced using other writers, own experience and own arguments. Reflections and independent thoughts.
- Theory is used to answer questions and pose questions.
- Demonstrate criticality, careful scrutiny of issues, highlighting limitations and the potential consequences of alternative perspectives.
- Question assumptions and suggest alternative schools of thought.
- Demonstrate the ability to question 'why?' and consider the 'so what?' factor encompassing the impact of strategies.
- Aim to demonstrate a coherent thread running through the writing with an ability to reflect on your personal work.
- Writing demonstrates what you have learnt at a deeper level.

Remember to use the guidance from your university of study and the numerous other online guides for writing at level 7. These sources are easy to access and will enable you to explore further the prompt list above in more depth. As always with online resources you will need to critically evaluate each source. As such, you may feel that university academic support units, sometimes known as 'learning services', are a good place to start. And remember to draw on the discussion points in this chapter, which include reflection and scholarly research to support and develop your criticality. Importantly, enjoy the writing process – it is an opportunity for you to share your knowledge. It allows you to develop as a professional and human being.

Reflective task

In preparation for writing at level 7, apply the knowledge gained from the above online self-study to construct a short piece that reflects the above guidance in relation to an issue, challenge or educational practice. Ensure that your piece of writing is not simply descriptive but demonstrates a level of criticality as outlined in the prompt list. Aim to reflect upon the techniques required for writing at Master's level. Consider what your challenges were and develop a plan to practise and strengthen your skills. Engaging with a process of peer review in relation to your writing may support you in creating an action plan.

Summary

This chapter has taken you on a journey that explores what it means to be a professional teacher in the twenty-first century. The role includes dealing with complex and unpredictable situations, research-informed practice and partaking in practitioner research to inform your practice. We have equated this profile of a high-level professional to someone who is *operating* at Master's level. In this way we have avoided the narrow definition of 'Master's level' as simply being a qualification.

As a trainee teacher, you are starting out on an exciting journey, and this chapter has provided you with ideas about the ways in which you can develop. The process of writing reflections on a regular basis will provide you with an insight into your learning journey and how you have been shaped by this – for example, has your ideological position changed? We would argue that in order to explore other people's knowledge and build knowledge, you need to have strong insights into your own beliefs, motivations and ideologies, and how these are shaped and can change. It is also important that you read other researchers' work, which could be in the form of dissertations/theses, articles, book chapters and books. This will help you to explore the research and learning journey that they have travelled and will no doubt motivate you to carry out and disseminate your own research. Good luck in your level 7 study and your professional journey!

Questions for discussion

- Why can being a reflective practitioner drive your classroom practice forward?
- Consider the characteristics of teachers as change agents. How do they fit your strengths and areas for development?
- How and why can practitioner research improve practice?
- Identify research questions to explore in level 7 study.
- How is your professional identity linked to level 7 study?
- Can you summarise the ways in which you need to develop in order to successfully meet Master's level criteria, as expressed throughout this chapter?

Further reading

Bassot, B. (2013) *The Reflective Journal*. Basingstoke: Palgrave Macmillan.
This book provides a practical approach to developing the skills and understanding of writing reflectively. For example, in addition to an introduction to relevant key theories, it offers structured activities and prompts to encourage the reader to explore different techniques and approaches to writing more freely, and at a deeper level.

Bos, J., van Opijen, J. and Zomer, P. (2012) '"Are you talking to me?" Assessing discourses on reflection', *Reflective Practice*, 13 (5): 621–35.
The question of how to assess academic discourse on reflection from a dialogical point of view is considered. The researchers highlighted five overall modes of reflection that point to different lenses of processing experiences. Mode 1 'conscientious reflection', Mode 2 'confident involvement', Mode 3 'nondescript detachment', Mode 4 'accounted manifestation' and Mode 5 'professional approach'. Two of these modes strongly correlated with what is perceived to be 'good reflection', whilst the other modes related to lower rankings on a rating scale. It is suggested that the aforementioned may relate to a lack of involvement on the part of the student or overemphasis of the professional dimension. Recommendations point to a need to redirect attention to processes that contribute to the construction of reflexivity, instead of solely focusing on the qualities of the 'product'.

Chi, F.M. (2013) 'Turning experiences into critical reflections: Examples from Taiwanese in-service teachers', *Asia-Pacific Journal of Teacher Education*, 41 (1): 28–40.
This study explored how teachers turned classroom experiences into critical reflections via journal writings at three different levels: transitions, transformations and problematics. This facilitated the teachers' awareness of the close interrelationships between their experiences and teaching. The researchers also raise the notion of needing to be cautious about the danger of negative outcomes if reflection is excessively engaged in – the premise being that expecting teachers to reflect critically and systematically over a long period of time may be unrealistic, unless adequate support is provided.

Cohen, L., Manion, L., Morrison, K. and Morrison, R.B.K. (2011) *Research Methods in Education*, seventh edn. London: Routledge.
This insightful text encompasses a range of methods utilised by educational researchers at all stages of their research journey. It offers practical advice, underpinned by clear theoretical foundations, research evidence and up-to-date references. A key feature is the attention given to choosing and planning a research project, including material on sampling, research questions, literature reviews and ethical issues. The textbook is accompanied by a website: www.routledge.com/textbooks/cohen7e.

Duckworth, V. (2013) *Learning Trajectories, Violence and Empowerment amongst Adult Basic Skills Learners*. Research in Education. London: Routledge.
This study provides an 'insider's' position to offer a critical insightful analysis of the interplay between literacy, learning, violence, gender and social class. Drawing on a participatory ethnographic approach, it presents rich and critical life/story methodologies to create biographies sociologically. This book will inspire education researchers and reflective practitioners with an interest in learning and empowerment.

Wise, D., Selwyn, N., Smith, E. and Suter, L.E. (eds) (2017) *The BERA/SAGE Handbook of Educational Research*. London: Sage.
This high-quality research methods handbook has received very good reviews. With contributions from over 50 authors, many who are highly eminent in their fields, the authoritative, insightful content will be of interest to practising researchers, and those who are new to education research.

References

Bandura, A. (2001) 'Social cognitive theory: An agentic perspective', *Annual Review of Psychology*, 52: 1–26.
Boud, D., Keogh, R. and Walker, D. (1985) *Reflection: Turning Experience into Learning*. London: Kogan Page.
British Education Research Association (BERA) (2013) *Why Educational Research Matters: A Briefing to Inform Future Funding Decisions*. Available at: https://www.bera.ac.uk/researchers-resources/publications/why-educational-research-matters-3 (accessed 2 March 2017).

British Educational Research Association–Royal Society of Art (2014) *Research and the Teaching Professions: Building the Capacity for a Self-Improving Education System.* Available at: https://www.bera.ac.uk/project/research-and-teacher-education (accessed 2 March 2017).

Daly, J., Duncan, M., Gill, R., Hayes, C. and Whitehouse, A. (2014) *Developing as a Reflective Early Years Professional: A Thematic Approach.* St Albans: Critical Publishing.

Day, C., Elliot, B. and Kington, A. (2005) 'Reform, standards and teacher identity: Challenges of sustaining commitment', *Teaching and Teacher Education*, 21: 563–77.

Dekker, S., Lee, N.C., Howard-Jones, P. and Jolles, J. (2012) 'Neuromyths in education: Prevalence and predictors of misconceptions among teachers', *Frontiers in Psychology.* Available at: http://journal.frontiersin.org/article/10.3389/fpsyg.2012.00429/full (accessed 10 May 2017).

Dewey, J. (1910) *How We Think.* Boston, MA: D.C. Heath & Co.

Dewey J. ([1938] 2008) *The Collected Works of John Dewey: 1938–9 Experience and Education, Freedom and Culture, Theory of Valuation and Essays. Vol 13: The Later Works 1925–53.* Illinois: Southern Illinois University Press.

Duckworth, V. (2013) *Learning Trajectories, Violence and Empowerment amongst Adult Basic Skills Learners.* London: Routledge.

Kolb, D. (1984) *Experiential Learning: Experience as the Source of Learning and Development.* Englewood Cliffs, NJ: Prentice Hall.

Lave, J. and Wenger, E. (1991) *Situated Learning: Legitimate Peripheral Participating.* Cambridge: Cambridge University Press.

Leat, D., Lofthouse, R. and Reid, R. (2014) *Teachers' Views: Perspectives on Research Engagement.* Available at: https://www.bera.ac.uk/wp-content/uploads/2013/12/BERA-Paper-7-Teachers-Views-Perspectives-on-research-engagement.pdf (accessed 2 March 2017).

Le Fevre, D.M. (2014) 'Barriers to implementing pedagogical change: The role of teachers' perceptions of risk', *Teaching and Teacher Education*, 38: 56–64.

Medwell, J. and Wray, D. (2014) 'Pre-service teachers undertaking classroom research: Developing reflection and enquiry skills', *Journal of Education for Teaching*, 40 (1): 65–77.

Moon, J. (1999) *Reflections in Learning and Professional Development.* Abingdon: RoutledgeFalmer.

Nodding, N. (2016) *Philosophy of Education*, fourth edn. Boulder, CO: Westview Press.

Quality Assurance Agency for Higher Education (QCA) (2014) *Framework for Higher Education Qualifications of UK Degree-Awarding Bodies.* Gloucester: QCA. Available at: www.qaa.ac.uk (accessed 2 March 2017).

Roffey-Barentsen, J. and Malthouse, R. (2013) *Reflective Practice in Education and Training*, second edn. London: Sage.

Schön, D.A. (1983) *The Reflective Practitioner: How Professionals Think in Action.* Aldershot: Ashgate Publishing.

Taber, K.S. (2010) 'Preparing teachers for a research-based profession', in M.V. Zuljan and J. Vogrinc (eds), *Facilitating Effective Student Learning through Teacher Research and Innovation.* Ljubljana: Faculty of Education, University of Ljubljana. pp. 19–47. Available at: www.pef.uni-lj.si/ceps/knjiznica/doc/zuljan-vogrinc.pdf (accessed 8 March 2017).

Tarrant, P. (2013) *Reflective Practice and Professional Development*. London: Sage.

Teacher Education Exchange (2017) *Teacher Development 3: Transforming The Professional Education of Teachers*. London: Teacher Education Exchange. Available at: https://teacher educationexchange.com/publications/ (accessed 3 April 2017).

Tripp, D. (2011) *Critical Incidents in Teaching: Developing Professional Judgement*, classic edn. Abingdon: Routledge.

Van der Heijden, H.R.M.A., Geldens, J.J.M., Beijaard, D. and Popeijus, H.L. (2015) 'Characteristics of teachers as change agents', *Teachers and Teaching*, 21 (6): 681–99.

Van Looy, L. and Goegebeur, W. (2007) 'Teachers and teacher trainees as classroom researchers: Beyond Utopia?', *Educational Action Research*, 15 (1): 107–27.

20

Moving Forward

Hilary Cooper

By the end of this chapter, you should:

- have reflected on what you have learnt from this book
- have an understanding of what is meant by professional studies in education and that this is a fundamental, although 'fuzzy' concept
- have developed and be articulate about your personal philosophy of education and how to apply it in your teaching, within evolving statutory requirements and guidance
- be aware of the ways in which subject and professional associations can enable you to remain in contact with networks of like-minded colleagues, in your first teaching post
- understand the nature of a Master's level degree in education and the ways in which you have a good foundation for studying at this level and how this relates to doctoral study.

Introduction

This chapter will review the aims of the book and the theme which underlies it: that you should mediate changing statutory requirements and non-statutory guidance through your personal philosophy. It will consider the book as a whole and help you to reflect on what you have learnt through reading and interacting with it. It will reinforce your awareness of why 'professional studies' should underpin all your teaching. It will encourage you to articulate your personal educational philosophy, which, it is hoped, has developed through reading the book, and demonstrate the ways in which you are well prepared to undertake further study at Master's level.

The aims of this book

Throughout this book, you should have become increasingly aware that teachers are constantly responsible for making professional decisions related to teaching, planning and assessment, classroom organisation, behaviour management, and individual and diverse pupil needs, in order to provide equal opportunities that enable all children to reach their potential. You have been encouraged to reflect on and develop your practice and to make links between theory and practice through a raised awareness of controversial issues and by developing your ability to inform yourself about these, from relevant literature and contemporary comment. The book has aimed to promote practice informed by value judgements, promoting the educational development of the whole child: social, emotional and cognitive. It has aimed to encourage innovative and creative teaching and learning.

Statutory statements about professional attributes are inevitably succinct and prescriptive, and can be interpreted in simplistic ways if students are unable to appreciate the judgements and decisions that underlie them. If you are not able to bring informed professional judgements to bear on your work, your teaching across the curriculum will be the transmission of government requirements rather than being informed by a unique set of personal skills and understandings. If you are not able to analyse, reflect on and take responsibility for your practice, it will remain static rather than develop. And, finally, you will be vulnerable to constant political manipulation. This book has aimed to enable you to meet current and future government requirements within a broad and deep interpretation of the concept of 'professional studies'.

It is to be hoped that you are becoming aware of the ways, and many contexts, in which, as a primary school teacher, you need to think critically, make informed judgements and take responsibility for your own developing professional expertise. But do not worry if you feel overwhelmed by the proposition that you should do so. Since you are still at the beginning of your professional journey, it could not be otherwise. The Cambridge Primary Review (Alexander, 2010) has a section on 'Expertise and development: Ways of thinking' (pp. 416–20). It recognises that experience shapes us differently, as people and as professionals, and that by the time you retire you can expect to have a 'richly elaborated knowledge about curriculum, classroom routines and pupils that allows you to apply with despatch what you know to particular cases'.

The Review was critical of the framework by which this development was assessed by the Training and Development Agency UK (TDA, 2007), saying that this was unhelpful since teachers may demonstrate their expertise in different ways. The Review suggests that teachers' development is tracked better by evidence than government policy, which has implied that teachers use the same basic repertoire at each stage of their careers and that this depresses rather than raises standards. Development is seen by the Review as progress from novice, through competence, to expert, recognising that excellence includes such concepts as artistry, flexibility and originality, which are difficult to define precisely but instantly recognisable. So accept that you will gradually become expert by using the approaches suggested throughout this book. This criticism has been addressed subsequently in the Teachers' Standards (DfE, 2013), which see professional development as interpreted in terms of role and context, whereas the Standards for Wales, Ireland and Scotland define it more specifically.

Overview of the concept of professional studies

Having read this book, you should understand that 'professional studies' in education means a body of knowledge, understanding and skills, based on consideration of the values and aims which underpin the many decisions that each lesson requires. Professional studies encompass the pedagogy that brings educational aims and values to life, and translates the curriculum into learning and knowing which engages, inspires and empowers learners – or not. This body of knowledge and skills involves:

- communication, collaboration and relationships with pupils, colleagues and parents
- understanding how children learn and how to progress their learning, responding in a supportive way to individual differences between children
- provision of a learning environment in which all children can reach their potential
- taking responsibility for your own professional development through reflection on and evaluation of your experience and practice, your reading and interpretation of policies.

Professional attributes

These four themes are a synopsis of the professional attributes required for achieving qualified teacher status, which run throughout this book. Table I.1 in the Introduction (p. 5) showed you how this book reflects the Professional Standards for England, Wales,

Scotland and Northern Ireland, and invited you to use them to monitor your development as you read the book. You need to consider the significance of these themes in relation to your more detailed learning of how to teach each of the subjects on the curriculum.

However, it is important to remember that research (Alexander, 2010, pp. 450–1) suggests that there is no single definition of teacher professionalism because the concept is fluid, plastic and dynamic, and fails to recognise the 'more nuanced and dilemma-conscious private conversations of primary teachers … where feelings matter … and where subtlety and realism puncture the notions of "one-size-fits-all" and "good primary practice"'.

Reflective task

Take the plan for a lesson you have taught and the related evaluation. Highlight any of the Teachers' Standards that are reflected in the lesson plan. List the Teachers' Standards that you demonstrated as an integral part of your practice but did not need to state in the plan or evaluation. Are there any that, on reflection, you could have demonstrated but did not?

Analysis of the professional standards addressed in this book

It is clear from Table I.1 that professional attributes are not discrete. Most of them run through several chapters of this book. Analysis of the table shows that the professional attributes that are addressed most frequently in the book are personal qualities (the ability to work collaboratively and communicate effectively and to take responsibility for your own professional development) as well as personal values and beliefs (particularly in relation to behaviour management and equal opportunities).

Teachers' personal responsibility for developing their practice is referred to in Chapters 2, 3, 4, 15 and 16. The importance of constructive criticality is discussed in Chapters 1, 2, 9, 11, 14, 15 and 16, and provision of equal opportunities for children with diverse learning needs is covered in Chapters 5, 11, 12 and 14.

Personal educational philosophy

It was suggested in Chapter 2 that, while reading this book and relating it to your experience and other reading, you develop, review and adjust your personal educational philosophy statement. If you have done this, it will be helpful, as a personal statement is generally required as part of an application for a teaching post.

Reflective task

If you have not revised your statement of educational philosophy over time, write it now, drawing on discussions throughout this book. You might choose to use the following headings:

- My interpretation of the aims of primary education
- How I apply them in the following contexts
- Subject knowledge
- How children learn and how I support their progress
- Planning, monitoring and assessment
- Inclusion, individual differences and special educational needs
- Behaviour management
- Children's personal and social development.

However you decide to structure your statement, keep it brief. There may be 100 applicants. And do relate it to the advertisement for each particular post and school. The interviewers need to know that you are the one person they are looking for! Therefore, it is important to give a flavour of your personality and experience; what you have actually done in school in a variety of curriculum areas and with specified age groups. This will show you can make connections between theory and practice, and will give the interviewers a good idea of the things to talk to you about. Be prepared to critically evaluate what you tell the interviewers about your work in schools.

Reflective task

Read 'What is primary education for?' (Alexander, 2010, Chapter 12, pp. 180–200). Do you want to revise your statement after reading this?

Networks of like-minded colleagues

Subject associations

This book has been about critical reflection on practice in order to develop your own philosophy and resist manipulation. However, although you may feel that you have developed and can defend a robust personal philosophy, you may not be fortunate enough to find a school where this is shared by everyone. Teachers come from different backgrounds and are of different ages. In my experience it can be extremely frustrating when a belief in strategies and values you are convinced are sound is not shared by colleagues. Although the standards require teachers to continually develop their practice through reflection, research and collaboration, this is difficult to achieve. The standards also require us to work together with colleagues and parents. This too is often treading a tightrope! You want to fit in. You also want to fulfil your ideals – indeed, your potential. So the pressure to compromise, or even to give in, is very great. You want to continue with your professional development but there is little funding for this, so where do you turn?

The answer is by joining and taking an active part in a professional and/or a subject association (membership can be set against tax!). Here you will find the support of like-minded and idealistic people, opportunities to meet and work with others or to do so online, and receive up-to-date information and advice in dealing with issues and finding good resources. Subject associations provide a link with universities and research and best practice – offering a source of advice and a feeling of being part of a large and vibrant intellectual community, which may be missing when you are no longer in a university environment. Examples are given below.

Mathematics

The National Centre for Excellence in Mathematics (NCETM) (https://www.ncetm.org.uk) is funded by the Department for Education (DfE) (you can register online). It provides high-quality continuing professional development (CPD) resources and encourages collaboration among staff, by sharing good practice locally, regionally and nationally, through courses, regional networks and online, and supports teaching in schools. It also funds, supports and disseminates research. The personal learning section includes a professional learning framework, self-evaluation tools and a personal learning space for anyone who has registered. Partners include:

- Association of Teachers of Mathematics (www.atm.org.uk)
- Children's Mathematical Network (www.childrens-mathematics.net)
- Further Mathematics Support Programme: provides support for students and teachers' CPD (www.furthermaths.org.uk)
- Mathematical Association (www.m-a.org.uk).

English

- The National Council of Teachers of English (www.ncte.org) aims to support work with pupils and families to promote lifelong literacy, to help with resources and materials and with confronting issues.
- The National Association for the Teaching of English (www.nate.org.uk) provides national and regional courses, and CPD resources.

Science

- Primary Engineer (www.primaryengineer.com) works with schools to provide courses that develop technology, science and mathematics.
- The Association for Science Teacher Education (http://theaste.org) provides regional and national networks and resources and is a forum for debate and promoting excellence.

History

- The Historical Association's resources include the journal, *Primary History*, online CPD modules, lessons and exemplars, as well as conferences and forums and opportunities to comment on policies (www.history.org.uk).

Geography

- The Geographical Association (www.geography.org.uk) supports teachers and students through journals, publications, training events, websites and lobbying government about the importance of geography (incorporating the performing arts).

Music

- The Schools Music Association (www.schoolsmusic.org.uk) organises events, awards, training, grants and resources.

Sport and physical education (PE)

- The Association for Physical Education (www.afpe.org.uk) develops PE-related policy and offers professional support for members through high-quality professional development opportunities, journals and national working parties.

Art

- The National Society for Education in Art and Design (www.nsead.org) promotes and defends art, craft and design across all age phases, defines and reassesses policies, disseminates new ideas, research and good practice, and provides a forum for discussion.

Religious education

- The National Association of Teachers of Religious Education (www.natre.org.uk/) is the key network for RE.
- The Religious Education Council (http://religiouseducationcouncil.org.uk/) works to strengthen RE in schools and higher education settings publishing newsletters, blogs, and responses to policy documents.
- RE online (www.reonline.org.uk/) publishes quality lesson ideas and links with other helpful websites.
- RE today (www.retoday.org.uk/) also provides support for RE teaching and learning.

Organisations supporting the safeguarding of children

- National Society for the Protection of Children (NSPCC)(https://nspcc.org.uk/what-we-do/). This is a leading childhood charity, specialising in all aspects of child protection: not only children you work with but also all babies and children in England Scotland, Wales and Northern Ireland.
- Charity Commission for England and Wales (https://www.gov.uk/government/publications/safeguarding-children-and-young-people) gives advice to staff and volunteers in organisations working with children.
- Links to a range of safeguarding organisations are given at www.safecic.co.uk/your-scb-acpc/2-uncategorised/37-useful-organisations and at https://www.keepingchildrensafe.org.uk/.
- Links to many organisations dealing with different aspects of child abuse and to research and statistics can be found at https://www.gov.uk/topic/schools-colleges-childrens-services/safeguarding-children.

Professional associations

These are non-profit-making associations seeking to further the interests of pupils, teachers and lecturers in primary education.

- The National Association for Primary Education: this is concerned with the learning of children from birth to 13 (http://nape.org.uk). It works with teachers, parents, governors and schools, through sharing good classroom practice, conferences and the journal *Primary First*. It brings groups of like-minded colleagues together, enables discussion about innovative strategies and issues, and participates in discussions at the highest level with other organisations.
- The Association for the Study of Primary Education (ASPE): was founded on the belief that one of the best ways to advance primary education is through professional collaboration and action (www.aspe-uk.eu). Members are early years and primary practitioners, advisers and consultants, Local Education Authorities and university teachers. The journal *Education 3–13* reports on cutting-edge research. The emphasis is on collective study, collaborative activity, theoretical study, scholarship and informed debate.

Teachers' unions

You may not be sympathetic to all their campaigns but, as my father, a committed member when unions were less activist, always said: 'when one of your pupils is involved in a serious accident while you are in loco parentis, you need all the support you can get'.

- The National Union of Teachers (NUT) (www.teachers.org.uk) offers legal advice and insurance, and also provides learning opportunities for newly qualified teachers, and for CPD.
- The National Association of School Masters and Union of Women Teachers (www.nasuwt.org.uk) offers legal and professional services, and guidance on dealing with employment issues.

Work in school

Student: Goodness knows I'm not work shy – although I do think a consideration of work/life balance aids good teaching! But I have friends who have been expected to work on Saturdays (maths and language workshops for parents) and on a Sunday (performing a class play in the local church) and even to supervise school journeys in holiday time. Is this reasonable?

(Continued)

(Continued)

Mentor: The School Teachers' Pay and Conditions Document (STPCD) applies to maintained, foundation and voluntary aided schools. It specifies that a teacher must be available for work for 195 days, or 1265 hours, in any school year, at such times and places as specified by the head teacher, but should not be required to work on Saturday or Sunday. You should be given a calendar at the beginning of each calendar year setting out all your commitments. Usually there can be flexible and amicable negotiations about these. But if you suspect that you are being asked to work for longer than the STPCD specifies, you should discuss this with your union representative – assuming you have joined!

Student: I'd really like to join all the subject associations but couldn't possibly afford to.

Mentor: Most have a school membership, so ideally persuade your head teacher and subject coordinators of its advantages. Or you might share the cost of membership with friends, or each join your own specialist subject association and share resources. I think it's really important to be part of a larger professional network outside your school.

Moving from qualified teacher status to a Master's degree

Many teachers told the Cambridge Primary Review (Alexander, 2010) that they wanted more time to reflect, research and study. This echoes the need for continuing professional development and for teachers who take responsibility for this. Most Master's degrees in education involve a research study, usually based on enquiry into your own practice. Throughout this book, you have been encouraged to think reflectively and critically.

Part 3 focused on this process in more structured ways, through chapters on reflective practice, enquiry and critical thinking and exploring educational issues in order to prepare a small research study. The later chapters in this book should help you to move through this continuum of level criteria. This will put you in an ideal position for study at Master's level. This usually requires a sustained investigation of a question of your choice, based on a critical analysis of the relevant literature, theory and previous research. It will include modules on how to collect and analyse data and present and evaluate your findings. Table 20.1 shows the progression from qualified teacher status to a Master's degree and how you could build on this at doctoral level.

So make a habit of reading, keeping up to date with critical professional thinking. Make it a regular habit to engage with the wide-ranging, challenging and thought-provoking

Table 20.1 Shows the progression in knowledge, skills and understanding from qualified teacher to Master's and doctoral level research

Requirements for the award of an honours degree in education studies (benchmark standards level 7) QAA (2007) (www.qaa.ac.uk)	Descriptor for a Master's degree (level 7) taken from the *Framework for Higher Education Qualifications for England, Wales and Northern Ireland* (QAA, 2010; Appendix 2a, England, Wales and Northern Ireland; Appendix b, level 11, Scotland) (www.qaa.ac.uk)	Doctoral degree characteristics (2011) Descriptor for a higher education qualification at doctoral level (level 8) *Framework for Educational Qualifications in England, Wales and Northern Ireland* (QAA, 2011) (www.qaa.ac.uk)
Knowledge and understanding Demonstrate a critical understanding of: • the underlying values and principles relevant to education studies and a developing personal stance that draws on personal knowledge and understanding • the diversity of learners and the complexities of the education process • the complexity of the interaction between learning and contexts, and the range of ways in which participants (including learners and teachers) can influence the learning process • the societal and organisational structures and purposes of educational systems • the possible implications for learners and the learning process	To achieve the award of a Master's degree students should demonstrate a systematic understanding of knowledge, and a critical awareness of current problems and/or new insights, much of which is at, or informed by, the forefront of their academic discipline, field of study or area of professional practice	For the award of a doctoral degree students must have demonstrated the creation and interpretation of new knowledge, through: • original research or other advanced scholarship, of a quality to satisfy peer review, extend the forefront of the discipline, and merit publication • a systematic acquisition and understanding of a substantial body of knowledge that is at the forefront of an academic discipline or area of professional practice • the general ability to conceptualise, design and implement a project for the generation of new knowledge, applications or understanding at the forefront of the discipline, and to adjust the project design in the light of unforeseen problems
Application Demonstrate the ability to: • analyse educational concepts, theories and issues of policy in a systematic way • identify and reflect on potential connections and discontinuities between each of the aspects of subject knowledge and their application in educational policies and contexts	Demonstrate a comprehensive understanding of techniques applicable to student's own research or advanced scholarship	Students must have demonstrated a detailed understanding of applicable techniques for research and advanced academic enquiry and a detailed understanding of applicable techniques for research and advanced academic enquiry

(Continued)

Table 20.1 (Continued)

- accommodate new principles and understandings
- select a range of relevant primary and secondary sources, including theoretical and research-based evidence, to extend personal knowledge and understanding
- use a range of evidence to formulate appropriate and justified ways forward and potential changes in practice

Reflection

Demonstrate:

- the ability to reflect on personal and others' value systems
- the ability to use knowledge and understanding to critically locate and justify a personal position in relation to the subject
- an understanding of the significance and limitations of theory and research

Communication and presentation

Students should be able to organise and articulate opinions and arguments in speech and writing using relevant specialist vocabulary

Students should be able to use information and communication technology in their study and other appropriate situations

Students should be able to:

- collect and apply numerical data, as appropriate
- present data in a variety of formats including graphical and tabular
- analyse and interpret both qualitative and quantitative data

Demonstrate:

- originality in the application of knowledge, together with a practical understanding of how established techniques of research and enquiry are used to create and interpret knowledge in the discipline

Demonstrate conceptual understanding that enables the student:

- to evaluate critically current research and advanced scholarship in the discipline
- to evaluate methodologies and develop critiques of them and, where appropriate, to propose new hypotheses

Students continue to undertake pure and/or applied research and development at an advanced level, contributing substantially to the development of new techniques, ideas or approaches

Communicate their ideas and conclusions clearly and effectively to specialist and non-specialist audiences

(Continued)

Students should have the ability to collaborate and plan as part of a team, to carry out roles allocated by the team, take the lead where appropriate, and fulfil agreed responsibilities

Improving own learning and performance
Students should be able to articulate their own approaches to learning and organise an effective work pattern including working to deadlines

Students should be able to process and synthesise empirical and theoretical data, to create new syntheses and to present and justify a chosen position having drawn on relevant theoretical perspectives

Demonstrate how to deal with complex issues both systematically and creatively, make sound judgements in the absence of complete data, and communicate their conclusions clearly to specialist and non-specialist audiences

Demonstrate self-direction and originality in tackling and solving problems, and act autonomously in planning and implementing tasks at a professional or equivalent level

Continue to advance their knowledge and understanding, and to develop new skills to a high level. Holders will have the qualities and transferable skills necessary for employment, requiring:
- the exercise of initiative and personal responsibility
- decision making in complex and unpredictable situations
- the independent learning ability required for continuing professional development

Continue to undertake pure and/or applied research and development at an advanced level, contributing substantially to the development of new techniques, ideas or approaches

Doctoral degrees are awarded for the creation and interpretation, construction and/or exposition of knowledge that extends the forefront of a discipline, usually through original research

Holders of doctoral degrees will be able to conceptualise, design and implement projects for the generation of significant new knowledge and/or understanding

Holders of doctoral degrees will have the qualities needed for employment that require both the ability to make informed judgements on complex issues in specialist fields and an innovative approach to tackling and solving problems papers in the *Journal of Philosophy of Education*. Recent papers deal, for example, with such debates as: What is fairness in assessment? What are educational rights? The subservience of liberal education to political ends. What does it mean to be educated? What is meant by religious education? Race, schools and the media and the relationship between research and practice and the kinds of educational research we should value. I hope this has whetted your appetite for further study! Good luck – and here's a final quotation from Alexander (2010, p. 512):

> Abandon the discourses of derision, false dichotomy and myth and strive to ensure that the education debate at last exemplifies rather than negates what education should be about.

Summary

This chapter has considered the aims of the book in developing critical and reflective practice and cautioned that, while you should understand the process, this must be seen as an area of CPD. The importance of articulating your personal educational philosophy, exemplified by your experience in school, when you apply for your first teaching post was discussed. Information was given about national organisations that will offer you professional support networks and opportunities for CPD. The chapter concluded by illustrating the ways in which engagement with this book and some experience as a teacher can place you in a confident position to apply for a higher professional qualification.

Children's experience of primary school in the future is in your hands. It is an exciting prospect – and a great responsibility.

References

Alexander, R. (ed.) (2010) *Children, their World, their Education: Final Report and Recommendations of the Cambridge Primary Review*. London: Routledge.

DfE (2012) (updated 2013) https://www.gov.uk/government/publications/teachers-standards.

DfE (2013) *The National Curriculum: A Framework*. London: DfE.

QAA (2007) *Education Studies*. Mansfield: QAA. Available at: www.qaa.ac.uk/Publications/InformationAndGuidance/Documents/Education07.pdf.

QAA (2010) *Masters Degree Characteristics*. Gloucester: QCA. Available at: www.qaa.ac.uk/Publications/InformationandGuidance/Documents/MastersDegree Characteristics.pdf.

QAA (2011) *Doctoral Degree Characteristics*. Available at: www.qaa.ac.uk/Publications/InformationAndGuidance/Documents/Doctoral_Characteristics.pdf.

Training and Development Agency UK (TDA) (2007) *Teacher Professional Development in England*. Available atL http://webarchive.nationalarchives.gov.uk/20111218081 624/http:/tda.gov.uk/.

Index